P9-DNB-273

WITHDRAWN
New Trier High School
Library

Marcia B. Siegel's dance criticism, representing almost thirty years of writing and lecturing, has been called "the most important body of critical writing on dance since Edwin Denby." Siegel has published a biography of the American choreographer Doris Humphrey, *Days on Earth*; and three collections of reviews, the latest of which is *The Tail of the Dragon—New Dance 1976–1982* (1991). She is dance critic for the *Hudson Review* and is on the faculty of the Department of Performance Studies, Tisch School of the Arts, New York University.

The Shapes of Change

Isadora Duncan at the Theatre of Dionysius, about 1904. Photo by Raymond Duncan.

MARCIA B. SIEGEL

The Shapes of Change

Images of American Dance

ILLUSTRATED WITH PHOTOGRAPHS

UNIVERSITY OF CALIFORNIA PRESS
Berkeley · Los Angeles · London

NEW TRIER H.S. LIBRARY
WIN...

University of California Press
Berkeley and Los Angeles, California

University of California Press, Ltd.
London, England

First California paperback printing 1985

Copyright © 1979 by Marcia B. Siegel

Reprinted by permission of Houghton Mifflin Company

Library of Congress Cataloging in Publication Data

Siegel, Marcia B
    The shapes of change.

    Reprint. Originally published: Boston: Houghton Mifflin,
1979.
    Bibliography: p.
    Includes index.
    1. Dancing—United States—History.   2. Modern dance.
3. Ballet. I. Title.
GV1623.S536 1985   793.3'0973   84-28039
ISBN 0-520-04212-3 (alk. paper)

Printed in the United States of America

2 3 4 5 6 7 8 9

Portions of this book have appeared in *Ballet Review* and as a
pamphlet in the series *Essays from the Sarah Lawrence College
Faculty*.

The photographs on pages 3, 6, 15, 18, 26, 45, 94, 103, 112, 147,
173, 273, 308, and 311 were taken from the archives of the Dance
Collection of the Library and Museum of the Performing Arts at
Lincoln Center, and are used with permission.

793,3
S571

For Edwin Denby

Contents

Illustrations

Introduction

CONTINUITY IN DANCE must be worked at. The minute you relax your efforts at preserving something you start to lose it. There's no such thing as setting aside an idea or a style or a work for a while and then expecting it to be intact when you come back to it later.

This is also true of a dancer's body and of a critic's memory. Preservation — or the losing battle we fight with it — may in fact be the basic issue of American dance. The immediacy and the ephemerality of dance are its most particular qualities — they are the reason for dance's appeal as well as its low rank on the scale of intellectual values. People are thrilled by it because it is so singular an occurrence. When you have seen a dance, you've done something no one else will do again. But for this very reason scholars can't get hold of it. Dance leaves them with nothing tangible to analyze or categorize or put on reserve in the library.

In some way that isn't entirely perverse, dancers appreciate their own elusiveness in the culture. Their attitude toward filming their work is one of mistrust, and beneath their toleration for critics lies an unarticulated hostility. I often feel dancers would rather not have us see deeply into their work or meditate on its implications. They prefer to remain inaccessible to scholarly analysis, to exclude themselves from the normal processes of historical evaluation. They do what they do for their time, and their achievement is somehow exempt from being downgraded or superseded by later developments. If a dance makes a good impression, that impression tends to remain, and even to grow more splendid, in the minds of those who saw it. No one can go back and ask whether the impression was a mistake, or whether someone's success was due to a lack of sophistication in the audience or to any of a dozen magical accidents that happen in the theater. But we have no way, either, to review and strengthen our perception of things whose significance originally escaped us. No one can unravel or debunk the myth of Isadora Duncan or Ruth St. Denis or Nijinsky. Myths those dancers will remain, becoming more and more ethereal as the eyewitnesses to their work disappear. Nor do we really want to topple these gods, but we lack the means to consider their work for ourselves.

American dance is essentially without a history. Besides a written history, it also lacks anything except the most rudimentary and selective sense of its own past. For the first time, in the 1970s we are beginning to see a fairly widespread interest in the choreography of the early modern dancers. But the revivals being done are already watered down, taught by second- and third-generation dancers or even by notators who have never seen the dances at all. The audience is required to depend on steps alone and on our contemporaries' interpretations; we are asking the post-McLuhan generation to reveal the 1930s and 1940s to us. It's unreasonable, and it really doesn't work.

So the creative distinction of a Doris Humphrey — or even of a José Limón, who lived fifteen years longer — escapes us even though their contemporaries assure us of their importance. We try to be happy with a pale image of a Doris Humphrey work because that is the only image before us. We develop a callousness toward the simplest devices of history: documentation, attribution, the identification of sources and the establishment of background. We're used to seeing old works revived without benefit of program notes about their context or even their vital statistics. We are seldom told who was responsible for casting, teaching and rehearsing a revival, let alone by what method the choreography was reconstructed. Anyone who undertakes to establish what an old dance was steps on shaky ground — but we all attempt it in our own ways. We must.

For almost three quarters of a century in American dance, the most intense, individual pursuit of dance expression has been going on, an almost prodigal invention that often has spent itself leaving no real relics — generations teaching themselves to make it all new, only to be absorbed into later generations. The security and status that have benefited European dancers have thrown them into an almost complete paralysis of choreographic imagination, but the perilous existence that keeps American dancers outsiders has kept them free. They haven't had to please anyone, repeat their past successes, reinforce societal norms, or refrain from shocking people. They have been free to dance as they saw fit to dance. Since Western society has not come up with a way to have both security *and* creativity for artists, I prefer the way we've had it.

A critic of dance is in some ways a self-appointed historian. None of the documentary devices presently in use is as accessible, as highly developed, or as reliable as good on-the-spot dance criticism. The qualities of dance that make it so resistant to the conventional means of recovery are the ones that are the most intriguing to its critics. What many of us try to do is capture some essence of the dance; our writing is directed toward this rather than to the more cool and Olympian certitudes of critics in the other arts. For us, immediacy and accuracy of observation rank absurdly high, both in what we hope to achieve in our own work and in what we value in the work of others.

I began this book because of a desperate and continuing sense that not enough was being done to impede the extinction of yesterday's dance. Leaving so few and inadequate artifacts behind, dance is always in a way reinventing itself. It doesn't stay around long enough to become respectable or respected. Its ephemerality is mistaken for triviality. Because it is inherently always new, it's considered not to be profound.

I wanted to look at a wider range of dances than is usually available to be surveyed and see if I could uncover some of the sources of greatness by understanding what those dances were. I didn't start with any overall theories to prove, and I don't think I've found any explanations on which I can hang everything. Many forces, many influences, have been at work; if I found themes, they are the themes of America itself: diversity, independence, the lack of social stratification or any inviolable tradition, and an unapologetic openness to what in a more refined, less interesting society would be considered earthy or common or even coarse.

In trying to determine what makes American dance American, I decided not to observe the conventional ways of grouping dances. It seemed to me that dividing them up by choreographers, or following a strictly chronological sequence, or separating the world into "ballet" and "modern" would be just as artificial a way to account for what happened as looking across the board at how our major themes and forms got started. Even when ballet and modern dancers were angrily closed off from each other, their work represented a response, an argument, a refutation of what the other stood for. Now that the two "schools" have eased hostilities, we can see that they even had some things in common all along, and I thought that if I could find out what some of those things were, I might get at the American quality that underlies them both.

I think there are two basic approaches to stage dancing — the academic and the expressive. Academic dance is dedicated to the preservation of a style, a code of manners, a representation of society and art. Its appeal comes from its familiarity, its recognizability, and even its predictability. The audience goes to academic dance to be regaled with its own excellence, to be reminded of the world's perfectability even in imperfect times. And, of course, the audience is limited to those who can understand the language of academic dance and applaud its message. Most European stage dancing is academic, as are the court dances of the East and, probably, the ancient Greek rituals.

In expressive dance the style is only one of several possible means to state one's idea. The dance may want to tear down the society it comes from or endorse that society, but in any case it makes its endorsement or its protest without concern for proprieties. Its audience is looking for revelation of some kind, not reassurance. Most American dance has been expressive in the sense that it has been looking for new forms to express ideas or modifying the old forms when they stand in the way of ideas. And ideas can include visual, musical, kinetic, and other nonverbal concepts as well as intellectual ones. The European-born ballet choreographers who have contributed most to our dance were experimentalists, not fully successful or comfortable in their native ballet environments — Antony Tudor and George Balanchine are notable examples. And academically minded Americans like Glen Tetley, John Butler, Robert Cohan and John Neumeier have gravitated to Europe, where stability and formality are more highly prized. The more traditional influences from abroad (Massine, Ashton) have remained quite self-contained here, not inspiring new developments but instead adding to our raw materials in a general way.

I realize it is dangerous to categorize so broadly, and I hope the reader will think of this distinction as flexibly as it has been made.

Academic dance is often expressive, and expressive dance often uses the academic language. Alongside the most individualistic developments there has always been a popular European strain here, but even this has taken on a different kind of energy in its American interpretations.

I would also note that what survives is what has been best preserved, and when an effort at preservation is made, the prospects for survival increase. We know most about the academic dance of history because its business is to stay in business. The expressive dance only lives through the tradition of a continuous society, whether that is a tribe of Pacific islanders or a modern dance company. For all I know, there may have been a strong expressive strain in European choreography at one time, but it is not evident today except for those remnants of the relatively recent Central European modern dance that survived World War II.

Not only did American dancers not have much respect for academies, the ones they finally developed were identified with individuals rather than with anonymous traditions. "Classical ballet" or "modern dance" is part of every dancer's education, but there is no classical or modern school that constitutes a passport to success in the professional world, as for instance graduation from the Kirov or Bolshoi schools does for a Russian dancer. Our key schools are oriented to specific styles and lead the student to companies associated with those styles, like George Balanchine's School of American Ballet and New York City Ballet, Martha Graham's school and company. Usually the dancer has to undergo a transitional period with further specific training in order to enter a company outside his original orbit.

If the training of dancers has not become institutionalized, neither has the organization of performing companies themselves. Not until the mid-1960s did any dance company attain even quasi-public status, and this via financial subsidies that must be renewed from one year to the next. Official support for dance is only as permanent as this year's season; it can be withdrawn and funds cut in a poor budget year. The corporate identity of dance companies rests on the individual founders or directors of the companies rather than on any governmental unit. The existence of almost every one of our major dance organizations, including the repertory and the jobs of the dancers, has at some time been gravely threatened by the illness or death of one of its directors. I suspect a European would be puzzled by this. Characteristically, though, our companies seem to prefer it that way. A young choreographer in America invariably feels he must leave his home company and found his own group rather than mature under its wing. Since 1964 American dance has become noticeably more public, more "commercial," more stable and safe — and less independent and creative. It looks, almost everywhere, more and more like its European progenitors.

This book could not have been written without dancers, even though its main movers are choreographers, and I thank them for continuing to create the choreographers' visions for us. If there are too few dancers mentioned by name here, it's only because choreography must be able to outlast dancers in order for us to have a history. By this I do not mean that dancers and choreography can be separated. That the choreographies in this book will "live" somewhere, in some definite form, eternally. Or that, if they do live, the dances in this book and no others constitute the history of American choreography in the first three quarters of the twentieth century.

The works I chose to include — or to leave out — were selected only partly through a judicious screening of those seventy-five years of achievement. Some are undeniable landmarks, but epochal works like *Primitive Mysteries* and *Serenade* are so rare they cannot constitute a history by themselves. Many important works I have never seen, like Hanya Holm's *Trend,* or anything of Holm's work before she turned her creative hand entirely to musicals. Many that should be included are no longer in repertory, like Paul Taylor's *Scudorama,* and I wanted only works that I could study fresh for this book.

I've noticed that what I remember about a striking performance is impressionistic, and that I seldom retain enough specific information to back up my impressions or to give me any new thoughts about the work. So all the dances treated in detail here I have seen live at some time and have studied either live or on film during the writing of this book, and I've tried to indicate exactly which performances form the basis of my analysis. If no specific film or performance is referred to, the source can be assumed to be live performances by the dance's "home" company during the seasons 1974–75, 1975–76 and 1976–77. My second series of thanks goes to the managements and press representatives of those companies, who gave me the opportunity to see performances repeatedly with no immediate prospect of reviews, and to all the custodians of film and videotape who made it possible for me to view and make notes on those documents.

Even this outline of my sources will not satisfy the most rigorous requirements of historical research. The fact is that there really is no absolute form of a dance. Not only does a dance change subtly with different casts and in different theaters, but choreography undergoes a constant metamorphic process from the time it's made. Steps and designs change little by little, interpretations grow sharper or fuzzier, things get forgotten or inadvertently added, and — again *because* the dance is not a fixed, finished artifact — the choreographer who has second thoughts can change a dance from season to season in trying to improve it or adapt it to the resources at his or her disposal. The best a scholar can do with an old dance is to regard it in its present state and try to ascertain the source of its past or present greatness, taking into account whatever changes we're aware of. One "reads in" a style if it's not there and is supposed to be. In some cases I've compared past and present versions because to describe only the original would mislead people who've seen only current, greatly changed interpretations.

Nor is there any absolute way to describe a dance. Each critic and each member of the audience sees, feels and rationalizes a dance according to a highly individual complex of skills and sensibilities. I am "objective" only insofar as my eyes will allow me to be. Someone else could look at the same ballets and could describe and analyze them in a completely different way. In fact, I hope many more studies in this area will be made.

My discussion of these dances comes from an actual consideration of the dances as I saw them; I have made very little reference to the observations of other critics, since they can be read elsewhere. I have, however, drawn heavily on resources made available to me by many individuals and organizations. Most important of these is the John Simon Guggenheim Memorial Foundation, which granted me a fellowship to begin the work. For other materials and support I would like to thank the American Dance Festival, Sharon Bouck, Lucia Chase and Daryl Dodson of American Ballet Theater, Selma Jeanne Cohen, Merce Cunningham and the Cunningham Dance Foundation, the staff of the Dance Collection at the Library and Museum of Performing Arts in Lincoln Center, the Dance Notation Bureau, Jim D'Anna, Agnes de Mille, Jeff Duncan, Stella Giammassi and Harry Forbes at WNET/Channel 13, Martha Hill, Elizabeth Kagan, Linda Kohl and the NYU Video Center, Lewis Lloyd, Frederick Morgan, Harry Rubenstein at New Dance Group, Jane Sherman, Ted Steeg Productions, Ernestine Stodelle, Greg Tonning, Martha Wittman, and Shirley Wynne.

Andrew Mark Wentink, who assembled the illustrations, has produced a remarkable document of American styles both choreographic and photographic. I am very grateful for his contribution.

For the indefinable but most appreciated stimulus of their ideas, insights, arguments and enthusiasm I want to thank my friends and colleagues Arlene Croce, Cecily Dell, Senta Driver, Ann Fisk, Charles Fisk, Ellen Jacobs, Deborah Jowitt, John Mueller, Robert Pierce, Charles Scupine, Laura Shapiro, Suzanne Shelton, and Nathaniel Tileston. I am especially grateful to Robert Cornfield for his devoted guidance and understanding, to my editor at Houghton Mifflin, Jonathan Galassi, and to Dr. Richard Kavner for helping me to see.

The Shapes of Change

Rehearsal

Nijinsky is probably an All-American half back—
gone wrong.

— *from an interview in a*
San Francisco newspaper, 1917 [1]

*W*HEN DIAGHILEV's Ballets Russes, embodiment of all that was
new in European ballet, made its only two visits to the United
States, in 1916 and 1917, the company met with a very mixed reception — hostility from competing managements, jocular put-downs
from nervous journalists, boycotts of its high ticket prices, in-
frequent discerning criticism. The guardians of morality registered
shock at its decadent scenarios while pleasure-starved provincials
indulged in its color and design. Cultural snobs announced that
Pavlova's company represented *real* ballet.

America's response to the Diaghilev revolution says a great deal
about where American dance was going to go. At the turn of the
twentieth century, when American dance began, there were no
schools, no academies, no companies, no tradition handed down
through a royal line. Up to that time classical dancing had been imported from Europe by touring companies and by dancers who
emigrated here and established themselves as teachers. American
ballets, even when performed by American dancers, imitated what
the European companies had shown us. Even the demeaning practice of maintaining ballet companies only to provide accessory
adornment in grand opera was accepted in several cities.

But something was different here. The state opera house and the
subsidized, officially sanctioned high art it represented were not
American institutions. Impresario Sol Hurok, who was responsible
for so much of the dance and the audience for dance in America,

said that when he arrived here in 1906, "I found a people who neither sang nor danced. (I am not referring to the melodies of Tin-Pan Alley or the turkey-trot.) I could not understand it. I was dismayed by it. I was filled with a determination to help bring music and dance into their lives; to make these things an important part of their very existence."[2] Hurok attempted at the outset to make a distinction between art and entertainment. Yet his own career proved that he understood where so much American vitality was coming from; he would exploit that energy whenever he could but never call it by name.

When the ballet companies started coming, we had a great deal of our own stage dancing: in vaudeville, minstrel and variety shows, musical comedy, exhibition ballroom dancing. "Opera house" was often another name for a music hall, except on those rare occasions when a visiting Fanny Elssler or a traveling grand opera company took up a brief residence. Exotic dancers, tap dancers and ballet dancers appeared on the same stages in touring shows. In the big cities where there was a functioning opera company, touring ballet dancers often shared its bill, as Anna Pavlova and Mikhail Mordkin did with *Werther* at New York's Metropolitan in 1910. But ballet was just as likely to appear as an act in a revue; in 1916 Pavlova played the Hippodrome in New York with circus acts, drill teams and an ice show.

At first, most Americans must have seen ballet as merely an entertainment done on a stage, not as an aesthetic experience to be viewed with a deepening discrimination and taste. Our serious dance has always partaken of the popular arts; it has always come directly *from* the people or the times — or whatever constitutes our American environment — to a much greater extent than European dance comes from its environment. American dance expresses people; European dance, when it attempts to be popular, is created *for* people. I think the whole development of our dance up to the present time can be understood in the dynamic between these two attitudes. We have gone through periods when artists felt they had to remove themselves from any taint of the popular in order to do serious work, because in our country there was virtually no middle ground between commercialism and starvation. But even the most determinedly uncommercial, depopularized choreographers have drawn on the resources of the American character rather than on images dictated by other cultures and eras. Throughout the five

The Chester Hale Girls, from a musical revue in the 1920s.

most important decades of our dance history, ballet and modern choreographers have been heavily influenced by their work in movies, legitimate theater and television. The early modern dancers often created serious works to be performed as part of Broadway or nightclub shows. Jazz dancing fed directly into the vocabularies of ballet and modern dancers, and ballroom-exhibition styles have been used very successfully by stage choreographers. This constant stream of vernacular and popular material flowing into our art dance, sometimes by design and sometimes inadvertently, is one of the major sources of the creativity of American dance.

We had, at first, little reason for thinking of ballet as a serious art. If it had any symbolic or ceremonial meaning to Europeans as representing a moral order that could be attained through the workings of a class system, Americans had rejected that system, had denied, at least in principle, the obligations and rewards of a world where master, peasant and slave each keeps to his own place — the constant message of most nineteenth-century ballet. The traveling dancers who carried this message here were appreciated not as products of revered academies or as ornaments to crown a whole city's cultural achievement but for their more superficial qualities of physical attractiveness and offstage charisma. In nineteenth-century puritanical America, dancers were presumed to lead immoral lives. Genteel women did not go to the ballet at first. Whatever respectability ballet later acquired seems to have been connected to the humility Americans of cultural bent have always felt toward anything European. Ballet was patronized by the rich and admired by an awed middle class. But it was not ours; it was foreign, confirmed by long tradition; that was its appeal.

As a culture, America was just waking up around the turn of the century. Technological and economic improvements were putting people in touch with national and international styles and ideas in fashion, entertainment, homemaking — the automobile, telephone, radio, phonograph, movies and rapid long-distance travel all came within reach of middle-class Americans by 1925. It was during this first quarter of the twentieth century, concurrently with this dramatic broadening of our access to ease and refinement — and perhaps partly because of it — that the allure of European dance began to be felt strongly enough to be seen *as* a style, moreover as a style not native to America. People began to perceive that dancers were doing something besides impersonating supernatural or superhuman creatures and looking glamorous; that what they did came from a centuries-old tradition of discipline with different types and degrees of practitioners; that this discipline could be grafted onto American bodies. And quite soon, they made the further crucially American assumption that this tradition need not only be used in traditional European ways, and in fact need not even be the only serious discipline through which a dancing mystique could be expressed.

The two most potent European imports of the period were the conservative, star-centered dance of Pavlova and her company, and the exotic, sensual, and also star-centered modernism of the Ballets Russes de Diaghilev. Besides being a great artist, Pavlova was an independent, an original personality. Not an artistic innovator, she was a popularizer in the same sense as Nureyev is today: by her great personal charisma and artistic gifts she drew people into the theater who might not have come otherwise. Pavlova made quite a few films, some of them in Hollywood, and from them it appears that she reinforced the star image associated with ballet, but not by styling herself as a flamboyant personality at the center of a great stage spectacle. For her many tours the repertory consisted of short divertissements that gave her a chance to display her acting versatility and her technique in a variety of guises. Though she did reductions of the classics too, they were evidently arranged to highlight the solos and the corps de ballet work, with elaborate scenic and staging effects taking second place. Though contemporary critics praised her technical abilities, the films show that Pavlova — in her own dancing and in what she arranged for the ensemble — used only a few steps among the atmospheric floating tulle and expressive hand and face gestures. She seemed to walk on her toes endlessly, she posed prettily, took little flying jumps back and forth, focusing unusual attention on these technical accomplishments. In sum they might not have been very virtuosic, but Pavlova insisted that they be reckoned with. For years, Americans popularly believed that ballet meant "toe dancing," balancing on the toes for as much of the dance as possible while moving the arms gracefully. This was aesthetic. This was art.

Pavlova was also important for us because, although trained by the Maryinsky, Russia's greatest official ballet institution, she chose to operate outside the European state ballet system. After a season or two with Diaghilev, she even slipped out of his loose organizational framework. Nor did she simply travel around as a guest star for permanent companies. She supported and maintained her own company, and thus set a model for American dancers who wished to circumvent the artistic norms decreed by others. Her example was especially significant for women; unlike the nineteenth-century free-lance ballerinas, who were choreographed, managed, and produced by men, Pavlova added a more solid kind of self-determination and dignity to her sensational onstage success. Her ideas may have been conventional, but she set up her roles to suit herself and kept herself apart from personal scandal and business altercations.

The Ballets Russes appeared in New York and on tour in 1916, then returned the following year with Nijinsky as nominal artistic director. On both visits the company seems to have been in a depleted condition because of the war, and the second time Diaghilev stayed in Europe, leaving the enterprise in charge of the star whose absence from the first tour had been severely criticized. Nijinsky did create *Til Eulenspiegel* in the States, but his precarious mental condition hurt the faltering company he was so ill equipped to manage.

The repertory for both tours consisted largely of ballets on fantastic Russian themes — Russia at that time was considered as barbaric as China — and strange tableaux that transported audiences to exotic lands, customs, passions. Leon Bakst, an early principal designer for Diaghilev, helped create the luxurious image that was a

The Diaghilev company in a pose from SCHEHERAZADE.

company trademark. Bakst's designs — almost the direct antithesis of Isadora Duncan's natural line — show the dancer's body distorted, with opulent breasts and buttocks, elongated limbs, sinuous torsos, small delicate heads, and joints that could apparently rotate 360 degrees. He emphasized exotic features — the black skin and long slinky fingers of slaves, the slanted eyes of Orientals — and he dressed the dancers in a profusion of colors, textures, designs, and ornaments. From the many photographic and verbal accounts that remain of the Diaghilev period, it appears that the costumes were only one element of a deliberate effort to create an unusual aura for ballet, to make the dancers look unearthly, pagan, or superhumanly sensual.

Not only were the scenarios racy, the settings lush, and the musical scores rich and rhythmically insinuating, but the action of these ballets was removed to another time or place. The characters could transform themselves or indulge in behavior prohibited by proper society. Vicariously, so could the audience. In some American cities the sheriff was on hand to check on the reported miscegenation, homoeroticism and unrestrained passion, and some of the ballets were adjusted to satisfy the requirements of civic morals. What the Ballets Russes showed America was perhaps no more suggestive than what could be seen in the music hall or in some of the early silent movies, but it called itself art. This has always made Americans self-conscious. The ultrarefined, Beardsleyesque sensibility of the Ballets Russes at that time made people uncomfortable, as much for its implications about the exhausted condition of art as for its liberated moral behavior.

In the next decade or two, America became a refuge for artists fleeing the political upheavals in Europe and for dispersed elements of the Ballets Russes who were left without a company after Diaghilev's death in 1929. Naturally, they brought European ballet with them — founding schools and doing choreography modeled after the Imperial example, and touring the country in imitation Ballets Russes troupes. A generation after Diaghilev failed to conquer, hand-me-downs from his company and from Pavlova had permeated the American consciousness as "real" ballet.

The first American innovators found a welcome in Europe. Loie Fuller, as much a stage inventor as a dancer, created nonliteral images by manipulating lengths of cloth under special lighting effects. Fuller hardly danced at all, but what audiences saw were the swirls of gorgeous material illuminated in ways that had never before been seen on stage. She evoked fantasies of flames, luminous insects, sunsets, water. It was to be many more years before Americans could appreciate the sensuality of pure design. Fuller's work, with its emphasis on texture, flowing line, modulating color, and repetitive patterning, said more to Europeans in the throes of art nouveau than to Americans of less sophisticated, less jaded tastes.

Ruth St. Denis began her career in musical revues and never lost her flair for what was flashy and theatrical. Very early, she decided it was her calling to combine in her dancing the visual beauty and the spirtual message of various non-Western cultures. Her first program, in 1906, which was also said to be the first solo dance program ever given in New York, included three Indian portraits, *Radha, The Incense,* and *The Cobras.* She did these dances and others all over Europe for the next three years, and her glamorous quasi-mysticism proved neither threatening nor esoteric for the audiences she won there. Returning to the States in 1909, she began touring with the spectacular pageant *Egypta* and other works, under the management of a Broadway producer, Henry B. Harris. Throughout her career, St. Denis had a fascinating ability to combine practicality and idealism, and she could exploit her latent commercialism to further her high-minded purposes. She said, on returning home: "I had returned to America, full of love for her, determined to bring the best of my art; so I refused to be put off by any psychic difference between hurrying, moneymaking America, and the calmer, more aesthetic Europe."[3]

Isadora Duncan withstood the pressures to "go commercial." Though she too started out dancing in plays, once she had found her own inspiration she refused further commercial work. Paradoxically, although Duncan is considered the mother of American modern dance, she discovered her conceptual models in the museums and salons of Europe. In her endeavors to return through her dancing to the purity and harmony of Ancient Greece, in her association with prominent artists and thinkers of the early 1900s, she impressed herself on society as a serious artist too, albeit a dancer. There was an incongruity in this for Americans. Ruth St. Denis had intellectual pretensions but she was also a very beautiful woman, and she put on a good show. Duncan was unrelentingly earnest and made no concessions to glamour or spectacle, except the spectacle of her own compelling presence. Her American tours were not highly successful. Not only was she presumptuous enough to dance solo and unprettified, she wanted to be taken seriously too. There is a proselytizing tone that fills Duncan's writings and that must have filled her dancing, and then as now Americans hated to have art thrust on them.

In addition, Duncan's politics and her moral conduct infuriated American puritans. Though a professed artistic reformer who tried to cleanse dance of excess and phoniness, she gave antiestablishment speeches from the stage and made no secret of her unconventional love life. Though she supported relatives and hangers-on as well as a succession of schools with her concert earnings, she also lived on an extravagant scale. What a tragedy it is that no films exist of her dances so that we might see her work for ourselves, so that we might assess her directly, not colored by the strong emotional reactions she provoked in her contemporaries.

For an individualist like Isadora Duncan, European classicism constituted not a technical instrument or an aesthetic model but a confining mold to be broken. Until Duncan, dancers probably tended to express their independence in their personal lives rather than through their artistic activity. Duncan led an unconventional life, but she also thoroughly denied the aesthetic norms of her day.

Duncan is sometimes considered important because she danced barefoot or in loose clothing — she's thought to be a symbol of self-expression, of the triumph of the dancer's ego over tradition. More than that, she challenged the very image of the dancer by refusing to adopt the ballet dancer's "look" for herself — relinquishing the pulled-up rib cage and sternum, the turned-out legs, the placed arms and pointed feet. By her very stance, the solidity of her presence, she affirmed her connection to the ground rather than contriving to deny it. Duncan was rounded where the ballet dancer was straight, fleshy rather than tightly corseted. She was monumental; sculptors of heroic figures captured her: Maillol, Bourdelle, Rodin. Instead of twinkling delicately on the petals of flowers, she loomed solid before her audience. She proclaimed the verities of the ages, the material things that endure, rather than the ephemeral, spiritual mysteries that pass before they are understood.

It was important, after the codified escapism of nineteenth-century ballet, that a serious dancer should say this. Whatever else it was about Duncan that influenced Fokine, Nijinsky, and the other ballet modernists, the concreteness of the image she created must have impressed itself on their minds just as it still does on ours. And this image, because it was so at odds with the traditional ideal, was particularly important for women to have before them as an alternative to the decorative, inconsequential stereotypes that had preceded it.

The other thing about Duncan that was so crucial to the development of our dance was her commitment to teaching. Although in her contrary way she paid only sporadic attention to the schools she founded, she really based much of her thinking on the idea of transmitting her dance ideals by instilling them in young people. She thought in terms not of techniques that would prepare the student to perform repertory, but in terms of philosophy, aesthetics, health. She wished to belong to history not by means of theaters, documents, records, or reproductions of her performances, but through a legacy of action that other generations would carry on after her. Modern dance adopted this credo as early as the establishment of Denishawn in 1915, and for most of its history it has maintained the Duncan tradition that making stage work is inseparable from teaching an approach to dancing, and that both activities are based on individual points of view rather than on a merging of the individual into some overall mainstream of academicism.

Duncan placed more emphasis on performing and teaching than on choreography. Her dancing seemed inspired, unpremeditated, rather than rigidly planned. We even read accounts of her doing whole dances without any preparation other than listening to the music. Yet, in the photographs and written descriptions we have of her, it appears that she never looked like just an ordinary person dancing. She looked like a special person, a dancer, and this was to give later generations of American dancers the courage to look different again. Duncan showed how dancing could reflect an individual rather than a set of formal rules. She was an American pioneer, breaking away from Europe again, this time to make an art and, she hoped, a new society.

The Denishawn Succession

> Any technique is sufficient which adequately ex-
> presses the thought intended by the artist.
>
> You should *think* of the Dance as Art although you
> may have to *do* it as business.
>
> —Ruth St. Denis[1]

*I*N SPITE OF THE FIRST modern dancers' drastic efforts to reject
and reform the influence of Denishawn, we can see with the
perspective of time that the philosophy and achievement that was
Denishawn has filtered down through our whole dance history.
Denishawn, the school and company founded in Los Angeles in
1915 by Ruth St. Denis and Ted Shawn, was the first assertedly
American dance institution. Eclectic by choice, philosophical and
idealistic by temperament, Denishawn became identified with a
whole mystique of dancing and dance performance. Almost every
major modern dance choreographer can be traced back, via at least
one chain of development, to Denishawn.

The Denishawn engagement with myth and mystery extended
through Martha Graham, where it focused on the individual psyche, to the diverse points of view of Anna Sokolow, Anna Halprin,
Glen Tetley, Paul Sanasardo, Meredith Monk, and others. St. Denis'
music visualizations, attributable partly to Doris Humphrey, de-
scended through Humphrey-Weidman-Limón, and helped kindle
the musicality of Paul Taylor, Twyla Tharp, and Laura Dean. May
O'Donnell and Merce Cunningham carried pure-dance, kinetic experimentation from Graham, and so, in another way, did Erick
Hawkins, and in the present generation that line is being further
animated by Trisha Brown and Douglas Dunn. And Denishawn's

predilection for spectacle, for high-class glamour, was continued in Jack Cole, Lester Horton, Katherine Dunham, Alvin Ailey, and today's popular dance.

Besides laying out the ground for the next fifty years' work by the seriousness of their concerns, I think Denishawn lent American dance much of its unique character, established many of our dance's aims and limits. It was, after all, the first nonacademic school and company to capture the attention of the public. It was the first to announce itself as seeking to transmit what was genuinely American through dance, and thus it became a focal point for young people who wanted to dance but could not identify with the imported ballet of the time. Perhaps in spite of itself, American dance institutionally and philosophically has followed the lead of Denishawn, even when it has surpassed Denishawn artistically. Denishawn became a model for a tribe that wanted no models. Not until the contemporary era has our dance community begun to look back to Europe for a pattern of organization and an aesthetic that are more politically accommodating, more conventionally professional.

Several things fortuitously came together in Denishawn to make it the American institution that it was; its character still exerts an influence, it seems to me, because we still identify with these things even though we now can conduct our affairs in a more mature, rational manner. There were, first of all, the backgrounds of the two leaders. St. Denis and Shawn were all-Americans born and bred, bumpkins we might say, she coming from New Jersey and he from Kansas City. They had no urban sophistication and no family predisposition toward the arts. Before their meeting in 1913, and after they separated in the early 1930s, they went very different ways. St. Denis, attracted from childhood to the stage, won huge success, first in Europe, as a concert dancer, and fashioned respectability for herself by emphasizing the spiritual values in the lush, exotic dances she performed so seductively. And Shawn, a theological student with a he-man physique, took up dance as therapy after an illness and dedicated himself to combating society's two strongest fears about dance — namely, that it was immoral and that it was effeminate. Neither of them appears to have been an outstanding choreographer, particularly when arranging for a group. Yet they both made a serious pursuit of the art, St. Denis augmenting her native musicality and performing flair with the study of

Ruth St. Denis in 1927. Photo by Arnold Genthe.

yoga and Oriental religions, Shawn investigating the expressive gesture-language of Delsarte. They both sought out existing dance forms from all over the world as well as other kinds of human movement that they could adapt for dancing.

Only in the few years since their deaths (St. Denis died in 1968, Shawn in 1972) has the American dance community been able to consider them as anything but the beloved — or detested — parent-figures they were for so long. I have only seen them dancing as elderly people in films. But enough of their legend is remembered, enough of their choreography has been documented, for us to see them in a different light now. There was in both of them a certain amount of pretension. They both harbored and transmitted ambiguities concerning sex. Shawn, a homosexual, promoted male dancing in a variety of muscular portraits that seem crudely chauvinistic today but that impressed early audiences accustomed to jock athleticism in the movies if not the arts. Somehow in Shawn the desperate need not to be thought "queer" got mixed up with the altruistic wish to repair the weak, accessory role that men had been playing on ballet stages during the nineteenth century.

St. Denis' position was in some ways the complement of Shawn's. A beautiful woman, and also a gifted and ambitious one, St. Denis didn't take the easy route to success, through show business. Perhaps she feared her own sexual power; it seems that most of her lovers and her husband, Shawn, were younger men of doubtful heterosexuality. She neither concealed her physical attractiveness nor exploited it openly; she played the goddess — not just the icon-object but the source of mystical wisdom. Both her role and Shawn's were to be replayed by others, with variations, down the modern dance years, even after the relaxation of the puritan uneasiness that drove St. Denis and Shawn to fabricate these sexual guises.

It also occurs to me that they adopted these rather exalted responsibilities for themselves because they both may have had some self-consciousness about being artists. Perhaps they were too close to the workaday, plain and honest America to be altogether comfortable in the realm of high culture, and so they had to take on special missions to explain to themselves why they were spending their lives in that realm. Americans have always felt a little unsure about art and intellectualism. Our entertainments are full of zany professors, affected prima donnas, and lunatic thinkers; and in the period

EGYPTA (*St. Denis, 1910*).

of movies and radio from the 1920s to World War II, the distinctions between popular art and serious art were severely drawn. Isadora Duncan and Loie Fuller made their careers in Europe, where no one questioned a serious dancer's popularity; they never had to resolve this question. St. Denis and Shawn were breaking ground. For financial reasons alone, it wasn't easy for them to avoid being tainted by mammon. They made movies, even the biggest of them all, D. W. Griffith's "Intolerance." Regularly they had to install Denishawn numbers in Broadway shows and traveling revues in order to make enough money to keep going. But they consoled themselves with their idealism; they were made for purer things. In her autobiography St. Denis wrote about the aftermath of Denishawn:

It had apparently served its purpose and now came the inevitable upward path for the two individuals who had, like one of the threefold planes of Hindu life, been "householders," done their duty as parents and educators of their children, and made the contribution to their race. We had come together for the purpose of artistic birth; we had achieved that purpose, and now found ourselves once more solitary souls seeking even deeper meanings out of life. [2]

Denishawn was a vortex of dualities, many of which derived from its original home, California, the meeting place of East and West, cult and consumerism, poverty and play. Although it is easy to think of American culture, particularly dance, as emanating from New York and the European Judeo-Christian heritage, there has always been a strong Oriental influence in our dance. Both aspects of Eastern culture — the ornate and sensual, the monkish and spare — had their effect on Denishawn, just as Eastern thought and aesthetics later had great importance for Martha Graham, Merce Cunningham, and the whole line of American modern dance.

Ruth St. Denis found the blend of mysticism and ornamentation that suited her at the very beginning of her solo career. In the small works with which she astonished her first American and European audiences, as in the dances and larger spectacles to come, glamorous costumes and décors not only established the proper mystery, but probably covered for some fairly amateurish dancing as well — or at least dancing that must have been rudimentary in comparison with the period's ballets or chorus lines. The Denishawn dances that have been reconstructed in our time indicate to me that despite their classes in St. Denis' and Shawn's eclectic styles, the Denishawn dancers were not highly trained, even for their time. Some must have been good natural dancers, like St. Denis herself, able to project a mood, an intensity, however inauthentic or limited their skills. The others could do what they were required to do without the highly tuned, stretched agility and strength every professional dancer has today. St. Denis' choreography demanded a certain amount of flow and focus, a sense of line, but it couldn't have been hard to do. Shawn's vocabulary was made almost entirely of academic ballet steps, with character steps interpolated for variety or color. He seems to have had a minimal sense of flow — he didn't connect steps so that they could become an organic whole apart from the dramatic tension created by narrative.

Yet the company did dance and was successful, bringing its particular artistry to an enormous audience throughout the United States, Canada, Europe, and the Orient. Denishawn had lasting implications for dance in the towns across America; it played Sandusky, Ohio, and Gainesville, Florida; Bismarck, North Dakota, and Yakima, Washington; as well as New York and Los Angeles. For many provincial Americans, Denishawn was the first dance they ever saw, or it was an experience on a par with Pavlova's touring company or the Ballets Russes — or a vaudeville production by David Belasco. To them, the quality of the dancing was not important, the theatricality was what counted.

Without more documentary evidence, we can only guess at what would have been considered high-quality dancing in 1920, but we can say that ballet dancers had an academic standard to aim for. In every age, there has been some evolving code ballet dancers could agree described good dancing. The nonacademic dance had no such norms, and has none to this day. What came to be called modern dance meant a dance that fulfilled the needs of its leaders. Martha Graham's early company was a group of women with muscular legs, powerful feet, arms, and pelvises, and little subtlety in the upper body. The early Humphrey-Weidman dancers had exceptional fluidity in their arms and legs, rhythmic sensitivity, a feeling for the pulse and swing of their own weight.

By not demanding academic perfection, Denishawn opened up dancing to generations who might never have danced. Even today it's not uncommon to find professional modern dancers who started dancing in college. The commitment to dance isn't required so early as it is in ballet. The aim is not so narrow and the path not so straight. Distinctions between professional and nonprofessional dance are not so clear-cut. The nonprofessional factor in American dance is something few Europeans understand — that is, they don't understand how interwoven it is with the strictly professional. Denishawn was a model nonprofessional company, in the contemporary American sense. Because it was independent, the company's finances were precarious, and dancers were paid little and had to do their share of the company's housekeeping chores. On the long 1925–26 tour of the Orient, some dancers actually got no salary and paid their own expenses in order to be taken along. Perhaps the only Denishawn dancers we would think of as career professionals were those old enough and mature enough to teach in the school. The others were very young women — usually with middle-class families able to subsidize their classes and augment their poor earnings — who would perform for a few years and then go back to college to learn another profession, or who would marry or open a dance school of their own somewhere.

There was and is a constant interplay between performing modern dance companies and provincial dance on the college or studio level. This is where modern dancers, and many ballet dancers today, come from rather than from large state conservatories. It is where they return, with the exception of a determined and gifted few who stay in the professional arena. In many communities, college students or star pupils at the local ballet studio are the source of most dance performance and are loyally appreciated by their audiences. The nonprofessional local companies know they are building a dance audience, and touring remains the principal source of work for modern dance companies and many ballet companies as well.

We also have a strong salon tradition in American dance, which owes a lot to Denishawn. A dancer cultivated a special artistry that didn't depend on a big organization for a showcase, and that dancer could continue to dance as a soloist, or with a few devoted young followers, long after he or she could no longer maintain a financially solvent company. In the last years of his life Charles Weidman performed new and old works every Sunday night, with students, in the minuscule space where he lived and taught. Some people found his circumstances depressing, but others were in-

THE LAMP (*St. Denis, 1928*). *Ted Shawn, center.*

spired. I think he believed in what he was doing as much as if he'd had a big thriving ensemble and a theater to work with.

The key to much of Denishawn and its legacy is the idealism that the founders transmitted to the many young people they trained. The entire nonacademic succession has carried with it a sense of dedication, a sense that dance needs to create its own image and believe in that image because it has renounced the established forms and all the rewards to be had for preserving those forms. Modern dance has been innovative not because of some native American stubbornness or originality, but because that is how it defines itself.

By now it's an article of faith that the modern dancers intended to discover a dance form that would be expressive of America. But I'm not sure we really know what we mean by that, or what those dancers did in the early days. Notwithstanding the tremendous volume of creation in the immediate post-Denishawn years, 1930–40, almost nothing survives to demonstrate how the moderns went about their work and what they discovered.

People actually wrote about dance quite a lot in those burgeoning years. Dance criticism had not attained the depth and pertinence that much of it has today, but thought had not yet been discredited. People thought about dance, as civilized people think about any modern art, and they wrote books on dance theory, dance appreciation, philosophy, current history, aesthetics. But the dances themselves did not survive. In the course of a year you can perhaps see four or five live performances of modern dances composed before 1945. A handful of others were filmed in their original versions and can be seen. It is, essentially, this handful we should study to gain a picture of how and what the early moderns danced. But it's much too limited a selection, and even the best film omits the important factor of live presence. So we go to later interpretations, in revivals or on film, and try to project on them what seems to have been lost as the work came down through later dancers. Finally, there are dances that were never filmed or reconstructed, which we can only read about and try to imagine.

In the total careers of the individual choreographers, many of these lost works may deserve to be forgotten. Maybe Martha Graham had to do twenty character studies before she made *Frontier*. Maybe Humphrey's *Life of the Bee* was only a sketch for *New Dance*.

And maybe *Frontier* and *New Dance* were only a prelude to *Clytemnestra* and *Missa Brevis*. But I think we make a serious mistake if we assume that what we cannot see had no importance in itself. This is a dynastic view of art, a view that says we need not concern ourselves with history because what's taking place now is the highest development to which the art has attained. It says that anything worth surviving will survive, and the part that doesn't survive didn't deserve to.

This view cuts us off from our roots. To adopt it in modern dance is especially tragic because of the economic, social, and cultural conditions that surrounded those first, prodigious steps toward an American dance form. Then, as always, the preservation and recording of any dance work held a low priority; unless someone was willing to risk the effort and expense of a film or a notated score, the dance was ultimately abandoned. There wasn't money enough or public sympathy enough for any modern art to get a grip on society in the thirties. Government funding, via the Federal Dance Project, was washed away after a couple of years in a flood of political bickering, both internal and external, and what was accomplished there was tainted with socialism-by-rumor. The cooperative energy it generated among dancers ran out with the money. Dance was still associated in the public's mind with sexual license and immorality; dancers operated at the fringe of society socially as well as economically. Men shied away from dancing either because they couldn't make a living at it or because they would be considered homosexual, or both.

Yet, creatively, this was a period of enormous and rapid development, a progression from ideas to larger ideas, with much left unsaid and unexplored. There were no schools or academies to do the exploring. A choreographer trained other dancers in order to have people to produce her work. "Technique" came from one dancer's way of moving or rationalization of the movement process, and in many instances, certainly that of Graham, technique consisted largely of accretions of movement phrases and ideas from choreographed dances. There were no company structures as we know them today. A choreographer created and produced her work on a group of devoted dancers whose attachment to her she had to cultivate so they wouldn't drift off somewhere else in the periods between concerts. I suspect this fact alone — the absence of a permanent, economically sound company system — accounted in large part for the accusations of cultism and insularity that were heaped on modern dance later, and for the real bitterness and feuding that resulted at the breakups of these relationships that were personally instead of professionally rooted.

Yet, works were created and concerts given in New York with greater frequency than they are today. Some companies did some touring, but there were no established college circuits and of course no financial subsidies as there are now, so a modern dance company made its home and did its work in New York. In 1935, for example, the year Doris Humphrey made *New Dance*, Martha Graham showed new group and solo works at the Guild Theater in February, April, and November and did a group work at Bennington School of Dance in the summer. Helen Tamiris and her group premièred *Cycle of Unrest, Mass Study,* and *Harvest* at New York theaters in January, March, and November, in addition to appearing three times in concerts with other dance companies and giving a program of the dancers' compositions.

It might take Doris Humphrey several months to make a huge work like *New Dance*, but in their early years, the modern dancers created several works — solos and small groups — for a program. These dances were often very brief. Elizabeth Selden, who wrote a thorough contemporary account of modern dance aesthetics, *The Dancer's Quest*, said that she once gave a seven-minute dance, and it was considered rather long for that period — only one or two dancers performed, and they needed time to breathe.[3] But each piece was an exploration, an experiment. Having learned whatever was to be learned from it, the choreographer might keep it in repertory for a few seasons and then discard it, much as our avant-garde dancers do with their new works today. Once dropped, the great majority of these dances were lost.

With the establishment of the summer dance school at Bennington College in 1934, a certain sense of solidity came to modern dance, even if the anchorage was only provided for a few weeks a year. Those choreographers and their companies who enjoyed residencies at Bennington began to luxuriate in the time to work it afforded them, and began to think of dances on a bigger scale. The first six parts of *New Dance* were given at Bennington, as were Humphrey's *With My Red Fires* and *Passacaglia;* Hanya Holm's *Trend;* Graham's *American Document, Letter to the World, El Penitente, Deaths and Entrances;* and many other works. Ideas that had been suggested before on a smaller scale could be consolidated; a choreographer didn't have to make many little dances to keep her company busy, she could undertake bigger projects.

Bennington also became one center for the development of "American" dance ideas. A strong patriotism prevailed there in the years before the war. After a couple of seasons, German-born Hanya Holm was shipped out to start a new modern dance summer school in Colorado. Bennington was hostile to ballet, but Lincoln Kirstein's Ballet Caravan gave its debut performance there in 1936 — due, in large part probably, to Kirstein's avowed intention of building an American classical dance form.

Beginnings

I have tried to combine emotion with intellect.
Some call my art tragic, far removed from
sweetness and prettiness. I have tried only to interpret modern man and his fate.

— *Mary Wigman* [1]

IT'S NOT POSSIBLE to identify the real beginnings of a phenomenon as diversified and as organic to our American cultural development as modern dance. Some people automatically consider
Isadora Duncan as the founder, others give the credit to Ruth St.
Denis, but we could as well trace some of the roots of American
dance to the levees of the Mississippi or the free-thinking religions
of the nineteenth century. The works I've chosen to call beginnings
are significant because they represent surviving formative work by
some of our primary choreographers, and they all look very different from the Denishawn/Duncan work that preceded them. There
are no traces of the secondhand balleticism or the formless expres-
sivity we associate with the earliest American dancers.

While Duncan seems to have relied on her instinctive musicality
and her body's gift for plastique, and St. Denis and Shawn modified the balletic language they inherited, we see Graham,
Humphrey, and Tamiris setting out to visualize clear, unexplored
ideas and forms, and devising languages through which those ideas
could be conveyed. What is perhaps most striking about these
dances is that they all employ the dancer nonrepresentationally.
That is, what the dancer is doing stands for something else: *Water
Study* illustrates the play of natural forces, *Life of the Bee* duplicates
a social structure in microcosm, *Lamentation* projects an emotional
state, not the person who is experiencing it. Even *Air for the G*

String and *Spirituals*, while they bring the audience directly in touch with the performers, are working toward abstraction to a far greater degree than did the exotic visualizations of Denishawn.

The early modern dancers seemed suspicious of "just" dancing; it smacked of showing off to them, or of worse kinds of exploitation. "I'm tired of darling little dances and I long for a good thick juicy beef-dance-steak that I can chew on hard," Doris Humphrey wrote in 1927.[2] Humphrey made pure-dance works at all stages of her career, but these always tried to express what she heard in music. She thought that to do a Japanese or a Spanish dance for stylistic variety was false to the experience of an American dancer.[3] Graham began with salon studies in the Denishawn manner, in which she posed and sculpted herself into innumerable porcelain geishas and Greek bacchantes. But as early as 1927 *Revolt* leaps out at us from the list of her dance titles, and within a couple of years the languid poses are gone, the subjects begin to require more of the viewer than casual viewing. Even Helen Tamiris, the most glamorous and physically outgoing of the early moderns, placed her immense attractiveness at the disposal of her intention to show the conflict of modern life.

Denishawn can hardly have been as aesthetically corrupt as the European ballet against which Duncan rebelled, but to Graham and Humphrey and their contemporaries it seemed trivial, overdecorative, and above all restrictive. Denishawn was no dignified tradition, entrenched beyond personal criticism, as were the European ballet academies. It was Miss Ruth and Papa Ted, who insisted on loyalty from their dancers, and who would countenance no deviations from their methods of teaching and choreographing. Young dancers wanted the freedom to be themselves. The beginning of modern dance was at one and the same time a purification of Denishawn decadence and an insistence on the validity of individual dance expression.

Air for the G String (Doris Humphrey)

Doris Humphrey choreographed during her Denishawn years (1917–28), doing solos for herself and group works, some in collaboration with Ruth St. Denis. She and Charles Weidman were sent to New York to run a new branch of the Denishawn school, and they gave concerts consisting of Denishawn work and their own. *Air for the G String* was first seen at the Little Theater, Brooklyn, in March 1928, in a concert given under the Denishawn aegis. But the two artists had been chafing under the Denishawn oligarchy for a long time, and shortly after this first major New York performance they broke completely with their leaders.

Humphrey no doubt was already feeling the urge for independence when she choreographed *Air for the G String*. Although it has some of the surface gloss of the later Denishawn period — I think of the chill perfection of St. Denis' *White Jade,* for instance — this little dance has definite leanings toward the compositional originality that became Humphrey's distinction. Fortunately, the dance was filmed in 1934; complete with Leopold Stokowski-ish orchestration, its handsome Hollywood treatment was the sort of high-class, reverent gesture the mass media often made toward the serious arts in those days. This film preserves not only the choreography but an exquisite Doris Humphrey dancing in the central role. (She did not dance in the original performances.) The work has been reconstructed in recent years, most notably by Ernestine Stodelle, a former Humphrey dancer who also appears in the film, for a summer workshop at New York University in 1976. Stodelle's production restored the original color concept to the dance: costumes of gold, pale peach and blue with warm lighting, an effect she says was based on the paintings of Fra Angelico.

The dance, set to the familiar music from Bach's third orchestral suite, consists almost entirely of walking patterns for five women dressed in plain floor-length shifts with extremely long swags of material attached to their shoulders and trailing behind them. As with so many of the Denishawn dances, when the curtain goes up on these voluminous costumes, the audience knows immediately that no "real" dancing is going to get done. But Humphrey does more than model the dancers in beautiful arrangements of draperies.

With a careful eye for the fold and swirl of the heavy material, she designs processional patterns in which the women are continuously sculpting the space in precise lines and flowing curves. The dance neither stops to pin down any tableau or position nor skims over the movement that facilitates change. It seems to me that one of the turning points in concert dance occurred when choreographers began to be as interested in the visual possibilities of traveling as

Ernestine Day in AIR FOR THE G STRING (*Humphrey, 1928*).

they were in static positions or attitudes of the body. Humphrey's dancers create a metaphor in motion rather than a set of pictures. Even on the occasions when the dance collects itself into a solid grouping of the women, their arms continue lifting and the curves of their body postures keep the viewer's eye flowing out into space, continuing the line they have momentarily suspended.

The other interesting thing about the dance is its suggestion of "character." Denishawn adopted material from other cultures in much the same way that nineteenth-century ballet masters had: they copied more or less authentic dance movement, ritual behavior, or scenes from art history, modified them for their own stage requirements, and took care to surround them with enough costume, props, and acting information so the audience could recognize them. Humphrey instead concentrated on a few elements, almost moods, indicative of Renaissance maidens, and simply let these color the style of her own dance. George Balanchine and other ballet choreographers developed the same device on a classical base.

In *Air for the G String*, Humphrey incorporated the tilted pelvis and slightly tipped-back upper body of the fifteenth century as well as the delicatedly molded, showy arm gestures. It's necessary to keep the pelvis moving forward through the whole step and shift of weight in this walk, or the body will lose its line. And this is a definitely nonvertical line, something Humphrey employed over and over again in her later work. Here, as the women incline backward, they give a hint of piety. It's fascinating to me, though, that the dance is not about pious women or a saintly ritual when it so easily could have been. Why these women glide around in orderly paths; why they sometimes gather around the central woman, who may or may not be their leader, bending and lightly entwining wrists and arms; why they have such an ethereal look, seeming to float above the floor despite the undeniable attachment to the ground provided by their costumes — all these are things one wonders in the seven or eight minutes it takes to perform the dance. Ruth St. Denis could make an ordinary dance seem mysterious and seductive by the way she performed it; Doris Humphrey showed that the dance could create its own enigma.

Water Study (Doris Humphrey)

Only a few months later Humphrey and Weidman were on their own, and in a New York concert in October 1928 she showed what is still one of the most extraordinary works in American dance, *Water Study*. As small and strange as it is, *Water Study* is a masterpiece of the choreographic art.*

It has often been observed that Doris Humphrey's great talent was for choreography while Martha Graham was greater as a performer. We really don't have enough information to accept this easy distinction. Neither artist's early work has been fully enough documented; Humphrey became disabled by arthritis quite early and had to stop dancing by 1944; and the very different personalities of the two women probably determined a lot about how their careers developed.

*Although *Water Study* has been notated, it has been given recently in more than one form. I am chiefly describing the version reconstructed by Ernestine Stodelle for students at N.Y.U. in 1976.

Yet, there seems to be truth in this truism. Graham, before the institution of her first real company, made many more solos than group dances. There would be an occasional trio, or a trio-plus-Martha combination, but mostly her concerts were a showcase for herself. She didn't choreograph for men at all until Erick Hawkins joined her in the late thirties. Humphrey from the outset made as many group dances as solos, and she conceived of the group in many different ways, from duets between herself and Weidman to women's ensembles of various sizes, sometimes with herself and/or Weidman at the head. As early as the 1928 Brooklyn concert she was working with seventeen dancers, which even today is large for a modern dance.

There's a big difference between doing group choreography to provide audience relief from solo showpieces or to extend ideas beyond what a soloist can do, and finding the group a more interesting and expressive medium than your own body. Humphrey's firm sense of design and musicality must have been strengthened because she was able to sit out in the audience and watch what her dancers were doing. Her book *The Art of Making Dances* (1959) is ample testament to a lifelong concern with composition. Unlike Graham, she was able to get outside the dance to construct it.

Rather than leave the development of what they hoped would be a serious art form to the random instincts of its practitioners, some leading modern dancers codified their work and linked it philosophically with other forms of modern art. The chief theorist and proselytizer of the movement, musician Louis Horst, worked as an accompanist at Denishawn and left in 1923 with Martha Graham to become her musical director. Horst began teaching dance composition in 1928 at the Neighborhood Playhouse, advocating a return to "natural" movement and body awareness that would be disciplined to create new forms of communication. "The realistic gesture or posture is taken as a point of departure on which to construct a poetic metaphor," he wrote in *Modern Dance Forms*.[4] By "realistic" Horst meant that the body was to have more latitude of expression than under the prescribed rules of classical ballet. In this early period of modern dance the Americans were the closest they ever came to the expressionistic modern dancers of Europe, and *Water Study* would not have surprised the followers of Mary Wigman.

To a modern audience, the first look at *Water Study* must be a very strange experience. Its nearest relative in contemporary dance is the choreography of Alwin Nikolais, but it has no need for all the costume and lighting paraphernalia that Nikolais uses to create natural imagery. *Water Study* is an impersonal dance, the most abstract of all Humphrey's surviving works. It is an example — perhaps a very extreme one, because it is so well fulfilled — of what the modern dance theorists were proposing when the fires of idealism burned strongest in them.

Water Study is a collection of images of water. In silence, fourteen dancers create these images both collectively and individually, using movement that does not *describe* the movement of water but corresponds to its energies and spatial configurations. Humphrey told critic Margaret Lloyd that she began "with human feeling . . . with body movement and its momentum in relation to the psyche and to gravity, and as it developed the movements took on the form and tempo of moving water."[5]

The dance is not specifically symbolic; that is, you cannot say one dancer represents the wave and another the spray, or even that one part of the stage is the shore and another the ocean. Each dancer contains within herself all the elements of all the images, so that she is creating simultaneously the ebb and flow of energy, the evolving design of an expanding and shrinking body shape, and a changing stage landscape as she travels through the space. The group as a whole does the same thing, breathing and shifting together to keep a continual ebb and flow of energy, changing its total outline, and traveling together to make new arrangements of the space. Doris Humphrey had a genius for microcosm. She could reproduce the overall form of a dance within the activity of a small group or the steps of an individual dancer. Her dances fit together like wonderful geometric structures, interlocking, overlapping, reflecting, multiplying, wheels within wheels.

When the dance begins, the dancers are spaced evenly around the stage; each is curled tightly into a ball, resting on her knees. One by one, beginning to the right of the audience, a ripple passes across the space — the dancers slowly rise a little off the floor, keeping a low crouched position. The last person makes this move and settles back down again, and the bodies fold and sink in succession back across the space from left to right. This slight rising/sinking motion is initiated in the center of the dancer's body, the pelvis, and forms one of two basic movement seeds for the whole dance. It is repeated four times; each time the trunk lengthens a little more, the arms spread, and a tendency toward propulsion becomes more pronounced and more urgent. Each dancer times her move with her own breath rhythm, which is in accord but not necessarily synonymous with the rhythm of everyone else. Each dancer begins to move individually and waits in a kind of suspension until the movement passes back to her. The effect is to make the watcher's eye travel across the stage, following the movement like a current or a wave. But there is, here and throughout the dance, an undercurrent of energy always present in the suspended forms of the waiting dancers, and the audience can almost hear a surging rhythm like the flow of a calm sea.

At first, nothing in the shape of the dancers' bodies actually looks like a watery shape, but as the impetus builds, some of them throw their torsos into a backward arching curve on the upward push, then fold over again into a lunge, the arms flinging first back and then over the body like a cresting wave. On the fifth rise, the dancers pull up out of the lunge to stand and quickly divide into two groups that run to opposite sides of the stage. Without breaking the breath rhythm, some people run to the center from each group and break into a big arching-back jump facing the center, sliding sideways flat to the floor as they land, while the remaining dancers on both sides continue the rising-lengthening-arching-folding cycle out of which the jumps have emerged.

The jumpers change places with the other dancers, who rush forward and jump as the first group did. After four sets of jumps, one half of the center group falls onto their backs as the others jump. The jumpers bend forward as they land and grasp the hands of the women on the floor, pulling them to their feet and taking them with them to the right side of the stage. One repeat of this sequence gets the whole group together. For the first time the stage is not full, and one feels the emptiness to the left as a vast expanse.

Facing the open space, the group forms two lines, one standing and one kneeling on one knee. They lift, swing back, arch forward, and run straight across the stage, the lower group staying low to the ground and somersaulting forward the last few feet of the distance. The standing group pulls them up and across to the right, where they begin again.

After the somersaults, the whole group runs diagonally across the stage, wheeling on a suspended breath and flocking back the other way. After the fourth cross, five dancers emerge from the rear of the group. Holding hands in a chain, they circle in front of the group and around to upstage, where they stand in a line facing away from the audience. Quickly and without pausing to consolidate this new floor pattern, the five dancers move in sequence, each one beginning a split second before her predecessor has finished. Each one's move is an evolution of the one before: the first dancer jumps straight into the air, the second jumps up with both arms slightly curved to her left, and this sideways tendency continues into a spiral, with the third dancer flinging her arms around her waist, the fourth twisting to face behind her as she flings her arms, and the last spiraling down to the floor where she makes a complete circle with her upper body and then reverses direction to spiral up to her feet again. Meanwhile, all the remaining dancers have gathered in a close group, sunk to the floor downstage of the standing group, and made one cycle — falling back from the knees and circling around the side of the body, back to an upright kneeling position, at half the speed of the standing group.

This sequence is the most complex development of *Water Study*'s second movement motif, the circle around the dancer's body. Spatially, we could see the whole dance as being made of two kinds of circle. One surrounds the dancer like a wheel in front, below, behind, and above the body. Its complete form is the somersault, but usually we see only pieces of it, the upside-down U of the opening moves, the arched-back jumps. The other circle encompasses all the space horizontally around the body. It's seen every time the dancers twist their upper bodies from a kneeling profile to face the audience, in the circular recoveries on the floor in the counterpoint section just described, and also in the path that the five dancers take to reach their position upstage. The sequence of five overlapping moves takes us uninterruptedly from the arching forward and back cycle to the horizontal cycle, with the three-dimensional spiral movements of the middle dancers providing a connection between the two space patterns. As the eye follows it, the sequence makes a flowing curve that changes level and direction — from the first dancer standing and facing upstage to the last one falling toward downstage.

After this exclamation, but proceeding from it without a break, the group once more coalesces into unison ebb and flow as everyone faces the audience and shifts from standing foot to foot. They spread their arms out to the sides as the torso expands, and close them in toward the body as it shrinks on the exhalation of breath. The individual dancers change position imperceptibly, one step at a time in this sideways-swaying interlude, giving the effect of a mass that is pulsating and gently shifting without actually changing shape or location.

The momentum begins to subside then; the tempo slows down, the dancers sink to one knee, then to both, as they continue to sway from side to side, and in one motion they pivot into profile again, once more spread out to fill up the entire stage space. One more spurt of energy passes over the group, this time reversing the pattern established at the beginning. Starting to the left of the audience, the dancers fling themselves up and backward and hover, suspended back on their knees. The folding begins from the right after the last figure has spent itself, each dancer reaching around with an arm and circling her upper body around to the front, and at the same time lowering the pelvis to the floor until each is closed into a ball again. The opening wave begins once more, but instead of curling up after rising, each dancer crawls a few steps in a lunge and falls slowly forward. When all the dancers are prone on the floor the dance is over.

To me, *Water Study* is almost as powerful a musical experience as a visual one. An unfortunate revival several years ago by the now-defunct National Ballet of Washington had the dancers inhaling and expelling their breath so loudly that the audience could actually hear them. I think Doris Humphrey's idea about breathing was that we should *not* hear it but feel it, internalize it, so that the flow of events on the stage becomes as natural to us as it is to the dancers. The dynamic variety implicit within this flow should be no more surprising than the crash of a wave against a rock or the heavy drag of a receding tide. The fact that the dance is done in silence requires each performer to participate in the build-ups and dissolutions of energy. There is no counted-out unison in the piece; each dancer times her moves in relation to the other dancers, both pace and interval can quicken and decelerate at different points in the dance. The group must constantly remain aware of itself, and the dance as a whole is unusually cohesive — the mass moves and the sense of the mass impels individual dancers to move. The dance is constantly in motion, collecting and spreading itself, but never still.

Life of the Bee (Doris Humphrey)

Premièred six months after *Water Study,* in March 1929, *Life of the Bee* was a much more ambitious composition, and I think a less successful one. It is important, however, because it indicates the complexity of Humphrey's ideas and the communicative range of which she thought choreography was capable. The only production I have seen was staged by Joyce Trisler for the Danscompany early in 1975, based on Humphrey's own 1958 Juilliard Dance Theater revision.

It was not until a 1955 Juilliard revival that Humphrey set the work to music, Paul Hindemith's Kammermusik #1. In keeping with one of the most emphatic principles of the new dance, Humphrey thought dance need not depend on musical accompaniment, that as a primary expressive art it could do without accompaniment or dictate its own musical terms. *Life of the Bee* was originally performed to offstage humming through combs and tissue paper, but its rhythm was established, as in *Water Study,* by the collective thrust of the dancers' energy.

Doris Humphrey was doing several important compositional things in *Life of the Bee.* It seems odd that she, who was so pragmatic and so little given to fantasy or poetic ornament, would have been inspired by the turn-of-the-century symbolist Maurice Maeterlinck, but she seems to have found in his work a way of thinking about the human life cycle that was not tied to specific characters or incidents. At this point she seemed to need to interpose a nonhuman agent in order to make the translation from cosmic organization and universal emotion to a dance metaphor. A few years later, *New Dance* accomplished much the same thing as *Bee,* but in a more natural and direct dancing mode. Critic Margaret Lloyd astutely observed that "in these early works Doris intuitively struck theater while striving to reach autonomous, abstract dance."[6] This is certainly true of *Bee,* where the struggle against literality is so determined that it results in contrived-looking movement, and the viewer hangs on to the "story" for dear life.

Humphrey did a lot of research for *Life of the Bee,* investigating the social habits and the biological structure of these fascinating insects. Once again she tried to produce movement and staging patterns that would express some human equivalent to the behavior of natural phenomena. She saw rhythm first, and like *Water Study* this dance is pervaded with a continuous, fluctuating current of energy, the ceaseless activity of the hive. Where *Water Study*'s energy comes from the center of the dancers' bodies and can be generated in place without any locomotion at all, the basic energy in *Life of the Bee* is peripheral; the dance seems to keep constantly in motion by means of steps, going at a pace from moderately fast to very fast, often overlaid with a second pulse in the arms. *Water Study* feels self-contained, plastic, able to flow in any direction and still hold together; *Bee*'s energy is bottled up, full of inner conflicts but limited in the shapes it can take when it breaks out. Humphrey seemed to want the dancers not to look like people; the movement and the characteristic uses of the body in this dance are strange, distorted, often exaggeratedly large or abnormally fast and small.

The dance falls without pause into four sections: the nurturing and birth of the new queen; the queen's coming to life; the battle between the new queen and the old, with the challenger victorious; and a dance of celebration presided over by the new queen. In terms of human drama, this scenario has possibilities for four different kinds of dancing. First is the highly organized, purposeful opening group dance, in which the activity is clearly directed toward some as yet unrevealed goal, the bundled figure on the floor of whom they're so solicitous. Next is the young queen's solo, in which she begins waveringly, unable to control her actions, is supported by the group, and gradually grows in strength and opens her body into space at the same time. The duet for the two queens is unique in my dance experience, a fierce fight between women. And the closing group dance is of a completely different character from the first, though it retains much of the movement material introduced earlier.

Within this program Humphrey found additional ways to differentiate the group: small individual solos arise out of the ensemble patterns, and a trio with its own leader serves as a sort of inner-circle escort to the young queen. In the Danscompany production three men performed these duties — the program listed them as Drones. Humphrey choreographed the work on an all-female company, so we can't tell whether she intended the moments when they surround and lift the queen to refer to sexual impregnation, although the idea would have been reasonable. She might also have intended the movement of the young queen and old queen as variations on a theme; the contemporary version uses the old queen's solo as rechoreographed by Joyce Trisler when she was dancing with Humphrey in the fifties. Both antagonists work, as do all the dancers, with a body attitude strongly divided between right and left sides. There is virtually no gestural crossing over the body's midline, no twisting horizontally, no oppositional tensions; the working arm and leg are usually on the same side. But where the young queen strives for openness, the old queen crouches over, swoops, and dives, one leg flying high into extension, hands locked together, arms lancing down or back behind the body.

The dance as a whole replicates the theme of unfolding that evolves in the young queen's body. In the first scene, the workers fan the queen — or more precisely the queen-egg, a dancer who lies on her back, her legs folded under and her arms pressed flat along the front of her body. The workers characteristically move in a squatting second position, skittering in lines from side to side, often with their outstretched hands vibrating. But this dynamo energy can also be transferred to shaking heads, pumping arms, or a bouncing of the entire body initiated in the pelvis. The formations are constantly changing, but the queen is always at the center. At this point the dance has a very compact feeling even though there's a lot of motion, much of it very large motion. We are looking at a cell, with hot, active molecules streaking around inside it.

When the queen is "born," members of the group lift her, still rigidly folded together, and continue to fan her until she puts her feet on the ground. Then they withdraw to the outskirts of the stage, enlarging the cell but still enclosing her as she makes her first wobbling essays in space. They collect at the left side of the space and remain motionless during the battle of the queens except for the penultimate sequence, when the opponents plunge right into their midst. For a moment there is a roiling, disorderly mass, tightly packed, with the women thrashing at the center. Then the enemies emerge, the young queen dragging the old queen by the neck. The loser's torso is arched backward, and as she rolls out of the hive she wrenches and bends her body as if it would break in the middle.

In the celebration dance, the sense of enclosure is broken entirely as the new queen presides over a prancing, running processional along ramps and a platform at the back of the stage. Two at a time, the workers tumble down to the front, each pair exploding with a different movement — rolling, jumping, falling, swinging the leg in big gestures. The queen whirls among them as they form small, finicky group patterns in different parts of the stage — fragments perhaps of their former corporate geometry — and at last she leads them up the ramps and out in a line, arms stretched straight out, bodies slightly tilted as they run into the open air.

Assuming that the general outlines of the dance are intact, we can see that it was hampered by its insistent bilaterality of body attitude and by a tendency toward overregimented floor patterns. Humphrey was not entirely satisfied with the dance, although it was an immediate success. She tried to "build it better than it was originally" when she revived it in 1941. She must have been aware of dramatic inconsistencies when she wrote in a letter: "The whole point is to build up the choreography sufficiently so it will not matter what it is about." [7]

The human analogy sometimes breaks down if we try to follow the sequence as a narrative, but if we look at the dance as a purely abstract structure, the dancers' humanness gets in the way. The movement is too grotesque; the patterns look arbitrary and Germanic. Humphrey's work throughout her career showed traces of a too-stubborn design sense, but most of the time she was able to

LIFE OF THE BEE (*Humphrey, 1929*). *Photo by Soichi Sunami.*

transcend this by setting movement that could move freely and still carry out her visual intention. These three surviving works before *Shakers* show her grappling for the first time with what to her were the main issues of choreography.

Lamentation (Martha Graham)

Martha Graham may have made pieces as radical as *Lamentation* before 1930, but the photographs and descriptions that survive indicate she was proceeding gradually, not radically, away from the Orientalisms of her Denishawn background. She was finding her way toward an expression "purged . . . of the superficial prettiness of the past," in the words of Robert Sabin.[8] Writers spoke of her severity, the seriousness and emotional intensity of her work, its angularity and unusually high dynamics, but the photographs of those earliest works show her being expressive in acceptable terms for a concert dancer of those days.

One film, *Flute of Krishna,* survives from her post-Denishawn days. Made for her students when Graham was teaching at Rochester in 1926, the dance shows her idea of a vignette from Indian myth — the Lord Krishna wooing Radha and three other young women. As she had seen St. Denis do often, Graham took her pictorial cue from Indian paintings and other artifacts. The setting is an archway with an overall painted design, perhaps more Persian-flavored than Indian, and the costumes are flowing trousers for the man and harem pants and tops for the women, with skirts that convert into shawls, veils, and other elements of decoration in the course of the dance.

Graham typically started with poses from statuary and paintings, although she was none too scrupulous about copying them literally. But instead of having her dancers glide around in the same poses or try to rearrange themselves smoothly to achieve a succession of poses, Graham seemed to be looking for ways to animate the poses. Instead of having the women sway from side to side, she tried other movements that took them on excursions through space before they arrived at the next position. We see the beginning of the spiral — the body moving three-dimensionally rather than on a flat plane — which she employed so brilliantly as an expressive device later on. In the *Nautch Dance*, Ruth St. Denis had worked to keep her body consistent with those arm and torso configurations she thought of as Middle Eastern. She swung her voluminous skirt because her hips and legs were making it swing as they swiveled from one side to the other. Graham's dancers carried the diagonal tendency beyond the point where St. Denis would have reversed the body to reassemble on the other side, and got into turning, into backward arcs of the head and upper body, with one arm closing provocatively across the chest. The transformations of costume seem to come out of this exploration of the space around the dancer's body, too, instead of from some preconceived idea that the costume must be gracefully manipulated.

By the time of *Lamentation,* Graham looked very different from this, and from all the commonly accepted theater dance forms of the time.* Lincoln Kirstein, coming from a background that he only later understood as a deteriorating phase of Russian ballet, has described his initial disappointment with Graham:

I went to Graham expecting to be shocked further than by the collaborations of Picasso, Cocteau and Massine. I was unequipped for her simplicity and self-blinded to her genuinely primitive expression. For me the primitive was the primitivistic, the Stravinsky of Sacre and Noces, with all their attendant resources of complex colour, historic reference and elaborate orchestration. The archaic was the archaistic of the Afternoon of a Faun: *the contemporary was the Chic of* Parade *or* Les Biches. *This solitary dancer, not even a girl, with her Spartan band of girls seeming to me to press themselves into replicas of the steel woman she was, appeared either naive or pretentious, which, I could never fully decide.*[9]

Perhaps no dance up to 1930 — certainly none that survives today — so thoroughly destroyed the conventional image of the dancer as did *Lamentation.* Even *Water Study,* so radical in its concept of what bodies could be made to do on a stage, preserved for most of its duration the dancer's capacity for locomotion. I think ev-

*Graham revived the dance in 1975 for two of her company members, Janet Eilber and Peggy Lyman. Being contemporary dancers, trained in both ballet and the softer, more peripheral Graham style of today, and also being tall, lyrical women, their dynamics were quite different from what we see in Graham herself, doing the dance in two films made in the 1930s.

erywhere in the Western world, right up to the present time, our idea of dancing includes some picture of a person on his feet. Dancing is running, jumping, leaping, skipping, bourréeing, bowing, promenading, tapping, shuffling, waltzing, two-stepping, tangoing, and even walking or standing still. *Lamentation* is dancing sitting down.

Not only is the dancer sitting down, she is encased in a tube of lavender stretch jersey with only her feet, hands, and part of her face and neck showing. Graham thus limited her motion possibilities and deprived the audience of one of the sights it expected to see, the dancer's body — limbs, waist, arms, torso, all of the suggestive physical apparatus upon which the ballet depended so heavily. This deliberate closing of the obvious channels for artistry must be part of what Kirstein meant by "her genuinely primitive expression." Certainly Graham was not then, or ever, primitive in the sense of elementary or unsophisticated.

What she achieved by restricting herself in this fashion was an unnaturally intense concentration on the body's dynamics. It's not just that she makes herself into an odd shape, but the minute she starts to move, the tube gets pulled into diagonals that cross the center of her body; as she tugs asymmetrically in opposition to the rounded forms of her back, her head, her arching rib cage, the jersey converts the energy of stress and distortion into visible shapes and lines.

The dance's opening image is a prelude, purposely basic. The figure sits on a bench, legs and arms spread and flexed, feet rooted into the ground for leverage as she rocks from side to side. Monolithic, as if it had taken a cosmic push to move her, she shifts the mass of her body off its vertical axis, all of it together, then hefts it over to the other side, her head swinging through a forward arc. Gradually she pulls herself over more violently, skews an arm up toward her head, hitches a leg up and out, gets almost off-balance on her seat. The pulse of her rocking has built up into a momentum that destroys rather than preserves equilibrium.

Except for the rocking pulse that thrums through her body, she resists any fluidity. The dancer's body looks hard, braced against itself. The limbs work as if on hinges, in one piece, from the big hip or shoulder joints. A foot starts to pull off its mooring, but only the flexed toes and metatarsal come up; the heel digs even more firmly

Martha Graham in LAMENTATION (*Graham, 1930*). *Photo by Barbara Morgan,* © *1969*.

into the ground. She lifts one leg, knee bent, the foot sickled inward in some primal gesture of grasping.

Gestures that have no literal counterpart emerge out of this dis-
tended, nearly inhuman shape. She wraps her flat, closed hands in
the cloth, mummifying them, and places them against each cheek.
She touches the shroud with flat hands, worshiping it. She clasps
her hands in front of her, conflicting energies suddenly collected,
and plunges them straight down into the jersey between her
legs — a symbolic dive into a grave perhaps, as if she herself were
the earth or a pit with no bottom. She spreads her elbows until her
whole head disappears in the folds of cloth, and twists her upper
body as if it were dangling from a noose. Because she does nothing
else, these gestures assume almost mythic importance, suggest the

collective grief of whole societies. Though she sits, her posture is that of ancient tribes squatting in the dirt.

Yet she is a white Anglo-Saxon woman. And it is a particular kind of grief — confined by its costume and its rhythm, and by the design that Graham wants the audience to see this body making. It's a very ritualized, depersonalized kind of grief, one that allows the woman no real release. At two points in the dance, when she seems about to tip or pull herself off-balance entirely, she draws back into the stability of a symmetrical pose. She finds comfort in form and balance, not in letting go. She seems to be referring to heaven or to some cruel power outside of herself as she rocks back and later stretches an arm high overhead. Now she's standing; now she puts one foot on the bench as if she would climb up and claw down the thing that is responsible for her condition. Again, no release. No jump, no explosion. With the upraised hand she pulls the cloth down over her head, pulling her body over with it, until she sinks to the bench. Continuing this folding-forward motion, she pitches over, stopping only when her fist touches the floor.

Graham tried a new ending for Lyman and Eilber: they slid off the bench knees first, straight, narrow, to the floor, fitted finally to a coffin. But she later reinstated her original, more iconic conclusion. The figure remains a symbol of grief in our final image of her; she doesn't succumb to her tragedy. In the films of Graham doing the dance, she doesn't pretend to cry or distort her face in mimed sorrow. She makes no effort to communicate anything to the camera with her face; her face is an expression of some process going on within her, one that is deeply satisfying if painful. She looks almost ecstatic.

Negro Spirituals (Helen Tamiris)

Helen Tamiris was an outsider, a very different breed from the other matriarchs of modern dance. Like Humphrey and a later descendant in the Humphrey-Weidman line, Pauline Koner, Tamiris began her career in ballet. After five years in opera ballet companies, she gathered an eclectic dance education that included classes with Michel Fokine, instruction in Duncan technique, and an apprenticeship in the commercial dance world of shows and nightclubs, before she gave her first New York concert in October 1927. Tamiris had ideas she knew she couldn't work out while dancing in revues or musicals, but she didn't disdain the world of entertainment. She choreographed her first musical in 1929 and appeared at Radio City Music Hall in 1933, when Graham and Humphrey had renounced the popular stage for good. Tamiris continued to find a fruitful creative outlet in the theater, particularly on Broadway, until her death in 1966, choreographing such successful shows as "Annie Get Your Gun," "Up in Central Park," and "Plain and Fancy." This activity took her out of the group who dedicated themselves solely to the concert dance. She was in good company — Agnes de Mille, Jerome Robbins and Donald McKayle are only three of the many serious choreographers who have made valuable contributions in both the "art" and the popular fields of dance.

Tamiris paid a price for this dual career, however. She had a succession of concert groups, but did not maintain either a long-term school or company that could give her work continuity. Nor did she teach for the purpose of codifying a technique or transmitting a repertory. She didn't participate in the prestigious Bennington School of Dance, the focal point of modern dance activity. In those days you had to have your own company, cultivate your own students; it was the only way of making sure your work could be passed on to the future. I also suspect Tamiris was the victim of a subtle snobbery and clannishness among the "in" modern dancers. She enjoyed life and she enjoyed dancing. The clique thought her rather vulgar.

Yet she identified herself with modern dancers, and during her lifetime she led many efforts to produce their work under more favorable circumstances. She kept organizing producing units to present a number of modern dance companies under one roof; none of them succeeded for more than a couple of seasons. She was a staff choreographer under the Federal Dance Project and gave countless benefits — alone and with other dancers — to help liberal causes. She was a founder of the Stage Directors and Choreographers union.

In an excellent monograph and chronology of Tamiris' work, historian Christena Schlundt points out that she never lost her attachment to the social, urban life of which she was a part. She wanted to make dance for the public, not for an exclusive coterie, and she used popular dance idioms and themes, as she used her own beauty and vitality, without self-consciousness. Schlundt feels she personified the "modern" in modern dance: "a responsiveness to the unformulated will of an epoch, a drive to do what the time requires,"[10] but it was just this temporal involvement that has made her an unknown quantity to the present generation.

Strangely enough, though, it is Tamiris' philosophy and her ideas about dance and its audience that have had the greater influence on the modern dance companies of today. Graham and Humphrey gave techniques to dancers — movement languages from which dances could be written — but their deepest perceptions about their purpose as artists are only dimly remembered now. The present generation of modern dance companies are, almost by definition, popular companies. They were created in a time of public subsidy and they exist because of their ability to make an immediate impression on large, untutored audiences as they tour the country. Like Tamiris, they trust in glamour and a dynamic delivery. She choreographed about her time, the problems and aspirations of society; they choreograph about neurosis and commercialism and sexuality. She used Negro songs and jazz; they use rock and country music. Tamiris did not come from Denishawn; she didn't mask her popular appeal with high-flown theories or mysticism, so she was thought to be somehow less of an artist. I think she was simply more comfortable with a tendency that has been present in every phase and every area of our dance development.

Tamiris started choreographing Negro spirituals in the very beginning of her concert career. *Nobody Knows* and *Joshua* were given at her second New York concert in January 1928. She added more over a period of fourteen years until there were nine such dances of her own and a few choreographed by members of her group. She presented these short dances in various combinations on concert programs throughout her career, and in 1959 she filmed five of the solos.* To my knowledge, this document is the only remaining primary-source example of either her concert or her commercial work.

The spirituals have been controversial in our time, as is all white interpretation of black material. They were extremely successful

Go Down Moses (1932), *Swing Low* (1929), *Git on Board* (1932), *Crucifixion* (1931), and *Joshua Fit the Battle of Jericho* (1928).

when Tamiris first presented them, and at the end of her life, when she set them for a racially mixed group of students at New York's High School of Performing Arts, they were greeted respectfully. But when her nephew, Bruce Becker, reconstructed six of the numbers, his performances in the mid-seventies received boos as well as applause. I want to comment mainly on the choreographic aspects of what Tamiris was doing in her film; its racist implications or egalitarian rhetoric may have more to do with our style than hers. From what we know of her life, she seems hardly to have been the type to patronize or exploit this kind of material. She responded to it, and in her own way. Perhaps her lack of guile is what we miss as Becker so artfully tries to imitate her.

Tamiris' concept of the spirituals was pantomimic in the ballet sense: she made up abstract, gestural equivalents of the words. Although Louis Horst accompanied her first concerts, Genevieve Pitot joined her in 1930 and was responsible for the piano-vocal arrangements that accompany the film. The music is a concert version of the simple songs, and the singers have warm, rich, almost operatic voices, but this is the way much black music was presented at the time, by black singers as well as by whites. Pitot adjusted the tempi in odd ways to accommodate the dance, and Tamiris interpreted them literally.

What is striking to me, however, is her very selective and controlled use of the body at a time when this material would surely have been jazzed up or made pretentious by everyone else. In the film, at least, she confines her expressive medium to her own body's gesture; she hardly travels at all, taking only a few steps that seem to well up out of a need to make the gesture bigger if only her limbs could do it. Space is not the instrument for projecting energy or feeling — as it is in Alvin Ailey's *Cry*, for instance, a contemporary treatment of similar themes. We concentrate on this dancing figure alone, as we do in *Lamentation*, because she doesn't send the dance away from herself. Whatever happens happens *to* her, is absorbed into her spirit. When, at several points, she seems to see or hear someone from outside herself, we don't become curious about who it is or what she's reacting to; it is her reaction that captivates us.

Each song has a few thematic gestural ideas that the dancer varies as the verse continues; most of these gestures are either directed toward the body or directed outward to no particular place, being simply declamatory. The arms swing open and closed from the elbows in *Git on Board*, reminding us of a door or a gate, and also in an abstract way of a large, motherly embrace. She digs her hands, straight-armed, in toward her hips in *Crucifixion*, suggesting both the image of the Cross and the piercing wounds of the Crucified. In *Go Down Moses* she alternates a stern finger-pointing-in-the-air gesture with a bent-over, quavery, shrinking stance that could refer to old Pharaoh. And in *Swing Low, Sweet Chariot* a big waving gesture becomes a drop-swing of the whole body from side to side. The one really clear outward-pushing gesture in the film, throwing down

Helen Tamiris in ''Jericho'' from NEGRO SPIRITUALS *(Tamiris, 1928). Photo by Thomas Bouchard.*

the walls of Jericho, is preceded by a wind-up that grows bigger and bigger, so that the final push becomes not the climax of the statement but its aftermath almost.

In devising these abstractions, Tamiris did something that was quite common among the modern dancers. Her point of view shifts. If she is acting out something, it's not always the same thing. In *Moses,* at first she's God commanding Moses, then she becomes Pharaoh. Later in the song she represents the oppressed people trying to free themselves ("When Israel was in Egypt land . . ."). In *Swing Low* she seems merely to be dancing joyfully at the approach of the "chariot," but then for a minute we glimpse the "band of angels" and finally the big swings that are nothing more than a very direct physical expression of the title. It is common in East Indian dramatic dance for the dancer to take several roles in succession, and in the West mimes often do this too. Tamiris has an exceptional clarity of motivation when she makes these changes, so we never become confused — we know when she switches from being God to being the person God is talking about.

Her economy and precision in choosing gesture are also notable. Each move is carefully planned to be specific enough to carry the intended connotations and also to be capable of nuance when slightly modified. She tends to eliminate everything except the one telling agent of change. Setting her body in a position, she may move with imperceptible steps, changing only the position of her arms or head. Tamiris places a great deal of stress on connecting movements. Not only must they be in character, they must be clear. In the *Spirituals* we can also see the way she pays attention to tiny, transitional movements, brings them to the surface, and enlarges them so that they also can become gestural. A preparation becomes a huge wind-up, a tiny rocking reverberation becomes a swing of the whole torso, an invisible push through the spine to the neck and head enlarges to a forceful thrust of the head. Except in the matter of these transitional ideas, she devised her movement by subtraction or condensation, making a strutting or shuffling step so small you could barely recognize it, eliminating the curves or the droop of relaxing muscles from ordinary shapes to make them angular and flat, stopping the flow of a gesture's path precisely at a certain place instead of letting the movement dribble away as it does naturally.

I want to look at only one dance of this group in detail. *Crucifixion* is the starkest and to me the most interesting musically and as a design, but it contains all the devices I have mentioned. The dance is stationary. The dancer shifts the direction in which she faces but does not travel at all. Not only that, the whole dance is done in the upper body, the legs serving only for support. Her body is always asymmetrical; perhaps she was trying to avoid the literal picture of a cross, although I think she also had a natural preference for the off-balance pose. I also have a strong impression that she was deliberately keeping her body wide through the chest and shoulders. The consistent body image that projects to us is one of inflexible, massive power in the upper body, dangling, useless legs, a head that droops listlessly to one side, and arms that enact the whole drama while the back and lower torso writhe in agony.

She stands with her arms hanging slightly away from the body, palms facing in, fingers pressed together. ("They crucified my Lord, and he never said a mumbling word.") With a hyperextended lower back, she leans backward, as if she has been pushed hard in the chest, and falls back twice more with two smaller pushes or repercussions. As the music repeats, she starts to bend back again, her arms lifting, then really falls and has to take a step to recover her balance. Then she drops her arms, palms out toward the camera, and slowly turns her upper body from the waist. ("Not a word, not a word, not a word.")

Without changing the shape of her torso or the relationship of her arms and hands, she pulls one shoulder up, then the other, quickly several times, with some big tugs, some small. This pulls her whole body into diagonal tension. ("They nailed Him to the tree . . .") At the end of the refrain she returns to her initial pose, finishing with arms held away from the body and her hands breaking at the wrists so that the fingers point toward the thighs.

In the musical rest, the arms lift farther away from the body and then begin to dig hard toward the thighs, once very harshly, then with a few afterblows, though they never touch the body. ("They pierced Him in the side . . .") Her hands spring open with small vibrating bounces, and the verse begins again. With it, the sequence repeats, the head bobbing too this time on the reverberations. She turns away, one shoulder pulled up, the other arm dangling, weight resting heavily on her right foot.

Then she turns again into profile, stands on both feet, her body drooping forward slightly, arms open as before. ("The blood came trickling down . . .'') From her back, she pushes her body backward several times with big and small pushes, she droops, rises and pushes, falls off-balance and recovers. At last she turns to face the camera straight on and opens her arms into the horizontal, hands hanging from the wrists, head drooping to one side, and stands that way as the music ends.

Ritual

An Elder sister led the band,
With sounding timbrel in her hand,
While virgins move by her command,
And after her they danced.
                                    — *Shaker hymn* [1]

MANY PEOPLE THINK dancing has its source in man's spiritual being. Mary Wigman and the German modern dancers were also digging their way back to these roots in 1931 when the two religious masterpieces of American dance were composed. They were Martha Graham's *Primitive Mysteries* and Doris Humphrey's *The Shakers*. It's hard to believe that two such radical dances could have originated in the same year, and that they should be as different from one another again as they were from the conventional works of the time.

Graham and Humphrey were already recognized as leading innovators in what was then called the New Dance. Their audiences were fanatically loyal — and intolerant of each other. If you liked the Graham approach, you couldn't possibly like Humphrey too. Young dancers had to decide which of the two schools they were drawn to, and having decided, they seldom switched. Modern dance then was a matter of personal identification, not merely of whether you liked the teachers or thought their choreography was inspiring. For Graham and Humphrey it must have been a source of tremendous power and creative growth to work with dancers who wanted to look as much like them as possible when they moved — like multiplying yourself several times over. The unifying power of all this idealism and devotion flowed into *Primitive Mysteries* and *The Shakers*. Devotion to a godlike presence was what both these dances were about. Although to modern audiences they may seem slight (*Shakers* is only about nine minutes long) or obscure or underproduced, both dances have an authentic spirit of communion seldom attained by forty ballet dancers doing Petipa.

Perhaps the closest precedent for these two works in ballet was Nijinsky's *Le Sacre du Printemps* (1913). That massive, revolutionary ballet did not survive, so we can't be sure exactly what it did, but it seems to have concentrated on the driving power of the group; the ecstasy inherent, but seldom discovered, in form; the savage beauty that is unlocked when man reestablishes his connection to cosmic forces. Bronislava Nijinska's *Les Noces* ten years later fitted these earthy currents of energy into the personal dilemma and fulfillment surrounding the celebration of a wedding; thus it led right back to the more conventional ways of treating religious subjects, as story or character ballets showing particular experiences of faith or revelation. Even after *The Shakers* and *Primitive Mysteries* had been done, few modern dancers probed this area again in search of thoroughly new forms, although many have returned to ritualistic sources for subject matter.

Primitive Mysteries and *The Shakers* both resulted from the choreographers' interest in American folk practices, and both refer to Christian belief. In going straight to the ritual rather than to the charismatic personalities or events of the sects that interested them, Humphrey and Graham chose a more difficult course than most of the later choreographers who wished to celebrate the American character, and the dances, perhaps for this reason, are more abstract and impersonal than much of the work that followed them.

Primitive Mysteries (Martha Graham)

Primitive Mysteries is not an enjoyable dance.* It is not a dance you go to in order to be entertained — satisfied, yes, uplifted, mystified, moved. It is a terse, severely disciplined dance, not a kinesthetic joyride. Excitement is brought to a certain pitch and then immediately modulated into different intensities. Something of great import is constantly claiming your attention. There are no lapses or blurred moments in the choreography when you can let your emotions subside except for two complete stops, when the

*This analysis is based in large part on a study of the dance as revived and filmed at Connecticut College in 1964, with Yuriko in the leading role created by Martha Graham.

stage is cleared and the audience is left to stare at emptiness and absorb the impact of what has just occurred. Graham controls the stage event absolutely, and intends it to have the same effect as a religious service.*

There are specifics that are known about the dance. It was one of several works Graham devised after studying the Indians of the Southwest, American natives who had been converted by the Spanish missionaries and whose religion combined Catholicism with the more elemental beliefs of their earlier faith. But the dance gives you few direct hints of these sources. There are no overt references to the magnificent, violent desert landscape that constitutes a major force of life in the Southwest. The people who enact this drama and the forms of their observance seem fabricated out of whole cloth. Sometimes you catch a glimpse of a familiar motif — an attitude of prayer, perhaps, or a pose remembered from a catechism — but the images are transformed, sharpened, purged of all the sentiment with which memory endows them. Although there is clearly one central figure, her relation to the group is ambiguous. She seems at times to be leading their worship ritual, at other times to be telling them a story, and at still other times to be passively submitting to their adoration. Despite Graham's Protestantism, *Primitive Mysteries* seems to be one enormous Hail Mary.

It took eleven years of looking at this dance, live and on film, for this symbolism to become thoroughly clear to me. Not that it isn't available once perceived, but the patterns and energies of the group have more often drawn my attention away from the central figure. In the conventional method of staging a ballet, when the main characters are present they do most of the moving, and the ensemble makes decorous rearrangements of its shape to complement but not overwhelm the central action. In *Primitive Mysteries*, the main character either acts responsively with the ensemble or changes position in the pauses between their actions. It is the pagan vitality of the group that animates the icon, and this has a lot to do with what Graham must have perceived about the Christian Indians.

The first section, Hymn to the Virgin, begins in silence — a processional, lines of women, four at a time, striding forward into the

*She evidently had different ideas about this when she revived it in 1977. Here, as throughout, I am trying to get at first creative impulses, rather than nicer, neater, more acceptable second thoughts.

arena, heels down first. Alone between two of the lines walks another woman, different from them in her costume and in her solitariness but in nothing else. This way of introducing the dancers occurred again in *El Penitente*, another of Graham's dances about the Indians, and suggests the presentation of a mystery play where the townspeople enact sacred roles. Graham opened and closed each of the three episodes in *Primitive Mysteries* with one of these processionals, each in a different formation. The effect, besides setting apart each phase of the dance, is to keep reestablishing the common identity of each participant in the rite, to reassert the possibility that any one of them might play a crucial role in what is to come. Not even their costumes foretell what they are to do: the twelve women wear dark blue dresses with tight-fitting bodices, short sleeves, plain, round, collarless necklines, and flaring ankle-length skirts. The single woman wears what might be a plain version of a party dress for a Southern belle, in white organdy with flowing panels and sleeves, a dress that is almost demurely feminine yet conceals the shape of the body. The woman wearing it could be a matron or a teen-ager.

The three groups of four women station themselves in three straight lines, one at the back of the space, the other two facing each other across it. A flute and piano speak and answer in short phrases, and the woman in white hurries from one group to another. The woman and the group gesture responsively to each other; the phrase gets longer and the gestural dialogues contain more information. They speak of praise and prayer, of blessing and comfort. Each small group works as a unit to answer the Virgin and to complement the designs she makes. A few times near the end of this sequence she fixes her arms in an open pose and becomes rigid like a statue; the group supports her from behind as she leans back or launches herself forward. Two of the groups come close together and form a double file through which the Virgin passes. Each woman in turn receives a benediction and acknowledges it. The sacrament performed, all the women process into a large circle around the Virgin.

They begin strutting backward and forward around her to a marcato five-count melody that the piano and flute play in unison but in different registers. At each end of the groove that they're digging by backing up and treading forward, they lash their arms around their bodies, clasping them behind and pulling back on the forward

PRIMITIVE MYSTERIES (*Graham, 1931*). *Graham (c) and company. Photo by Barbara Morgan, © 1969.*

step, and clasping them in front, pulling the upper body toward the gound, when striding back. Though it's a five-count phrase, the steps and turns are set up so that each woman remains in the same segment of the circle, making no headway in either direction.

The phrase gains a beat and accelerates. As if the regularizing of the beat — from five to six — had fortified their intention, the dancers begin making a complete turn on their back-and-forth pathway. They begin emphasizing the vertical, jumping into the air or bouncing down to the ground on each turn, at the same time as they pedal their hands up and down in front of their bodies. They seem to be pushing off from the earth, being sent heavenward by a great propelling force. The bodies have stopped wrenching forward and back, and have become straight and taut, like arrows shot into the sky.

Suddenly, on a cadence in the music they stop, turn to the center of the circle, where the Virgin has been sitting. She rises, keeping her arms in the same iconic position, and they fold their bodies from the waist and bow to the ground. After a pause, they march off the stage in formation.

In the second section, Crucifixus, the group paces back and forth while the piano marks every step and the flute mourns in sustained high tones. The Virgin stands upstage center, flanked by two women from the group. They seem to be posing: the Virgin holds both hands to her face, as if terror had interrupted prayer; the two guardians are lunging forward with one hand resting peremptorily on the back hip and the other stretched toward heaven, with the index finger pointing.

The patrolling women in the group seem to be waiting, agonized, for something to happen. Their elbows are pulled together and held in front of their chests; the upper arms are folded back toward the sides of their faces. As they stalk around in this odd pose, you notice that the Virgin and her two companions — guards or heralds or accusers or disciples, whatever they are — have been imperceptibly advancing downstage. There is an abrupt hold in the music, the women in the group bring one hand up flat to their foreheads, and as the music-steps begin again they back into a circle and sink to one knee with the other leg extended back. On a cadence the two women fall away from the Virgin and she suddenly stands with her arms spread out, palms forward, center of the body contracted. Is she the crucified, or is she merely empathizing with an unseen figure on the cross? My guess is that Graham had both meanings in mind — the crucifixion scene itself, so often depicted in art, and the more human, personal feelings of the mother who had to witness the event.

While the Virgin stands there, a woman from the group steps out into a slow-motion leap and run with her hands clasped behind her as in the earlier circle dance. One by one the others follow and the pace gradually accelerates. There's almost no describing the suppressed fury of this dance. The huge leaping-forward step is initially confined and distorted by the slowness of the music. Then, like a broken movie projector, the momentum builds and seems to run away with itself, until all ten women are running and jumping ahead into space but held back by their own arms tightly clutched behind them, pulling back their shoulders, tugging backward against the forward thrust of the upper torso; they don't get anywhere except around, in that once-jubilant circle.

Then the pointless race is abruptly cut off. On a cadence from the piano and flute playing in two keys, the women suddenly fall to both knees facing the center, their hands clasped in front again. The Virgin's two companions turn to go, look over their shoulders once toward the sky, as if dreading another blow, then turn away. The group gets up and forms a processional to leave.

When they return for the last section, Hosannah, there are only eleven women, one of whom immediately detaches herself from the group to become the Virgin's partner. This entire section is a dialogue between these two figures, the woman from the group perhaps standing in for Christ. The story is told in a series of picture-book poses that recall the Crucifixion, the Pietà, and the Assumption of the Virgin. The sequence is like stop-action photography, with the chorus dancing a bouncy celebration to repeating sixteenth notes in the music. Their dance is interrupted so that the duet can continue into another pose, and the duo's action is held while the dancing continues. Thematically the group moves with traces of earlier motifs: their arms are pulled down in front of them, hands clasped, as in the first section, but their bodies now are vertical, springing in a direct line from earth to heaven.

Later the group does a series of big flourishing bows and praising gestures with their arms while standing in place, and as the drama reaches its climax, the crowning of the Virgin, they advance around the two protagonists, then fall to their knees. The Virgin's final beatification is enacted as she stands and lifts her arms while the accomplice, seated on the floor behind her, lifts *her* arms in unison. Graham used this symbolic gesture elsewhere for renewal and the reunion of earth with heaven. The group witnesses this, not on their knees, but seated with legs open and knees drawn up close to the body, arms clasped around them. As they rise to leave, they go over onto their knees and fold their bodies up completely, touching heads to the ground, in a gesture of utmost worship.

Although I have given much of this description an emotional coloration, it must be made clear that nothing in *Primitive Mysteries* is dramatic or pantomimic in an acting sense. Two kinds of movement devices put across these ideas without literally imitating them. One is the isolated gesture, a pointing finger, hands touching the body, hands clasped. These are treated in a design sense, without being given full support from the rest of the body and the face, and their very detachment from the action of the person as a whole makes us notice them and see them as symbols.

The other expressive technique is Graham's use of the whole body in a nonliteral way to create a metaphor: the slowed-down, held-back frenzied runs in the second section; the centered symmetricality with which the Virgin presides over the ritual and with which the group pays her homage, the varieties of locomotion, none of them quite realistic — the deliberate striding and long pauses between steps in the processionals, the Virgin's exaggerated skipping as she visits one then another group of worshipers, the flatfooted, springy walks of jubilation that seem to reestablish the dancer's contact with the earth even as she bounds into the air. Gravity and space do certain things to the body when it moves in certain ways, and to the spectator, who feels an answering sensation in his own body. Graham's early choreography was based very largely on these universals; that is why it was so moving to some people, so repellent to others, even when it told nothing in a representational sense.

Not that *Primitive Mysteries* is untheatrical. Graham may have rejected the spectacle, the physical exploitativeness and the vague mysticism of Denishawn, but she was fully aware of how effective the Denishawn works were on the stage. In *Primitive Mysteries* she had already assembled most of the techniques and devices that were to confirm her as one of America's most gifted stage directors. Her use of rhythm and dynamics was particularly masterful in this piece, and she was greatly aided by Louis Horst's score, which was dependent on the dance and supported the action at all times. The music, like the movement, is not continuous, but is often interrupted to allow the event to change. There is no thematic development, no rhythmic pulse that is allowed to go on long enough to automatically propel the action.

The use and type of the phrase in both music and movement are very expressive of the dance's meaning. At first, a series of short, declarative responsive statements; then the hesitant but increasingly affirmative circle dance. In part two, the protracted sense of doom, the women's tense, sustained walking as the main figures get nearer and nearer. Then, after the awful event, the leaping, running circle that accelerates and is suddenly cut off at its peak of effort. And the springy, elated activity that begins the third section, subsiding gradually as the women settle into one spot, then sink to the floor and become immobile, totally in subjection to the miracle that has taken place. The silences, during which all the processionals and many of the key dramatic visions are enacted, are tremendously important. The viewer notices them more, too, because the score avoids melodic development and predictability. The silences break in rudely, commandingly.

The movement language of *Primitive Mysteries* is untranslatable in the terms that had served theater dance audiences up to that time. It wasn't narrative. It wasn't a codified system of abstract steps that could be appreciated for their aesthetic value. It had none of the joyful abandon associated with folk or ethnic forms. Nor was it expressionistic in seeming to come directly out of the emotions of the dancers. It was austere, formal, controlled. The dancer's body line was never allowed to soften; the face was a blank, not to betray the message of the body.

The hands are cupped stiffly in right angles, not in curves. The arms jut at the elbows, strain backwards from the shoulder sockets. The body bends in the middle or lunges forward over a projecting knee. The feet flex. Graham uses angularity for its own sake, not as a transition into some position that's easier to look at. The body or the limb that makes the gesture is kept emphatically clear by moving in one unit. There is no fussy adjustment, no small equivocation, no rippling or displacement of small parts. Change occurs all at once. Even when some transition occurs over a long interval, the dancer assumes as much of the shape as she can right at the beginning, so that in part three you see a straight body, hinged at the knees, sinking backward into the Virgin's arms and echoed by the group walking tilted back the same way. The shape of the part two run-leaps is imprinted long before their speed coordinates with it. Graham does not want you to see the body unfolding sequentially, seductively. She does not want you to dwell on the body but on what the body is invoking. Having arranged the body in some striking attitude, she keeps it until it gathers the extra weight of long holding or the extra substance of a collective voice.

The spatial forms and floor patterns, like the body line, are piercingly clear, never disorderly or erratic. The women dance in unison most of the time or in simple follow-the-leader sequences. They don't touch each other in the ordinary ways — clasping hands or linking arms — but move shoulder to shoulder, arm against arm. An energy flows between them, even when they aren't making this contact.

One can hardly think of the dancers in *Primitive Mysteries* as anything other than vessels, instruments for the divine message they are acting out. They must not express or interpret the movement individually; they must not stand out from the group. In fact, if they are women at all, they are a breed apart. They have not taken up dancing to be looked at as beautiful, sexually attractive, ingratiating, or in any way idealized or "feminine" figures. Yet the fact that they *are* women, fully capable of conducting a religious observance, that they do not need male priests or teachers to channel their worship or intercede for them with God, is one of the boldest of *Primitive Mysteries'* many achievements.

The modern dancers were trying to get away from the surface histrionics they found in ballet, and *Primitive Mysteries* may be one of the first — and one of the last — dances to project dramatic content in such an abstract way. Innovation in the arts seems to follow an inevitable course from strangeness and arcane significance to greater and greater clarity. Once the groundbreakers show us something new in the art, we want to see that new thing done in more accessible ways, applied to more situations, made more widely available. The new thing gets thinner and thinner as it is absorbed into the old familiar thing, and soon it disappears. Nothing in dance today remotely approaches the rigor and intensity of the vision in *Primitive Mysteries*. The audience wouldn't stand for it.

The Shakers (Doris Humphrey)

Manipulation of rhythm, tempo, and silence was a primary device in *The Shakers*, too. This is a dance about religious purification achieved through the ecstatic state, and Doris Humphrey condensed all the elements she saw in the Shaker observance into a very short period of time while giving the appearance of a realistic Shaker service. In those dedicated, not to say didactic, early days of modern dance, the idea of doing anything representational was repellent. To take a religious service and exploit it by putting it bodily onstage would have been anathema to Doris Humphrey. What she did in *Shakers* was to extract the essence of Shaker belief, practice, and psychology, to clothe all this in a form apparently so simple and direct that the audience is overcome before it realizes how much meaning has accumulated.

Humphrey's interest in the Shakers has been explained in various ways. I can think of many reasons why this utopian sect appealed to her, and it is perhaps because the Shakers concentrated so many of her own tendencies that they evoked a dance of such power from her. She herself said that their preoccupation with form interested her,[2] and that she liked the idea that they expressed their faith through dancing.[3] Her biographer Selma Jeanne Cohen has pointed out an aesthetic compatibility between Doris Humphrey's temperament and the simple, uncluttered, and unadorned Shaker style.[4] And there was the desire that many modern dancers had at the time to find American themes, to look for subjects expressive of the pioneering American character.

Much of Doris Humphrey's choreography sought an egalitarian world where neither men nor women played a dominant role — or a world where women could be leaders. The Shaker religion, founded by a woman and administered by female priests called eldresses, seems to have been just that sort of world. In it, equality was achieved through the sacrifice of sexuality. The Shakers were celibate, propagating their small communities by adopting orphan children and converting adults. Becoming a nonsexual being is one of the alternatives open to a strong woman when she tries to be independent in a male-dominated world. Sexual repression and ambiguity are and were a fact of life in the dance profession, and in the 1930s the extreme choice might have felt possible or even necessary. Certainly Doris Humphrey struggled with the conflicting demands of art, family, and sexual identity in her own life. Perhaps she felt the Shakers had succeeded in arriving at a productive, co-operative way of life, and considered sexual deprivation not an undue price to pay for the spiritual fulfillment and domestic harmony they achieved.

Both the deprivation and the fulfillment are in Humphrey's dance, although the degree of sexual desperation has varied from one production to another. I suspect that Humphrey saw the sexual frustration as a stimulant to an already passionate spiritualism. Dancers in the sexually permissive 1970s have tipped the balance of the dance a bit, giving the impression that spiritual ecstasy is only a sublimation of denied sexual release.

Floor pattern is the first and most obvious thing Doris Humphrey used in *Shakers* to define the character of the society she was presenting. When I first saw the dance, in a student repertory production at Connecticut College sometime in the 1960s, the strongest impression I had was of an invisible line or a fence down the middle of the stage, which the dancers could never cross. This boundary was so well established that it seemed almost a protection. The dancers conveyed the idea that they weren't ashamed to feel desire for the opposite sex because the limits of that feeling were so clear, the outlets for it so well prescribed, the compensation so well known — and preferable. Years later I asked students who had danced in a revival at Ohio State University how it felt to do. They said they hadn't liked performing the dance at all because it was so restricted. Humphrey's message survived four decades; what had changed was the young people's attitude toward limits, forms, and authorities.

As the dance begins, the group is kneeling in a boxlike formation, the men on one side of the stage, the women on the other. The stage remains divided throughout the dance, the women to the left of the audience, the men to the right. Two women and two men are placed down close to the edge of the stage, facing upstage. The other dancers are stationed along the sides of the stage in two facing lines. Up center, seated on a bench or box, is a woman, the Eldress. Music begins — a wordless soprano, accompanied by a harmonium, singing a hymn tune. The pace is very slow and the lines of kneeling men and women rock toward the ground in time to it, their hands clasped, stiff-armed, in front of them. The downstage groups rock from side to side, the others back and forth, and their motion is antiphonal in a subtle avoidance of unison. Over and over again in *Shakers*, Humphrey withholds total unison from the audience until the moments when it will have the maximum impact.

While the group is rocking slowly, the first paroxysm of rapture bursts from a man. In double time he rises, yanking his arms back and forth across his body, as if struggling with a tenacious adversary. Abruptly he pries his hands apart, opening his arms to heaven, then sinks to his knees again. The group continues its rocking and praying. Soon the man jumps up again and repeats his gesture, joined by another man. These outbursts don't disturb the regular rhythm of the group, but the tempo accelerates. Suddenly the man closest to the center downstage is seized with joy and wrenches his hands free, but as he lifts them to God, he sees the woman kneeling next to him.

The group stops moving. As their companions stare, frozen and in silence, the two face each other, hands describing a narrow, rigid channel very near their own faces. Still looking at each other and straining slightly forward, they rise and begin stepping sideways, stiff-legged, on the balls of their feet, doubling each beat. As they move upstage, the rest of the men and women march along the edge of the space to meet in the same spot at the center, confront their opposite numbers, and move off in the same stiff manner. It's like some congealed version of a grand march at a ball.

The last to come to the center is the Eldress, who has no partner. Exhorting them with a finger pointing skyward, she moves back up to her bench while the men and women, in arm-linked pairs, form two Texas starlike patterns, and as they wheel, they again encounter a member of the opposite sex. The outside arms of the pairs reach out from the elbow, hands stretching tensely, as they pass each other going away from the audience. They are still stepping on the balls of their feet, almost bouncing, and the bounces begin to carry them into small jumps with the legs opening and one finger pointing in imitation of the Eldress.

As the jumping grows faster and more active, a man's voice breaks out from the group and everything stops: "My life! My carnal life! I will lay it down — because it is depraved!" The jumping begins again, growing faster, only to be halted by the Eldress. She stands on her box and claps her hands several times, then shouts: "It hath been revealed. Ye shall be saved. When ye are shaken free — of sin!"

As she begins to speak, the group falls to its knees; the men bow with both hands flat on the floor, the women bend backward, arms open. After her words, the Eldress begins a motion that is so slow, it's hard to tell what it is. Bending from the waist, she folds her whole upper body over and throws her arms down with it — a gesture of resignation and a certain disgust. After an instant's pause, she straightens up, spreading her hands and twisting her upper body as if searching the air for something. Another pause, and she lifts her torso and arms high and wide. She repeats this sequence several times, accelerating each time, until she arrives at about the same tempo at which the jumping began. The group on the floor accompanies her, falling onto their hands, then bending back with arms open. Again their motion is antiphonal.

The Eldress' interrupted-spiral motif, her body folding down and

THE SHAKERS (*Humphrey, 1931*), *contemporary reconstruction by the José Limón Company. Photo by Martha Swope.*

opening up, contains the entire symbolism of the dance and the basis for all of the movement — the polarity between earth and heaven. The earth and its carnal temptations pull the dancer down, literally and figuratively. She expresses both her contempt for earthly ties and her vehement effort to get rid of them by this peculiar "shaking" out of the hands. The lifted opening up of the body can only come when the dancer gives herself totally to God. It is typical of Doris Humphrey's compositional genius that she did not introduce this theme literally at the beginning of the dance, although it appears in variation from the start. It's also typical of her humanistic approach to insert that hesitation into the path between sin and salvation.

The Eldress comes down from her bench and begins the "shaking" dance. Bending slightly forward, in a double-time rhythm she stamps twice on one foot, then the other. With each stamp she throws her hands toward the ground and emphasizes the change of weight by slapping one foot on the upbeat. The thrust of the downward energy is renewed with each shift of weight, and for the first time a drum is heard, underlining each beat. The motion has the "digging" quality you see in the dance of some Australian aborigines or North American Indians. It is rhythmically and physiologically primal. The dancer is hurling his whole energy into the ground with his upper body and pounding it home with his legs — the earth is his enemy. But with each step he is also reinforcing his basic *affinity* with the earth.

This downward concentration of energy begins to build. Stamping and shaking at a tempo that is slower than their previous speed, the men and women back off to the sides of the stage. The Eldress and one man begin a sequence horizontally across the floor, joined quickly by the rest of the group. Throwing their hands forward and down with elbows bent on each step, they advance to the center line. Just before they meet, they pivot toward the audience. Resorting to the rigid abstinence that squelches their erring thoughts, they tilt their heads up and step sideways out to the edges again, shaking their arms down at their sides on each step. Several times the lines of men and women cross the stage and retreat from one another in this fashion.

They keep it up as a man suddenly breaks out. Rising, he lifts one arm, whips his whole body around in a huge backward-leaning spiral that sinks and finishes in one vigorous shaking gesture very close to the ground. This phrase is a summing up of the conflict that the dancers have been stating again and again throughout the dance — the person's desire to escape the evils that rule his life, his reaching for heaven but being drawn again to the earth and emptying out his revulsion for earth even as it pulls him. The dancer is poised between heaven and earth, leaning over backwards to get out of the straight-and-narrow existence that is his only mortal way of avoiding temptation. And as he plunges down again he seems as if he would like to shed his very skin if only he could be free. This complex phrase, in nine continuous counts as opposed to the percussive, regular, eight-count shaking and retreating phrase that everyone else has been doing, comes as a kinetic shock to both the group and the audience. The man steps back to his place only to begin it again. Then four men join him, then a few at a time, the women.

As if seized by a contagion, the dance gets faster and more vigorous as more dancers pick up the phrase. But they do it in counterpoint, the men's side of the stage turning and plunging into the ground while the women take their small shaking steps, and vice versa. After they have all done the turn several times, the Eldress and the entire group of men plunge toward the center line at once. Suddenly, in an intensified version of their earlier encounters, all the men and all the women confront each other. They jump into a squatting position, their upper bodies straining forward, and their hands fly together, locked in prayer or repression. They pull their upper bodies away from temptation. They stagger back a few steps and with great exertion pull their arms apart. They lean backward as if to praise but the momentum of their struggle propels them forward again, where they catch themselves by clasping their hands.

Each series of these struggles becomes bigger and faster and more in danger of falling completely off balance until, after the fourth time, the group all plunge at once toward the center in a circle and fall on their knees. In the center is the Eldress. Completing the spiral at last, she begins to spin, with her arms open and her upper body slightly tilted, her face and palms raised. This seems to incite an even faster and more vigorous shaking than anything the group has done before. They stamp and make individual gestures, including shaking their hands, this time with the fingers upward, palms in front of their faces. The group moves into two lines upstage and they pause for an instant, all with their arms open. They finally attain their release from the ground. Facing the audience, they begin jumping forward, split jumps, with legs and arms out to the sides, higher and higher, wider and wider, their bodies folding forward so their hands can almost touch their toes at the top of the jump.

While the group does this, the Eldress comes out of her spin, changing to a turning phrase of four counts that she begins with her arms doubled up close to her body and ends in an open position. Each turn she reverses direction. This finally slows down the tempo. One by one the men and women become spent, make one last flinging jump into the air, and sink to their knees with their arms open. When the last man has come down, they all clasp their hands in prayer and circle them high above their heads from one side of the body to the other, while the Eldress, spiraling with her upper body, slowly points into the air as the soprano sings an ascending amen.

Although there are only two or three moments in the entire dance when the whole group is doing the same motion and also maintaining the same focus — the circle on the knees when the Eldress begins spinning, the split-jumps coming forward to the audience, and the final amen — the dance has a remarkable unity. Within prescribed confines of space, tempo, and gesture, Humphrey allowed tremendous variation to occur, even permitting the dancers to improvise on her themes at specific places. She made extensive use of simple and complex contrapuntal patterns. But no matter how many things are going on at one time, you never lose the shape or motivation of the moment because everyone keeps the same tempo and usually does the same steps. Humphrey built a tremendous cumulative intensity into the dance through her use of accelerations, stops, and beginnings-again at a slower tempo than before the pause. She seldom had everyone begin a new idea all together. Each development in the progression is introduced by one or two dancers, then picked up by individuals or small groups. When she did introduce a stopping place or let things come together by relinquishing counterpoint, she wanted to underline a change in the ritual. A lesser choreographer would have set much more unison movement in *Shakers* and thought the effect was stronger.

The other thing Doris Humphrey did so splendidly — it is perhaps seen best of all in *Water Study* — was to make movement that evolved from simple to more complicated ideas. In *Shakers* the dancers' hands do only three basic things: they clasp together, they open, and they flatten out. (The Eldress' pointing gesture is literal, exhortatory, and is used only for that purpose and in that form.) Between the obvious symbolic relationships of open hands meaning freedom from carnal bondage and closed hands meaning prayer and resistance to temptation, there is the use of the hands that is never seen: touching a person of the opposite sex. Every time the occasion presents itself, when the hands wander from the straight officially sanctioned paths, the person makes an effort of will and restrains himself by making his hands rigid and parallel, or clasping them together, or pulling them open. The only time the hands are not almost vibrating with tension is when the dancer is shaking them out. Humphrey then makes variations on these gestural motifs, sometimes enlarging them to involve the whole body, sometimes confining them to the hands and arms alone to create different dance patterns that ride over the rhythm.

In support of the polarities of Shaker life that Humphrey is trying to show, there are only two kinds of floor patterns through which the dancers travel across the stage: linear and circular. With the exception of the wheeling Texas star, there isn't a curve until the Eldress begins spinning. People travel in processional patterns along rectangular routes, and they do their dancing-jumping-shaking back and forth in short pathways, from upstage to down and back again, from the center line out to the wings and back along the same line. It seems as if they would trample a groove into the ground, as the aborigines do, there is so little deviation in their course. I think the limitations of these pathways also permit the build-ups of energy by which the dance gets from one type of activity to another. There isn't any way for the dancer's concentration on his objective to get sidetracked or diffused.

The circle of religious ecstasy — and its further development, the spiral — of course represents release and freedom from earthly temptation and the necessity for self-imposed control. This is a universal symbol as well as an effective choreographic device. In *Shakers*, the Eldress is the only one who spins, being in direct contact with God, but the other communicants partake of the circle when they kneel around her and when they swoop their arms and upper bodies around in the process of getting free.

Over and above all the specific incident and movement pattern that take place in *The Shakers*, there is drama. The dance is one surging progression to a climax. The progression, though inevitable, is not a constant upward curve. Just as Humphrey avoids overstating her case by saving unison for rare occasions, she pulls back on the tempo often so that it doesn't run away with itself. I'm sure the religious reasons for this are just as strong as the theatrical ones.

But she plants ideas. The end of the first section of the dance comes when the man and woman look at each other. It's like the first test of their spiritual vows. At that moment, the group of men and women freeze and look at the erring couple. For the first time since the dance began, the group are all doing the same thing: though they've been following several different space designs with their clasped hands, at this moment they are all holding their hands stretched out in front of them. Later this shape will be exaggerated as the men and women confront each other at the beginning of the final struggle. Similarly, all the downward and upward motions are built into the movement from the beginning of the dance. Only at the end do we see just how strongly opposed these two tendencies can become in their claim for the domination of man's spirit, and how, short of death, he can only resolve them within himself by literally pulling himself apart, by suspending himself for an instant as a horizontal line in the air instead of as a vertical line connecting earth and heaven.

Neoclassicism I

> Their thrilling dances then gave me a sharp pang
> of yearning to get a closer view of things immea-
> surable and unattainable, such as no poem of
> Heine's, no prose of Poe's, no fever dream has
> ever given me, and, since, I have had the same
> sensation, at once sub-conscious and acute, which
> I attribute to the silent and nebulous precision of
> all they do.
>
> — *Lincoln Kirstein* [1]

IT IS NOT SURPRISING that modern dance got an earlier and stronger start on American soil than ballet. Modern dance at its inception was essentially a protest, a statement of incompatibility with the aristocratic assumptions of European ballet. If the American character had been congenial to these assumptions, a classical ballet tradition surely would have taken hold long before it did. In the other arts, Americans were insecure about their ability to discriminate, to identify cultural excellence, or maybe even to have a culture, and they attached themselves to the proven culture of Europe, its music, painting, and literature, before they acquired the confidence to invent their own. But the first American dancers were not imitators, they were explorers. Even those who worked within the classical ballet vocabulary seemed to want to reshape its syntax.

Dancers are physical beings, and when they began choreographing seriously in this country they were physically removed from the European classical tradition. For once, the difficulty of recording and preserving dance worked in favor of progress. In America dancers did not have the models before them in the form of scores or books, and in any case what they had seen or engaged in most recently in Europe would have been affected by the powerful modernism, the antiacademicism of Diaghilev. Ballet is cumbersome and expensive to produce; dancers are not prepared in a few weeks' rehearsal; audiences must be cultivated. And choreography, more than any other creative art, is a cooperative process. One could not study in the academies of Europe and then come back and expect to make ballets. The art has so many components, it was bound to mutate when it started employing so many new raw materials, even if there had been a strong drive to emulate the established models. Many of the Europeans who immigrated here in the 1920s and '30s did have a grounding in the traditional repertory, but they may have felt that crossing the ocean separated them symbolically as well as literally from their roots. Certainly Balanchine and Antony Tudor, our most influential transplanted choreographers, must have felt they had entered a climate more receptive to experimentation.

Throughout our brief dance history are many examples of works that are trying not to look like other works — modern dances that don't want to look like ballets, abstract ballets that don't want to look like narrative ballets, modern ballets, antiballets, antidance modern dances. Until recently we have had, it seems to me, much less tendency than the Europeans to take the givens as good, to reconstruct the past or to make new versions of old successes. Perhaps as an outgrowth of our native skepticism, we have been — at least in the twentieth century — more open to new ideas in art and much more capable of reinventing the modes of art.

Serenade (George Balanchine)

George Balanchine came to America in 1933 at the urging of Lincoln Kirstein. It was Kirstein's intention from the first to develop a school and a ballet company headed by Balanchine. The plan was sidetracked many times, and the performing-teaching institution now known as the New York City Ballet and School of American Ballet did not assume its mature form until 1948. The school was started almost immediately after Balanchine's arrival in New York, and has continued to operate under the direction of Balanchine, Kirstein, and the late Eugenie Ouroussow up to the present time. The company, however, went through various incarnations before being adopted into the City Center of Music and Drama, an umbrella organization now totally misnamed, since its main constituents are the New York City Ballet and the New York City Opera, neither of which performs in the theater known as City Center.

In common with most modern dancers, Balanchine appears to have thought of his school as a medium for training performers of his ballets. While other Russian expatriates operated ballet schools to earn a living, with performing groups as a sort of by-product, a necessary outlet to give students some stage experience, Balanchine thought of choreography as the end-product and of a school as the means for developing dancers capable of executing his choreographic ideas.

Already a modernist when he left Russia in 1923, Balanchine was not a rebel in the sense that the modern dancers were. I don't perceive in any of his choreography that insistent need to be different, to find new ways of dancing that could be satisfying in his own personal terms. The classical ballet vocabulary was expressive enough for his needs; the norms of ballet classicism — its attitude toward the dancer's role and purpose and image — provided Balanchine with a framework adequate for his investigations. He made modifications in that basic language. But once he came to America — or perhaps once away from the novelty-crazed atmosphere of the late Diaghilev era — his ballets seem to have been less bizarre, less smart, and more steadily, concentratedly experimental.

Over the years his dancers came to look more angular than softly rounded; he exaggerated the transfer of weight from one leg to the other by bringing the hips and pelvis into play; he gave more articulation to the foot; his dancers' line became subtly distorted to make us more aware of the connections between different parts of the body rather than of the body as one smooth, harmoniously working whole. These and other features distinguish a Balanchine-trained dancer from other ballet dancers, but you would never mistake a Balanchine dancer for a modern dancer. To Balanchine, the traditional mode of training and using a dancer is a liberating asset, not a limitation. This is why he has been, at one and the same time, a great innovator and a great classicist in the American style.

Serenade was Balanchine's first choreography in America. The story of its creation now belongs to what has become an extensive and colorful lore of Balanchiniana. The choreographer intended it to serve as a sort of classroom demonstration by his students at the new School of American Ballet. It was first performed outdoors at the Westchester estate of Felix Warburg, father of E. M. M. Warburg, one of the company's early benefactors, on June 10, 1934. (It rained on June 9, the scheduled performance date.) The first public performances took place in Hartford, Connecticut, in December of that same year and in New York early in 1935. The work took shape in the rather haphazard but expedient fashion of most American companies, where dancers were not paid for rehearsals and people would be absent when they could get other jobs. Balanchine is said to have included accidents, anecdotes, and other fortuitous events of the rehearsal process in the final choreography. Whether he actually made capital out of his liabilities or whether all along he intended *Serenade* to be very free in form, it certainly turned out to be an odd-looking ballet.

Serenade is like a stream-of-consciousness monologue, an impressionist painting. From its first stage tableau, Balanchine seems to have just let himself go, following up whatever the music (Tchaikovsky's Serenade for Strings) and the available dancer-resources suggested to him. The ballet's classicism is found in its basic vocabulary of steps, its references to staple works of the ballet repertory, and its tendency to return to familiar formations in space, as if all of these were well-loved landmarks by which the dancers and the audience could find their way and renew their courage while pursuing a strange new journey. The form of the ballet itself is unique, the distribution and use of the principal dancers doesn't follow any known patterns, and the content of the work — its aesthetic or narrative message — is cryptic.

Like all Balanchine, *Serenade* is musical, but it doesn't follow a logical structure. From the beginning to the end it doesn't progress in a cumulative way — building one huge structure out of four smaller units as *Symphony in C* does — or toward kinetic designs that eventually blend with each other as in *Four Temperaments*. If there is a progression in the ballet, it must have been suggested to Balanchine by the music, which begins with a slightly embellished but discernible descending scale. Perhaps this most simple of musical devices suited Balanchine's intention of presenting a sort of graduation piece, and perhaps this is why he took the liberty of transposing Tchaikovsky's last two movements: the third — here the final — movement is based on an ascending scale. Within these musical parentheses the choreographer seems to be showing us the rudiments of all the possible types of ballets: lyrical, virtuosic, dramatic, danced by solos, duos, and all sizes of ensembles.

The ballet is very eventful — all Balanchine ballets are — and has an undercurrent of something unsettling that is not precisely menace, and not fear or agitation, for the dancing is serene even when it is precipitous or sad. I think one reason we feel this vague expectancy is that it keeps changing. Most especially, the roles of the dancers keep changing. Balanchine doesn't tell us at the beginning of the ballet who the main dancers are going to be; once he introduces some, he doesn't arrange that they always do the same kind of thing or maintain the same relationships to the others; and right to the very end he holds out the possibility that new roles can be brought in, with dancers doing them whom he hasn't previously singled out. He seems to be saying something about the dancer's "place."

The first movement opens with seventeen women onstage, all facing front and spaced out over the stage so that we can see them all, but not lined up. Later, after this formation has broken and many soloists and ensemble combinations have presented themselves, the women return — maybe to their original positions, maybe not, but to a very similar floor pattern. Then another woman appears from offstage and wanders among them as they stand waiting. Just as the music ends, she finds her place in front, and we realize that a place has been empty.

This assertion about the theoretical equality of all dancers, about the right each one of them has to belong — to fit in and to stand out — is in larger scope one of the messages of *Serenade*, and indeed of Balanchine's philosophy for the company he was to create. There are three women soloists in *Serenade* (originally there was only one) and two men, but many of the other dancers enact brief but important parts. In various productions the women soloists have shared the choreography in different ways. Balanchine could almost be declaring his own independence from the undemocratic ranking systems of the old Russian companies, where this one is the Ballerina, another is the Cavalier, and others are the Corps or the Second Lead, and they never do anything more or less than their assignments.

This group formation with which the ballet starts is interesting in several other ways. It is didactic without being doctrinaire. Though the women are presented to us absolutely flat front, standing in position, as at the beginning of the center-floor part of a ballet class, they are not yet centered, poised and ready for the symmetrical, orderly sequence of events by which a dancer's body tunes itself day by day. Dressed in a long filmy blue dress, each woman stands with feet close together, legs parallel, not turned out. Each looks toward a point in space somewhere above and beyond her right side. Her right arm is extended toward that spot, the hand turned with the palm facing out, and the arm pulls the upper part of her body very slightly away from her center of gravity. There is something strained about this tableau — the pose is too angular and eccentric to match the formal way the women are distributed, and yet the way they all do it alike denies any realistic or dramatic ideas we might have about it.

The pose is held for a long time before it softens and begins to look like an ordinary port de bras, and as the music repeats a cadence three times, the dancers all suddenly spread their feet along the floor, from parallel into first position, heels together, toes pointing out. The clarity of this gesture is stark almost to the point of insolence, and yet it's possible to miss it altogether since the dancers keep the rest of their bodies perfectly still. It's like a code word flashed outrageously under our noses.

Finally the orderly progression of chords is broken, and the women move out of their ranks. The rest of the section has the group creating an amazing array of dance designs. Soloists appear; one woman in particular jumps and turns while the others watch. Dancers sweep across the stage; some of them leave while others cluster in odd parts of the stage, sometimes facing away from the audience. With one soloist missing, the rest make four sculptural groups, all alike, in a line across the stage, by running one at a time to pose behind one another, each succeeding dancer leaning out in a different direction. A soloist falls to her side on the floor surrounded by five lines of three women. The five formations do a classroom arm sequence while the soloist is still. In the rapid passage of events and dancers, we hardly have time to notice how odd they are, but later on, when many of them have developed into something more dramatic, they seem even odder.

Just before resuming their first formation, the entire group does a fast circle of piqué turns around the stage. Again I have the idea that Balanchine is suggesting some new kind of egalitarianism. Piqué turns are a showy, applause-getting device usually performed by the ballerina at the end of a pas de deux. Yet Balanchine says all seventeen of these dancers can do the step. And the trick, done by so many, looks less exciting rather than more. Balanchine plays down its flashiness, incorporates it into the standard body of material that a corps de ballet can do in creating its ensemble designs.

The second movement begins with the entrance of a man, who partners one of the soloists to Tchaikovsky's familiar waltz. Although the lead couple do many bravura lifts and combinations of steps, the section suggests the romantic ballet — *Giselle* or *Les Sylphides* — as well as the more virtuosic duets of the Imperial Russian style. The duet dips and flows with the music. Circling the stage at first, the dancers clasp each other around the waist with one hand, cradling the partner's head with the other. Though they are alone at the beginning, the corps de ballet soon returns. We never really lose the sense of the ensemble — the man's appearance after the first all-female section is surprising, and he never seems to belong, he is never more than an interlude in the woman's life. He isn't even on-stage for more than a few minutes at a time, leaving without her on most of his exits and returning without fanfare. The dance that the man and woman do together isn't some detached, singular occasion, but an event that can occur when the circumstances of the ensemble permit it or can absorb it.

Balanchine takes the position — unusual even now — that dancing is a perfectly natural thing for a dancer to do, and that one doesn't get to be a principal dancer because of the number of steps one knows. All his dancers must be excellent technicians, and they are chosen for leading roles because he likes other qualities about them. In his choreography he seems almost to go out of his way to avoid singling out stars. Two often-used tactics, seen in *Serenade*, are his emphasizing the importance of the ensemble by having them present and active during what would be the stars' time to show off and his dividing up the most spectacular choreography among several dancers. Even in his reworkings of the old Imperial ballets he has dispelled the feeling that the ballerina and her partner are the only reason for the enterprise. He often alternates the sections of a pas de deux with ensembles or other dances, and he often makes big works with separate sections, a different ballerina at the front of each. Balanchine also reduced the scale of many of his classical ballets so that with fewer dancers there would be more opportunities for all of them.

The third movement begins with a brief, touching image of solidarity. One of the principal dancers and four other ensemble women are left alone, standing side by side, arms lifted to frame their faces. Together they slide forward into a split. While they're on the floor, the woman in the center turns to her right side and offers her left hand to the woman next to her, then turns and offers her right hand to the woman on her left. The other women repeat the gesture until they are all linked with crossed hands. The group now resembles the four cygnets in *Swan Lake*, who dance in unison while holding hands in this way. But Balanchine, by adding one principal dancer to the group, is again showing that there is a place for her with the corps. Together the five women rise and, still holding hands, weave in and out of their own line, with circling pas de bourrée, finally winding tightly around the woman in the middle, then unwinding again. Balanchine has used this chaining pattern often in his ballets. Here it strengthens the bond among the five women.

The music moves from a rather melancholy refrain into a sparkling, fast motif. The women step off in all directions. More dancers enter and the soloist and her partner stand prominently in front of them. For a third time the group has assembled as they appeared at the opening of the ballet, but now another academic possibility presents itself: the man is supporting the woman in arabesque. As they break the pose, the ensemble organizes itself into geometrical formations, facing front — almost the only time in the ballet that the stage becomes clearly and formally balanced — and the principal couple dance in the center. The ballet up to this point has been an evolving series of stage patterns that seem deliberately to avoid the conventional lined-up designs that provide the background in nineteenth-century ballets. Not only does Balanchine stress asymmetrical designs, he often creates them with the dancers traveling. All the women start to form a diagonal line across the stage, but before the line is quite complete, the woman at its head begins "peeling off," and the others follow in sequence, rushing into the wings with a sweep of the arms. The images don't get fixed in our minds as static shapes, but rather as ideas that form themselves just enough to become coherent, then dissipate again.

This delayed assertion of classical order ought to be the smash finale of the entire ballet, and (Balanchine having reversed the order of the music) it is accompanied by Tchaikovsky's idea of an ending too. But the man unaccountably runs out — not to be seen again — and the women leap and prance together, celebrating perhaps the return of the soloist to their midst. Then in a flash they all run out. As they stream across the stage, one woman, usually the same soloist, falls on her side. She is left there as the music ends.

Now there is a strange anticlimax and what could be a different ballet begins. Having disrupted the flow of Tchaikovsky's music and finished it off prematurely, Balanchine now sets a whole new idea in motion. Except that, as it proceeds, we see that it has grown out of what came before. The elements are the same, but imagined in another context. In the slight pause before the music starts again, the audience has time to sense that a change has come over the ballet. A woman is lying alone on the floor. There are few occasions in nonnarrative dance where the ballerina falls or poses on the floor in such an exposed, emphatic way. It disturbs whatever impression of prettiness, diaphanous swirling skirts and romantic encounters the viewer has been accumulating for the past thirty minutes.

As the music begins, a woman and a man — not the same man as before — enter and cross the stage to the fallen dancer. The woman walks immediately behind the man, pressed against him, almost hanging on him. She holds him around the waist with one hand and covers his eyes with the other. This could be a specific reference to Orpheus and Eurydice. Balanchine had already shown an interest in the Apollo-Orpheus symbolism, and he was to choreograph his first Orpheus ballet, to the Gluck opera, for the Metropolitan Opera only a year after *Serenade*.

But this is not going to be a dance about the poet who tried to lead his wife back from the dead without looking at her. In fact, it is not going to be a dance about any story, though this story adds its resonance to the others already suggested. Continuing with its original intention of flowing easily along on the musical line, the dance now seems to turn into a more deliberate series of images, crystallizing and dissolving before they become too specific. The man with the woman on his back in this bizarre position is leading but he cannot see; the woman knows where they are going but her role is to follow. They're like a mythological creature with the attributes and disabilities of more than one animal.

When they reach the woman on the floor they stand behind her at first, and the man takes her hand. Again I have the feeling that unusual emphasis is placed on her being in this position: she must be someone special, but we're not told exactly who. While she's still on the floor, the second woman stands in front of her, and the man, now sitting on the floor, holds the upper part of his partner's leg — concealed by her skirt — and turns her while she stands in arabesque on pointe, so that she makes two complete turns without actually moving or being visibly propelled. As with the snap into first position that began the ballet, Balanchine designs something really odd to point out how the ethereality of ballet is achieved. He was to show the mechanics again and again in his "modern" ballets, but in the nearly conventional setting of *Serenade* the idea is still shocking.

Finally the woman gets up from the floor and the man dances with her and his first companion. In another part of the stage he lowers both women to the floor and the three of them form a kind of sculptural entryway. One woman from the ensemble, then another and another, come running across the stage and each in turn leaps over the women into the arms of the man. The third leaper is whirled around spectacularly as he catches her. This idea is repeated, this time with each leaping woman accompanied by one or more attendants.

Inexplicably, for the first time, four men appear and, with eight women, do a series of supported arabesques and pirouettes, each man addressing one woman, then another, in turn. It's as if Balanchine is reminding us that the decorous regimen of the dance goes on even while these more dramatic events are shaping themselves. Taking advantage of a persistent problem of ballet's early days, the lack of enough men, Balanchine makes this section extremely formal. The men's alternating between partners in identical steps reinforces what the corps has already shown us about the expansiveness that can be achieved by superimposition, duplication, and repetition of images. The men lift the women directly in front of them, grasping them around the hips, and they stand like totem poles or like bearers of idols. Each lifted woman steadies the arms of another woman standing in arabesque below her.

The first trio reappears, and the man dances an adagio with the woman who was on the floor. She spins fast in his arms, the turns growing more effortful. He holds her from behind and stoops over slightly, supporting her body in a long curve as if she were being cradled. She doesn't hold on to him at all, but one hand reaches back to touch his face as she sinks to the ground.

She is back in the spot where she first fell. Seeing her there again, with the man hovering behind her, is like returning to the start of a flashback in a film. Now we seem to understand how she came to be there, even though we *saw* how she got there the first time. The man and his companion pose as before, the man holding the fallen dancer's hand as before. The standing woman flaps her arms up and down a few times, a doomlike gesture recalling *Swan Lake* — the announcement of some curse that can't be staved off. Then she clasps the man again, covers his eyes, and they turn to go. As they walk slowly away, the man keeps holding the dying woman's hand until they can no longer reach each other.

Now four women enter, with another who hovers on her toes at the other side of the stage, facing upstage along the diagonal. The woman on the floor gets up and goes to the leader. She throws herself on the leader's shoulders, in a pleading-fainting gesture, and is gently but firmly lowered to her knees by the mother-figure. The implication of Giselle's doom here is inescapable. The Queen of the

SERENADE (*Balanchine, 1935*). *Melissa Hayden, Frank Hobi, Pat McBride in the early 1950s. Photo by George Platt Lynes.*

Wilis traditionally stands in the same place and refuses Giselle's plea for the life of Albrecht. Giselle saves her lover eventually but returns to the world of the dead. Similarly, in *Serenade*, the woman who falls gets no reprieve.

Now we're reminded that she was one of the larger group originally, and that although she may beg to resume her independent life, she will have to return to their midst. Three men enter and lift her straight up, holding her legs. The other women all face the upstage corner and move slowly away, walking straight ahead on their toes. The music rises higher and higher, and the woman being carried, in unison with the women on the ground, lifts her arms and arches her torso backward, opening her upper body to the direction in which she is being taken.

New Dance (Doris Humphrey)

Two great choreographers emerged in 1935. Balanchine, the pragmatist, worked with an established language and apparently with no other goal but to utilize its resources. Doris Humphrey, the idealist, invented a new language in order to promote specific social and aesthetic theories. Yet it is Balanchine, who has so few illusions and appears never to have uttered a high-minded word, who contributed incomparable poetic images to our stage; and Humphrey, for all her utopian rhetoric, who pulled dance down from its rarefied detachment and allowed it to speak concretely to us by way of our own richly descriptive and subtle but seldom analyzed energies.

Humphrey had already done this in *The Shakers* and in other early works, but with *New Dance* she was ready to make a major statement. According to critic Margaret Lloyd, "*New Dance* was the first modern dance work of extended length." [2] It was more than that. It was a dance of symphonic proportions and design that did not depend on any preexisting musical structure. It was the beginning of an ambitious scheme, a dance trilogy that would show society in its fragmented and dissonant state, with a blueprint for man's betterment. In the summer of 1936 Doris Humphrey completed her great work. The parts of New Dance Trilogy were never all performed on the same program, and substantial portions of the choreography were later lost. Today few dancers even dream such grandiose projects.

Others have written about Doris Humphrey, and she wasn't afraid of words herself, so we can read her ideas about dance and its possibilities in her published articles and notes and in her book *The Art of Making Dances*, published a year after her death in 1958. In one way, Humphrey's detailed verbalizing about her choreography has worked to her disadvantage. Dance is skeptical of the analytical mind. (A student once asked me if it bothered me to be called a critic.) Because she so often explained the underlying intentions of her dances, revealed the metaphors she was trying to create, she is thought of by many as an intellectual and therefore someone whose talent was opposed to the very nature of dance, and her works are condemned as somehow inferior.[3] The fact that they "mean" something is supposed to negate their value. Doris Humphrey's description of *New Dance* reads a bit like a tract forty years later.[4] She assigns motivations to many of the actions in the dance and invokes a social-political dynamic that isn't readily apparent in performance. As with any artist's program or platform, Humphrey's philosophical intentions gave impetus to her composition, but not necessarily in the specific terms she outlined. I feel she accomplished her purpose admirably in overall terms — the piece supersedes the economic and social problems that must have engendered it.

Many choreographers in the 1930s made dances of "social protest," but few were able to convert a social concept into abstract dance patterns as clearly as Humphrey. *New Dance*, although the first composed, was to be the last section of the New Dance Trilogy. The first part, *Theatre Piece*, has been altogether lost. Humphrey describes it in quite literal terms: "This dance depicts the world as it is today: a place of grim competition."[5] She goes on to picture what might be almost a pantomimic enactment of contemporary rivalries in business, sports, the theater, and love, with symbolic figures such as a dictator and an outsider who try to exert their influence over the crowd. Since Humphrey also assigns concrete characters and actions to the totally abstract *New Dance*, it isn't clear what *Theatre Piece* actually looked like.

The second part of the trilogy, *With My Red Fires*, reconstructed in 1972 at the Connecticut College American Dance Festival, told a story almost entirely in choral terms, with three soloists. Humphrey turned the ensemble into a dramatic instrument. The dance is about the pressures of tradition, as represented by a Matriarch and the anonymous members of a community, working to prevent what they consider an unsuitable marriage. After enduring the condemnation of their peers, the lovers are transfigured and the Matriarch is vanquished. The power of love prevails over prejudice, dissension, and violence.

The Variations and Conclusion from *New Dance* had been recorded in Labanotation and reconstructed periodically over the years.[6] The rest of the dance, however, disappeared when Humphrey was no longer alive to do productions of it. When Connecticut College undertook its revival in 1972, Charles Weidman and several former Humphrey-Weidman dancers attempted to piece it together from memory. Even the Wallingford Riegger score had disappeared. What they could remember, they remembered. Weidman filled in the rest. This is the only version of the whole work I have ever seen; it has the look of a masterpiece.

New Dance begins with a duet. Called by Humphrey the Introduction, it presents the two principals in a series of short dance ideas while an ensemble of men and women stand on boxes piled at the sides of the stage, watching them. Humphrey and Weidman frequently used white cubes in different sizes as a means of varying the stage space for their dances without the expense and backstage complications involved in conventional scenery.

This opening set of dances is vigorous and rhythmic. The man and woman are quite evenly matched in the shape and force of their movement designs. They're first seen posing in a stylized handshake. Later, they restate the triumphant final embrace of the lovers in *With My Red Fires.* They swing by the arms, run and stamp in divergent circles. They seem entirely complementary without working in unison. Although very obviously a concert dance, the Introduction suggests square dancing in its explosive energies and in the fellowship of the partnering.

This couple are to be the leaders and exemplars of the group. They gradually draw their companions into the dance, first the women, then the men, but for the ideal state of harmony to be reached they will merge with the group before the dance ends. The Variations and Conclusion is an expression of a group where each person has the chance to make a solo statement. This may seem to resemble the democratic atmosphere of *Serenade,* but the differences between Balanchine and Humphrey are as profound as the differences between ballet and modern dance, between "elitism" and "democracy."

With Humphrey the group is supreme. The whole of *New Dance* is a drive toward unifying all the energies into one complex organism that nevertheless permits subenergies to be expressed by individuals. Humphrey's soloists state ideas first, but the ideas cannot be fully worked out until they are adopted by the whole group. In Balanchine, the interchange works the opposite way: the group establishes the baselines upon which soloists go on to elaborate. Balanchine sees the group as a kind of germ culture, a breeding ground that gives rise to special individuals who carry out its most important business, make its decisions, express its highest ideals. Although a Balanchinian corps usually dances far more than its counterpart in conventional ballets, it doesn't carry the most demanding responsibilities. The group of circling piqué turns in *Serenade* would be comparable in effect to Humphrey's group work in the latter parts of *New Dance,* and with Balanchine the incident is striking because it's so rare.

Most of the movement motifs of *New Dance* are established early, perhaps in the first duet. I've already mentioned rhythm. The dance is rhythmic throughout, often in contrapuntal and polyrhythmic patterns that the audience would not perceive in any detail. What you do perceive is that a pulse is always going on.

Doris Humphrey employed rhythm far differently from any ballet prototypes. In ballet what rhythmic pulse there is usually comes from the music, most often the artificially regularized and homogeneous rhythms of the nineteenth century. The dancers may duplicate the music's rhythmic line by grouping their steps into phrases. The way rhythm changes or reasserts itself visually in ballet is when the movement pauses for an instant, the dancer takes a new direction in space, or the continuum of movement switches from one body part to another. Seldom in traditional ballet do you see a rhythmic pulse established by a downbeat, a push into the ground. This occurs most often when "character" material is introduced into the ballet — folk dances such as mazurkas and czardas, or jazz or social dance forms. Doris Humphrey worked with rhythmic impulses built into her movement.

By 1935, the breath phrasing that formed the basis of *Water Study* had developed into an intricate language of rising, sweeping, soaring, suspending, pitching, sinking movement phrases initiated and carried on the dancer's inhalation and exhalation of breath. The lifting and expanding of the body into space was often prolonged, not by establishing a balance point as a ballet dancer would do, but by continuing the lift of breath and the progress into space to a point where it seemed the dancer might tip over. Then the plunge downward, in a continuation of the spatial design, usually a curve or spiral of some kind. At the bottom of the trajectory, instead of letting go his weight and giving in to the drag of inertia, the dancer remobilized his energy to initiate the phrase again. Basically I am describing a swing, the whole body active throughout the phrase, supporting and creating the shape. But how unusual it was in those days to imagine that the body's own momentum could be fashioned into dance patterns. It was much more common for the dancer to learn to hold back her weight, to resist her affinity for gravity. This acknowledgment of the body's relationship to the ground was one of the things that made the early modern dancers seem so much more human.

New Dance is not a constant succession of breath phrases. Often when a soloist or a smaller unit from the group is in front, the others will keep a steady rhythm by stamping in unison, beating their hands on their shoulders, or by some other accompanying device. This is the folk dancer's use of weight; both Graham and Humphrey had used it before, but in *New Dance* it helped form an underlying propulsive texture and supported very complicated rhythmic counterpoint.

Humphrey tried to complement the "naturalness" that she had enforced rhythmically by deemphasizing the dancers' arms. She did this by establishing a few basic arm positions and functional patterns. No matter how active the dancers may be in their lower bodies, they keep their arms in the same positions, or, when it's necessary to change them, they use them in very simple ways: as a rule bilaterally, moving in simple, one-piece curves to the next position. This gives the dancers a somewhat disjointed look, but it focuses attention on their feet as Humphrey intended. It also announces very clearly that these are not ballet dancers, who often use their arms to decorate or frame the shape of the body. The arms in *New Dance* were to be severely curtailed, but they were not negatives. Even when static, they continue the lower body's energy, either throwing it off — into or away from the direction of the thrust of legs and hips — or containing the energy close to the body when the legs are designing rather than traveling.

For example, the female soloist starts a leg gesture that's later picked up by the others. The entire leg flexed at all joints from the hip down, she rotates in and out from the hip while bobbing up and down on the other leg. While doing this rather baroque figure, she curves both arms up, rotated outward so the palms of the hands face the audience, and holds them there. Later, the women do a whole series of tilts and spiraling thrusts in which both arms together swing from one position across the body and away from the direction of the chest and head.

Except for these rather rigidly prescribed arm designs, the stress of the motion throughout the dance is on its goingness, not its placement. The body is often thrown perilously off its vertical axis as the dancer swings, spirals, and plunges through space. Antiverticality is another of Humphrey's characteristics. It goes along with her phrasing — to prolong the moment of suspension between stability and reorientation the dancer is almost perpetually in a state of disturbed equilibrium. Again, this is antiballetic, anti the idea of divine classical balance and symmetry so hated by the modern dancers.

A by-product of this spatial leeway was that the dancers were not primarily concerned with body shapes or designs but more with the traveling designs they were making through space. The Humphrey-Weidman dancer did not aim for "stretch," or full extension of the limbs. In *New Dance* the body shapes are not inconsiderable, but those shapes are curving or obliquely angular rather than straight and perpendicular. The ballet dancer's long, straight line is expressive of what the avant-gardist Yvonne Rainer, thirty years later, called monumentality. Rainer said NO to making the dancer a superhuman, unnaturally big creature, and so did Doris Humphrey.

At the end of the man and woman's duet, the couple meet in the center, as they have several times before, and clasp hands, as they have before; but this time, instead of springing out into their own adventures as before, the woman pulls slowly away from the man, holding one of his arms and bracing a foot against his leg. This long counterbalancing tug of war decelerates the whole dance. The man leaves and the woman focuses attention on herself with repeated in-

NEW DANCE (*Humphrey, 1935*). *Photo by Thomas Bouchard.*

out leg gestures, like a tolling bell. One by one, the women come off the boxes and cross the stage with a vigorous sidestep initiated by tilting an upper body made more massive by keeping the arms immobilized and folded up toward the shoulders.

The soloist suggests movement ideas to the group, draws a few of them at a time into motion with her, starts small groups going and runs among the rest of them, throwing out her energy like a rallying cry. This First Theme is followed by a Second, in which the soloist majestically crosses the stage on a diagonal. She takes the entire distance to open her upper body, lean backward, and finally sink into an arching fall. The group follows her. When they are all on the floor, they develop their tilting theme into a full circle that takes them up and into spirals. They whirl, cluster for a minute in the center, then splatter out again, breaking their whirling to jump with both feet and reach toward the center. This whirling sequence is individually timed, and although the dancers do similar things, the space is organized spottily and emptied little by little.

The men's section, the Third Theme, was choreographed originally by Charles Weidman. The men enter and wait at the corners of the stage, then they echo the women who have left by launching themselves into turns, a jump, and a run to the opposite corner. Their dance is combative in feeling; although they don't actually attack one another, they frequently come face to face as if to challenge, or jump possessively into new territories on the stage.

The men's dance is related to the women's in its tendency to lean away from the vertical and in its use of a variation on the gesturing leg motif. But Weidman's use of the body is much flatter on the whole than Humphrey's, less oppositional in the directions of the upper and lower halves of the body. The arms and legs are more extended, giving more of a sense of balance and strength. Often the dancers propel themselves onto one leg and have to remain there securely. Their movement is full of two-fisted hoverings and pivots, punchy push-ups from the floor while supported on one hand and one leg, pelvic thrusts, and muscular stamping. They are accompanied by a slow drumbeat. Humphrey wrote that neither the women's nor the men's section was complete because it didn't include the other sex. Although she often used the sexes in an egalitarian way, she wasn't a doctrinaire feminist, and there were times when she made a choreographic point of the differences between men and women. *New Dance* is certainly one of those times.

The men retire to the boxes and the woman soloist returns, making a slow processional entrance with a pressing, sliding walk in which she leans back and at the same time twists her upper body toward the advancing leg while unfolding both arms with a firm, slicing motion, down and to the same side. This motion is repeated and carried all the way to the ground by the entering women's group and the men, who gradually join them. For the first time all the dancers are onstage and working together. Humphrey's movement device for bringing about this coalition, i.e., the female soloist's entering theme, is appropriate in many ways. First, it doesn't use the body in any way that hasn't been employed before — the tilt, the twist, the parallel arms, the sinking to the floor. Rather than introducing something unfamiliar to the group, she uses elements of a vocabulary they know, but her dynamics are slow, controlled, and firm. She moves along a straight path even though her body pulls away from a frontal, upright line. After all the scattered, agitated jumping and whirling, her action is like a wringing out of energy; she smoothes out their differences, draws them into more conforming patterns. The music for this section is two simple themes played in counterpoint to a regular beat by two pianos.

The group begins to circle the two lead dancers, who address each other in the center, linking arms and bending back in salute, then dipping their upper torsos forward, their back legs in attitude, in a kind of reverence. A few steps at a time, with halts in between, the group begins to run in a sweeping circle around the stage. By twos and threes they begin to cohere, like drops of matter in a centrifuge, then break off again. An orderly, wheel-like pattern is suggested but doesn't quite formulate itself.

Small ensembles group together. The woman soloist leads the men in a four-square, flourishing charge to the footlights, with the rest of the women flanking them. The men gather in the center, recalling their earlier dance. Then the women circle in the center, the men running in a bigger circle around them. For the first time in the whole piece these groups are arranged symmetrically, the visual order reinforcing itself again and again as the circle organizes itself in different compositional ways.

Briefly, the fragmentary wheel that was suggested earlier completes itself as all the dancers cluster in twos and threes and circle around. Together they all turn to the center and acknowledge the imaginary hub, to which they're all now connected. Humphrey called this dance Celebration, and it does indeed celebrate the unification of the two groups. But it isn't yet a complete expression of her ideal community, which must provide its citizens with a chance to express their individuality.

The curtain is lowered momentarily, and when it rises again the boxes have been moved from the sides of the stage and arranged in the center. The hub is now an actuality, a multilevel platform that is to focus the accumulating energy of the dance. The group wheels in a large circle as before, now condensing into a single spokelike line, out of which comes the first of several solo dances that seem thrown off by a force too strong to be contained. The movement of the solos is drawn from earlier motifs. Again the balletic process is reversed: not until the group has come together and gathered its collective dynamism can the individuals reach the inspired heights of their own powers. Nor does the group efface itself while these individual shouts of mastery are being made; it keeps up its pulse and its circuit around the center in constant support. The solos are brief.

They're not essays or meditations on a language's possibilities, but a language being used as an outlet for feelings.

This section, known as the Variations and Conclusion, is set to a very complex rhythmic pattern in which the group pulse is a steady 4/4 and the variations are in repeating phrases of six and eight counts. This creates all sorts of intellectually challenging possibilities for the choreographer — apparently the original dancers made up their own solos, although Humphrey must have exercised her editorial hand throughout. The meters are too fast for the audience to perceive their intricacy, however. What I do perceive is a most exhilarating and visually interesting stage space.

Although serving the same purpose as the finale of a big classical ballet — that is, to show individual and ensemble dancers in an array of flattering designs — the Variations and Conclusion could not look more different. The ballet participants arrange themselves in spread-out, decorative ranks, the better to set off the spread-out, presentational moves of the principals. The dancer in the ensemble moves in a contained way, changing the position of her arms or feet, or when traveling she aims for uniformity with her companions. As a group the ensemble serves to anchor the whole dance, to surround and possibly give limits to the risk and excellence of the principals. Within these limits, the dance is extended to allow for thorough exploration, for repetition and elaboration of ideas.

New Dance in its summation gravitates toward its own center. The pulsing pattern of the group around the boxes draws the dance in; sometimes the dancers look so tightly packed that it doesn't seem they'll be able to move at all. With the energy condensed in this way, its momentum seems irresistible. The solos are explosions — far-flung, Dionysiac, intensely personal. As each soloist finishes, he or she climbs onto the boxes, so that gradually the group traveling around the boxes diminishes and the group in the center grows bigger and stronger. Still, the group continues its pulsing support of the soloists. When all but the leading man and woman dancer have gathered on the boxes, this rhythmic ground-bass movement has spread and strengthened from the small syncopated traveling steps that took the group in their tours around the center. The dancer's whole body has become involved, changing on every downbeat, first the chest and arms thrusting forward in concave pushes, later arching back convulsively.

The circle is still a persistent idea, even though the group has given it up for a moment. First the male soloist, then the female, dance circular themes. The group in unison supports them with rhythmic pushing-forward arm motions, something like the *Shakers* theme; then they change to a big waving of both arms overhead that takes their bodies from side to side. Instead of going into spirals as she did before from this basic idea, the woman leader begins a pattern of turning and reversing, bringing the arms flat down toward her sides as she comes to face the audience, then lifting them and going the other way. As she steps into the place that has been left for her in the group, all the dancers simultaneously whip into this turn.

The turns are fast, two to a measure, and they serve as a background for a very brief reprise of each individual variation. When all the dancers have made their last mark, the group is whole once more, and the curtain goes down on all of them turning, reversing and turning again, a theme that is infinitely repeatable and has a built-in capacity for its own regeneration. When it's over I feel radiant, optimistic. *New Dance* confirms my failing hopes for action and change in the world. That is undoubtedly what Doris Humphrey intended it to do.

Passacaglia (*Doris Humphrey*)

Certain composers seem to intimidate choreographers by the magnitude of their accomplishment. Beethoven is almost unused in dance, but Brahms and Schumann have served often; Handel and Purcell are acceptable, but not Bach. The question of whether Bach's music should be used to accompany stage dancing was a very weighty one in the early days of American choreography. Virtually all of Bach is a dance, even when it isn't specifically built from court dance forms, but there is at the same time a spiritual quality, even in his secular works, that may have caused dancers to shy away. Bach fused emotional content with form, and also spoke to the dignity of the human being, to man's capacity for grandeur and positive resolution in the face of trial.

I think in *Passacaglia and Fugue in C Minor* (1938) Doris Humphrey was tackling the whole spectrum of Bach: his spirituality, his danciness, *and* his grandeur. Humphrey had choreographed Bach before, early in her career, but the evidence that survives indicates those were small salon pieces, of interest mainly as events in her development as an artist. She returned often to Bach after *Passacaglia,* and in fact was working on the Fourth Brandenburg Concerto at the time of her death. Charles Weidman and José Limón shared her love for the composer — Weidman choreographed several of the great choral works, and Limón, in addition to other works, set the Musical Offering with movement themes of Humphrey in 1963, as a tribute to his teacher.

Something about Bach's music must have especially appealed to Humphrey and her colleagues. This affinity probably has a lot to do with whatever distinguished the Humphrey-Weidman branch of modern dance from Graham and the others. Certainly structure was important. According to the contemporary critic and modern dance apologist John Martin, Humphrey's "genius for composition seems to go back ultimately to her ability to conceive her emotional ideas not only in terms of movement but directly in terms of form."[7]

In an introduction to Louis Horst's *Pre-Classic Forms,* published in 1937, Henry Gilfond noted that the modern dance, particularly that of Graham, was neoclassic "in the sense that it was concerned as America's dance was never before concerned with form as form; . . . in that it stripped itself of romantic emotionalisms, stripped itself of all the brilliance, the spectacular, the theatricality audiences had come to expect of dancing, and developed, *underscored* an almost Spartan restraint."[8] Too little of Martha Graham's work from the 1930s survives for us to tell whether she pursued the interest in formalism that she showed in *Primitive Mysteries.* In any case the formal concerns of her early work probably were largely the product of her association with Horst. When it came to an end in the forties, her work, perhaps by coincidence, evolved toward theatricality and away from pure form.

Humphrey remained in sympathy for her whole career with the formalist discipline of Horst, who attempted to rationalize this dance expression that bordered so closely on "self-indulgence." In his dance composition courses he worked from the examples of modern and primitive art and music, and "pre-classic" dance music forms — that is, the forms that antedated what we know as the classical ballet in Europe — to open up possibilities for dance structures that did not depend on the aesthetics of the nineteenth century.

Musically the passacaglia is a series of variations on a motif that is repeated over and over in the bass (basso ostinato). Humphrey devised a dance structure to match the thematic interweavings and complexities of Bach, but she did not attempt to mirror the music theme for theme, entrance for entrance, beat for beat.* Like the music, the dance makes an architectonic statement. It begins with all the building blocks present and in place, then takes them apart and shows you their different uses and shapes. Finally the elements, changed and expanded in form, are put back together to make a different but also logical result.

Without having access to all Doris Humphrey's intervening works, I see *Passacaglia* as a continuation of New Dance Trilogy, or a search into the implications of what *New Dance* achieved. *New Dance* represented society coming together as a mutually supporting and inspiring group; *Passacaglia* shows how this group of individually contributing members can evolve into an even more satisfying entity. The movement ideas seem both less complex and more interrelated, more harmonious. Everything in *Passacaglia* is of a piece; visually all the movement seems to come from the same palette. It's like a ballet in that way, except that rather than use the language of classical ballet, with a consistency and euphonious syntax produced by two hundred years of mellowing, Doris Humphrey invented her own idiom.

Passacaglia resists not only the time-honored forms of ballet but the passive redemption implied in traditional religious faith. This community takes nothing for granted. Its acceptance of a power beyond its own comes as an inevitable result of a collective probing, and it is to the group itself that tribute is paid at the end. *Passacaglia* is like a grand eighteenth-century argument in which the philosopher gains access to God through his intellectual efforts and then congratulates himself for having earned salvation.

The dance begins with a large group of men and women standing and sitting in a symmetrical arrangement on tiers of boxes. During the first statement of Bach's eight-bar theme, they remain motionless, facing the audience, their arms above their heads, with one

*John Mueller has provided an excellent detailed description of the dance from his study of the film "Dance: Four Pioneers," which includes a performance of a 1965 revival (*Films on Ballet and Modern Dance*, New York, American Dance Guild, 1974, pp. 23–43). I have used the same film for my commentary.

hand crossing the wrist of the other. One is always aware of the importance of arms in this dance, of what they are and are not doing. There is only one occasion in the dance when the participants open their arms and upper bodies entirely and unreservedly to the space above them. This happens at the penultimate moment of the piece, the great climax when Bach, after a long, suspenseful build-up, turns back to his original key to make one last reference to his theme. At all other times, the dancers gesture pointedly against the vertical, or pass through the open position in the course of a closing cycle, or lift only one arm skyward while using the other oppositionally to create a downward counterforce. I can't imagine a clearer statement of agnosticism. At the end of the dance, finally overcoming all their reservations, they accede to the heavenly presence, but no sooner have they declared their faith than they reaffirm their contentiousness, their mortality. Kneeling in a semicircle on one knee, they bow to their leaders, not to the unseen Power.

So the dance really celebrates humanity even though it concedes a higher existence. Even the man and woman who lead the group have no closer connection to God than the others, as has the Eldress in *Shakers,* for instance. These leaders are products of the group. All the major dance themes are presented first in germinal form by members of the group, then later enlarged and given back to the group by the leaders, whereas in *New Dance* the leaders encourage the group to become unified enough so that other individuals can emerge.

Two women are the first to move, in canon, turning and rising from the box where they sit. They open their arms vertically, like scissors' blades, until one arm is stretched straight overhead and the other is extended straight down with both hands flat, and the upper body is pulled slightly backward. People frequently unfold slowly into this position, from which they clang their fists together, and just before the end of the dance, the whole group in unison pulls back until they are half-kneeling in a semicircle behind the leaders, a sort of final, tension-filled denial before the giving in.

The two first women join both hands in an ice skaters' position and walk with stately, slow steps across to the other side of the group. Their steps expand to become large leg gestures that take the body off balance backward and forward, with small accommodating steps in between these rocking strides. This walk is also the forerunner of a motif that is repeated often as the group processes through the space. Sometimes the body is held tensely against the step, rocking back and forth with both arms pulled down behind pinched shoulders. At other times, the body fluidly curves back and scoops forward in either an exaggerated walk or a real plunge forward and down or a pitched-back fall to the ground.

The women, in their initial turning and coming forward, have also suggested a characteristic arm position — both arms folded in front of the body, held straight and parallel about six inches apart. This horizontal shape, so strange and antinatural, occurs as the women change their arms from the vertical stretched-up-and-down gesture to the crossed handclasp with which they walk together. It is used most frequently by the group in unison, sometimes only as a held position, other times as a shape that is pushed to the side on two beats of the music's three-beat phrase. The push takes the whole upper body with it, again carrying the dancer off his or her vertical center. I see these folded arms as a visual contrast to the Gothic arch suggested by the opening position of the dance, an underlining of the earthbound condition of men and women. Humphrey keeps reasserting this double horizontal, either as a separate gesture or woven into the sweeping, gathering-together gestures that accompany much of the locomotion.

The first pair of women bring into play one more motif in the course of their journey across the front of the boxes, a course that occupies the first three musical variations, twenty-four bars. As they are returning to their original place from stage right they turn, still holding hands, and take a few steps sideways instead of walking forward in profile to the audience as they have been doing. These side steps consist of unfolding the leg in second position, flat out to the side, and bringing it down as the whole body sinks into plié. In this step, both arms either strengthen the side to which the leg is lifting and descending or create a strong oppositional force to the leg.

After two more women from the other side of the stage greet the first pair in a courtly little dance, the male soloist makes his first move. Rising from his place in the midst of the group on the boxes, he steps forward through the group and down to the stage level. Like the female soloist, who enters at the next variation, he has been indistinguishable from the group up to this time. The soloists wear the same costumes, only asserting their importance by their actions.

PASSACAGLIA (*Humphrey, 1938*). *Humphrey and Charles Weidman in front. Photographed in performance at the Bennington Armory by Sidney Bernstein.*

Once the leaders have stepped forward, they immediately begin to enlarge on the ideas suggested before. The man clears huge circular horizontal planes with his arms as he steps forward, lifting and opening the plane into big scooping-back and gathering-forward spheres. Together with the woman he makes a small processional in which they bring their arms in circles overhead and down in front of them. The man lifts one leg and the arm on the same side into a high extension that drops into plié with both arms folded. Together the man and woman clasp their hands in front of them and push to the side, then, letting one arm swing up while the other keeps its folded shape across the chest, they go into a turn standing on one leg. They do fast little running circles and sideways jumps with their arms folded. In their last statement of this series, they give up locomotion and take positions, the woman downstage and the man directly behind and above her on the boxes, a different expression of the underlining-by-paralleling device we've seen in the use of the arms. Together they do a succession of large changes of body shape, first tilting from side to side on one leg with arms open and lifted, then stepping into lunges to the side with the arms scooping basketfuls of space, then standing on one leg and unfolding the other leg to the side while they open their arms straight into the horizontal. They tip their heads back and look up during this last opening. This is an image of contradiction, for while the face looks to heaven, the arms affirm the earthly plane, and the whole image is not even a definite position but a phase in a cycle that is closing into the arms-folded plié we saw earlier.

During these variations (numbers six through ten), the other members of the group have come off the boxes and gradually processed into a semicircle behind the soloists. Now they form a sort of clump at the side, and the soloists join them with twisting leaps across the stage. The female soloist and two women introduce a new idea: allowing the downward pull of their clasped hands to propel them into a turn. Up to this time, turns have been initiated by the upflung arms and leg or by the clasped hands twisting the body around its own axis. From the relatively simple, flat linear shapes and directions of the opening sequence, Humphrey has now evolved three-dimensional shapes and paths that arise from the body working against itself or allowing one tendency to spread and grow to include much space and many body parts. She has also begun to use the factor of weight, as either a downward pull or an upward lift, where earlier in the dance she merely depicted the ground as a static entity or a dividing line. Next she begins to combine these highly developed ideas.

With the group ranged behind them on the boxes, the soloists circle each other in a sort of formal reunion. Then they begin the motif of lifting one leg and arm, but before coming to a full extension they go into a suspended turn on one leg and end in a gathering lunge. The phrase is getting longer, as elements lead into one another. This lunge unfolds, and as the body rises one of the arms begins to pull backward from the elbow, leading the whole body into an off-center turn.

The leaders move to the sides and two small groups of women from the ensemble crisscross the space sideways with fluid, swaying motions of the trunk that take them into jumps, suspensions, turns, and reverses of direction. Then the leaders do a series of large one-legged turns, which they reverse by pushing both folded arms away from the spin, carrying the upper torso and then the whole body into the opposite direction. In a second series of turns they unfold from the arms and go into backward turns with a horizontal stress. Three men from the ensemble jump with their legs spread out to the sides, then scissoring in front and back of them as they beat their fists together from above and below. Four women run in a smaller circle with syncopated steps while the music plays a rather fast triplet, and as this, the eighteenth variation, ends, they pair off and link arms to the side; the opposite arms curve above their heads, recalling the courtly greeting with which the dance began.

In the last two variations there's a great deal of massing and regrouping by the ensemble — restatements of the various swing-down and pull-out motifs. The soloists introduce the famous bell turns, a development and combination of two earlier motifs. As one leg and arm swing up and the body pivots on the standing leg, the dancers beat the opposite fist against the thigh. The leg swings down and on the third beat of the measure they take two small recovering steps to the side, extending both arms forward. Then they lift and turn again to the other side. After the leaders have announced this idea, they are joined in it by the whole group for four repetitions. As the passacaglia section ends in a long ritard, the whole group goes back to the boxes and, turning in profile to the audience, they step into a lunge, with their arms straining behind their bodies.

The fugue section is built on a musical interweaving of the same theme and its embellishments. Like Bach, Humphrey has returned to the starting point. The group is arranged on the boxes as at the opening, the soloists indistinguishable from the ensemble. The dancers' arms are linked together now, and they push their upper bodies from side to side in tandem. Again, members of the ensemble are briefly singled out. A woman on the stage-left end of the top tier of boxes stands and, holding on to the man next to her, steps out expansively into space, stretching her leg and arm, and is pulled back into place before she falls. A man stands dead center in the group, reaching straight up as the male soloist did when he first appeared in the same place, then sinking and turning into a bent-kneed arabesque and pulling both arms straight forward. A woman on the floor level clasps both hands and lifts them in front of her, tipping backward as she reaches up. People support her as her whole body falls back. Then she slides one leg forward until she is sitting in a semisplit, one arm folded across the chest, the other reaching forward, one leg folded under her, the other extended in the ultimate exaggeration of a step. A woman steps forward from the stage-right top of the boxes, again seemingly groping in thin air, but this time people have bent down in front of her, and she steps onto their backs. The male soloist stands by her side and she leans on his hand as she makes a rather grand descent.

The soloists and small groups briefly elaborate further on these themes. The musical unit is four now instead of eight. Again they go from simple ideas, like standing in place or walking, to more complex ones, such as changing shape with a pivot or tilting off-center, and to allowing one idea to lead into another, as when they push both arms to the side, then pull one arm back in opposition and follow it into a sideways jump.

The female soloist and two men repeat the bell turns, which they end sliding to the floor. As one man on the boxes leads two women down with steps that begin with a big leg gesture, the whole group, now off the boxes, goes to the floor. First the trio, then the male soloist, move through their companions, who change positions every few bars. All of the floor positions are variations of the initial semisplit.

Now the music builds to its climax and the stage activity gets fuller. The group takes up a formation on the boxes similar to its original pose, then they all whirl into the space again with the reverse turns seen in *New Dance*. After a series of big unfoldings of the body where we see again the adamant folded parallel arms and the almost ecclesiastical raised arm with a palm now facing the audience, the group goes into a series of bell turns. The soloists' turns are continuous while the group, in a semicircle around them, pauses between turns to acknowledge them with a leaning-back, stretched-out gesture. From this position they all drop to the back knee, fists clenched, arms apart, one raised high and the other pulling down, as the music hits a huge question mark — a long-held chord in a different key.

Then Bach returns to his original key for the finish. The group rises, a few at a time, tilting their whole bodies from side to side with their hands locked together above their heads as in the first pose of the dance. The soloists carry this idea into a tilt with a strong downward swing of their clasped hands. Suddenly they lean back and open their arms, at the same time sliding backward down to the floor. This is the same kind of open gesture seen in *The*

Shakers at the moments when the worshipers finally get free of their earthbound state. The group follows the leaders canonically one measure later, so that as the soloists hit the floor the rest of the group opens their arms. The soloists immediately rise to their knees, beating their fists together, as the group descends to the floor. On the last musical suspension the group kneels, right arms raised in the blessing gesture, and as the music finishes, the soloists turn away from the audience to face the group. As the curtain falls the two are lunging forward with straight backs, bowing toward the center of the group, and the group, kneeling on one knee with the other leg extended behind, also pitches forward toward the center.

It is possible to see *Passacaglia* as a mere polemic. Dancers sometimes find its movement arbitrary and false. Indeed, it must feel especially unnatural to them today, when the balletic line is so ingrained in modern dancers and the sense of weight is so habitually avoided. I'm sure Humphrey meant the dance in part as an argument against ballet. The insistent pulling of the body off its vertical axis, the undoing of careful upright alignment with twists and oppositional stresses through the torso, the frequent throwing of weight as a means of propelling the body or the limbs through space, are all pointedly antiballetic ways of using the body. But the movement doesn't seem any less natural to me than ballet itself, only something we're less accustomed to.

There's something about Doris Humphrey that reminds me of Frank Lloyd Wright, the stubborn oddness of her visions perhaps. Like Wright, she thought people were capable of doing better if only they could be given the modes to help them. Her movement might have been uncomfortable because it denied the known forms, but it suggests higher possibilities that even now haven't been fully developed.

Concerto Barocco (George Balanchine)

During the 1930s Balanchine choreographed movies and Broadway shows, his efforts to establish a ballet company in abeyance after a disastrous two-year liaison between the American Ballet and the Metropolitan Opera. Kirstein turned his attention to Ballet Caravan, a company whose intention to create specifically native ballets on native themes was perhaps more suited to those patriotic days. Balanchine did a few "free-lance" ballets for other companies, but his only serious choreographing with his own dancers until the founding of the Ballet Society after the war came in 1941, when Nelson Rockefeller sponsored a good-will tour to South America. *Concerto Barocco* and *Ballet Imperial* were created for this occasion.

All during this period the various second-generation Ballets Russes companies were touring the country with productions of the nineteenth-century classics, hand-me-downs from the Diaghilev repertory, and neo-Russe ballets epitomized by the work of Léonide Massine. According to historian George Amberg, these companies consisted essentially of transplanted Russians and carried on the ballet tradition as they had known it in Europe; they never assimilated American ideas until Balanchine became associated with the third incarnation of Ballets Russes under Sergei Denham in the forties. "Russe" was America's idea of ballet in those crucial years. Says Amberg: "Massine's American career contributed immensely to the ballet education of this country but, for all its brilliance and fecundity, did little to further the growth of a native tradition."[9] Indeed, the last Ballet Russe de Monte Carlo actually survived into the early 1960s, leaving its imprint on audiences and scattering its retired dancers around the States to found Russian schools and regional ballet companies that extended a welcome to a new wave of European émigrés in the 1970s.

There were similarities between Massine and Balanchine. As young dancers, they had both excelled in character work, and they both explored musical forms in their mature choreography. They both went through a period of doing commercial work in America — Massine at Radio City Music Hall — before picking up the threads of their prolific former careers. Even Lincoln Kirstein admired Massine's work with Diaghilev and immediately after the Diaghilev era, as part of the modernistic trend Kirstein thought was needed to save ballet.

By the late thirties, during Balanchine's period of eclipse, Massine was dominating ballet here with his two types of choreography — symphonic and character ballets. Kirstein published a passionate defense of what he and Balanchine were trying to do, *Blast at Ballet* (1937–39),[10] in which he accused the traditional Russian ballet dancers and their promoters of blackmailing the American public into believing in old, worn-out formulas instead of searching for new forms that would express their own time and place. By that time he thought Massine's character ballets were all repetitions of the same number with different costumes,[11] and his symphonic pictures "gratuitous illustrations, or vignettes, free fantasies on well-known themes."[12] These did not satisfy Kirstein's vision of an American ballet. ". . . we want a new *idea*," he wrote, "a new *use* of paint or music, a *feeling* in gesture . . ."[13]

If we read the rhetoric of that period now, read what the two choreographers said they were doing and what critics said about them, it may not appear that Massine and Balanchine were all that different. But from the glimpses I've had of the Massine symphonic ballets on film, it seems that by the mid-thirties he and Balanchine had taken entirely divergent paths in pursuing the expression of music through a classical vocabulary. Massine's impulse seems to me to have been essentially dramatic. His so-called abstract ballets are abstract in the modern-art sense, as the artist's commentary on another phenomenon. The English critic Ernest Newman, in an early apologia for Massine, called his ballets "purely choreographic creations that run parallel throughout their design with that of the symphony, and at the same time set before us, in logical cohesion and sequence, a train of poetic associations that have been set up in Massine by the music."[14] Music calls to Massine's mind scenes, events, encounters — the Poet's quest for Love, the Creation, Man Against Adversity. He designs individual and group movement to express these themes. I find Balanchine's approach more modern — he relates to music as sound, texture, rhythm, phrasing, the way many visual artists use paint, canvas, metal, plastics. In each case the artist tries to express the properties of his medium directly, not to give his interpretation *of* the medium.

Massine's ballets were busy, explosive, full of great rushes and charges of energy. They must have been enormously appealing to the audience's emotions — you can sense a kind of Broadway programming of the sensibilities, the great sweeps of emotion and the long pregnant pauses, the melodramatic multiple pirouettes. Massine was fond of large choral groups, which he designed in harmonizing or contrapuntal masses, in the manner of the modern dancers, except that he used less original movements. Edwin Denby described the qualities he disliked in Massine in a 1942 review of *Aleko*: "— an agitation that seems senseless, a piling up of scraps of movement and bits of character like so much junk from Woolworth's, patterns but no room for them, accent and meter but no rhythm and flower of phrase."[15] It's easy to see why American audiences were captivated by the spectacular Massine and puzzled by Balanchine.

Concerto Barocco must have been startling when it was first seen, even in the original decorative costumes and headpieces by Eugene Berman that have since been discarded in favor of white practice clothes, for it had neither plot nor character nor philosophical pretext. The curtain rises on a small corps de ballet arranged in two parallel lines of four women, standing one behind the other straight upstage from the footlights. I suppose now we take chamber ballets for granted, but in 1941 this size and austerity must have been amazing. Although Balanchine chose the Bach Double Violin Concerto, he didn't design a virtuoso piece for soloists. *Concerto Barocco* is very much an ensemble work. The corps is the constant, remaining onstage throughout, with the man and two women principals serving more as a kind of embellishment of the corps patterns rather than the corps existing as a frame for them. When the principals are onstage they are the focus of attention, but the moments when they enter and slip away are so understated that it's hard to remember exactly how and at what point they occur.

Yet another surprising feature is the way the eleven dancers are distributed through the dance. I have read descriptions of the ballet in which the soloists are said to duplicate the musical line, each principal woman being assigned to one of the two violins. It seems to me that this is only a taking-off place for Balanchine; he is far less programmatic in *Concerto Barocco* than Humphrey is in *Passacaglia*, or even than he himself is on other occasions. The two women do enter with the violins in the first movement, generally addressing and answering one another as the music does, but for much of the ballet they interweave so closely that one can scarcely distinguish individual statements. The music acts in a similar way — the soloists overlap and follow each other so that often they could be one continuous line instead of two — but the correspondence between the music and the dance is seldom literal.

In the second movement, except for an opening theme and its almost identical recapitulation, one of the two women doesn't appear at all while the other dances a pas de deux with a cavalier. The choreographer preserves the balance between the two women by giving the second soloist some passages and jumps of her own to do later. Rather than conventionally bringing the entire cast together for the end of the piece, Balanchine omits the man in the third and final movement, returning, in a different spirit, to his first image of the corps with its two female leaders.

Instead of imitating the music, Balanchine expresses its essence by giving it a visual shape. The first movement, with its strong downbeat, has a lot of emphasis on the ground, with the corps working from solid foot positions. Even when they move out of place, they often step from downstage to upstage, swinging one leg and then the other out and behind, so that we get an impression that they remain stabilized as they go from foot to foot even though they are actually traveling back. Both the first and third movements are very lively in character, enclosing the slow, deliberate middle section. But the last movement is built on a double upbeat, created by a triplet with its last note falling on the first beat of the measure. Balanchine has converted this into a dance of bouncing pointe work that contrasts with the planted feeling of the feet in the opening.

In the middle section the two violins play a continuous contrapuntal duet, switching off so that each one plays the melodic line and the ornamentation for the same amount of time. The rest of the ensemble maintains a steady, walking beat below them, their three combined rhythms giving a sense of momentum without haste. Balanchine sets only the two slower rhythms, leaving the sixteenth-note ornamentation solely to the music. All the choreography in this section is built on the step. At the beginning, the second soloist leaves and the man enters to escort the woman through the corps, which has arranged itself in two diagonal lines. Everything in the duet stresses connections: the soloists and later the corps leading each other by the hand in long chains. The continuity of stepping is never interrupted, even when the woman is lifted in the air, but merely stretched over a longer interval. The ballerina turns slowly and smoothly under the man's arm, unfolding without pause into arabesque. She goes from pose to pose without stopping to adjust her weight but continues moving from one foot to the other, the poses growing one out of the other.

This very smooth, untroubled and unadorned section makes a great contrast to the two outer movements, which are sharp, almost fierce, in the agitation and precision of their stepwork. As a matter of fact, if there is one quality that the ideal Balanchine dancer has, it

CONCERTO BAROCCO (*Balanchine, 1941*). *Janet Reed and Frank Hobi in the late 1940s. Photo by Walter E. Owen.*

may be an almost incongruous combination of attack and lyricism, the ability to sell and the ability to yield. It's a truism that Balanchine idealizes women, and his ballets have been called sexist on occasion. But I find it fascinating that along with a rather cloying femininity there is invariably strength and independence. The female roles in both surviving pre-1933 Balanchine ballets, *The Prodigal Son* and *Apollo,* are one-sided: the conniving temptress of the Bible story and the three muses who submissively offer all their talents to the service of Apollo. Already in *Serenade* we begin to see these patterns being differentiated, in the mysterious woman who leads the man by covering his eyes and in the compassionate but firm Myrtha-figure whom the ballerina embraces before she dies. But in *Concerto Barocco,* without benefit of any dramatic signposts, we can see women in expressive modes of vehemence and playful unison as well as in the more traditional guises of lyricism, skill, and decorativeness. It seems to me that the ways in which the corps work together in *Concerto Barocco* owe something to the spunk and kinetic intelligence of Broadway chorus lines.

Though the solo and duet work make a powerful impression on the audience in *Barocco,* it is essentially a ballet of ensemble, an extension of Balanchine's ideas about the group in *Serenade,* and perhaps his first major exposition of that unit's possibilities. Perhaps it was Bach's music that helped Balanchine to formalize his visions of the diversity and detail inherent in a small group of individuals — he has not choreographed another Bach ballet since *Barocco.* In any case, *Concerto Barocco* came at a time when audiences were accustomed to the regimented ranks of classical ballets and the symphonic metaphysics of Massine.

Classical ballet's concept of the corps is extremely dehumanized. The function of the corps is to provide visual weight and mass for the stage, to symbolize the community with which the main characters are associated, and to exploit the possibilities of repetition on a large scale. All this is usually done by treating many people as if they were one. Anonymity, unison, and an emphasis on strict patterning are what we expect from the corps in *Swan Lake* or *La Bayadère.* Balanchine immediately makes the corps more personal by reducing its size. Instead of seeing it as an unobtrusive sort of second layer to the main action, like the lower parts of a string section in an orchestra, he imagines the corps as an instrumental colleague of the principals, with a complex texture of its own, like a piano. In *Barocco*, some of this complexity is almost thrown away, as when they dance in canon behind the principals; hardly anyone in the audience can comprehend this kind of intricacy, but most of us sense another sophisticated organism at work behind the soloists. At other times, the stage is cleared of solo dancers so that the corps' maneuvers can be seen without any other claim on our attention; what we may have sensed before as an intriguing presence is now revealed in its own right.

Balanchine's idea of the corps as a choreographic element interesting in itself comes from Petipa; he realizes the sure-fire effect of people all lined up facing the audience and filling the stage with mass motion, and many of his big ballets end this way. But he has also elaborated on the kind of formation patterns that had been achieved by a group, such as the Entrance of the Shades in *La Bayadère* or the Garland Dance in *Sleeping Beauty*. *Concerto Barocco* is notable for the variety and logic of these designs. In the first movement the corps is placed symmetrically in the two halves of the space, and they remain divided, working in linear groups, until the end of the section, when they form a semicircle behind the soloists and bow deeply. This arrangement gives an impression of simplicity, but it's kept from looking rigid or too severe by the individual dancers' movements, which are frequently off-center, the body pulling away from the gesturing leg.

The semicircle opens into two diagonal lines in a V-shape for the exit of the second solo woman and the entrance of the man. Once again the formality of the line-up is immediately refuted by the actions of the dancers. The solo couple thread their way through the lines, but each passage is different. One line of women stands, the other kneels; the ballerina winds in and out of the first with big unfolding leg gestures, then merely walks through the other with her partner, changing the position of their clasped hands. During the rest of the dance, the steps, the floor patterns, and the relationships among the dancers grow gradually more expansive without, however, becoming elaborate. Having once differentiated itself, the corps is able to split into even smaller units. One by one, the members of one of the two diagonals walk under the arms of the couple, and in pairs they kneel on either side of the stage as if they were the piers of an invisible bridge, along whose arcing span the man lifts the woman again and again.

In the process of making this formation, the corps has now, for the first time, destroyed the symmetry of the stage, and they and the soloists begin a gradual process of coalition. The remaining four women pass between the man and woman as they execute a series of supported arabesques in alternating directions. Six corps members gather on one side of the stage, against the soloists backed up by the other two on the other side, and the woman falls backward into her partner's arms from side to side. The male soloist leads them together again until all eight are on the same side of the stage. They all mingle together in a trailing, tightening circular procession of clasped hands that somehow ends in two parallel diagonal lines on the stage-left side, with the soloists at the head of the lines. These lines form a counterweight to the series of spectacular lifts and pirouettes that the solo couple do next.

In a transition so quick you can't tell how it happens, the stage reverts to the way it was at the beginning of the movement and the whole sequence of the second soloist's exit and the man's entrance is run off again, with slight differences. The music is repeating too at this point. The ballerina and her partner return to their opening sequence — except it too is different, and after some leanings and arabesques from side to side at the apex of the V, the dance leads quickly back to the asymmetrical arrangement it had reached before the flashback. This brief recapitulation is almost mystical — a return over the same ground, in which we quickly learn that it is not the same at all — and the stage arrangement in which the principals and the corps make their final bows differs completely from the one that ended the first movement. Now the corps is not backing up the soloists but is massed asymmetrically along the up-left-to-down-right diagonal that they themselves have created, six women in the upstage portion and two downstage, with the soloists almost extraneous to their design.

A second later the soloists leave, and the corps begin their most complicated dance of the ballet. They return to symmetricality —a cross in stage center that will be the design motif for the last section of the ballet. The whole process of reorganizing the stage into a stronger and stronger diagonal in the second movement suggests that the corps is mobilizing its force to nudge the principals out of the way, and symmetricality, with all its implications about balance, order, hierarchical focus, has to be ousted with them. Having tipped them off the seesaw, the corps can then return to symmetricality. Now they play a series of intricate canonic games with the fast, swooping port de bras that began the ballet. Except that instead of pulling the dancers toward the ground, as the arms did initially, the port de bras here lifts them onto their pointes, to rapid hops in fifth position.

The two women soloists enter, and the rest of the dance is a fast-moving succession, almost a competition, of solo and corps ideas that have been suggested earlier. The soloists at times complement the corps, at times join them; the corps constantly regroups into variations of its half-stage diagonals. Finally, they form two parallel diagonals, just as they did near the end of the second movement, and the soloists join their hopping port de bras, one at the head of each line. But startlingly, the ballet ends in a formation that has not been seen before, at least not in this very untraditional ballet: all the women make two lines across the footlights, with the soloists in front, and, kneeling, make a gesture of acknowledgment to the audience.

Despite the musical precision of the ballet, particularly in the last movement, *Concerto Barocco* doesn't give the set feeling of most classical ballets, where the corps or the soloists enter, line themselves up, take a preparation, and *then* begin to move. The dance is always in the process of developing ideas and forms out of what came before — and each new idea seems to materialize as another one is dissolving, certainly a cinematic idea. Balanchine's years in the glamour factories were definitely not a loss for art.

Americana Ballet

I frequently hear music in the very heart of noise.
— *George Gershwin* [1]

THE CONCRETENESS of American art is one thing that distinguishes it from its European forebears. Even in the neoclassic refinements of Tharp, Taylor, and Cunningham we see an irresistible craving for the real. The European painters wanted to improve on the landscapes they saw, and washed them with the sentimentality of the picturesque, restrained them with devices of composition or light. Walt Whitman might have been speaking of all American art to come when he said of the pioneering Thomas Eakins that, unlike other painters of his day, he "could resist the temptation to see what [he thinks] ought to be rather than what is." [2] Eakins endured the scorn of late-nineteenth-century Philadelphia because he didn't romanticize or flatter his subjects; he showed them slumping, frowning, squinting, with all the tensions or skepticism he found in them as they sat for him. Charles Ives put ragtime and discordant hymns into his music with the same directness, and encountered the same hostility because of it.

For Ives and Eakins — and for the enormous wave of Americana artists of the first half of the twentieth century — the American landscape, its sounds and inhabitants, was a perfectly logical subject matter, a scene that needed no embellishment or classical associations to make it interesting. European painters celebrated the efficiency and the technological power of the machine age, the dynamism and color of music halls or amusement parks, the voluptuous curves and shadows of plastic and metal. They made these things glamorous, awesome, as if their practicality, their plainness, ought to be glossed over. Only Americans accept the matter-of-factness of grain elevators, winches and cranes, bait shops, soda fountains, trolley cars, bridges, and gasoline pumps; only we see so penetratingly into the commonplace. Only America could have produced Gertrude Stein or Robert Rauschenberg.

Choreographers did not consciously begin searching for an American expression until a lot of groundwork had been laid. It was first necessary to establish the plausibility of the personal movement style and the independent creative artist, and to sense the beginnings of a potential audience. With the Depression came a period of introspection and patriotism in all the arts, and by the mid-1930s the idea of finding an American dance had become institutionalized in the Graham and Humphrey-Weidman schools and companies, the New Dance League, the Bennington School of Dance, the Federal Dance Project, the Ballet Theater, and Lincoln Kirstein's Ballet Caravan. Each was to find it from different sources — Humphrey and Weidman in American social behavior, Graham in American rituals, Tamiris in our ethnic roots, the transplanted Russians in our American enterprise.

Frankie and Johnny (Ruth Page and Bentley Stone)

When the Federal Theater Project of WPA came to Chicago, Ruth Page and Bentley Stone were named codirectors, and together they choreographed *Frankie and Johnny* in 1938 and *Guns and Castanets*, a modern-dress version of the Carmen story set in the Spanish Civil War, the following year. Page was already a key figure in Chicago, having worked with Adolf Bolm in Ballet Intime and the Chicago Allied Arts, two of the initial attempts to establish ballet companies on American soil. She had toured with many important artists, including Pavlova and Harald Kreutzberg, but her career was and continues to be centered in her home city. Page had money and connections and a flamboyant style that attracted at one time or another most of the dance talent in Chicago and an impressive array of international composers and designers. With Stone, who was also a native Midwesterner with experience in ballet and opera, Ruth Page formed the Page-Stone Ballet in 1938. She has headed a series of companies in Chicago ever since, many of them connected with opera companies, and all centered around her own choreography.

Besides her abundant energy and cheerfulness, Ruth Page has the virtue of nerve. It seemed, especially as she began choreographing, that there was nothing she wouldn't try and no historical precedent too sacred to break. With scant regard for the niceties of decorum or aesthetics, she updated legend and literature, including the Bible, in primary colors. In addition to her productions in Chicago she choreographed for other companies, danced her own solo programs, and traveled extensively. Although most of her ballets have not been seen or discussed by serious dance writers, one gathers from contemporary accounts that she put on a good show and did not add much to choreographic progress.

Frankie and Johnny seemed to be about equal parts pop art and dance theater. It was not the first ballet of its kind, but it was the earliest example in active repertory in 1976, when I went to see the Pittsburgh Ballet Theatre's revival. The reconstruction was staged by PBT's co–artistic director Frederic Franklin, another old colleague of Page, and appeared on a curiously regressive Bicentennial program as one of three ballets on "American life and times, and balletic styles as they have developed in this country."[3] In the company of an uninspired dance-drama and a tribute to the city's steel industry done in 1920s Euro-mécanique style — both newly choreographed — *Frankie and Johnny* exuded cockiness and authenticity, the vitality of its own intentions. It looked as though it came from the beginning of an era, not the end. Raw, raunchy, and proud of it, the ballet parades its lack of refinement. It's a *Dodsworth* of a ballet, hailing from mid-America when "culture" was still suspect. People liked it in 1976, and they liked it when it was made. Margaret Lloyd called it "a ballet that is good fun, if not precisely good form."[4]

Frankie and Johnny, the old barroom ballad about a woman who shoots her two-timing lover, is part of a healthy American lore of rough-and-ready frontier types noted for their exploits just on the brink of the law. The lyrics in general circulation don't actually say that Frankie and Johnny's relationship is that of prostitute and pimp, although their precise occupations are less significant than the quick passions and quicker revenge of which they're capable. But Page and Stone spell out this situation right away, with no subtlety at all.

The scene is a back street somewhere — a saloon, a lamppost, a dingy two-story house, with Nellie Bly hanging out of the upstairs window and Frankie living below, their rooms red-lit, with window shades that they pull down when they're engaged. Johnny, sharply dressed in vest, pants, a bright-colored shirt and spats, lounges on the "boarding house" stoop. Three Salvation Army ladies march in, take up a position at the side of the stage, and start the narrative in operatic voices. Burlesque is what the whole thing says, and burlesque is the style of the ballet — at least in the production I saw.

The choreographers didn't see *Frankie and Johnny* as a tragic love story or a gruesome tale of immorality and retribution among the dregs of society. Instead they told it in the manner of a traditional tall tale, with the slapstick disrespect of a minstrel show. You can't pinpoint its locale or its period because it has none. The characters have no more psychological depth than the types in a Mack Sennett comedy. The dancing, with the exception of a balletic solo done by Johnny, is almost entirely borrowed from vaudeville, musical comedy, and the dance hall, with mimed action and signature gestures incorporated for particular characters. There's a chorus-line corps de ballet made up of assorted denizens of the neighborhood and transients. They don't do much more than provide a likely looking crowd against which the story happens.

The dance is uneven in construction and proceeds by a variety of expository means. There are scenes where a lot of things happen quite fast — Johnny drums up clients for the girls, taking their money and conducting them to Nellie's or Frankie's door; Johnny steals a dance with Nellie while the crowd hides them from Frankie, then sneaks up the stairs with her while Frankie is having a beer. There are conventional numbers in which the main characters express their feelings at some length. Frankie and Johnny's love duet is a slow, stretched-out, acrobatic series of embraces, a sort of apache, that starts on the stairs and quite skillfully slides from realistic attitudes into danced elaborations of them. Johnny's solo is the danciest part of the ballet, blending fast pirouettes and jumps with the shimmy and other jazz steps and bits of byplay with the other men. Frankie's fit of anger at Johnny's betrayal is aptly designed for her character: stomping around bent-kneed in her high-heeled shoes, sheer black stockings, and slit-to-the-waist skirt, she shakes her fists, tears at her dyed-red hair, pounds on the floor with her hands.

FRANKIE AND JOHNNY (*Page-Stone, 1938*). *Bentley Stone and Ruth Page.*

Here begins the best part of the ballet, the murder and Johnny's boisterous funeral. Again I am reminded of silent movies with their sight gags and exaggerated situations. Frankie goes barreling up the stairs, turns suddenly, and gnashes her teeth, scuttles down the stairs again to get a more ferocious start, and stomps up again, clutching both banisters. Johnny and Nellie lift the shade and peek out, proving what Frankie suspected. She goes into her room, comes back with a gun, climbs a ladder to Nellie's room. Hanging onto the windowsill with one arm and kicking her trailing kimono out behind her like a horse twitching its tail at an insect, Frankie shoots Johnny just as he and Nellie are rushing out the door.

Dying, he takes his time falling down the stairs, and reaches the bottom with his feet in the air. Frankie is immediately stricken with remorse, pulls his legs down, and kneels by him until he finally expires. Then she goes into another paroxysm, grabs a shroud that the bystanders have brought, and tries to hang herself from the lamppost. Just then Nellie appears dramatically at the head of the stairs with an enormous wreath of lilies. Seeing Frankie, she runs down and grabs the shroud away. The two enemies embrace tearfully as the mourners celebrate in the bar. A coffin is brought and the women shove the now-stiff victim into it. Finally the grief subsides, the mourners shuffle away, Nellie goes upstairs with the policeman, and Frankie is left sitting dejectedly on the coffin while the Salvation Army lassies tell us you can't put no trust in men, and lift mugs of beer.

Filling Station (Lew Christensen)

Considering Lincoln Kirstein's background and aesthetic interests, it was natural that Ballet Caravan should stick with a fairly conventional mode of movement and presentation. Its productions made use of American themes, characters, locales, décor elements, gestures, and even American dance steps as "character" indications, but they didn't attempt to find an American movement style as the modern dance was doing. Nevertheless, the two surviving Ballet Caravan works show that its choreographers were picking up more of the American style than its surface manifestations. By Kirstein's design, Ballet Caravan's repertory tried to make a direct appeal to audiences, providing them with characters and situations they could identify. This is the sense in which Kirstein thinks of ballet as being "popular," and in fact Ballet Caravan's most American attitude probably was its egalitarian view of the audience.

After a play of his had failed in 1940, Tennessee Williams lamented "the failure of the theatre really to explore the many levels of society except in the superficial and sensational way of 'Tobacco Road' and its prototypes, which please the carriage trade inversely to polite drawing-room comedy by representing their social inferiors as laughable grotesques."[5] This seems to me to represent fairly well the appeal of *Frankie and Johnny*. Ballet Caravan, while it didn't see its mission as sympathetically projecting human degradation, didn't feel the necessity of ridiculing the "common man" either. Unlike European ballet or the many transatlantic descendants of the Ballets Russes, the Ballet Caravan wasn't set up for the pleasure of the rich and the aristocracy. Kirstein intended it as a touring company for the college-educated audience, and he planned to use all types of American entertainment media as choreographic sources.

Ballet Caravan may not have acquired a mass audience in its two-year existence, but it attempted to be a people's ballet.

I went to Detroit to see *Filling Station*. It was being revived by Ballet West, and that was the closest the tour was coming to New York. I hoped there might be some poetic justice in this ballet and this city coinciding, but neither I nor the audience seemed to find any particular added enjoyment in the identification. Maybe even in the Motor City the automobile no longer represents the adventure and the expansiveness it did to Americans in 1938. What was first and most obviously American about *Filling Station* (score by Virgil Thomson) was its theme, setting, and characters. Its librettist, Lincoln Kirstein, has noted that the characters are familiar from movies and comic strips,[6] and this, perhaps, is a clue to the ballet's style and its ultimate significance.

The people in *Filling Station* are types. The sturdy, adaptable Mac; the brassy tourist family consisting of henpecked Dad, portly Mom, and their bratty daughter; the two rich drunks on a party; the truck driver pals; and the hard-bitten cop and the tough holdup man.

FILLING STATION (*Christensen, 1938*). *Photo by George Platt Lynes.*

These characters are not drawn from life but from codified representations of life — Babbitt and his missus, Jiggs and Maggie, Little Caesar and Scarface. The choreography is designed to let the audience identify these types while at the same time enjoying balletic entertainment.

The hero of *Filling Station* may only be a gas station attendant, but he's an American hero, and he dances in a classical style suited to the heroes of traditional ballets. Mac's opening solo and later thematic dance interludes are full of jumps, beats, pirouettes, barrel turns — the whole range of danseur noble achievements. "His acrobatic brilliance showed him capable of treating any emergency that might come up, with brilliant resourcefulness. He was the type of self-reliant, agreeable and frank American working-man," says Kirstein.[7] Perhaps only an aristocrat could seriously believe this — or an audience that accepted the conventions of classical ballet.

For his other characters choreographer Lew Christensen adopted the typically European practice of setting variations on an already identifiable dance or mime attitude that fits the situation. While waiting for his wife and daughter to use the rest room, the tourist pulls out his golf club to take a few practice shots. Ray and Roy, the truck drivers, get interested and ask to have a try at it. They do some swings in rhythm.

Fred Astaire's golf dance in "Carefree" wasn't in circulation until later in 1938 — but what a world of difference in the two ways of handling this reference to a popular pastime. Instead of incorporating a few typical gestures into the continuity of a completely alien dance form, Astaire turned the whole movie, the whole dance, into a golf game for that moment. The shots he takes at a row of balls teed up are real. He uses whatever amount and distribution of energy he needs to send them soaring down the fairway. The tap-dancing steps he takes in between swings are like by-products — the golfer's follow-through — as if he's using up the overflow of energy or gathering together a new supply to hit the next ball. In *Filling Station*, just the opposite happens. The golf swings are reshaped and reenergized to fit into the rhythm of the ballet steps that surround them.

I suppose Astaire's attitude, that his dancing drew its impetus from whatever plot situation he happened to find himself in, is what enabled him to dance so often and so effectively in so many films. We never feel we're looking at a contrivance. We're never sure what turn of events will cause Astaire to break out in a dance next. He could as easily have danced in Walking the Dog ("Shall We Dance") — or *not* danced in Edward Everett Horton's hotel room ("Top Hat"). The approach Christensen used — and that so many choreographers use to this day — limits the range of subjects you can make a dance about, and also limits the ways the specialty dance can be integrated into the ballet so that it makes sense.

Christensen found an unusually large number of such occasions in *Filling Station*. When Roy and Ray appear, they greet their buddy Mac with somersaults, and the trio do a sequence of tumbling, flips, and other acrobatics. The choreographer wants to show us people of high spirits and daring — it doesn't matter what form this vivacity takes. The tourist's daughter can do a toe dance because she's a showoff, and toe dancing is showoffy dancing. I think the symbolic associations of the signature forms were more important to Christensen than their appropriateness for his characters. Certainly mechanics don't ordinarily burst into multiple pirouettes.

The drunken couple also resort to a classical form, the pas de deux. The girl is in fact conveniently wearing toe shoes with her evening gown — the only nonrealistic item of costuming in Ballet West's production. Here Christensen created a comic dance that relies almost entirely on distortions of the classical technique. Again, Christensen counted on some sophistication about classical ballet from his audience. Weaving and lurching, their spatial relations wrecked by alcohol, the couple grab for each other and miss, or contact the wrong body parts. They set themselves up for a supported pose, calculate wrong, fall free for an instant, then collapse against each other. The girl achieves a perfect line in arabesque and locks herself into it while the man ducks confusedly under her leg and comes up on the other side, still holding her up. These are gags, but they're more than gags. In satirizing the precision of placement and trajectory that makes a classical pas de deux work, the dancers have to use an equal amount of precision. Their erratic approaches and off-balance teeterings are almost as lovely to watch as the coordination they can't achieve.

As this dance is ending, Mac and the other men — and later the women — get caught up in it, at first throwing the drunken girl around like a beanbag, which she seems to enjoy, and then coalescing into a rhumba and what Kirstein has called a "sublimated Big Apple." This is frankly a "number" — Christensen made no effort to preserve the fourth-wall illusion here as he did, minimally, in the rest of the ballet. Everyone dances in unison, facing the audience. The scene moves without pause from a situation that has some dramatic context or rationale into a dance that couldn't possibly occur under realistic circumstances — a typical device of the Broadway musical.

Just as the ensemble is building up to its highest pitch of rowdy exuberance, the gangster rushes in, initiating the last few minutes of the ballet and its entire plot. The bandit drives all the gas station denizens into a corner and, holding his pistol on them with one hand, places a bucket on the floor. Ony by one they come up and dump their valuables into it, each according to the character that has been established for him or her. When he's picked the group clean, the robber leaves, and the place is suddenly plunged into darkness.

During this blackout Christensen set a dance lit only by flashlights. Other choreographers were to make use of a blacked-out stage — Merce Cunningham's *Winterbranch* is perhaps the most notorious — but Christensen may have been the first to attempt it. Presumably the holdup man has pulled the gas station's fuses to immobilize his victims while he makes his getaway. Somehow flashlights are located and what we see is a wonderful confusion of lights sailing through the air, crisscrossing and colliding, with shadowy figures popping up and disappearing as everyone runs around in panic. The scene ends as abruptly as it began, with a gunshot. The lights come on again to reveal the handcuffed burglar crouching center stage, covered by the trooper's gun, and the drunken girl lying wounded or dead in her escort's arms. In a quick finish, the entire party forms a procession — totally abandoning realism again — and solemnly files out behind the cop and his captive. Mac remains — thinks it all over, and goes back to his newspaper.

Since the original Ballet Caravan production and the 1953 revival by the New York City Ballet, the work has undergone some changes. Ballet West (formerly the Salt Lake City Ballet) is directed by Willam Christensen, brother of *Filling Station*'s choreographer, and credits its production to Lew Christensen's San Francisco Ballet. It is hard to tell at this point whether Christensen choreographed the buoyancy and spaciousness into the role of the filling station attendant, whether he intended the unclassical look that seems to have connotations of athleticism and virility as well as a connection to American soft-shoe dancing, or whether this quality rubbed off on the role when Jacques d'Amboise danced it in the fifties. The last-minute resuscitation of the rich girl's corpse — she sits up and winks at Mac as she's being carried out — is a show-biz touch contributed by Balanchine, who is always ready to sacrifice reverence for the dead in the interest of comedy. Kirstein has written that Balanchine suggested this twist in lieu of Kirstein's more lugubrious idea of having the girl accidentally killed by the gangster, but it isn't quite clear whether this change was made before the première or for the New York City Ballet revival.[8]

For all its boisterous realism, *Filling Station* leaves big holes in logical narrative. Is it a fairy tale? A morality play? In its present condition it might be a daydream or a flashback that Mac goes through while waiting for his next customer. Kirstein tells us he chose the comic strip as the appropriate idiom for *Filling Station*, and the original costumes, in plastics and cutout shapes, were designed by Paul Cadmus, who had worked in an advertising agency and whose paintings tread that ambiguous territory between illustration and art. The producers were aiming for a synthetic look, a kind of pop modernism, that was entirely lacking in Ballet West's version. A moderne painted backdrop, uncredited, recalled the period, with a suggestion of chromium and curves, but the clothes didn't even attempt to preserve a 1930s look, let alone Kirstein and Cadmus' cartoon-thirties whimsy. Writing a decade after *Filling Station*, George Amberg deplored the poor, styleless revivals of Fokine's works in America and hoped that contemporary classics would be spared that fate. Better to let the works die, he thought.[9] We still have not solved the problem.

Billy the Kid *(Eugene Loring)*

Eugene Loring's *Billy the Kid* is the first great American storytelling ballet. Like *Letter to the World, Undertow,* and *The Moor's Pavane*, it invents its own particular form rather than follow the traditional forms of narrative ballet. Created in 1938 for Ballet Caravan, it went along with Loring to the newly formed Ballet Theater in 1940 and has remained in repertory intermittently since then.

Billy the Kid is very much like a film Western, but a Western of a subtlety and seriousness that Hollywood was not to attain for another fifteen years. Loring wasn't trying to make a ballet that looked like a movie, however. He was trying to use film techniques on the stage, and the resulting work is both very odd and very interesting. Though created in the same year as *Filling Station,* it represents an enormous advance in its conception of what a ballet could do and what it could use to develop its imagery. Other choreographers were to adopt Loring's methods of cutting and continuity, but no other ballet has ever looked quite like *Billy the Kid.*

The Dance in America version, shown nationwide over National Educational Television in late 1976, correctly identified all the peculiarities and problems of Loring's conception, as well as its relation to Hollywood. Instead of preserving the ballet as it was made, Loring and the telecast producers converted it into the Western it had so carefully tried not to be. At every point where Loring had originally worked with the proscenium stage and the ballet medium to create a nonliteral image, TV substituted narration, camera techniques, and cinematic editing to draw attention to the story, sacrificing most of the dance innovation that had distinguished the piece.

The ballet opens and closes with a procession of pioneers marching across the footlights, doing canonic movements abstracted from frontier activities like roping and riding, scouting, cradling babies, praying. *Billy the Kid* was Aaron Copland's first big Americana score, and the open fourths and fifths of his harmonies, heard as Loring's westward army surges past, provide an enduring image of distances and inexorable progress. This procession is really nothing more than a musical introduction and conclusion, but it has the effect of transforming Billy's story — a real story from our folklore — into a kind of parenthetical incident in the panorama of American history. The dancers in the procession are depersonalized, isolated; they stand for large forces. Later they become more individual, but they will merge into the processional again when their several stories have been told.

The procession is unusual too for its restricted use of the stage area. Loring arranged it to move straight across the front of the stage instead of along a diagonal. The diagonal is the more conventional way of staging this type of group action — for the very good reason that it encompasses more distance. Loring's downstage traverse does several things to the procession. Instead of moving toward or away from the audience as they cross, and thus changing the way we perceive them, the dancers stay in the same horizontal plane; their figures remain flat, in the same perspective, like the flat images on film or an unfurling olio in a music hall. They can use only a few feet of the stage depth, and that way their numbers look dense, crowded, and by inference desperately in need of elbow room.

The stage opens out for the first scene, and the anonymous caravan turns into a frontier town full of cowboys, outlaws, Mexican girls, dance hall girls, mousy women settlers, all strolling through their newfound space. Edwin Denby described this scene in 1943: "The wandering individual floor patterns by not emphasizing a fixed place on the stage and the gestures by not emphasizing a climax in rhythm give the sense of unfenced spaces and of all the time in the world. Nothing could be more characteristically American or more original as a dance conception." [10]

Each type of character has his or her signature movement pattern. The cowboys come in astraddle, elbows out, gripping imaginary reins. They canter to a six-count syncopated Mexican rhythm. The badmen hook their thumbs into their belts and sink into the advancing leg with an exaggerated, truculent shift of weight. The Mexican girls fold their arms and swing their hips. The dance hall girls rest their hands on their padded buttocks and shove their pelvises forward. The pioneer women's walk is the most interesting of all. Bending forward slightly and keeping their arms folded a little distance from the body as if holding a baby or an armful of laundry, they step carefully, placing one heel on the ground and rotating each foot in, then out, before advancing the other one. This peculiar step has the quality of irresolution followed by deliberateness. The women are both hesitant about where they are going and firm about where they are.

Into this bewildering thoroughfare comes the young Billy in overalls and a straw hat, clutching his mother's skirts and gawking at everything. As they make their way through the crowd, two men start a fight over a woman, a shot is fired, and Billy's mother is accidentally killed. In a panicky rage, he snatches up a knife, kills the gunman, and runs away. When next we see him, he has become a desperado, killing and escaping by his wits until he is tracked down in his hideout and shot with his boots off by his old friend, Sheriff Pat Garrett.

Loring tells this story in a series of fast, tense episodes, most of which depend as much on various cinematic uses of space as they do on pantomime and character. At first viewing, *Billy the Kid* is confusing to many people. The action is neither literal nor sequential. The miming is abstract as often as it is realistic. The dancers frequently use their hands flat to stand for objects. Billy holds one flat hand next to his cheek, with his head turned away, to represent hiding behind something. Playing cards are mimed by flat hands rather than by hands holding imaginary cards. The mailman distributes letters by patting the back of one hand against the palm of the other and then flipping the top hand, still flat, out to one side. Loring was able to say a lot very economically by thus doing away with the mechanical business of handling objects. When someone wants to snatch someone else's gun — Billy tricks at least two of his enemies this way — he merely slaps the other man on the hip where a holster would be.

There are more conventional pantomime gestures too: Pat Garrett calming the crowd after Billy's first revenge killing, the Mexican girls showing their claws to each other during their folk dance to symbolize their fiery tempers, the shuffling of cards and the aiming of rifles and the mounting and riding of horses. Through combined literal and nonliteral gestures, the transactions between people unfold. Billy cheats on Pat Garrett in a card game. Here Loring also uses dance itself as a dramatic device in the tap-dance challenge Garrett throws to Billy after their disagreement about the game. Captured in an ambush, Billy tricks his jailer and escapes. An Indian scout leads Garrett to the hideout.

The large scenes are harder to follow because Loring sets up the stage as if he were combining several camera shots that in a movie would be shown in separate takes. The best and most wildly imaginative of these scenes is the ambush, when Garrett leads a posse to capture Billy and his gang. While the four outlaws stand center stage, in plain sight but "hiding" behind their hands, a large group of deputies gallops on. They take up formal positions in two lines, prone and facing each other as if stationed on high rocks above a

Ambush Scene from BILLY THE KID (*Loring, 1938*). *Daniel Levins and American Ballet Theatre. Photo by Louis Péres.*

canyon or a road. Billy and his cohorts run this gauntlet one at a time, and they're all hit, except Billy, who emerges at one end of the corridor only to be grabbed by Garrett.

There is no way to look at this scene realistically. It's even more unbelievable than the eyeball-to-eyeball confrontation of hunters and swans in *Swan Lake,* Act II. One has to understand that Loring is condensing into one small stage space and one fixed viewing position what would be spread out and seen from several angles on the screen. The same process underlies the celebration that follows the ambush and Billy's capture. The members of the posse and their partners do a sort of Virginia reel, a very mechanical, doll-like, and completely unnatural barn dance. I've never understood this dance very well, but early reviewers of *Billy the Kid* talked about it as a danse macabre. As performed now by Ballet Theater, it has no particular feeling; the dancers just set themselves in flat, spread-out positions and hop fast from foot to foot or bob back and forth, not changing the position of their arms.

But in the floor pattern of the dance Loring's intent is clearer. The lines of partners don't stay in one place as in the usual Virginia reel; the whole ensemble shifts together into different circular and linear orientations on the stage. Finally both lines exit into the wings, bobbing sideways. It's as if, given the limitations of fixed perspective, Loring is turning the dance around so that the audience can get different views of it. Then, instead of moving the viewer's attention away from the dance and on to the next scene, he transports the dance out of the viewer's range.

Loring's many scene changes in *Billy* are similarly cinematic. The stage fills and empties with crowds of people. One group fades away while another slides in. The scene of Billy preparing for sleep in his final hideout overlaps with the scout leading Garrett to him. This is very simply done by dividing the stage into two areas — Billy in the down-left corner, and the scout beckoning Garrett across the empty expanse of the rest of the stage. Again, thinking filmically, you have to imagine that they're traveling over miles, not just going in a big circle. And of course you have to accept the convention that neither the sheriff nor his quarry is aware of the other although both are in sight of the audience.

Loring asks us to do so much of this kind of seeing-without-seeing that when Billy dances with his Mexican sweetheart, it's easy to accept the notion that he is merely asleep and dreaming of her. At first they dance back to back, and during much of his supporting action she is in a position where they can't make eye contact. Even when they can see each other, they have a far-off look, their contacts are remote. When they think they hear something outside, they draw together, the way we cling to sleep when something threatens to wake us.

When *Billy the Kid* is performed well, most of these dramatic scenes have a dreamlike quality. Whether alone or among others, the principals in each episode create a strange kind of quiet around themselves, as if even in the wide open spaces they feel hemmed in. In a movie these scenes would be close-ups, or a camera would move in on them after first establishing their locale. In the traumatic fight scene, where Billy's mother is killed, Loring had the astonishing idea of making the two antagonists and the woman they are arguing about move in slow motion while the rest of the crowd's speed is normal.

Apart from the expositional first scenes and the final pas de deux, the only time we see the mother-sweetheart is when she crosses the stage in a series of arabesques pliés, making a calling gesture by lifting her cupped hand to her mouth and then extending her arm into the distance. This entrance occurs during the posse's celebration dance after Billy's capture, and has the effect of a photographic double exposure. This scene is a flashforward, rather than a flashback, like the momentary glimpse we have about midway through D. W. Griffith's "Way Down East" of the river and waterfall that are to have such an important part in the movie's climax.

Choreographed during a period when psychoanalytic ideas were very much discussed, *Billy the Kid* is an effort not only to depict an era in American history, but also to explain — and with considerable sympathy — the reasons for Billy's murderous career and for his personal attractiveness despite his contempt for society. The 1930s saw a fascination with bank robbers and kidnappers, the beginning of the cult of the outlaw. Billy the Kid was not only a badman but a frontier hero, the forerunner of John Dillinger.

Loring makes a convincing case that Billy's criminality stemmed from a perpetually unsatisfied desire for revenge against his mother's killer. All of his victims are played by the same dancer, under the name of Alias. All the different Aliases threaten Billy in some way and one of them, the Indian scout, brings about his downfall. By this device Loring presents Billy as not simply a criminal, shooting his way out of every tight spot, but as a man haunted by a kind of madness. As if in a nightmare, his enemy won't stay dead but pops up again and again to steal his precarious safety.

Less stressed, but consistent with this interpretation, are the recurring images of Billy's mother and his father-figure, Pat Garrett. His mother represents his primal innocence and security. The same dancer plays his Mexican girlfriend in the last scene, and I find here further substantiation for the idea that Billy is dreaming the pas de deux. He is in his last hideout, about to be dealt his last betrayal, so his last visions are of safety and love. His relationship with his mother is not shown in any depth or range, and neither is the relationship between him and the Mexican girl. Both are idealizations. The dual role is also, of course, consistent with Oedipal theory.

Garrett is a very interesting character whose significance in this psychological knot is often obscured by the dancer doing the part, but in recent years William Carter of Ballet Theater has made his

relationship to Billy very clear. We see him first as a leader and pac-
ifier, who calms the crowd after the shooting of Billy's mother, and
as a figure of compassion, who tries to comfort Billy, then lets him
go free, and then carries away his mother's corpse. In the card-play-
ing scene he is more than a friend; he is the partner who trusts
Billy. Billy pushes his credibility too far, but even though Garrett
suspects Billy of cheating, he stops short of a real fight. Later he
becomes a sheriff, capturing Billy after the ambush and finally dealing him the ultimate blow after his escape from jail. Garrett is
the lost father who can't ever really think badly of his son but who
also represents authority and morality, the community Billy has renounced.

Anatole Chujoy, in his 1953 history of the New York City Ballet,
thought that *Billy*'s librettist, Lincoln Kirstein, was interested in
showing the taming of the West through law and order.[11] Perhaps
the ballet's final episode before the westward procession resumes — a scene in which the Mexican women file past Billy's coffin — is meant to show the unimportance of a life lived outside society, even such a flamboyant life. Billy's destructiveness could not
impede the development of the nation, and after his death there
was no one to mourn him except other outcasts. Today we tend to
sympathize with the antihero, but intensely patriotic pre–World
War II American audiences probably felt Billy got what he
deserved.

Rodeo (Agnes de Mille)

Remembering *Billy the Kid* and *Rodeo* (1942) after many months of
not seeing them, my mind retains entirely different sorts of impressions. I can picture *Billy*'s stage patterns very clearly; I could almost
block the action for every scene — how many dancers there are,
where they come from, and where they go. Loring's stage setups
are not only clear and unusually effective, they're tied in a cinematic manner to the narrative. So that you can't even imagine the
murder of Billy's mother without seeing the townspeople crowding
around watching Alias and the other man quarreling in slow motion, and Billy and his mother all alone out in the open on the other
side of the stage, perfect targets. What I remember about *Rodeo* has
almost nothing to do with the floor patterns of the ballet. I recall

what happened but it doesn't matter *where* it happened. *Rodeo* is cinematic in its portrayal of characters and in the type of action its characters engage in. Loring uses film techniques. De Mille uses film sensibility.

Whatever the term "Hollywood" means to an American who grew up in the first half of the twentieth century, no choreographer can have been more immediately Hollywood's child than Agnes de Mille. When she was five or six and already stage-struck, her family moved to California, where her father, a successful playwright, went to work for his brother, Cecil B. de Mille. Reading the lines, and between the lines, of Agnes de Mille's many books on her choreographing and dancing career, one can see how she developed the same sentiment, the idealism, the social consciousness, that became the unspoken foundation of American films; one can see how "Hollywood" was once a very real thing, how it still is a very real thing to Agnes de Mille. She writes about her life as if it were a movie scenario, with all the drama, the hard work, success, failure, rivalry, love, death, suspense, and gusto of a rip-roaring script, starring herself as the indomitable heroine. And though it sounds like a clichéd Cinderella plot, for de Mille it really happened. She did come from a rich, famous, and brainy family; she did meet and work with the great stars; she did experience fabulous success after long discouragement, and in the very manner most of us would find incredible, by hearing the unexpected, thunderous applause of thousands in an opening night audience.

Introducing a performance of *Rodeo* on a 1952 Omnibus television program, de Mille tells us: "The theme is old, American, and basic. How to get a suitable man." I think, when she made *Rodeo*, de Mille believed that, just as everyone believed it who consumed American movies of the time. The values of *Rodeo* seem absurd to me now, even pernicious. Yet I can still have a good time watching the ballet because of its bounce and good humor, which are also part of the American myth.

The heroine, the Cowgirl, tries to imitate a group of Cowhands in their roping and riding stunts. They ignore her or tell her to shove off. Admiring girls from town arrive, and when the men show off for them, the Cowgirl tries even harder. She's bucked off her horse, made fun of by the girls. When the boys and girls pair off for the dance, she's left alone. The Champion Roper tries to cheer her up in a big-brotherly fashion, but she yearns after the Head Wrangler, a handsome, conceited fellow who of course has snagged the prettiest girl for his date. At the dance, the Cowgirl has two left feet when the Champion Roper tries to get her to join. She runs away in embarrassment and returns in a dowdy dress. Even though the dress hasn't a single ruffle, the Champion Roper and the Head Wrangler are instantly smitten and fight each other over her. The Champion Roper wins her with a stunning tap dance, and they do a hoedown to end the ballet. She becomes a woman, gets her man, and learns to dance, all in one magical evening.

I don't know why *Rodeo* hasn't been denounced and picketed by

RODEO (*de Mille, 1942*). *Christine Sarry and Terry Orr of American Ballet Theater. Photo by Louis Péres.*

women's liberationists. The heroine doesn't want to be a woman — God knows, the women in her community are simpering fools — but she shares their one ambition in life, to get that man. When she tries to be a man, she's no good at it, and neither the men nor the women will accept her. But when she gives in to appearances and tries to conform, clumsy as her attempt is, she's immediately rewarded with her heart's desire. The Cowgirl is the worst sort of misfit, a sexual misfit, and in a highly conformist society she must be shunned until she gives up her peculiar notions.

One of the most striking differences between *Billy the Kid* and *Rodeo* is in their views of the communities they portray. Loring's characters are types, even archetypes. They don't develop or change during the ballet. But what a varied population these types comprise. Loring distinguished them in several ways, by their occupations, their temperaments, their racial origins. He represented in a very condensed way, like the background landscape in a Renaissance painting, many of the kinds of activity that go on in the community: people are homebodies; they raise children; they provide services for others; they are adventurers or hard workers; they are peaceful or break the law, or they administer the law; their life contains faith, entertainment, danger. Looking at *Billy the Kid,* you think it might have been wonderfully exciting to live in a town like that at such a time.

De Mille's community, on the other hand, is entirely homogeneous. In fact, the moral purpose of her ballet is to show the error in being a nonconformist. All the cowboys do the same movement, usually in tight, unison floor patterns. Spraddle-legged, one hand gripping imaginary reins in front of them and the other swinging an imaginary lariat, they gallop back and forth, jerk up and down violently to show they're riding unmanageable horses, and stand a long time on one leg with the other drawn up in front of them when they've succeeded in taming their broncs. The girlfriends from Kansas City are ultrafeminine, walking or skipping with small steps, wiggling their shoulders, making lots of little fussy gestures that draw attention to themselves. You can tell they have always lived in houses, walked on sidewalks in more or less civilized towns.

Rodeo personifies all the conventional ideas about courting. In trying to be like the men, the Cowgirl loses their respect; they want their girls to be mysterious, unpredictable, helpless, to wear bows in their hair and not smell of leather and horse sweat. They don't want the Cowgirl as a friend, either, because she can't keep up with them in their horsemanship, and they don't like her horning in on their bunkroom camaraderie. De Mille hasn't given the Cowgirl any dignity in her independence — although when the choreographer herself danced the role, she seemed a great deal more solid, confident, and capable than the small, slight dancers who have taken the role in revivals by Ballet Theater and the Joffrey Ballet. When they attempt those big strides and strenuous jumps and falls, they look inadequate. You feel protective about their pathetic little gestures, their imitations of correct male, and later female, behavior that are always missing the mark. Only when this contemporary Cowgirl dances with the Champion Roper at the barn dance do we feel she's completely in command of her situation, and of course, then she's got her man.

Agnes de Mille seems always to have been preoccupied with social behavior, and often in her ballets social niceties — the proper execution of polite gestures — seem to lead to social acceptance. Growing up as a parvenue movie daughter in Hollywood, de Mille was extremely conscious of the small distinctions between classes that could not be glossed over by money. She developed a strong social conscience, but somehow she became stuck there. She couldn't make manners stand for a whole sensibility, as Antony Tudor did; in de Mille, manners stand for manners; to be correct is to belong, and belonging is all.

The people in *Rodeo* are always glancing sideways at each other to make sure no one is out of line. The Cowgirl usually is, and she is scorned for it. When she gets thrown off her horse, the men all ride away, and the women stand around her prostrate form and giggle behind their hands. When she's alone, she tries to cheer herself up; she doesn't seem to find herself bad company. But whenever she has to do anything when other people are around, they glare at her and she gets clumsier and more confused than ever. Her eventual transfiguration is accomplished not through anything she learns or any crucial event or any sympathetic help from her peers. The Cowgirl turns her life around when she gives in and puts on a dress. Then everything comes to a stop, everyone stares, and in an instant she has earned not only the acceptance of this narrow, rigid community but the admiration of two men as well.

The lure of conformism, and the sense that the outsider is not only dangerous to the community but perpetually out of sorts with himself, are very strong in American life. Certainly they pervaded Agnes de Mille's Hollywood, and they influenced frontier life in an earlier period. The square and folk dances that constitute the second half of *Rodeo* also give evidence of these feelings. It's thought that folk dances reflect and transmit the social patterns of the culture that produces them, and the Virginia reels and running squares that de Mille reproduced in *Rodeo* do express many of the values that are set forth dramatically in the early part of the ballet. The floor patterns are straight and orderly. Every person has a partner of the opposite sex, and the dance requires the participation of each couple in order to be accomplished. The steps are prescribed in advance and are simple enough so that with a little practice any energetic person could perform them.

Except for the fast square set with a caller that four couples do in silence, de Mille doesn't use these dances as showpieces, which they aren't, anyway. She keeps them going, interspersed with a waltz, a galloping polka, and a big circular figure, as a background while the rest of the story unfolds — the unhappiness of the Cowgirl as she sees the Head Wrangler dreamily embracing and lifting his pretty partner, her embarrassment at being without a partner in a reel, her flight and transfiguration. There are more incidents that reinforce the sexual stereotyping: girls come in and out by twos, primping and whispering; one cowboy kisses a girl and she runs out crying; another girl gets dizzy from dancing too fast, and her partner lifts his eyebrows indulgently.

The Champion Roper's tap dance that wins the Cowgirl is the most individual and most persuasive gesture in the ballet. In fact, de Mille has recorded different versions of it on film, based on different dancers' abilities. Here for the first time in the ballet a character does something out of inspiration rather than an instinctive desire to be like everyone else. The Cowgirl and Roper create a great surging tide of steps and awakening pleasure in each other. When the Cowgirl, impressed but still undecided, wavers between him and the Wrangler, the Roper grabs her and gives her a big kiss — the perfect Hollywood clincher — and the audience feels satisfied to see the whole silly business resolved in the right way and with the most basic argument. Of course, the Cowgirl sees the light too, and jumps back into his arms for one last rousing fling before the curtain falls.

Rodeo is a very entertaining ballet, and the accessibility and Cinderella sentiment of its story have made it a favorite with audiences. De Mille's use of American folk dance material probably was
not a great breakthrough in choreography, but she combined the
dances with the story so ingeniously, and her choice of folk themes
was so consistent and appropriate, that the ballet is remarkably
unified. The plot never seems to get interrupted for dancing, nor
does the dancing ever seem out of place or phony. De Mille was to
revolutionize the musical comedy a few years later by using the
same technique in "Oklahoma."

From her own account, she must have identified strongly with
the wallflower-misfit-Cinderella heroine, because she made *Rodeo*
at a time when her life was turning a corner. She felt herself to be
neither a ballet dancer nor a modern dancer. Too bright not to
create, too creative to be accepted in the middle-class world, and
too typically American to make the grade with the aristocratic tastes
that dictated what ballet ought to be, de Mille was like the Cowgirl.
She couldn't make it in traditional dance, and she couldn't be a lone
creative martyr like her friend Martha Graham. Suddenly, with
Rodeo, she was a success. Oscar Hammerstein wanted to see her.
The audience threw flowers. No wonder she endorsed the Hollywood myth.

Fancy Free (*Jerome Robbins*)

Like Ruth Page, Lucia Chase was a woman of wealth and good family who pursued a dance career. In 1939, with Richard Pleasant, she
reorganized the old-style Mikhail Mordkin Ballet to form the Ballet
Theater. Her initial policy was to gather the best contemporary
dancers and choreographers as well as the classics of the past in
order to build an eclectic international repertory. Chase didn't
choreograph herself or attempt to promote any one aesthetic or discover special trends, but inevitably Ballet Theater provided an outlet for American talent that did not find a natural home with Balanchine. Jerome Robbins' *Fancy Free* was probably the greatest of
Ballet Theater's ventures into Americana.

If de Mille represents one kind of classic American success story,
Robbins personifies another. The son of Jewish immigrant parents,

he grew up in Weehawken, New Jersey, about as far as you could get from either the frontier West or the socially sanctioned enclaves of European culture. Robbins is city-bred; he grew up with access to all kinds of dance and he studied everything that was available, as well as acting, piano, and violin. He knew the Borscht Circuit and Broadway. A member of Ballet Theater almost from its inception, he was known for his character roles. He had a gift for character; he was gutsy, street-smart. In 1944 he emerged from the hustle of the rapidly developing American dance scene with his first ballet, *Fancy Free,* and it was a smash hit.

It seems to me that no one thing in *Fancy Free* was really new as an idea — choreographers had used jazz and popular dance idioms before, they had tried devising contemporary-looking stage movement, ballets had been done in modern dress, and scenarios had tried to capture everyday experience. What Robbins did was to create a reflection of the time, and so sure and unified was his personal imprint that his use of all these devices seems incidental. It was wartime; his characters were sailors, which automatically linked them to their audiences. But most important, these sailors behaved in something like an ordinary way — at least, with the exaggerated ordinariness of Broadway, rather than with the stylization of the ordinary usually seen in ballet.

One of the primary distinctions in dance aesthetics in those days, and perhaps also now, was the degree of "reality" that could be expected or tolerated in a dance. One of the great Russian lines of development presupposes very little reality at all: ballet is supposed to be fantasy; dancers are supposed to be sylphs, or steel ingots. The other European line, that of classicism, which led to Balanchine, does away with fairy tale but still assumes the dancer is not a being like the rest of us, that, in fact, he can tell us about ourselves because he performs our actions in a heightened or more beautifully organized way. American choreographers had been struggling to get away from these restrictions, and the modern dancers had already created more directly expressive dance images and a whole new dance literature. But ballet choreography still had to contend with the ballet body and the ballet vocabulary, neither of which produced people who moved on the stage in anything like the way people in the audience moved. Robbins, like Loring, made a clean sweep of the current preconceptions as to what a ballet could be. But his background was much more eclectic than Loring's; he had fixed the varied shapes and faces and rhythms of urban America in his eye much more tenaciously — they rang truer to him than the formal, aristocratic attitudes of classicism.

Another tremendous asset of Robbins is his nearly infallible sense of theater. As early as 1944 he was proposing a stage work, *Bye Bye Jackie*, that would constitute "a new form toward fusing the potentialities of ballet and theatre. It employs three mediums of expression: dance, music and voice."[12] Some of his most ambitious projects in the ensuing years were aimed at realizing this fusion, and his ballets and musical shows probably constitute several different examples of total theater-dance in themselves. *Fancy Free* was certainly conceived as an integral mix of theater, dance, and musical inspiration. Although Robbins is now opposed to letting the public have access to documentation of his works, he did allow his scenario of *Fancy Free* to be published in George Amberg's *Ballet in America*, and it was reprinted more recently in the first edition of Selma Jeanne Cohen's source book, *Dance as a Theatre Art*. Without naming a single ballet step, it describes the action in language that incorporates the kinds of characters, the kinds of thing they do, and the energies that motivate them, all within a theatrical shape that builds, subsides, and finally whirls away in exhilaration.

At its best, Robbins' dance has always been a dance of incident. You can see from this scenario that he imagined *Fancy Free* in terms of what was happening to the people in it, and that he wasn't worried about what dance steps he would use to transmit those happenings. His sense of the characters and their milieu was so complete that the right steps did come, and they are as integral as everything else in the stage event.

Briefly, the ballet goes like this. Three sailors are out on a pass in New York City. They're looking for fun, for girls. They approach one girl and she seems not averse to being followed, so two of them head off in pursuit. The third sailor hangs around until he picks up another girl. They're just getting to know one another when the two buddies return with their girl. The sailors have a dance competition to see who will win the two girls. It ends in a fight, during which both girls stalk out in disgust. Somewhat the worse for wear, the trio takes up its post on the street corner again, looking for new adventures.

The stage is deserted when the curtain goes up on a cutaway sec-

FANCY FREE (*Robbins*, 1944). *American Ballet Theater in the 1960s. Photo by Martha Swope.*

tion of a bar, designed by Oliver Smith in slanty moderne style and placed catercorner to the footlights and slightly off center, a lamp-post just outside its entrance. The bartender reads a newspaper or does busywork, and the sound of dance music comes from his table radio. All we have time to take in, really, is the quietness, and the sense — if we know anything about cities — that this is just a momentary lull, that things never stay quiet around there very long.

The pit orchestra begins Leonard Bernstein's score with a couple of raps on a drum and some syncopated trumpet notes, like the start of a jam session, and the three sailors "explode onto the stage," in Robbins' words.[13] The curtain has been up less than a minute, and already we perceive the whole ballet — the identities of the characters, their situation, and the irrepressible, inexhaustible spirits that energize them. With the economy of the Broadway master he was soon to become, Robbins has presented them to us swiftly and unmistakably, not just as sailors but as sailors true to type — on the make, rowdy, and less experienced than they'd like to let on.

In the trio that follows, we learn that they've been around some together and are used to each other; they haven't just teamed up for the evening. They boast a bit to each other — each one dancing a scrap of his best line — but it's not really competitive. They dance a conversation about what to do next, interrupting each other, and at one point two of them suddenly pick up the third man and hold him in the air for a split second. He continues his thought, kicking his heels together in a suggestion of a sailor's hornpipe and simultaneously adjusting his cap, before they put him down. They lean against one another; one pulls a pack of gum out of his pocket, offers it; the others each take a stick without thanking the donor. They unwrap the gum and put it in their mouths; they crumple up the wrappings and idly flip the pellets out between two fingers to see who can send them the farthest.

This is one of several ritual games they play together — it's repeated exactly at the end of the ballet. Another game is matching to see who pays for beers. Once again, two of the sailors team up and trick the third, who never seems to catch on to their deception even though they always con him the same way. This kind of camaraderie, in which the partners understand that the outward challenge or the practical joke really stands for a more forthright — but taboo — expression of fondness, could only be American.

Although the sailors are not given names, they begin to exhibit individual qualities as the ballet progresses. The one who stays behind during the first girl-chasing expedition seems a bit softer, more romantic. He's often the fall guy when the other two play their tricks. When the second girl appears and he takes her into the bar to buy her a drink, the entire tempo of the ballet slows and cools down. As they sit at the bar, he romances her, invites her to dance with a gesture of holding his arms above his head and tapping one hand appealingly into the other palm.

The courtship is halting; the ground keeps shifting as they acknowledge their attraction for one another. The music, a slow blues, progresses in brief snatches and pauses. The girl is reluctant, the sailor thinks he's come on too strong, she relents, he grows warmer, holds her tighter, she pulls back. The dance swells into a waltz of Viennese proportions, then quickly dies down again — they're still not sure there's anything substantial between them. If they could have a whole evening together they might find out, and when the rest of the crew shows up, the sailor tries to duck out with her. But it's too late; the friends see them and won't let them get away. Still, you feel they're slightly relieved not to have had to risk getting more intimate.

The five pals now take a table in the corner of the bar and the sailors compete in earnest for the girls' approval. The first one is all flash and bravado; he does a dance full of pyrotechnics — high kicks, spins in the air, standup skids on his heels from a running start. Finally he jumps up on the bar, starts a series of fast turns, downs a shot of whiskey for fortification while keeping the spin going with his finger, continues the stunt, and jumps down to land in a split at the feet of one of the girls. This role was created by Harold Lang.

The second sailor (John Kriza) is the one who danced the pas de deux, and in a way his solo is a continuation of his attempt to win over the girl he found. To a quiet, insinuating melody announced by two clarinets, he seems to be beckoning her back into his arms. His dance is softer, more fluid than the others', but also more complicated rhythmically, the metre shifting almost every measure, like the subtle emotions he's been trying to match up with those of the girl.

The final solo — danced originally by the choreographer — is Latin in beat, although the rhythms are again irregular. Perhaps the second sailor's dance has suggested the dance floor to him, but he fancies himself an exhibition dancer, one who can manage without a partner. He gives an exaggeratedly sexy version of a rhumba, hips swaying, glance tipping provocatively over his shoulder. In the liberated 1970s this dance has become probably a good deal more suggestive than would have been possible at first. Where Robbins indicated "a strong passion and violence, an attractive flashiness and smoldering quality,"[14] we more often see leers and bumping buttocks.

The sailors have gotten all heated up by their dances, and what starts as a kidding argument over who gets to sit next to which girl turns into an all-out fist fight that provokes the girls' huffy departure. When the men exhaust themselves and realize what's happened, they philosophically take up their place by the lamp post, chew their gum, look around. They spot another girl, debate whether to go after her, think better of it, then do a last-minute switch and race off around the corner in her direction.

I think what *Fancy Free* did most impressively was to integrate classical and colloquial dance within a context of carefully observed character. The dance shifts constantly between made-up movement that suggests the exuberance of the sailors on a spree, to mime and literal gesture, to popular dances, to virtuosic display dancing, and the viewer is scarcely aware that the idiom is changing. *Frankie and Johnny* was aiming at this sort of amalgamation; Robbins achieved it for the first time in a contemporary ballet. He gave gesture and the actions of real people the same validity on the concert stage that Fred Astaire gave to dancing in the quasi-realistic milieu of movie romances. Interestingly, both choreographers affected their rapprochement of styles through rhythm. Astaire's dance rhythms have the regularity and rebound of ordinary activity, like walking or swing a cane — *his* walking, anyway. Robbins stressed the irregularity of rhythm — the syncopations, the shifting metres, the pauses and pushes and gliding transitions of jazz — and infused even his literal gestures with a jazzlike emphasis. His next ballet, *Interplay*, did the same thing to the classical vocabulary, with only the slimmest of realistic implications.

Bernstein's score for *Fancy Free* — brassy, exciting, retaining a vernacular sound in spite of its concert hall proportions — is ideal, possibly the best symphonic jazz score that Robbins ever had. Robbins has never used authentic jazz or pop music, although he's made many jazz ballets, because his musicality seeks richer textures, more calculated effects. He is, above all else, a theater man, and I'm convinced that his rhythmic irregularity — his tendency to shape the phrase with the heightened dynamics of complex naturalistic actions rather than the more easily counted, more predictable walking-breathing-ballet-studio rhythms — is an essential factor in the theatricality of his ballets. And their success.

Crystallization I

A painter paints a sunset — can he paint the setting sun? . . . Maybe music was not intended to
satisfy the curious definiteness of man."
                                    — *Charles Ives* [1]

BY THE END of the 1930s, most of the experimentation with radical new dance languages, forms, and subjects was done. That
brief, brave period that often occurs when an idea is taking hold
had come to a close. The movies had experienced such a period
during the 1920s; television would experience one in the decade
after World War II. It had been for dance a time when the imagination could range freely. Audiences were small but eager. Companies were loosely organized, modestly financed, ingeniously produced. I think it is important to understand how little of the world's
conventional recognition or rewards were available to dancers at the
beginning; they could not gain status by any means, but neither
could they lose it by being radical or esoteric.

The freewheeling invention of the thirties, as well as the strong
but often nonconforming social/political attitudes that surfaced in
dance, evolved quite understandably into more accessible statements of national pride and purpose during World War II, and
came out the other end as a grown-up art form. Before the forties
was over, all of the models for our various types of dance institutions had been set. Our two major ballet companies had been established, with essentially the same character and goals they project
today. Regional ballet had taken hold as an indigenous activity,
closely allied to its community's big cultural institutions, especially
opera, in Chicago, San Francisco, and Philadelphia. The pattern

had been set for modern dance companies as variants, in descending degrees of size and elaborateness, of the Graham, Humphrey-Weidman, and Lester Horton companies. Training patterns had been established, with modern dance securely functioning within universities as well as in individual studios, and moving in summer to programs based on the Bennington School of Dance. Ballet training acknowledged a more direct relationship between school and performing outlet.

Modern dance was already understood to be the less exacting discipline and could be taken up when a person was in his teens or even later because its fulfillment didn't depend primarily on a technical foundation. Modern dance was the more cerebral or expressive art, the more "democratic" in its openness to new ideas and new practitioners, and also the more individual and personal in its range and appeal. Ballet was more traditional, more "elitist" in its technical requirements, and appealing to a broader sector of the public because of its past associations with European culture and its conservative aesthetics. Modern dance had come to be regarded as the choreographer's art, ballet as the dancer's art.

The basic lines of creative development had also been drawn by the turn of the 1950s, with the sole exception of the avant-gardist explorations spearheaded by Merce Cunningham and John Cage, which were still to come. The main threads of modern dance were well delineated: Graham, Humphrey-Weidman, Wigman-Holm, Tamiris and the politico-folkways choreographers bred in the Depression, Lester Horton on the West Coast. Ballet was clearly committed to the threefold aesthetics of Balanchinian neoclassicism, narrative-character ballets in the old Russian tradition with American subjects, and the expressive classicism imported from England via Antony Tudor.

By the end of this period of consolidation, television and Broadway had begun siphoning off some of the choreographic talent from ballet and the concert stage. Dancers found paying work there, and learned how to dance like extroverts. The initial creative drive of modern dance began to slow down; a second and less revolutionary generation was emerging. Working conditions, at last, began to improve and individual artists found it easier to work together. The qualities that had made choreographers and styles so distinct, so individually strong, began to meld and blur. American choreography began its gradual evolution toward internationalism.

The works I'm about to discuss show their choreographers gathering some of the main ideas for which they've come to be known and setting them in exemplary form. They are works, all of them, that rest on the perilous edge between invention and repetition, between innovative strangeness and overaccessibility. For each successful choreographer, that knife-blade moment of perfection comes at a different period in life and lasts a greater or lesser time. Some of these choreographers have made other kinds of work besides those we're looking at here; some may have created better examples that can no longer be seen. But for the genres they represent, these works cannot be surpassed in current repertory.

Frontier to *Appalachian Spring* (*Martha Graham*)

It's easy now to think of *Frontier* (1935) as merely a sketch for *Appalachian Spring* (1944). It is the nature of dance history that we tend to think a choreographer's later works better than his earlier ones, that small-scale works are merely incomplete or unfulfilled conceptions. We place too much onus on present-day dance and dancers by refusing to allow the past its own validity. Although most of the dances contemporary with *Frontier* are lost, we know that Graham and others were doing things like it in the late 1930s. To consider them as merely a passing phase leading toward a somehow higher, more mature art is to deny every artist's achievement. An artwork belongs to its time, is not insignificant simply because it leads to something else.

Whenever an early dance is reclaimed from someone's memory, both dancers and audience want to see it modernized, at least to the extent of fitting it out with today's long-legged, presentational performing style. Martha Graham herself has disavowed the film made at Connecticut College of Ethel Winter in the 1964 revival of *Frontier*, saying that 1976 dancers Peggy Lyman and Janet Eilber were doing the "authentic" version.

As similar as *Appalachian Spring* and *Frontier* are in theme and sentiment, and as romantic in style as they both look now, it seems to me they show the choreographer in two distinct states of mind, about her subject, about her craft, and about herself. Both dances draw on the American pioneer experience, which absorbed the interest of Graham and so many others. *Frontier* is a comment, an abstracted recital of the circumstances and feelings of the pioneer woman. It is a dance of identification — Graham the dancer *was* a woman whose heritage goes back to the frontier. The dancer of *Frontier* is a more specific personage than the protagonist of *Lamentation* but not yet an objective, theatricalized being. Again I find evidence for the cultlike, personal character of early modern dance in *Frontier* and works like it — Jane Dudley's *Harmonica Breakdown* is one I've seen, and we can read descriptions of others by Graham and Anna Sokolow and Doris Humphrey. They are fascinating because, while they are obviously about specific personalities, feelings, or events, they are not fictional. The dancers who did these solos not only created character, they became the characters they danced. That was part of what it meant to do the dance. Most people who danced the works later missed the mark somehow. It's not just that they weren't Martha — they weren't the Martha-persona who *was* the dance. This is particularly true of today's dancers, because for them there has never been any middle ground between theatrical dancing — doing a role as an actor would do it — and dancing for the dancing alone, being simply yourself in a role, in the manner of Merce Cunningham.

Frontier is structured in the form of a loose rondo. When the curtain opens, a woman in a long, plain dress is standing with both arms pulled back, leaning on a log fence. There is no other scenery but this, and two ropes fastened to the floor behind the fence and stretching up and out into the wings. This extraordinary image, the first of many sets designed for Graham by Isamu Noguchi, centers the woman in a limitless, temporary universe. She can put up another fence in another place; she probably will. Yet this is a place where she can feel stable. She makes three excursions away from it, returning to lean, rest back, and finally settle herself firmly on it. You feel the inadequacy of this spot to serve as an anchorage; it's only the woman's determination that fixes its use.

Louis Horst's music, for a small wind ensemble, drum, and piano, begins with a fanfare. This woman rises and sinks slightly to its rhythmic pulse, holding the rail behind her with both hands and looking out in all directions. She gradually lifts one foot up onto the fence and begins to lean back almost luxuriously on it. The music

Martha Graham in Frontier *(Graham, 1935). Photo by Barbara Morgan,* © *1969.*

now is playing a sort of excitable march, and the woman rises and comes off the fence with a sweeping circular gesture. She parades down to the foot of the stage and back, beating one leg and one arm up and down very broadly, then makes a circle around the stage-right half of the space, lunging forward and flinging herself up and back on alternate steps. The straightness of her body in the first phrases contrasts with its bending and bowing in the second. She could be asserting her claim over this land and then worshiping or celebrating it.

She goes back to the fence, this time lying back on it almost languidly, as if she were bone-weary at the end of a day's work. She swings off it again and rocks from side to side, brushing her gaze and eventually her whole body closer and closer to the ground. She kneels and inclines straight back from the hinges of her knees, almost touching the ground with her shoulders, then sits and brings her legs around in front of her. In a series of big, circular, straight-limbed gestures, she pivots around on her sitting-bones —

opening her legs and arms and then closing them, pausing after each rotation around the axis of her ramrod back, with legs together and hands clasped at arms' length in front of her. If this is prayer, it's an unyielding, all-encompassing kind of prayer.

She rises to dance a vigorous, bouncy version of her first marching theme. This section has the flavor of a square dance, of flirtatiousness, as the woman relinquishes her straightness and grows more and more serpentine in her movements, more playful, until she's running and skipping with arms behind her back, shoulders flouncing.

Suddenly the music interrupts her with a single prolonged flute note that is soon augmented by a mournful suggestion of a hymn tune. As was to happen over and over in Graham's American dances, the dancer's moment of physical abandon or play is cut off by the intervention of puritanism. Here the woman immediately narrows her body and straightens it, facing square to the audience with her arms pressed tightly to her body, elbows bent up, and she takes tiny steps on her toes in a rectangle — back, to the side across the space parallel to the fence, forward, sideways to center stage, and backward to the center of the fence again.

Once more we hear the fanfare, and once more the woman pumps up and down rhythmically and comes toward the audience. This time she combines the vigorous assertiveness and the curving, flouncy body line in her variation of the opening theme. In mid-jump the hymn tune nails her again, and she twists to a stop, her body narrow but angled in several directions at once. Then she bourrées along the same path as before, rocking her folded arms in front of her body as if she held a baby in them. This time when she returns to the fence she sits on it, takes possession of it slowly and deliberately, and, in a definitive gesture, as if she were hammering in a stake, brings one fist down to clasp her knee.

Compositionally, *Frontier* is as interesting as *Primitive Mysteries*, brief though it is (it lasts seven minutes). Graham used a very limited movement vocabulary based on the idea of the contrast between large, straight, circular movements and small, twisting, adaptable movements. Whether she is sitting, standing, on the floor, or in locomotion, she is consistently involved in either clanging her body open and shut on the space or wending her way through space more pliably. In the last variation these two tendencies have combined. It's one of the few times in Graham when two opposing ideas are able to accommodate to each other within the body; usually in the later works this situation results in conflict, contradiction, and neurosis.

Whether she is dominating space or embracing it, the woman in *Frontier* sees space as her element. She scans the horizon, reaches far out around herself, bows to the ground, explodes into the air, and at the end, perched on the fence like a nesting eagle, she surveys the distance fearlessly. To me, *Frontier* is about openness; *Appalachian Spring* is about enclosure. Graham herself confirmed this when she discussed the two dances in 1975. *Frontier,* she said, "has to do with the plains, the distances, the vista. It's about roads that disappear into the distance, or a railroad track. Welcoming distance means freedom and a sense of openness, while the frontier is a barrier in Europe. *Appalachian Spring* is essentially a dance of place. You choose a place . . . part of the house goes up . . . you dedicate it. The questing spirit is there, and the sense of establishing roots."[2]

The setting immediately tells you something entirely different about the dance that is to come. Noguchi has once again sketched a structure, a framework, but this time much more is suggested than a place of demarcation on the open land. There is a section of a wall, with a bench along it, a porch, and a rocking chair to one side. There's a section of fence too, but this time it's placed downstage left, separating the house and yard from the prairie beyond. The dance has moved in from the frontier. The people have put down roots and begun to live a life that allows for some crude rest and comfort; they no longer feel exposed to the elements. They have put shelter — and community — between them and the unknown.

This says a lot about Graham's evolution too. While the house and family may have been implied in *Frontier,* she didn't feel the need to show them. She was preoccupied with the woman's state of mind, her very isolation and the dreams with which she peoples it. In *Appalachian Spring* the dreams have materialized.

Appalachian Spring is a theater dance and a pivotal work for the choreographer. It is the last of her specifically American works until *The Scarlet Letter* (1975) and, in form, the model for all the Greek works to come. Its core is the woman's soliloquy — although here, for perhaps the only time, she also explored the emotions of male characters with some subtlety. But curiously, this woman at the center is not the same as the woman in *Frontier*. It's as if, having felt the need to actualize the characters surrounding her by making theater pieces, Graham lost some of her firmness and independence. As if, perhaps, she gave decisiveness and strength over to other people and was happy to have done with them. She was in her fifties by the time she made *Appalachian Spring*, and physically she was no longer the indomitable, enduring, protean figure she had portrayed. The other theater pieces that preceded *Appalachian Spring* — *Deaths and Entrances, Letter to the World, Every Soul Is a Circus, El Penitente* — also present their female protagonists in a softer, more passive, often irresolute role as compared to the invincible beings of the earlier works.

The dance begins with a processional — as so many of Graham's theater pieces do — first the Revivalist, then the Pioneer Woman, the Husbandman, the Bride, and finally four female members of the preacher's entourage. They all enter gravely and pass through the door frame, the husband pausing to smooth his hand over the side of the house. The dance has no real story; it's more a documentary of an event, the marriage of two young people at the edge of the wilderness. We see an austere ceremony, very plain and brief; we get an idea of the demons that will prey on the couple and the solace they will be able to find. But most of all, we see what all these people are like and what kind of sustenance they offer each other.

The dance is episodic in form; extended narrative or choral development was never Graham's style. Rather than create one flowing statement through which many themes could interact, transform, accumulate, and reorganize infinitely, Graham made dances for discrete voices, developed her ideas through successive expositions of the characters' feelings. Each contact between individuals is its own statement, a duet, sometimes a trio, entirely apart from other characters or relationships. No solo character ever adopts the movement motifs of any other; each is always herself or himself, reiterating or elaborating on private thoughts, or, in the later, more dramatic dances, taking the specific action that moves the plot into its next phase. In *Appalachian Spring* only the Pioneer Woman shares movement with other characters, usually the Revivalist's four followers, who, presumably, will one day inherit her role in the community.

Appalachian Spring may be the most unified of Graham's theater pieces in terms of time, place, characters, and action. Yet even

Aaron Copland's famous score consists of broken rhythms, independent themes that are interrupted in midphrase to make way for other themes. Melodically too it is worlds away from the *Passacaglia* music, for instance, where a single thematic idea pervades the entire piece.

As the solos take place, all the other characters lapse into their own private reveries about the event they've come to witness. Nowhere in Graham are these tableau backgrounds so well motivated as in *Appalachian Spring*, perhaps because here the dance is clearly focused on a single event, with no jumps in time. The solos are interspersed with bridging action — processionals and celebratory exclamations — and with encounters between two of the characters. Only at the beginning and end of the dance, and at the moment when the marriage vows are taken, do all the participants really act in concert. The bride doesn't join in either the prayers or the rejoicing of the others; the parishioners are unaffected by the preacher's hellfire exhortations; the preacher doesn't acknowledge the Pioneer Woman's benedictions. All the characters are curiously isolated from the others, yet they are interconnected by means of their common ceremonies, myths, and aspirations.

It seems to me that the characters define themselves as much in terms of time as of space. This farm, this frail bulwark against the forces of nature, is already a *place* for them. They use it casually, familiarly. Having acknowledged its existence, they don't have to keep establishing their affinity with it, as the woman in *Frontier* does, ritualistically. It is their source of material necessities — shelter, rest, potential wealth — and it can be threatened, and its loss would be a real loss to these people. But what motivates them and distinguishes them from each other at this important moment in their lives is related to forces outside themselves, to the future and the past as well as to the present.

The Pioneer Woman is very earthbound, very solid and reassuring; even the joyful dances she initiates are slightly serious. She is moderate and smooth in all her approaches. She always seems to have her arms open, ready to pour forth sympathy, praise, or comfort. She is the most iconic of the characters, either exercising her soothing influence over the others or watching from the sidelines, waiting, accepting, inspiring, but never revealing her own thoughts. Alone of all of them, she makes no solo statement. She is also the bringer of benedictions, the exorciser of curses. She will probably be the midwife when the babies come. She has a kind of spiritual calm that might be partly drawn from associating with friendly Indians. Certainly the open, uplifted arms and undisturbed verticality with which she whirls and jumps in praise are very different from the uptight Calvinistic piety that dominates the others.

The Husbandman is also very down to earth, a practical man who is proud of his skills at farming or ranching. You feel he will be a good provider and protector, but he may not have much humor or imagination. His back is too straight, his legs too stiff, his body too square to bend very much. You feel he doesn't often cut loose as he's doing on his wedding day, when he swings his bride into a lively hoedown. He will often have to comfort her with his physical sturdiness, but he won't really share her flights and fears.

The husband's movements are large and expansive. The actual steps he does when he first takes center stage are a conglomeration of knee-slapping, rein-pulling mime motifs; balletic turns in the air; and leggy, traveling jumps, reachings, and stampings. You feel he's showing off, but not in a narcissistic way; rather, he's giving vent to his happy feelings and pride, his natural assertiveness and drive.

APPALACHIAN SPRING (*Graham, 1944*). *Erick Hawkins, Martha Graham and Company.*

He keeps breaking off these shouts of celebration to kneel and clasp his hands reverently. His actions toward the Bride are protective; he leads her down from the porch where she's been watching his dance, and side by side they walk together, pray together, kneeling. After the wedding vows are taken, they promenade around each other in an exuberant sort of square dance. After both duets, they return to the porch of the house, which is where they will be at the end of the dance too.

The husband is a kind of dreamer, a practical, American dreamer, looking out over the fence toward the acres of land he'll someday tame. He also has a conventional religious feeling, a strong, unquestioning faith and an almost naive susceptibility to the preacher's threats of damnation. It's interesting that, although the wife is his partner in the formal devotions they perform before the wedding ceremony, when he gets really frightened by the preacher's hellfire he turns to the Pioneer Woman for help. Her straightness and symmetricality help him get control of himself. In other words, it seems that his strength is going to sustain his wife, but she won't be stable enough to bolster him when he wavers.

The Revivalist is one of Graham's most interesting creations. In a few telling strokes she gives us a portrait of the circuit-riding ministers of the nineteenth-century backwoods. The character also personifies Graham's ambivalent feelings about formal religion. Like the Ancestress in *Letter to the World* and the Christ figure in *El Penitente,* he represents absolute authority that is often cruel, denying, and frightening, but also like them he has a sympathetic side. He does not temper his punishment with compassion as they do, but he is vulnerable nevertheless. The preacher's weakness is vanity. He loves being the central figure in the dramatic events of these people's lives, and he revels in the adulation of the female hangers-on. Perhaps he's been alone too long with the Scriptures; he may have a wife somewhere back in town; but as an itinerant pastor, he has no real congregation of his own. He comes to each little cluster of souls every few months, maybe, to preach the gospel and administer the sacraments, and he stays a night with a family and moves on. You can see that he doesn't know these people well, and doesn't know how to be easy with them.

You can also see that he is the victim of his own terrors. Absorbed in questions of sin and retribution, he thinks of himself as one of the damned, and his sermon after the bride and groom's dance of celebration is a convulsion of self-hate, wrenched and ripped out of his guts and hurled at them through shuddering fingers. This outpouring of passion seems to be the only way he can express himself. Otherwise he's comfortable only in the prescribed forms of ritual, and in playing the role of the adored, respected, fussed-over visiting divine.

The preacher is an outsider, alienated even from this world of self-willed, independent people. He never uses the house in a familiar way as all the other characters do — he neither goes inside it, nor leans against it, nor sits on the porch rocker or on the bench along the side. A sort of pulpit, a tipped-up round low platform that might represent a fallen tree stump, is placed upstage and serves as his home base. He stations himself there during much of the action, standing a bit haughtily with head tipped back, chest lifted, elbows stuck out, thumbs hooked in his lapels, and his back turned to the rest of the company. He has come there for one purpose only and is disdainful of the socializing and emotions that surround the occasion.

He is susceptible, though, to the four girls who flutter around him. Graham has given the preacher-followers a comical, angular kind of movement, not precisely childlike but with the feeling of a child's mechanical toy. The women take tiny waltzing or promenading steps; they scuttle along in sixteenth notes, sometimes while squatting on their toes. They beat their cupped hands together near the sides of their heads. They twirl their skirts coquettishly. To this the preacher responds with condescending ecclesiastical gestures. He allows himself to be included in their dance of celebration. He sinks down into a squat, then immediately springs straight up in the air, several times. In his stiff way he grows more excited, kicking one leg to his opposite hand, does a kind of Grand Right and Left, slapping palms with the girls, and finally rolls on the floor into their laps and lets them cuddle him, though all the while retaining his anchorite rigidity. Then he lifts one of them straight into the air by the elbows and circles with her while she gazes adoringly down at him, and her companions make a ring around them.

The preacher is literally straight and narrow. He seems locked into this body attitude. The only time he lapses from it is during his orgy of denunciations and predictions of doom. The sermon begins ominously, as he rivets himself to the ground, standing on one leg and holding a clenched fist stiffly at his side, and literally smites himself, slamming the other fist and leg, foot flexed, back hard into his body. For the first time the center of his body caves in, and he runs with one hand in front of his eyes. In the grip of his apocalypse, he throws curses in all directions, crawls frantically on his knees, runs with his legs splayed apart, jumps with his body all crooked. At last the Pioneer Woman puts an end to the mania with her hallelujah jumps. The preacher resumes his aloof decorum immediately, even recovering his composure enough to dance again with the followers once the excitement has calmed down.

The wife seems untouched by any of this. She responds neither to his violence nor to the Pioneer Woman's ministrations. When the others pray, she doesn't bow her head. She seems remote from all that moves them. This Bride is a curious entity among Graham's characters. I have already mentioned that she seems greatly diminished in power and initiative from the women in *Frontier* and *Primitive Mysteries*, and that Graham's central characters seem to have become more dependent as she developed her theater dances, even before *Appalachian Spring. Spring* is almost unique, though, because the woman is more nearly the equal of the other characters. With certain contemporary casts, I have thought of it as being a dance about the husband, not the wife, and even in the film that Graham made in 1958 (with Stuart Hodes as the husband, Bertram Ross as the Revivalist, and Matt Turney as the Pioneer Woman), the dance is not totally dominated by the wife's presence. I think this demonstrates that she was able to build psychological complexity into roles other than her own. One of the great puzzles of Graham's later career is why she did not choose to do this more often. Increasingly she kept herself at the center of her dance by surrounding herself with one-dimensional characters who always did or represented the same things, whose actions referred to the Graham-character's thoughts, and who in that way acted for her while she watched or paced up and down remembering.

It seems that Graham increasingly saw her role as that of making visible a psychological process rather than taking concrete, here-and-now action. In *Spring* the other characters act — but the wife, except for the few times when the husband draws her out of her reverie, is entirely caught up in her own thoughts, her feelings about what she's doing and her imaginings about her future life. She sees the other people as a reflection of these feelings or as instigators of formal protocols in which she must play a role. She is a person for whom "real" life takes place in the mind; mundane life is a formality. This, of course, links her intimately with Emily Dickinson and Emily Brontë, about whom Graham had also choreographed in the years preceding *Appalachian Spring*.

The wife has two solos, both of them interior monologues. Whereas the husband and the preacher want to communicate something to the other characters when they make their solo statements, when the wife dances the others don't "hear" her, even though she frequently refers to them. Her first dance, which occurs well into the ballet, after the husband's dance and the preacher's interlude with the followers, is a dance of excitement, but not the large joyfulness of the husband and the Pioneer Woman. As the music plays a fast, tripping theme, she hops and skitters downstage, tapping her hands to her shoulders on each beat. Even in these first few bars we get an impression of littleness, of a tight, nervous person, a prim, "feminine" woman who was brought up not to be noisy or get in the way. She is positively afraid of space, afraid to spread herself or her emotions out in it.

She runs a few steps toward each of the other characters, a lurching, almost falling run with her center body contracted, as if she couldn't bring herself really to reach out to any of them. She does some of those bouncy kicks to the side that we saw in *Frontier*, then pivots in a sweeping arabesque but with her upper body plunging toward the ground; she twitches her skirt coquettishly at the husband. This dance is quite similar in progression to the opening Emily Dickinson solo in *Letter to the World*. Though more specific in its references to the realities of the character's life, it has the same mercurial quality, the inability either to stay still or to investigate one feeling at length. The wife suddenly thinks of a baby; she runs to the Pioneer Woman, who seems to be holding one in her arms. The wife takes it, rocks it a few times, gives it back, runs to the husband again, and finishes her exclamation by falling all the way to the ground in arabesque, and ending up on the porch at the older woman's feet.

This character is beside herself with excitement, but frantic because she doesn't know how to express it. Her world is not safe and she wants it to be. You might say that what happens to her in the dance is that she's enlarging her space, but only somewhat. What has been her personal universe grows to include her husband and her house, and she sees both these things as shelters for her, not as spaces she will take possession of.

Her second solo, after the hellfire episode, is filled with foreboding. All the things that earlier awoke her repressed delight now become laden with terrors. It's not the unknown, the supernatural, that frightens her, but the known — the baby, the husband, the house — will it burn down, will there be droughts, plagues, Indian raids, maddening loneliness? The music plays a sort of stuttering version of her first playful dance, and she runs as if in panic to the house, touches it, rolls down the steps, circles the yard, gestures the baby, the husband. And, back on the porch again, she distractedly twirls the rocking chair around and finally sits in it, leaning back and kicking one crossed leg up and down. It's as if she foresees some agonized night when she'll be waiting for a child's fever to drop or for the snow to melt, powerless, impatient, but willing herself to hang on.

Fortunately for her, the husband understands her dilemma, and again and again in the dance he shields her from the terrors of space. At the end of this solo he carries her off the porch and takes her down to the fence. There, with the fence for protection in front and his bulk enclosing her from behind, she can be calmed. During the final prayer, the wife again panics, running to each of the characters as they kneel, facing away from her, and for a moment she stands alone, unshielded, looking out into space. Then the husband comes up behind her, closes her arms with his, and surrounds her in an embrace. Now she accepts that this will be enough, and, when the others have gone, he stands behind the porch rocker and she goes up and sits quietly in it. Together they look out over the land.

Pillar of Fire (Antony Tudor)

American dance never developed a tradition of full-length story ballets, the kind that dominated nineteenth-century ballet in Europe. Acknowledging the successful modernism of Diaghilev, our ballet and modern dance is almost universally based on condensed forms of twenty to forty-five minutes. Graham's *Clytemnestra* (1958) is perhaps the only example of an extended theater form in a non-European idiom. (I am leaving out the contemporary works of Robert Wilson and Meredith Monk because they seem to me to place strong emphasis on graphic, verbal, musical, and dramatic expression, not principally on dance.)

Until the eclectic, no-style ballets of the 1970s, narrative in American modern dance has mainly been conveyed through the symbolic psychological shorthand of Graham or the development of character by means of musical organization and shading, explored by Humphrey and Limón. In ballet the devices were those of tradition: mime and other symbolic languages such as the ballet vocabulary itself; indications of period, place, or station through "character" dance gesture. In the 1930s and 1940s, words, both spoken and sung, were used in narrative ballets and modern dances, as were preexisting scenarios from literature, poetry, legend, and even ballets. But in Antony Tudor, American ballet gained another dimension.

Tudor came to this country in 1940 at the instigation of Agnes de Mille, who had worked with him at the Ballet Rambert in London. American Ballet Theater had recently been founded and was in need of choreographers. Tudor is not a prolific choreographer, but most of his major works after 1940 were made for ABT. More important, his works profoundly influenced the dramatic style of that company and many of its later choreographers. His early ballets *Dark Elegies* and *Jardin aux Lilas* became staples of the Ballet Theater repertory, and *Gala Performance* (1940), *Romeo and Juliet* (1943), *Undertow* (1945), *Shadowplay* (1967), and *The Leaves Are Fading* (1975) have also been significant works for the company. But *Pillar of Fire* (1942) is Tudor's signature work, the model for a whole "school" of American narrative ballet.

The story of the ballet is easily told; there is just enough of a plot to keep the interest of the literal-minded in the audience. Hagar is a shy, sexually repressed woman, afraid of both the Victorian spinsterhood of her older sister and the flirtatious abandon of her younger sister. In a desperate moment she allows herself to be seduced by a young man of bad morals. This adds guilt and shame to her already burdened psyche. But the man she really loves, an older, respectable type called the Friend, understands her torments and persuades her that he loves her in precisely the way that she needs to be loved.

I find it somewhat awkward even to recite this story today, but it may be that Tudor's view of sex and society was old-fashioned even in his time. The scenario is based on "Die Weib und die Welt," the poem that inspired the score, Schönberg's Verklärte Nacht, and both are heavy with a late-nineteenth-century Germanic indulgence in suffering and mystical transfiguration. Perhaps out of a desire to make the ballet's plot reasonable in modern terms, writers have interpreted the specifics of motivation, and even of the narrative itself, in widely differing ways. Or perhaps we can account for this disagreement by the depth and ambiguity of Tudor's portrayals. I find I need to adjust the dance's morality somewhat in order to make it credible, but Tudor allows for that, as does the contemporary ABT production headed by Sallie Wilson, who succeeded to the role created by Nora Kaye.

Tudor refocused the entire process of narrative ballet by putting academic technique at the service of character, instead of the other way around. Except where a place is made for showy dancing — *Gala Performance*, for instance, is about ballerinas giving a performance — no one in a Tudor ballet just goes out and dances a dance. Even in *Dark Elegies*, a pure-dance ballet with no plot or specific characters at all, the people lamenting the death of their children are dancing for *that* reason, and the dances are made to show us different kinds of lamenting, not different kinds of dancing. Almost any Balanchine ballet I can think of reverses these priorities.

In addition, Tudor deals strictly with a classical movement language. He has sometimes been aligned with modern dancers, but I think this is a great misreading of his craft. Nor does he adopt the usual "character" signs — literal gestures, folk or national dance steps and attitudes, or trademark pantomime. His people are inventions, not exact replicas of types we can immediately recognize and place. I think this adds to the mystery of his characters and to their ability to represent universal emotions rather than the concerns of a particular period. If they are "dated," then the viewer who dates them is probably overinterpreting them.

As the ballet opens, Hagar sits on the steps of her house. Legs together, feet flat on the ground, back straight, head drooping, she slowly lifts her right hand to the side of her head and looks up. Tudor is a genius at the loaded gesture — this one, like most of his others, is completely nonliteral. People have tried to imagine what Hagar is doing when she lifts her hand — fussing with her hair, touching a throbbing temple — and other choreographers have elaborated more specifically on the idea. Tudor's gesture leaves room for speculation. Hagar is not yet revealed to us except as one who is alone, who touches herself. Later we see that physical touch means a great deal to her; perhaps her own is the most comforting she has known up to now. This gesture tells us that she is literally a self-conscious person, not yet so far gone into eccentricity that she doesn't care what people will think of her actions.

People walk by the house — two ladies in long skirts with hats and gloves. They too have a characteristic nonliteral gesture: together they turn slightly behind them and pick up their skirts, carrying a fold of material around to the front and letting it drop again. The action is part of a whole constellation of adjustments that these women make to their clothes and that later the prissy older sister will also occupy herself with, especially when she is nervous or disapproving. It is also an eminently fastidious gesture, a withdrawal from someone they already suspect might be morally beneath them. As they walk, the two old maids rise on their toes and dip down, bending their knees, bowing and curtseying to Hagar and the older sister as they do. Tudor has translated the fundamental plié-relevé of ballet into a ritual of empty politeness.

Quickly Tudor introduces all the other parties to Hagar's dilemma. Her little sister twirls in, escorted by two young men, and runs to the house, where she spins into the older sister's arms, leaning back on her for a moment, then whirls away again, pausing just long enough to touch Hagar's outstretched hand. We see something about her — she is frivolous, she enjoys the attention of others and wins it easily, but she doesn't stay with anyone. She's always attracted to some other diversion. She could be selfish or malicious or just thoughtlessly adolescent.

The Man Opposite passes by, a muscular, sensuous type in shirtsleeves, and goes into the house across the street. The Friend appears, very straight and proper and noncommittal, and goes into Hagar's house with the two sisters while she is left outside. Immediately it becomes apparent that her distress is not only due to shyness or rejection, but is also sexual.

She sees through the windows into the House Opposite; an orgy is in progress — or what she thinks is one. Here Tudor makes a tiny slow-motion sequence — men and women moving through a succession of poses, holding each other in attitudes of abandon. Hagar runs to the windows and spreads her arms out along the side of the house yet shrinks away in the center of her body. At that moment the house goes dark. Then the man she saw earlier comes out alone, perhaps for a breath of air. She looks at him, fascinated and repelled, and he makes her a crude proposal, rubbing both hands along the inside of his thighs and spreading his legs. He does it just once; she might not have seen it at all, but she knows what he means, and, shaking her head no, she turns away in disgust.

Only one other time does the Man Opposite make a lewd gesture toward Hagar, at the climax of the seduction duet, when he stretches lengthwise on the floor, supporting himself by his hands and feet, and thrusts his pelvis at her. The rest of the time he merely dances like a ballet dancer, with expressive nuances. In *Night Journey*, Martha Graham made a whole solo for the man using phallic gestures. Tudor employs only these two; but the character's sensuality and danger are inherent in the way he sinks his weight into the ground and swaggers his shoulders when he walks, in his daring to touch Hagar when he knows how vulnerable she is to being touched, in his lifts and embraces that force her body into unaccustomed, exposed shapes.

After Hagar's first refusal of this man's advances, there begins a scene in which the romantic love she yearns for is elaborated, and her isolation from it is made more apparent. Six boys and girls, called Lovers in Innocence, appear, and while they are dancing together, the sisters and the Friend come out of the house. Little sister and the Friend join the young people and leave, the men carrying the women high in an airy, expansive lift.

A minute later the sister and the Friend stroll back, and the sister teases Hagar by urging her to show off for the Friend. Hagar is too shy, but the sister takes her by the hand and they dance for him together. Just as Hagar begins to seem confident enough to let him look at her, the sister pushes her toward him and she stumbles at his feet; he catches her and raises her from the ground. Perhaps the sister sees Hagar's crush on this man and wants to encourage them to get together; perhaps she wants to attract his interest to herself by embarrassing Hagar. At any rate, after Hagar's fall, she claims him again and they dance together, again ambiguously, in a trio with Hagar. The man is absorbed in the sister's demands, but he also partners Hagar with the other hand as she shadows their motions, bewildered and having a hard time keeping up. At last they

PILLAR OF FIRE (*Tudor, 1942*). *Marcos Paredes and Sallie Wilson of American Ballet Theater. Photo by Louis Péres.*

run off on either side of her, and the man's hand accidentally brushes Hagar's waist. After he's gone, she hugs herself as if she'd been lashed.

Now the Man Opposite comes out again and seduces her in a duet of angular, harsh body shapes; possessive graspings and latent indifference on his part, tentative, horrified advances and withdrawals on hers. The dance seems all circlings, undoings, rewindings, growing ever tighter. But when she goes into the house with him it is her own decision; in fact, she throws herself into his arms at the last minute when she sees he has lost patience with her hesitation. Even in taking this traumatic action, Hagar's motivation is only partly physical passion, for her capitulating step is an inversion of the little sister's careless whirl into the shelter of the elder's arm.

A minute later — or an eternity — Hagar comes out of the house again and falls to her knees. Naturally. This affair could only have produced guilt in such a frail ego. The older sister comes out and sees her standing all bowed over, her legs and arms pressed close. She senses something is wrong and at first glances around to see if someone might be walking away; then, looking closer at Hagar, she thinks it may be more serious and looks around again, this time anxious that no one passing by should see the family in disarray. Two women do go by, and the sister props Hagar up, forcing her to behave as if everything were all right. The minute they leave, she inspects Hagar again and understands the truth. Wringing her hands overhead, she walks up and down lamenting, as if she has been visited by an undeserved punishment from God.

At this point all the other characters appear, a few at a time, as if assembling for a judgment. The elder sister puts her arm around Hagar's shoulder protectively — or perhaps warningly. Tudor's socially obsessed characters often compel those who are wavering to conform to ritual gestures, with the intention of forestalling the suspicion of others or restoring them to their senses by observance of the proprieties.

The little sister puts on another one of her shows, pirouetting and extending a pretty foot first in front of the Friend, then coiling into the arm of one of the men from the House Opposite. Hagar puts her hand to the side of her head, as if she doesn't understand how her sister could move so easily between these two polarities. The dancers whirl away, and the sisters say goodnight to the Friend, who looks after them as the eldest sister closes the door the same way she pulled her skirts around her, and the lights go out.

This pause in the action is called for by the music, but even so it seems odd; it separates the ballet into two time segments and also two slightly different styles. After the break, the action seems less literal. Tudor evidently wanted to indicate the passage of time in this pause, but how much time, in a ballet where there's always some doubt about how literally the elapsed time is to be taken, is not clear. Some critics have assumed that enough time passes for the whole family to be considered outcasts on account of Hagar's disgrace. (In the source poem, the woman has borne a child by the time she is accepted by her true love.) In any event, the momentary lapse allows us to consolidate what we have learned about these people. It seems to me that the latter half of the ballet can be seen as a shift of focus: first we have seen these people as individuals with their own psychological patterns; now we see them in relation to each other and to their community. However, both aspects of the situation are apparent in both parts of the ballet. The more I studied *Pillar of Fire*, the more I became aware of how subtly Tudor interweaves his characters and cross-references their motivating passions.

As the second scene opens, the sisters are posing in a tableau, each in a characteristic attitude: the older sister stands in the middle, with her hand on the shoulder of each of the others; the younger sister hovers on one leg, pulling slightly away, with a hand coyly drawn up to one shoulder; and Hagar kneels on one knee, one arm down at her side, the other covering her breast. The older sister turns and spreads herself flat between the two, as if trying to shield the little sister from Hagar. But as she leaves, the girl skips around Hagar, flouncing her skirt at her, perhaps taunting her, perhaps only wooing her attention. When Hagar doesn't respond, she too leaves, as if skipping rope.

Some girls from the town come in and dance their airy, open dance. Hagar walks sedately among them. She tries to imitate their patterns but before she's caught onto more than a few phrases they're gone again. We might remember now that when the Friend and the sister went off together, they first danced with the boys and girls of the town. But actually it was the sister who danced, the Friend more or less stood around to lift her so she could be in unison with the group. The Friend has as much trouble conforming to this group as Hagar does.

As the girls leave, the Friend appears. He tries to comfort Hagar, and once more she recoils from his touch on her waist. She rises on pointe, but her leg doubles under her, and he catches her as she falls. In a swift series of lifts and carries, the Friend keeps attempting to reassure her, and each time she is lifted or held she tries to evade his eyes, but she is very conscious of his hands on her.

A couple from the House Opposite appear and begin nuzzling each other. Hagar grows acutely embarrassed, and the Friend leaves when he sees her shut him out again. Now the whole party of Lovers in Experience enters. Hagar's seducer has another woman with him. She tries to get his attention, to dance with him, but he brutally rejects her, first by ignoring and shrugging off her advances, finally by dragging her along the ground and leaving her by the side of the road.

Hagar cringes on the ground in a spasm of the most abject humiliation. While she is cowering there, the little sister runs in and sees her, flounces above her for a moment — the most callous instance of her insensitivity — then goes to the Man Opposite and deliberately dances with him. This act is the culmination of something Tudor has been suggesting all along: despite their differences of manners and temperament, the two groups of lovers have much in common.

Hagar seems to have discovered this very early, when at the beginning of her duet with the Man Opposite she ran toward him and he caught her in a spread-open jump that was only a stopped-action version of the running lifts of the Innocents a few moments before. The Lovers in Experience are earthy while the Lovers in Innocence all tend toward the air. One group has a decidedly downward tendency — you feel weight in all their lifts; the men bend the women down under them, press and drag them into embraces. The other group always seems to be lifting, jumping, running with their arms high, skimming in and out of contact with each other. But both groups are important to Hagar, and both present possibilities that she somehow cannot share. By the end of this dance all the Lovers are present, the two groups now intermingling, and while they dance Hagar runs among them and is lifted three times into the air by men from both groups in combination.

The young people go off; her seducer is the last to leave. He saunters right past her without seeing her; she doesn't look at him but reacts as if he had punched her in the stomach. She is growing more desperate now. She makes an appeal to the older sister, stretching out a hand to her. The sister starts to move toward Hagar, then changes her mind and goes off with her friends. Hagar is alone again, but the Friend returns. She tries to run away, or does she run *to* him and miscalculate? He seems to scoop her to him, holding her around the waist, and she folds herself over his arm.

This third and last of her duets is about accommodation. The first with the man across the street, seemed to be strained and over-difficult; she was not merely resisting him but making it as hard as possible for them to work together. When she first danced with the Friend she turned away, avoided confrontation, but did allow it to happen. Now she and the Friend seem to be trying to find ways to move together. In none of these pas de deux does Hagar really change her contrariness, her angularity, her rabbit-scared veering into new directions. But finally the Friend is able to find ways to support her tenseness and agitation. He lifts her so that the spiky, oppositional awkwardness of her limbs can become harmonious. First he holds her near the ground, as he did twice before when she fell, supporting her under the arms, and she covers her eyes, holds one leg out straight and the other drawn up. As he lifts her, the bent leg straightens until she is standing on pointe in a perfect arabesque.

Their final accord is a recognition of their likenesses. The man appeals to her from the ground — taking almost the same position as the carnal lover had, but instead of making a sexual gesture he merely rests back on his hands, exposing his whole body to her without defenses or threat. They have a kind of dialogue, each one kneeling before the other as if acknowledging and forgiving the sensual weaknesses of the past. As she kneels, he bends and kisses her, then lifts her to her feet, and they walk off together, strolling through the trees in the background, as women bourrée quickly across the far distance, floating light as air.

The gesture with which the Friend embraces Hagar tells everything about their coming relationship. Side by side they walk close together, and he clasps both her shoulders. He avoids putting his arm around her waist or embracing her frontally; probably he knows how dangerous a hint of sensual caress is for Hagar even now. This way of partnering is also a replica of the older sister's gesture after discovering Hagar's "sin" — it is protective and therapeutic, and it also contains an admonishment. It reminds me that the Friend is basically upright and law-abiding, that his love will help Hagar live in society rather than become so desperate she has to outlaw herself again.

The inherent saneness of conventional morality is a message in all of Tudor's ballets. He admits that there are mavericks in society, but he sees them as condemned to suffer. And having suffered, still the only way to redeem their lives is to adopt society's terms. The Friend who turns out to be such a good match for Hagar is not only a father-figure, more mature and presumably less sexual than the boys of the town, he is also very much like the sister who represents conformity. The sister, bloodless and stern, stands for passion rerouted into an unyielding code of behavior, and the hypocrisy of maintaining appearances when the morals underneath have collapsed. When Hagar calls on her for real affection, she has second thoughts, censors her instinctive sympathy, and turns away. The Friend gives me a similar sense — not precisely of insincerity but of withholding commitment. He appears on the scene blandly ready to accept the family's hospitality, to fall in with any plan they may have for him. He neither refuses nor solicits their attentions. He is so circumspect he might be a minister.

Tudor details a community that is changing — in its structure and its behavior. The three sisters are survivors of a family in transition, living on in a once-genteel neighborhood that is becoming infiltrated by immigrants who haven't learned to refine their tastes or repress their emotions. Already we can see the young people of the good families beginning to mix with the strangers, to share their pleasures. Hagar does not see this evolution of mores as an acceptable way to end her own estrangement. Maybe it will work for her younger sister, but she is either too old or too stubborn to modify her standards. Time and again Tudor gave his character the refuge of tradition or asceticism — in *Lilac Garden*, in *Shadowplay*, in *Dark Elegies*, they draw back from experience and risk, into the safety of tribal codes.

I think, in some way, Tudor's social concerns had an influence on the way he structured his ballets. He didn't make them character studies or encounters, the way Graham or Limón did, because they really were about whole societies in flux, the stabilizing effect of the community against the forces that threaten to destroy it. *Pillar of Fire* is diffuse where Graham's theater dances are specific. People run in and out constantly, and scarcely ever do the main characters get to be alone long enough to think. Only Hagar has any dancing that might correspond to Graham's soliloquies, and her solos are more like hurried notations than monologues, for the demands of others constantly crowd in on her privacy. Everything you know about these characters you learn from their actions — how they behave, what choices they make — not from the way they describe themselves. Graham's dances are self-directed, Tudor's are other-directed. Groups of people pass in and out of Tudor's world because to him, individuals are part of their society and share its ills and benefits. To Graham, I think, the individual is at odds with society in some way; a psychic life takes place apart from the group and must come to terms with itself before it can be lived at peace.

Tudor's individuals suppress their differences and learn how to fit into society. What he seems to be saying is that society is big enough to hold even the most divergent of them.

Day on Earth (Doris Humphrey)

By the time she choreographed *Day on Earth*, Doris Humphrey had relinquished three of the four main identity symbols of modern dancers: at forty-seven she had stopped dancing due to arthritis of the hip, and she had given up the Humphrey-Weidman school and company by the end of World War II, after fifteen years of struggle. The old relationships that had sustained the enterprise were disintegrating. But she could still choreograph, and she did, until her death, for the José Limón Company and the Juilliard Dance Theater.

As in her earlier career, Doris Humphrey continued to elude modern dance stereotypes. Alone among her colleagues, she worked for a company that didn't bear her name. José Limón, her protégé, made her the artistic director of his company and depended on her not only as a choreographer but as an adviser for his own choreographic work. Although Humphrey's basic movement ideas had already been developed, she choreographed all her dances after 1946 without being able to demonstrate what she wanted, so Limón, Pauline Koner, and the other dancers probably had a more equal role in creating Humphrey's late works than modern dancers traditionally did. For this reason, and for many others, Humphrey seems to me the first of the "egoless" modern dancers. Her works were not exclusively reenactments of roles she could visualize for herself (although, curiously, one can picture her doing some of the parts she never danced, like the woman in *Day on Earth*). They ranged further in theme and characterization, often cued stylistically to Limón's personality or to those of other dancers rather than to her own. The Limón company had begun to take shape during the war, and by 1947 its working methods were established, and so was its success. But it was the enormous courage and optimism of Doris Humphrey, in the face of the most crushing adversities a dancer can experience, that made *Day on Earth* what Margaret Lloyd called "a shimmering idyll."[3]

*

Day on Earth is for me just about the best surviving example of the combined humanistic and kinesthetic possibilities of modern dance. In a completely nonliteral, poetic way it compresses a world of experience into a small, spare form. Set to Aaron Copland's 1941 piano sonata, the dance has only four participants, a man, two women, and a child. The only décor is a large box and a cloth, and the costumes are simplified ordinary clothes in a color described originally as terra cotta. Descriptions of the dance usually sound pantomimic because the action is so clearly translatable, but what is truly amazing is the rich emotional tone that infuses its narrative content. The dance is remarkable to me because of the movement, not because of the story told by the movement, which is the age-old cycle of work, love, birth, loss, companionship, death, and continuation. It is a sort of "Our Town" without any detail or sentiment.

A man travels along a diagonal, making large, strong motions with his arms that could suggest many kinds of outdoor work: sowing, planting, harvesting, hauling, driving a plow. A young woman comes to him and they dance together playfully for a while, but the man is fundamentally serious, and the girl finally breaks away from his embrace. He returns to his work and is joined by another woman, who is a more compatible partner. Together they walk upstage; a cloth is spread on the floor in front of the box where the two women were posing at the beginning of the dance. The man and woman lift the cloth away and disclose a child lying under it.

The parents breathe life into the child, rock and play with her. Then they return to their work as the little girl skips around them. The woman leaves for a moment and the man plays with the child alone. After the mother's return, the child grows restless in her play and eventually slips away from her parents. The man comforts his grief-stricken wife until they both can take solace in their work once more. Then, ceremoniously, all the dancers slowly return to the box and form a concluding tableau — this time with their initial positions reversed, the child seated on the box and the adults lying under the cloth.

Although the progression of events is very clear and continuous, certain specifics are left out. For instance, all the characters are onstage at the beginning and end of the dance, and all of them leave the stage once and return during the course of the action. But all the exits are ambiguous. One can become distracted from the stage activity by wondering where someone has gone, but I think

Humphrey's intent was to leave room for many possibilities. Her characters are universal beings who can react and function in many ways. Their relationships and feelings about each other can change.

It seems to me quite unusual in dance to find a man who loves two women, neither one destructively. The women do not compete with each other, nor does one stand for his mother or his feminine alter ego or any neurotic desires. Humphrey shows us that the two women are very different types. The first is quick and lyrical. The man is attracted to her perhaps because she's so different from himself, the steady, down-to-earth plodder. They dance together for a time, but their impulses don't coincide for long. Inevitably, the man thinks of his work, of settling down; irresistibly, the girl is set for flight. When he finally draws her close in an embrace that could be for all time, she breaks away for good. Although the man is severely hurt by her departure, Humphrey does not offer the platitude of endless grief and loneliness for the man. How much more true to life that he should be able to love another woman later on.

Another scene that adds depth to the characters follows the brief separation of the man and his wife. Her departure is puzzling, but

DAY ON EARTH (*Humphrey, 1947*). *Ruth Currier and José Limón. Photo by Gjon Mili.*

not if we see the dance from Doris Humphrey's prefeminist point of view. Women can have minds of their own, can have things that they do in private or completely outside the lives of their husbands and families. Instead of showing us what the woman does away from the family — she doesn't feel it's necessary to account for that — she shows us the father and daughter who have been left behind. They have a relationship that can exist without the mother's presence.

Humphrey's excellent craftsmanship helped further delineate these characterizations. Her use of thematic gestures, like the man's work motifs, succinctly keeps facets of the people's lives in our view. The man keeps returning to these gestures — after the withdrawal of his youthful love, after the birth of the child, and again after the tragic loss of the child. The last time, his grief and anger turn these motions into slashing, twisting throws and hits; at one point he seems to be hurling whatever he has collected into the air. Then, at the peak of his fury, the habit of work not entirely lost, he pauses midway in a defiant series of jumps, then bends his body in the familiar pattern, curving his arm up around his shoulder, and you can almost feel him take up his life's burden again.

The wife has especially persuasive arm and hand gestures. When she enters the action, the man has left the stage, perhaps to repair the sorrow of his broken first affair. The woman draws him gradually back onstage with big beckoning motions very similar to those with which she will coax life into the child. After the child is gone, she repeats this gesture, along with others associated with the child's learning and playing. She also recalls some of the work movements, but now they are interrupted — the arms begin mechanically to gather in, but the circle breaks, the arms twist up and away from each other, the basket is empty.

The ways in which the various characters dance together are also indicative of their relationships. While the man and the young girl are seldom able to synchronize their movements, with the other woman he finds an immediate rapport. She moves more like him in the first place — smoothly and deliberately, with a sense of seriousness and of dealing with the space around her rather than of flitting through it. In their first encounter they go through a few poses, size each other up at arm's length, find that they can achieve unison easily. Most of their subsequent relationship is one of synchronous or complementary movements. A surprisingly large number of family events is suggested in a very brief time. We see that the man and woman share the child's upbringing, and, when she is able to romp around on her own, they share their pleasure in watching her antics. They work together; although they don't always do the same things, you feel that both partners are contributing to the life they have. It's not a case of the man doing the "work" and the woman keeping herself busy in the background. After the woman's absence, the family seems strengthened — the parents rock and swing the child more vigorously than ever, they work together more expansively.

But then, while they still seem caught up in the child's game, the little girl skips erratically around them. They make a sort of gate with their arms, but, instead of letting them catch her, the child pushes through the gate. She continues to elude them, and finally their close trio breaks open. The man and woman step backwards toward one side of the stage, and the little girl backs away to the other and goes out.

When the parents realize she isn't coming back there is a beautiful sequence in which the man holds and supports the woman as she reaches out futilely or spreads her body flat out in resignation. They become more and more agitated, tensely pulling away from each other and rejoining from an increasing distance until the woman flings herself forward across the box. Their suffering now subsides in long, alternating solo phrases. The woman's arm-twisting motions transmit themselves into the man's whole body and he throws himself into twisting jumps, landing face down on the ground, then drags himself up and starts to plant. The woman slowly pulls herself up and begins to fold the cloth in a gesture that is all in the same time poignantly sensual and practical — she holds the large piece of material against her body as women do when putting away sheets or blankets, and every contact with it is redolent of the child who slept under it. At last, with agonizing slowness, she drops the folded cloth onto her arched-backward body, and with it bends forward, kneels, and goes limp over the box. The man haltingly begins his work cycle again, and when he establishes it, the women all begin their final procession behind him, their movements becoming more and more formal. The child mounts the man's back as if for a piggyback ride, and he carries her to the base of the box and lets her down. The man plants one last seed, then gestures as though taking something heavy off his shoulders. Then he and the two women lie down at the foot of the box, pulling the cloth over them, as the child seats herself on the box.

The Moor's Pavane (José Limón)

After the war, a second generation of modern dancers began to establish themselves as independent artists. Some, like Merce Cunningham, Erick Hawkins, and Alwin Nikolais, made a definite break with the accepted themes and modes of choreographing. Others didn't seem to need the complete separation from their mentors but were content to work in greater depth or detail on one aspect or another of the aesthetic they had learned. Anna Sokolow concentrated on the psychological alienation described in Graham and framed it in contemporary images. May O'Donnell developed the rhythmic and bodily fragmentation of Graham, the irregularity and asymmetricality of form, to make mostly nonnarrative dances. José Limón particularized Doris Humphrey's humanism.

Limón, a Mexican-American, had originally wanted to become a painter. Throughout his life, his heroes were artists, the biggest ones — Michelangelo, El Greco, Bach, Shakespeare. Limón himself looked heroic, tall and upright with high, chiseled cheekbones and deeply set eyes, his head tilting back slightly so that his gaze always seemed to be directed downward. He had been Doris Humphrey's bullfighter in *Lament for Ignacio Sanchez Mejias,* the man in *Day on Earth,* and a long succession of other archetypes; but in his own choreography he developed characters with more specific identities. He seemed to need the limits implied by focusing on literary or historic persons whose deeds he could justify or illuminate. His gift was not to enlarge and represent but to explain, to dramatize, to become a hero for a while and play out that hero's role.

The Moor's Pavane (1949) is now probably the most widely performed of all modern dances. A number of practical circumstances contributed to its being adopted by so many ballet and modern companies twenty years after its creation. Limón's company was chronically in need of money in his last years — he died in 1972 — and he authorized some of his young dancers to serve as rehearsal directors to mount his works for other companies. *Moor* is an easy work to produce, having only four dancers and no set, with Purcell music played by a string ensemble. Most attractive of all, it is considered a vehicle. The work was a popular favorite from the beginning, when Limón and Lucas Hoving played the antagonists Othello and Iago, with Koner as Emilia and Betty Jones as Desdemona. Later dancers such as Bruce Marks, Christian Holder, Lawrence Rhodes, and Rudolf Nureyev have seized on the dramatic possibilities of Limón's tragic Moor. Over time, especially since the choreographer's death, the work has lost much of its dance quality. Ballet dancers performing it have not been able to capture the weighted tensions and balances of the Limón style, and these characteristics along with much of the choreographic detail have gradually lapsed while the acting was increasingly stressed. I feel these later versions do not reveal Limón's choreographic excellence, which consisted of more than providing an opportunity for great acting dancers to project their personalities.

The story is skillfully built through a series of duets between various sets of characters, interspersed with formal meetings of the whole group. Limón, Hoving, and Jones made at least two films of the work, with Koner in one of them, so their interpretation can still be seen. Undeniably they were powerful performers; they also possessed a subtle command of dynamics, of spatial and body articulation, and of gradations of intensity in gesture and facial expression, all of which are of equal importance with their acting abilities in creating the dance's powerful impact.

Limón translated the plot of Shakespeare's "Othello" by going to the play's basic dilemmas rather than by trying to duplicate its actions. He saw the individual tragedies of the various characters, each doomed by his or her flawed personality. But he also saw that much of the explanation for the tragedy could not be shown in a dance — not Iago's political plotting, nor his manipulation of people and events, nor the reasons for his hatred, nor the other characters' vulnerability. The dance concerns itself not with states of jealousy and envy, not with specific deeds of betrayal, but with a process of deterioration, perhaps several interrelated processes. Limón described it as being about "the destructive power of jealousy."[4] This development, or disintegration, of character can be and is depicted in the dance movement. Doris Humphrey fashion,

Limón chose his images so that they would work on several levels — the spatial form of the dance, as well as its internal order, undergoes a gradual breaking apart while the closely dependent relationships among the characters are also disrupted.

Louis Horst described the preclassic pavane as a dance of "ceremonious dignity, splendor and grave pride,"[5] consisting mostly of walking steps, and according to the great aesthetician of baroque dance, Thoinot Arbeau, this "honorable" form was used mostly for processionals and displays of majesterial splendor.[6] The form is ideally suited as an ironic ceremony within which Limón's characters destroy themselves through their own passions. His pavane, even in its initial presentation, seems less a closed, set ritual than a series of ideas by which the group formally asserts and describes itself. Events of plot significance take place during and between figures of this courtly dance, so that we get the impression the pavane is always going on — like the protocols of courtly power — defining the terms of rivalry and defense rather than being a separate event they enjoy when not engaged in more serious pursuits.

We first see the characters *as* a group, a quartet inextricably linked by clasped hands and clustered close together facing the center of its own circle. A moment later the Moor breaks this image of solidarity by circling his leg out behind him along the floor, and the other individuals follow suit. The group separates into pairs, the men and women addressing each other, then the married couples. This acknowledgment of the individual bonding relationships takes the form of bowing, nodding, and other formal recognition patterns and of advancing and retreating — initiated by the pelvis — in straight lines toward the person opposite. The pavane is never seen in quite the same form after the first time. Each restatement of these motifs — the inward-facing cluster, the mutually supporting handholds, the circling and approaching-in-a-line floor patterns, and the bowing-dipping acknowledgments — casts them in increasingly fragmented or disturbed form.

At first, the movement is very slow and smooth, the pauses and suspensions very secure. The predominant shape of the dancers' hand and body gestures is round, especially when they scoop and gather into the space between them, enlarging on the claspings of interdependence. But even as early as Othello's first leg thrust, small motions poke through the pavane's even surface. Iago gestures furtively toward the Moor, drawing his hand across the center of his body as if tugging at an invisible rope or invoking a silent spell. Emilia refuses Iago's first hint that she steal Desdemona's handkerchief by jerking her arms upward and twisting her head away.

The tight clump into which the quartet had first been gathered spreads out into space, the dance becoming more expansive, the dancers presenting themselves more grandly to each other, the movement overflowing into big spirals, turns, and falls, and into a big crossing pattern from one side of the space to the other. The earliest form of this sweeping advance is cut off: the dancers rise on the balls of their feet and halt their forward motion by withdrawing the pelvis, as if they've run into an invisible waist-high barrier. Later, the circular path and the long, straight, crossing path seem to become confused and intermingled, and in the last pavanes the dancers swoop erratically out to the farthest ends of the space in zigzagging runs that end in tight turns back to the center or huge, whole-body falls to the ground. Toward the end, they return to the center and cling together even more tightly while leaning outward. The stress of this figure, where the dancers have to hang together all the more strongly because they are veering away from each other, eventually breaks the group apart and they fall violently outward. Spacings that had been even and measured become either uncomfortably close or very distant. The dance that was once smooth, connected, and placid becomes clashing, jagged, increasingly random in its pattern, until it has disintegrated entirely.

Limón's plot centers around a handkerchief that Othello gives to Desdemona. It's dropped by her in the course of a pavane and retrieved by Emilia. She gives it to her husband, Iago, who returns it to Othello as proof of Desdemona's infidelity. But we don't see the other key persons in Shakespeare's drama. Limón's version centers on the personalities of the main four. Each is weak in some ways and strong in others, and these dualities are what keep the group connected even while it is breaking apart.

The women — as in Shakespeare — are pawns and victims in the struggle between the men. Desdemona is weak, unassertive. Her credulousness and inability to defend herself are like the feminine side of Othello's own weakness. Both need their idealized belief in each other, and both are too easily persuaded — Othello accepts her guilt as if atoning for something he hates in himself, and Desdemona clings to him blindly even when her life is in danger. Both perhaps mistrust themselves, to need so disastrously the supposed purity of the other.

Othello's self-condemnation is shown quite clearly in his hand gestures. Consistently, throughout the dance, he makes a fist and beats against himself in fury. But when striking out at Iago he uses an open hand. There is impotence in this, a misdirection of his power or an inability to use power against his enemy. When his suspicions against Desdemona are first aroused, he prefaces a duet with her by struggling with himself: he clenches his fists together in front of his face and pulls in opposite directions until his hands fly apart and his palms open.

Emilia and Iago are more confident, less introspective characters. Both of them know what they want and how to use others for their own ends. Like Desdemona, Emilia is engrossed in her husband. She is so anxious for his approval and his sexual favors that she doesn't realize his devious purpose. Emilia is a sensualist who can exert or withhold her charm, who keeps Iago's attention by keeping him in suspense, by knowing just when to give in. She makes quick decisions and positive ones, but they can always be changed. In fact, the changeability of Iago and Emilia, expressed in his case as deviousness, is one of the main differences between them and Othello and Desdemona.

The innocent couple is consumed by unwavering beliefs — she believes her husband will trust her purity, and he that he cannot trust it. They cannot compromise or alter these attitudes. Othello holds himself back from his anger and Desdemona is too passive to contradict. This ability or inability to accommodate is also probably related to their positions in their community. Othello and Desdemona are aristocratic, accustomed to command, to having other people wait on them or carry out their orders. Iago and Emilia are subordinates; their position depends on keeping in the good graces of their superiors. Iago is especially skilled at accommodating to Othello's wishes. He is that particularly repellant kind of creature, the sycophant. He is constantly bowing and scraping and apologizing to Othello, knowing he has planted his lies well. He is also a coward; he never fights Othello outwardly, but when the Moor becomes enraged with his accusations, he cringes, grovels, or throws himself bodily on Othello's back. With Emilia he bides his time, knowing she will give in to his wishes eventually. Having engineered the whole tragedy with his sinuous, grasping gestures, his hands go limp when he sees Desdemona's body. He takes no responsibility.

Limón made particularly effective use of responsive phrasing in the dance — often the characters in a duet make alternating moves in answer to each other. This may be a variation of the bow and curtsey pattern that is part of the pavane. Othello and Iago particularly relate to each other in this way in their antagonistic moments. Othello strikes, Iago scrambles away, Othello strikes again, Iago scrambles farther. At another time Iago stands behind him, his

THE MOOR'S PAVANE (*Limón, 1949*). *José Limón and Lucas Hoving.*

hands on the Moor's shoulders, and they jump up in the air several times, first one then the other. Sometimes they face each other and do the same gesture, complementing and conflicting at the same time. Even when there is no physical connection, this kind of alternating gesture keeps the two opponents bound together rhythmically and spatially.

Repeating gestures between pairs happen all during the dance, even in the final moments, when Emilia, then Iago, steps over Desdemona's body. With one large move each one accuses the other; then Othello grasps them both by the wrist, pulls them up one at a time to meet his fury, and thrusts each one away. Othello falls on the body of Desdemona, becoming one with the object of his preoccupation and insecurity. Nothing is left of the pavane circle except Iago and Emilia, who stand on either side of the fallen couple facing outward. They bend double, then rise, stretching out one hand, palm toward the audience — giving evidence in every way that the ring is broken, its shape along with its support, its continuity, and its harmony.

The Epic Graham

Glory is that bright tragic thing
That for an instant means dominion.
— *Emily Dickinson* [1]

*T*HE 1940S WERE Martha Graham's most fruitful years. Creatively she was at her peak. All but three of the dances from this period have been reconstructed in the past ten years, and each one carries enough impact to last a contemporary choreographer a lifetime. The works, in the order of their premières, were *El Penitente* and *Letter to the World* (1940), *Punch and the Judy* (1941), *Salem Shore* and *Deaths and Entrances* (1943), *Appalachian Spring, Hérodiade* and *Imagined Wing* (1944), *Dark Meadow* and *Cave of the Heart* (1946), *Errand into the Maze* (1947), *Night Journey* and *Diversion of Angels* (1948). Although Graham continued to be productive and made wonderful dances after that, nothing she did in succeeding years surpassed the dances of her midlife. It was a time of upheaval in the world and in Graham's own life, but perhaps the very disruptions she was undergoing caused her to look more deeply than she ever had or would again into her creative process. Whatever the reasons, in these years she brought forth what will probably prove to be her most enduring single work, and certainly the dance of hers that is easiest to love, *Appalachian Spring;* she began her long cycle of Greek tragedies; and she created what I consider her two masterworks, *Letter to the World* and *Dark Meadow.*

Choreographed only five years apart, these huge dances represent the two strains of aesthetic preoccupation on which Graham's whole career centered: the expression of personal feelings and national identity through recognizable prototypes of character and movement, and the abstraction of those feelings to a more cosmic level through the use of symbol, myth, and psychoanalytic exploration. These two concerns correspond very closely, I think, to the two main types of formal organization in contemporary dance as defined in the 1930s by dancer-aesthetician Elizabeth Selden: "stylized naturalism wherever the emotional rhythm predominates" and a "formalistic approach" where the emotional impulse is restrained; the outgoing tendency is resisted "in behalf of the will to conquer, to defy, to dissimulate, to inhibit — and sometimes to extol, as in ritual dancing."[2] *Letter to the World* summed up and virtually ended Graham's naturalistic, emotional period, and *Dark Meadow* linked her early, stark abstractions *Primitive Mysteries* and *Lamentation* with the monolithic Greek rituals to come.

Letter to the World (score by Hunter Johnson), based on the life and work of Emily Dickinson, is a documentary of the artist in a puritanical culture, of woman caught in convention, and of the beauty such a person can perceive and give back to her culture. It is the story, on one level, of Martha Graham. Because its characters and events are quite literal, its emotional changes openly displayed, it is perhaps the most moving of all her dances. *Appalachian Spring* is cut from the same cloth, but is more limited in scope.

But Graham started turning away from such direct self-revelation. Like most great artists, she saw the limitations of autobiography, however fictionalized, and chose to submerge her feelings in grander themes, less explicit images. *Deaths and Entrances* started her in this direction, but she may have been held back by the specificity of her characters, the Brontë sisters, and the dance projects essences and fleeting impressions rather than one consistent idea. *Hérodiade* is small but it makes the transition from literalism to abstraction. From there she went on to her tremendous Greek tragedies. Just before plunging into the myths of classical antiquity, she used the devices of abstraction to give substance to the myths of the unconscious. *Dark Meadow* is unique among Graham dances. Its characters aren't based on any historical or literary persons; its plot development is negligible; its message is obscure. Yet it clearly does have a meaning, and to convey it Graham made some of her most absorbing choreography. I love *Dark Meadow* because it is "difficult," and because its meanings are not circumscribed by legendary events. It throws us back on real human experience without looking like anything we might have experienced.

Letter to the World (Martha Graham)

It is hard to imagine how Martha Graham ever located the affinity between herself and the New England recluse-poet Emily Dickinson. On the face of it, the strong, passionate, worldly activist rebel of dance had very little in common with the shy spinster who buried her gifts for art and love because she lived in a society that could not permit them to flourish. But somehow the words of Dickinson opened avenues of lyricism, wit, and a large range of feelings that Graham rarely explored elsewhere. Dancer and poet did intersect at many points, the central one being the puritanism that dominated Emily Dickinson's life and obsessed Graham's thought. Dickinson bowed outwardly to propriety, wrote and collected her poems in secret. Graham steered straight into the traditions that blocked her, pursued her talents openly through the very medium that most thoroughly threatened the ancient repressions, the human body. And, ironically, by keeping her nonconformity to herself, Dickinson seems to have become free to express whatever she felt, but Graham seems never to have rid herself of the old reservations, never to have got done with her struggle against convention. Out of this insoluble struggle, in *Letter to the World* Graham created a flow of events and images reflecting the life of the woman artist.

The dance is built on a brilliant device, a double main character, One Who Dances and One Who Speaks. The dancing role created by Graham has been danced most often in the present version — reconstructed in 1970 — by Pearl Lang. After an unsuccessful première with an actress in the speaking role, Jean Erdman took it over, and she resumed it in the recent revival. The contemporary critic Margaret Lloyd described the dance as a fantasy in which "the poetic imagery of movement substantiates the poetic imagery of words."[3] The speaker invokes selected lines from Dickinson and the dancer interprets them with action. Their characters frequently merge in mirroring movements or in related dynamic qualities, but they are basically two very different personae. The One Who Speaks is mature, sedate, has her emotions well in hand. She is an observer; she distills what is happening to the other woman into controlled images, a narrative that has power but that can be told.

The One Who Dances is young, unrestrained, vulnerable. She is all action and feeling, and she has no words.

The dance, designed by Arch Lauterer, takes place in an open space surrounded by black drapes. To the right of the audience is a doorway, or perhaps a porch — a clapboarded side of a house, a trellis, a few low steps. On the other side is a wooden bench. A narrow backyard world, in which Emily Dickinson dreamed the boundless life adventures she never actually had.

The dance begins with a wonderful walking duet. Wearing long, full, Victorian-type dresses and holding their arms in squared-off, head-framing positions, the two women enter and stride through the space, acknowledging one another confidently. This walk of theirs has an amplitude and a weight that epitomizes the whole modern dance period for me. Younger dancers don't really achieve it. The dancer steps with her whole foot, and the weight of the body transfers as the foot is placed down, not after it has set its position — in other words, the dancer makes an immediate, firm contact with the ground through her foot and leg as she is traveling forward. Today's ballet-trained modern dancers hold back their weight from the stepping leg, and they look careful, correct. But they don't have the quality of assurance, of oneness with the space into which they're going and the ground to which they entrust their progress. People don't walk like this naturally, but as Graham designed these women they couldn't be anything but American.

The One Who Speaks leaves for a little while and the One Who Dances does an introductory dance full of flights and rushes, sweeping arcs and circles, changes of speed and direction following rapidly one after the other. This ecstatic Emily wants to try everything, be everywhere; she no sooner arrives in one place than she thinks of something else to do. Her alter ego returns and, walking in their calm, expansive circles again, they regard each other, accepting of each other's differences. "I'm nobody," says the speaker. "Who are you? / Are you nobody too? / Then there's a pair of us." They come closer together and clasp each other by the arm, then around the upper back, still circling, still seeing each other. Again I have an image of strength and affirmation that is peculiarly American.

There begins a rhapsodic first section peopled by Emily's homely delights: the New England landscape and its wild creatures ("The

LETTER TO THE WORLD (*Graham, 1940*). *Pearl Lang and Jean Erdman in the 1970s. Photo by Martha Swope.*

robin's my criterion of tune / Because I grow where robins do"), the neighbor children ("Let us play yesterday —"), and four young couples dressed for a party. She imagines an older man ("Life is a spell so exquisite / That everything conspires to break it"), who greets both her speaking and dancing selves and then dances alone, rather violently and harshly, with big lunging jumps and clenched fists. This figure, later Emily's lover, plays several roles in her fantasy, as do most of the characters. In this first solo, he evokes her straitlaced father as well as a potential husband.

Dickinson's allusive poetry often leaves you unsure of the roles of the people she's addressing or referring to. She often speaks of herself as a child, addresses flowers or birds as the Divinity and also as relations of hers — "summer sister, seraph, / Let us go with thee!"[4] Graham has made that ambivalence — or deliberate mixing — visible in the character she calls the Ancestress even more than in the father/lover or creature/playmates. Just when Emily's enjoyment of the natural world and the company of its denizens seems most complete, she breathes, "I'm sorry for the dead today!" There's a pause, and both Emilys, sitting on the bench, stiffen and grow serious.

The dream turns into a "gay, ghastly holiday," with the dancing couples returning dressed in black and gray as if for a funeral. The One Who Speaks shouts, "It's coming! The postponeless creature!" and scuttles away, while from out of the shadows a hulking woman dressed in black bears down on the One Who Dances. Graham combined in this character all the grinding authority and unreasoning negation that the world's free spirits have ever encountered. She is death, tradition, parents, iron discipline and blind morality all at once. Even her costume combines all these notions — a completely unadorned long-sleeved dress that encases the straight lines of the upper body and conceals the legs, and a strange black head-covering lined in white to frame the face, like the bonnet of a nurse or a nun.

This behemoth advances with rigid, clumping steps, her arms spread stiffly in ominous parody of a crucifix. She chases after Emily, who can run faster but who is defeated by the other's size and power. The pursuer stands behind her prey and, without touching her, encircles her with arms set in angles; she clamps Emily inside this jail-embrace with devouring jerks, and Emily shudders each time as if she's being punched. When the Ancestress has subdued her, she takes her over to the garden bench, picks her up in her arms, sits down with her legs splayed wide apart, and rocks her with the same percussive tenderness, her whole body locked in a frozen, mothering shape.

This first encounter with the life-denying force of the Ancestress takes place during a long, macabre death sequence that is in many ways the obverse of the previous party scene, a quickly changing succession of images, some very clear, some dissolving almost before they form. The young ladies and gentlemen cross the space in somber reflection of their party dances and reception lines. A band plays a gospel hymn, "Blood of the Lamb," and they form into funeral processions, sometimes lifting Emily as the corpse, sometimes carrying the two little girls in her place. There are confused moments of dispersal, some of them with only a clattering sound from offstage — the women run all bent over with the arms curving behind them and back toward their bodies, black veils over their faces, looking like harpies or furies. The Lover comes back and tries to revive Emily by lifting her and setting her in motion, but before he succeeds, the dream rushes on, carrying him away with it.

I don't think Graham ever achieved a quality of nightmare as well as she did here, even though in many other dances she worked with fragmentary ideas, clashing dynamics and characters from different times and places. After the death sequence, the piece becomes much more focused, almost narrative, although it never loses the feeling of artificiality, never becomes realistic.

The One Who Speaks dissipates the death orgy at last by taunting the Ancestress with blasphemy: "The Bible is an antique volume, written by faded men at the suggestion of holy spectres. . . . In the name of the bee and of the butterfly and of the breeze. Amen!" Emily returns to her rambles in the countryside, dresses up in a sort of sailor outfit and dances a sort of hornpipe (The Little Tippler), plays hide-and-seek with an exuberant March. They're caught at their rowdy games by the Ancestress and March is banished, while Emily imagines herself as a decorous, most impossibly beautiful fairy queen ("Court is a stately place" . . .). March dances a brief reprise with one of the young girls; then the mood turns elegiac.

The two Emilys appear on the porch holding white veils above their heads and admiring the moonlight ("Lightly stepped a yellow star / To its lofty place"). A subdued yearning comes over the One Who Dances. "My river runs to thee: / Blue sea, wilt welcome me?" She thinks of infinities beyond even her rich imagination and offers herself to this unknown. Is it spiritual mystery that lures her, sexual and emotional fulfillment, or suicide? She dances a quieter but broader dance than her first solo, a dance that sends her forward in big searching, circling walks, that propels her in sweeping turns with one leg rising around her own axis, the outward arc extended by the flare of her dress.

Young men enter, bow to her, as if presenting a possibility, but she doesn't find it interesting. Then the Lover comes back. Although more mature than the other suitors, he seems less conventional — he doesn't wear gloves or a jacket, and he doesn't make the empty gestures demanded by etiquette. With the Ancestress watching from around the corner of the house, they address one another hesitantly; he is still full of conflict, she of doubt. The Ancestress poses herself against the Lover, and when Emily chooses him after a brief hesitation, the authority figure retires.

Their dance of love ("There came a day at summer's full / Entirely for me") is curiously restrained. It's as if even in her fantasy Emily cannot open herself to experience with another as fully as she can alone. After the spacious longing of her previous dance, she now becomes narrow in the body. She doesn't embrace the man, she permits herself to be embraced by him, from behind, in an echo of the Ancestress' clenching grip. Her motions become smaller, the phrase shorter, the gesture more tense. Clasping his hand, she keels over, corpselike, and is pulled upright. The dance culminates in a strange lift — the Lover collects Emily, who holds her body long and narrow and tight; he supports her stiff-armed, horizontally across his midsection, and whirls around with her very fast. This is another graphic example of Graham's puritanism — she portrays the moment of sexual ecstasy with rigid bodies; the dancers are prevented by the mechanics of the thing they're doing from giving in to their pleasure or letting go of their reserve.

When he puts her down they stand embracing for a moment. The Ancestress comes up behind them and, using her hand like a machete, chops them apart. Emily runs away and the Ancestress disposes of the Lover once and for all by marching him back to be swallowed up in the same void from which she first emerged.

There is a long dance of violent Old Testament grief. To an even, ticking sound, the One Who Dances moves one step, one gesture at a time. She lies on the floor on her side and slams her forearm, then one jabbing flexed foot, into the ground. The One Who Speaks, out of control for once, hurls herself across the stage. "Of course I prayed — And did God care?" The One Who Dances, still moving without connectedness, wrenches her body in all directions, beats on herself with her fists. "Mirth is the male of anguish!" Sitting on the bench she does a grotesque imitation of her Little Tippler dance. She tries to calm herself by pacing. "After great pain a formal feeling comes —" but her anguish is still not spent. "Soul! Wilt thou toss again!"

At last, she faces the Ancestress, wrestles with her, and breaks apart the viselike embrace. Released from everything that bound her, she spins lightly like a dervish. The One Who Speaks can imagine, "Hope is the thing with feathers / That perches in the soul," and "Glory is that bright tragic thing / That for an instant / Means dominion." They walk together for a few moments, in mutual support and completeness. Then the dancing Emily goes to the bench while the speaking Emily crosses and goes out saying "This is my letter to the world." The one who is left folds her hands and lowers her eyes, as though she is ready for eternity.

So much of Emily Dickinson and of *Letter to the World* is tied to the American experience. It seems in many ways more revealing than *Appalachian Spring*, even though that dance announces itself as a frontier documentary while *Letter* centers on one individual's life. The American spirit in *Appalachian Spring* is a familiar one — cherished but not particularly surprising. The portraits are not necessarily one-sided, but the sides have been explored before. It's a celebration, not a revelation.

Letter to the World goes inside a society, speaks of the way people lived. If Emily Dickinson in her later years did not appear in society, she had a lively traffic with it in her imagination. The spinster of good family and some education was supposed to be involved in town life, to carry out charitable work or teach school or organize social events. She was not supposed to retire to her garden and write poetry. How well Martha Graham must have known the scenarios of gentility; almost a hundred years later the daughter of a doctor in Santa Barbara, California, was supposed to enter the same kind of society.

If the weight of popular opinion went against women artists in the nineteenth century, the simple volume of mundane activity they were expected to engage in must also have sapped a lot of their creative drive. Emily Dickinson *could* live enfolded in a family that loved her, shielded her from responsibilities that she did not wish to undertake in the world; and in that family cocoon she was free not to grow up, not to regiment her fantasies, and not to expose her work to the judgment of the world. There is no fear of rejection in her "This is my letter to the world, / That never wrote to me" . . .[5] Graham, out in the world, had infinitely more to prove.

Deaths and Entrances (Martha Graham)

The party and funeral scenes of *Letter to the World* appear to have provided the working format for *Deaths and Entrances*. Graham wanted to explore the inner relationships of a family of isolated women artists. She was undergoing Jungian analysis at about that period, and she used the techniques of dream recall and symbolic objects to bring to the surface events that had long been buried in the psyche. *Deaths and Entrances is* a dream, with the unexplained shifts of scene, the juxtaposition of characters and times, the dramatic and inconclusive gesture that characterizes most dreams.

Critics have singled out this dance as one of Graham's best works, but I'm unable to grasp its totality. Most contemporaries remarked on Graham's own performance, and Edwin Denby, although conceding the dance's disordered structure, thought that Graham herself held it all together because of her "lucid concentration." As the Emily Brontë figure she was "a personage to whom all the actions on the stage are completely real."[6] I first saw the dance in its 1970 revival, with Mary Hinkson in Graham's role. The year 1970 was a particularly painful one for the Graham company; the choreographer was absenting herself more and more frequently from rehearsals, and in fact she was to leave for two years of illness and struggle before she resigned herself to not trying to dance anymore and resumed her leadership. *Deaths and Entrances* and *Every Soul Is a Circus,* reconstructed in the summer, and *Letter to the World,* done for the fall 1970 season at Brooklyn Academy, were brought back from record films, from memory, and with the coaching of former members of the company. Under those circumstances, *Letter to the World* stood up as a great work while *Deaths and Entrances* seemed ill defined.

I think Graham was working in *Deaths and Entrances* to depict a middle ground between the experience of specific characters and the universal experience that applies to us all. But the devices of her telling were too specific and the characters too individual to be recognized. In *Letter to the World* the components of the dream are already types — they have appeared before in the dance, they are identified verbally, and they act consistently and definitely in accord with their symbolic roles. In *Death and Entrances* the characterizations are less clear — even the three sisters, in the revival, were not that different from one another. You couldn't see what they meant to each other or why they caused things to happen, only that the three of them were shut up together and had nowhere to go when they got on each other's nerves except into their fantasy-past. Nor could you see why certain objects were brought on or moved from one special shelf to another with an almost religious care; that

DEATHS AND ENTRANCES (*Graham, 1943*). *Matt Turney, Phyllis Gutelius, and Mary Hinkson in 1970 revival. Photo by Martha Swope.*

is, you could see that they meant something to the characters, but not *what* they meant.

Graham must have realized the dilemma into which she had led herself. The great themes she wanted to dance about were essentially literary and intellectual. The link between herself and the cosmos existed perhaps too much in the mind for dancing on a stage. She knew what the connections were, and in the words of her program notes, her notebooks, the images she gave to her dancers, she could convey them. She might have made wonderful films, novels, plays. She was reaching for grandeur, for tragedy, for madness and fulfillment. I think she had the same large sense of herself and her time as Eugene O'Neill. But O'Neill had words at his disposal, and although he too resorted to myth occasionally, he was often able to tell his epic visions in the cadences and images of his own time, his own life agony. I don't see how Graham could ever have created a "Long Day's Journey into Night." Dance alone wasn't enough to tell the whole story, and Graham knew it.

So she turned from contemporary themes and characters to myth, legend, the Bible, and history. There she found her grand human themes already personified and set in parables that the audience could be expected to know. She gave them movement and stage action that spoke of her time and in that way told the audience of its own universality. The fact that she chose these legendary characters and that she danced the heroic roles herself for twenty-five years inevitably removed her, elevated her somehow, from the ordinary run of mortal artists. She became a myth herself. Her messages became Olympian, but not so recognizably American. She began to speak to us on a higher plane.

Hérodiade (Martha Graham)

The mirror was a potent symbol for Graham. Like the dream, it held out the possibility for self-knowledge, and Graham's mirrors always contained more than her characters first perceived about themselves. After *Hérodiade*, mirrors didn't actually figure in the dances, but it was frequently the business of the central character — the business of the dance — to find that hidden soul behind the character's deeds.

Graham originally called this work *Mirror Before Me*, then

changed it back to the title of Hindemith's music. The score had been written as a setting of the poem by Stéphane Mallarmé for a woman's spoken voice, but Graham dispensed with the words. I don't know if she used them initially and then found them uncongenial, but her dance is far different in tone from the symbolist fragments of Mallarmé's dialogue. They could not have sped the flow of the dance as Emily Dickinson's lines contributed to *Letter to the World*. Dickinson's concreteness, her compact, emotionally spare phrase, suited Graham's rigorous temperament; the sensuality and emotional indulgence of the Frenchman did not. Graham needed words to anchor her work, to give it limits, not to make it bigger or more elaborate; that she was quite capable of doing for herself.

In Mallarmé's Hérodias Graham found a character, a relationship, and a decisive moment. The heroine waits in an antechamber for an unknown event to happen to her, with a servant to help her prepare. I'm not sure whether the dance takes place before or after Hérodias has committed the bloody deeds for which she is known. Mallarmé seems to place her at the moment before her marriage; Graham could be seeing her just before her death, but it doesn't really matter. The deeds are within her, whether or not she has already done them.

The dance opens on an empty stage furnished by three Noguchi props: a bench of extremely eccentric shape, like an implement devised for a particular form of torture; a V-shaped stand with some material draped across its well; and a sculpture made of branches, cutouts, curves, and straight lines, jutting and closing in all directions. This last piece, the mirror, represents the complex, convoluted interior of the woman who is trying to subdue her inner turmoil, to smooth out her conflicts by means of ritual.

The woman enters from behind an upstage panel and begins pacing along a path that she sets for herself — straight down to the front of the stage, across to the mirror, back up the other side. Feet flexed, legs straight, one arm flung up to frame her head, fingers closed and cupped, she moves one step at a time, adamantly maintaining the shape of her body. She is like a prisoner with a long term, exercising just enough to keep herself sane. As she perambulates the space, she confronts the mirror, sometimes in an attitude of worship.

The woman dances a series of soliloquies, meditating perhaps on the evil fortune that awaits or that has already befallen her, or perhaps just taking stock of her own resources. Her attendant stands by, trying to offer comfort, to forestall the moment of departure. But the woman repulses these gestures and finally commands the maid to prepare her traveling vestments and leave. Alone, she makes one last obeisance to the manifold images of herself that she has so painfully exhumed, then decisively wraps herself in a black cloak and stands ready for her fate.

Much of *Hérodiade* is ambiguous, including the end. In the revival staged for Graham's New York season in late 1975, I saw Pearl Lang and Diane Gray dance the title role. Lang, a passive, rather bland performer at this stage in her career, seemed doomed from the start and resigned to her fate. When she put on the cloak, her motion was unmistakably one of suicide — she gathered it around herself and quickly pulled one end up so that she looked as if she were hanging. Gray made me aware that the woman's emotions were changing, her resolve strengthening, and as she put on the cloak and turned away from the mirror, it was clear she was in charge of herself, that she would confront whatever was to come without flinching. However the dancers interpret this work, the basic form of Graham's choreography gives us the opportunity to study two contrasting characters, to feel who they are without the literal events of a story to lead us.

How do we know, for instance, that the woman is capable of passion, even violence, while her attendant is much simpler and unavailing in her desires? The maid moves characteristically in a wide posture. She rocks in a squatting position with legs spread far apart; she makes a big enveloping circle with her arms; she moves her upper body in broad spirals. Her idea of center is huge; she could warm hemispheres. But the mistress doesn't want her compassion. In fact, that is the last thing she wants. Her narrowness is self-imposed; she must contain her feelings because they are dangerous. She works for linearity, but even her straightness is jagged; her elbows jut, her feet angle harshly into the floor. The shapes she makes are taut, tense, sometimes overstretched into inside-out bowings of the shoulders or the spine. She does odd, ritualistic tasks. She wraps one end of her skirt tightly around her pelvis and hips and confronts the mirror, as if vowing chastity.

As the maid touches her hair, her foot, she flings her away, insisting that she too rein in her feelings. She pushes her into the chair as if to get her out of the way. Later she sits on the chair herself, arching backward over one wing of it and hooking one leg forward over the other; she might be positioning herself for immolation. She gestures with one hand splaying out from her mouth for the nurse to get on with it, to begin the robing part of the ritual. Her dance becomes more violent, her body almost ripping at itself, arching, circling backward, and at the end of this, the nurse kneels and embraces her feet. At last she takes pity, lifts the woman who loves her, and makes her resume the ceremony.

The maid solemnly walks twice around Hérodias, touching her shoulders, her body, unfastening her dress, then slipping it off to reveal a white dress underneath. She takes the black cloth from the rack and lays it on the bench, then leaves Hérodias to carry out the final investiture.

The women's roles are further defined by how they use the space. *Hérodiade* takes place in limbo — a space neither inside nor outside, neither a room nor a hall nor a lobby, but any or all of these. Graham's dances never spelled out their locale; the abstract ones like *Primitive Mysteries* and *Dark Meadow* have no place attached to them except the conceptual places of the air and the ground. The more dramatic dances preceding *Hérodiade* are placed by emblematic props — the garden bench and porch in *Letter to the World*, for instance. With *Hérodiade*, the dance that is said to have initiated the "theater of Martha Graham," she conceived of space as a flexible entity, a nowhere that becomes somewhere in the minds of the dancers who move through it. Sculptural scenic elements, many of which could be manipulated by the dancers in the course of the action, become landmarks of geography, places where specific functions were carried out, or home bases identifying different characters. With *Hérodiade*, too, she symbolically announced her new theatrical emphasis by allowing a prop to obstruct the open space of the stage. Hérodias' bench occupied dead center.

But the two characters move through this landscape differently. The nurse spreads out in it, letting the compass of her movement and her attention fill it to its invisible boundaries. The mirror and the clothes rack are not awesome objects to her, she stands by them casually. The only time she gives a sense that her operating territory is constricted is when Hérodias forces her to play her part in the ritual.

Hérodias, on the other hand, moves in straight lines and

squared-off angles, the mirror her focal point. Whatever the size of this space is, the woman is conscious only of the discipline she works on herself, on the task she has come to do. In the area around the bench she is most vulnerable — perhaps it signifies rest to her, a letting down of her determination — and it is here that her greatest struggles take place. She refuses to rest. She concludes her ordeal treading the straight-and-narrow path. Her self-purification completed, the closed ceremonial track becomes a way out.

Dark Meadow (Martha Graham)

With *Hérodiade*, all the elements that were distinctive to Graham's theater had crystallized. The stage, an empty expanse, would have no real boundaries. Whatever objects we might find there at the rise of the curtain were at first no more than abstractions, forms that would reveal their purposes only in the context of the drama. The first view of a Graham setting tells you almost nothing; it's like coming upon the cave paintings of an undiscovered race. She seems to take great pleasure in showing us how these cryptic objects are intimately meaningful to the characters who own or inhabit them. By the end of the dance, hardly a prop or a set piece has not been used — often they are transformed — in the course of what happens to the characters. In a very sophisticated way she exploits her and our childish enjoyment at seeing things accumulate meaning or become other things.

The ultimate something-from-nothing theater event for Graham was *El Penitente*, based on a traveling street show, in which the dancers carried on their equipment, and sketchy but recognizable locales and occurrences were created, then wiped out before our eyes. Yet even in the stupendous *Clytemnestra*, her most ambitious stage undertaking, she managed, in addition to using fixed scenery, to create very large settings and functional props out of very spare materials. For example, two long spears served, at various times, as Agamemnon's sedan chair, his ship, the entrance to his chamber, and other things. Graham's ingenious use of costume follows the same idea. She designed most of the clothes herself — and not only are they created for her movement, and symbolically appropriate, they often have the capability of being changed or manipulated to dress the character in a new idea or to become themselves elements of movement.

As for the structure of the dance itself, Graham proceeds by short episodes that are quite self-contained and clearly separated from what precedes or follows them. Even in a dance as continuous as *Letter to the World*, the key events are not blurred or mixed in with any other action. We may not be able to decipher what these events mean, especially in the abstract works, but Graham doesn't equivocate about the fact that they are taking place. What in other forms of theater would be devices for calling attention to a particular scene Graham uses as a matter of course; subtlety of presentation is not her style.

This tendency, which had shown itself in Graham's work sometime before the mid-1940s, was ideally suited to the presentation of Greek myth, which was declamatory more often than it was conversational or symphonic. In a Graham dance, people make statements; people dance in small groups together; rarely, people engage in dialogues, but more frequently they move and answer one another in formal, choral patterns. Graham was always in a sense choreographing for herself — solos, multiples of one, or inextricable combinations of bodies where two dancers make one image. I don't think she could have conceived a scene that required many different contributing forms of action, like the ambush in *Billy the Kid*. Nor, because she ordinarily sees action in separate units of contrasting intensities, could she have built a dance that sails continuously along on rising and falling energies, like *Fancy Free*.

The other thing that distinguished Graham's theater from other forms was its unnaturalness. In a sense you can almost see Graham and ballet going in opposite directions with respect to the performer's role or attitude. American ballet was becoming more relaxed, incorporating into its formal language more of the rhythms and motivating energies that belong inherently to the way any person moves. Graham was trying to formalize natural impulses, to abstract human feelings into a set, expressive language.

Dark Meadow (Carlos Chavez) looks like a stone desert at the beginning. Four Noguchi set pieces are placed around the stage. Similar in shape, but graduated in height and squatness, they are all basalt in color and smooth in texture. The tallest, thinnest one, upstage center, has a sharp point and an edge down its length showing part of a white surface as the curtain opens. In 1946, when Freudian symbolism was neither unexpected nor obscure, some of the audience could probably read sexual significance into these shapes even before any dance action took place. It isn't necessary to discuss *Dark Meadow* exclusively in Freudian terms, but it is evident that Graham was making phallic references both in the scenery and in the dance itself. *Dark Meadow* is essentially a long fertility rite, and the barren landscape where it takes place is transformed by the end of the dance. The austere shapes have all blossomed with color, opened like pods, or sprouted flowery appendages.

Graham gave the dance four subtitles: Remembrance of ancestral footsteps, Terror of loss, Ceaselessness of love, Recurring ecstasy of the flowering branch. These may describe the episodes of the dance or they may merely be a poetic accompaniment to the whole progression. *Dark Meadow* is long and eventful, yet its quality is not narrative. Each new encounter is invested with great importance; there are virtually no transitional moments when the eye can rest or the mind can reflect. Like *Primitive Mysteries*, it is less a dance than a pageant or a service.

The dancers are a woman, One Who Seeks; another woman, She of the Ground; a man, He Who Summons; and a chorus of men and women, They Who Dance Together. The only character who changes in any expressive way during the course of the dance is the One Who Seeks, originally danced by the choreographer. The other figures are symbolic and always serve the same general function in reference to the central character.

She of the Ground is dressed in a tight-fitting tube of textured brown material that restricts her leg movements. She walks flat-footed, narrow, prevented by the tension in her lower body from venturing very far into space. Usually entering by the same path across the stage, she announces changes, seasonal perhaps, is the bringer of love, fruitfulness, death, and comfort. She is an earth mother, but an impersonal one. She has none of the tenderness and nurturing quality found in the nurse in *Hérodiade*, or even the enveloping solicitude of the Ancestress. She represents forces outside the province of man, the enduring cycle of nature, the infinite power to re-create that provides solace and hope to mankind.

The chorus invokes the life force springing from these natural phenomena — the urge to dance and to mate. Graham created for these four couples a wonderful series of duets, which they perform mostly in unison, that combine rhythmic drive with beautiful intertwinings of bodies. In these choruses we can see the germ of Graham's best choreography in her later life. When she was no longer able to move herself, she externalized what she may have had trouble carrying out with her own body; her dance became highly sensual, often erotic, especially for the men in her company, stressing the shape and tone of body surfaces, the flowing, curving possibilities of movement. But in *Dark Meadow* this sensuality was very carefully controlled; the couples don't act out love scenes, they portray the modes of love.

However often the One Who Seeks catches a glimpse of this idealized relationship, however strongly the desirability of procreation is impressed upon her, she does not participate in any such harmonious union. The man who will be her partner is presented, like so many of Graham's early heroes, as a strong, even overbearing figure. He is bent on mastering her, not seducing her — or at least that's what she thinks. Their courtship is a struggle of wills, their lovemaking is brief, and the woman is left alone at the end of the dance. He Who Summons makes no profound impression on the woman's inner life; he serves his function, which the woman recognizes as a necessary one though she may not welcome it.

Dark Meadow is about this woman's confrontation with love, and it begins with an incantation by the women of the chorus as the protagonist watches. These women wear one of Graham's most surprising costumes: scanty tops, bare midriffs, and slim, wraparound skirts, the materials in bold prints of brown, black, and white. With their hair drawn back at the napes of their necks, they seem not severe but clean and basic, figures Gauguin might have seen in Amagansett. They position themselves and move with a strange, archaic assurance; they don't seduce you by emphasizing anything, but — like the men who come to be their partners — they act as if their bodies belong to them. Their whole tendency is angular; curving or spiraling motion might blur their power. Typically they hold their hands cupped in right angles, the fingers pressed close together. The arms are straight or used with elbows and wrists bent into angles, and often the whole arm juts obliquely forward from the shoulder. Keeping these deliberately inelastic shapes, they often touch parts of their bodies or their partners' bodies, and the effect is to emphasize the part being touched or the gesture of touching, but not the subjective feeling that inhabits the contact.

DARK MEADOW (*Graham, 1946*). *Chorus with Matt Turney and Mary Hinkson in 1968 revival. Photo by Martha Swope.*

At the opening, the women stand in a circle. In silence, developing a group pulse, they begin a slow stamping dance, stepping to the side and then jumping flatfooted into the ground. Accelerating, the dance seems to spring out of the earth. They make a sharp little turn and gallop for a few steps around the circle, beating their cupped hands against their buttocks, then turn and go the other way. They open their arms, then, with an inward rotation from the shoulders, close the forearms so that the elbows are spread out and the cupped hands are pressed against the breastbone, palms out.

The drumming rhythm of the women's foot and hand beats seems to set the One Who Seeks in motion. She dances the first of several solos, making her way with large, swimming motions through the forest of stonelike forms. It seems to be a familiar path to her; she travels it more than once during the dance and always in the same direction until the last time, when the direction is reversed. She of the Ground enters, crosses the stage diagonally with a strange, stiff-legged walk, one arm angling upward in front of her, the other jutting down behind. Then she goes to the upstage prop and leads a man out from behind it.

The woman has withdrawn to her home base, the downstage-right rock, the lowest, roundest one, and, leaning on it, she watches the man dance. He makes a powerful display, hopping backward in circles, jumping and slapping his hands into the ground, leaping out of the ground with his body spread in the shape of an X and his hands fluttering. She of the Ground appears, doing another odd traveling motif like an invocation to air and earth. With the chorus watching — they have entered in a procession, the men carrying the women all folded up like bundles in front of their chests — the earth mother takes a black cloth and drapes it over one of the big props. The One Who Seeks kneels before it and slowly drags the cloth off, revealing a decoration that has been planted on top of the rock, a wooden cross with two red triangular flags hanging down from its arms. The man stands behind this quasi-altar, and the woman periodically returns to him as if touching a talisman, during the extraordinary sequence that follows.

Placing her feet on one end of the black cloth — it's very long, like a carpet — and holding the other end, she walks along it, wrapping it around herself in various ways. She crawls on it, smooths it, wraps herself in it totally and rolls in it, pulls it up and caresses it. Finally she propels herself across the stage by sliding her feet along in it, and when she arrives near her own rock she sits on the cloth, having positioned it so that she can drape it around herself like an Indian blanket. The earth mother, who has been watching, upends the woman's rock to show that the flat side, which has been resting on the floor, is white. The woman lifts her upper body, still sitting cross-legged, and raises the cloth high above her head. Four chorus men take it out of her hands and put it on top of another set piece.

The woman goes to her rock while the chorus does its most inciting dance, full of pounding jumps, the men at one point lying on their sides and hitting the ground with their hands. He Who Summons pulls the woman from her refuge and dances in pursuit of her. Kneeling, he holds her waist and she pulls away. He stalks her with big steps and outstretched arms, and she flees. He catches her and stands behind her, stamping, holding her under the arms as she kneels. At last she escapes and throws herself in a crouching position against the flat of her upended rock, and the man falls massively from one leg, the other extended behind him, landing braced on his arms above the woman's folded-up body.

She of the Ground comes and takes the black cloth from the pillar where it was left, and goes off tossing it into the air and catching it in an embrace close to her chest. This seems to signal a lifting of the oppressive aspects of the courtship. Three couples appear briefly and leave, walking briskly side by side with a step that resembles the earth mother's first, stiltlike march. The man dances another solo, similar to his first, with big flinging jumps and fluttering hands, but this time his body seems less rigid and he ends with a series of spirals and twisting falls to the floor.

The woman, still apparently fearful of him, watches this from underneath her rock, which she has tilted forward and holds above her. At the end of the man's dance he comes to the rock, tilts it on end again, and stands by it with the woman as the four men from the chorus bring mysterious emblems attached to white sticks and plant them in the white face of the rock. The man then straddles the rock with one leg while the woman dances a solo that ends with the acquiescent gesture of bending her whole body forward and extending both arms to the man. They dance briefly together, the man lifting her from behind as he did earlier, under the arms, and whirling around with her very fast.

They exit together, and She of the Ground appears wearing a voluminous green cape. She turns the downstage-left prop around, revealing a bright yellow surface. Holding the edges of the cape, she wraps her arms around the phallus-prop, which is about the same height as she is, enveloping it as she slides down to the ground. Then she makes obeisance to the prop and goes out with spiraling turns that send the cape swirling out in huge arcs around her. The woman returns alone, still disturbed, and dances with jerky, angular jumps and sharp contractions, back turns initiated by a whipping circle of the head, two-footed jumps, and a running circle with her body bent over and her cupped hands slapping her hips. She gestures often to the ground, then kneels and turns her whole body into a hollow block, as if she'd been flattened by a giant's kick, her pelvis contracted and her arms jutting forward from the shoulders, palms cupped and facing out.

The earth mother comes in holding a bowl, which she presents to the woman. The woman takes a plum-colored cloth from the bowl, holds it for a moment — in some recent performances the dancer has mimed washing her hands with it — and puts it back. Margaret Lloyd, who assigned symbolic meaning to many of the props and actions in *Dark Meadow*, said this signified the menses,[7] but it could be any purifying or soothing influence, because after the earth mother takes it away, squatting on her heels and taking tiny, fast trundling steps while holding the bowl in her outstretched hands, the longest and most satisfying series of duets begins.

First the chorus couples. Their dance is more like a set of poses — a sort of Kamasutra — in which the pairs of men and women act as one. The positions are intimate, protective, supportive, yet for some reason not precisely erotic. The body shapes and contacts are not representational; the couples do not embrace face to face. As in their earlier dances, their shapes — now their whole bodies in addition to their limbs — echo and complement and conform to those of their partners, but their formality, their precision, is never relaxed. The men carry the women out hanging back to back on their outstretched arms, the women with their arms and legs wound around the men's bodies. This is the most completely yielding permutation of the principal man and woman's early encounter in which he stood behind her and held her under the arms.

She of the Ground brings a sort of flowering branch, inserts it in the top of the now-yellow phallic piece, and leaves after kneeling and bowing to it. The principal man and woman now dance their final duet. They enter from opposite sides of the stage. They do not embrace frontally either, but their contacts are more varied, more equally matched than before. They kneel on one knee side by side, clasping each other's arms, and advance together by bringing one leg, then the other, around from back to front. He lifts her and whirls her in a version of the chorus' last exit, but she does not rest symmetrically against him; one arm and one leg reach away as he spins. They kneel again, shoulder to shoulder, almost their only really close bodily contact, and after a sort of nuzzling gesture, the man rolls out from the embrace and offstage, with subsiding impulses, while the woman continues her knee walk alone.

The chorus passes through again, the men carrying the women in positions of stylized abandon. She of the Ground then leads the One Who Seeks in a procession through the props in the opposite direction from her accustomed one. They stand in front of the tallest white phallus, where the man first appeared. He steps out from behind it, then retires, so that only his arm is visible, rising straight out to the side and echoed by a branch with three green arrows that arcs out of the prop. The woman comes toward the audience, swaying and arching her torso and describing decorative circles with her hands as the curtain falls.

Errand into the Maze (*Martha Graham*)

Despite the cosmic scope of *Dark Meadow*, Graham had not yet perfected a form that would have both universal human significance and popular intelligibility. *Dark Meadow* was and still is strange, cryptic, its action traceable to the subconscious regions. The dances that offered clearer narrative or more identifiable characters, *Letter to the World* and *Appalachian Spring*, might be considered a bit lightweight — "feminine" — since they concerned women's lives and feelings. Their drama was not grand or aggressive; they didn't deal with power or even sex, except in subtle forms. If there is such a thing as the American frontier mentality, our national entertainments certainly manifest it: America is not the home of circuses, mime, fairy tale, fantasy, courtly pageant, or drawing room comedy, but of the Western and the cops-and-robbers thriller.

Martha Graham was moving into the blood and thunder business, into territory the power-oriented, male-dominated society could appreciate. She may not have done this consciously. She was still probing the female psyche, and her main characters continued to be women until she stopped dancing. But her attention fastened increasingly on the large dramatic themes of literature, the dilemmas and conflicts that had occupied writers and philosophers through the ages. The personal equity, her own response, was no longer the subject of her dances; it became instead a pigment with which she repainted the mythology that had always been transmitted to us by men.

Graham's Greek cycle, by which term I also include those dances she drew from Judeo-Christian tradition, from history and from literature, combined her insights into human behavior, her sense of ritual and abstraction, and her ability to create fascinating theater. Less than six months after *Dark Meadow*, *Cave of the Heart* had its première. In it she contained her visions successfully within a recognizable story, that of Medea and Jason, and the cycle was begun.

The duet *Errand into the Maze,* choreographed a year after *Dark Meadow,* was another backward look at personal sources, possibly her last except for some solos in the 1950s that have not survived. It was the last dramatic dance in which Graham invented the character she was to play; after that, her personal attraction for the heroines she chose had to be subordinated to the legendary facts already known about them. Although *Errand* was suggested by a myth, no character in the original story corresponds to the role Graham created. Once again she was divided between identifiable myth and exploring her own subconscious, and once again the ambiguity of her own intention resulted in a more unusual, more open work.

From its first performances, *Errand* carried a program note referring to the legend of Theseus, who went into the maze to battle the Minotaur, leaving Ariadne's thread in a trail behind him so he could find his way out again. The two characters in the dance, however, are not named. The male dancer originally wore a bull's mask and later a masklike make-up, and he had to keep his arms wound around a massive yoke across his shoulders; he was clearly the Creature of Fear that Graham referred to. But the woman was less specific. Although audience and critics tried to explain her as a counterpart to Theseus or even Ariadne, I think Graham had neither character in mind; her protagonist in this dance was any woman who had to encounter this monster. To me, the progatonist must be a woman, not a metaphorical hero, not a stand-in in women's clothes for some Greek warrior-king. I think *Errand into the Maze* is a dance about sexuality, although a case could be made that the Creature of Fear is a personification of death, oppression, madness, even censorship — anything that threatens the individual's identity and that it takes courage to turn away.

As the dance opens, the woman is standing upstage, in a place that belongs neither to the Noguchi shapes in the sky at stage left nor to the rope laid out on the floor in a wavy line leading to a bleached, crotch-shaped sculpture downstage right. The woman has her arms wrapped around her midsection and is cowering in a pelvic contraction. She keeps her body shielded this way except to turn periodically and gesture with one forearm toward the wings. In place, she does a little dance in which her attention shifts from some inner anxiety that makes her shudder and writhe and lose track of where she is, to the premonition of danger that keeps her checking a particular place to her right. The woman is restricted at the beginning, closed off. She sees that it's possible to operate in a wider sphere but is denied access to the outside by her inner fear. This fear is connected with sex, and the woman prepares herself for her journey with a gesture of spreading her hands open across her pelvis.

Seeing the rope on the floor, she picks her way along it, her legs so narrowly close together that they often cross as she follows the twists and turns of the path. When she comes to the branching structure that is the heart of the maze, she steps inside and can expand for the first time, opening her pelvis and swinging her leg in figure eights, as if she could be safe there in the depths — of what? Herself, perhaps. But while she's there, the Creature enters for the first time. The fact that he appears when the woman has withdrawn into her most private refuge indicates to me that he is a product of her own psyche, not something that threatens her from the outside. Graham emphasized the relationship between the woman and her enemy by designing his costume with the same zigzag motif as hers, but with the colors reversed.

With his hands and arms immobilized, the Creature has a dimin-

ERRAND INTO THE MAZE (*Graham, 1947*). *Clive Thompson and Matt Turney. Photo by Martha Swope.*

ished power and doesn't seem a formidable adversary for the woman, but she thinks he is. He stalks her around the stage with big, flex-footed, monster steps, looms up behind her with his clutching arms. She pushes him away and he rolls out. After a few moments she senses him coming back and quickly retraces her path into the maze. When she gets inside, she frantically pulls the rope in after her and slings it back and forth from one side of the opening to the other until it creates a sort of fence between herself and the outside. Just as she finishes the Creature appears again.

By this time the woman knows that her nemesis can get to her even when she's retreated to supposed safety. When she desperately flees to the stronghold and puts up the barricade, she may be acting out of old instinct, but she probably also realizes that she's locking herself *in* with him, and that the decisive struggle will have to take place here. Again taking the whole stage for the inner chamber the woman has established, the Creature pursues her, steps over her writhing body the same way she stepped over the rope, carries her on his back. She pushes him away again and, after a brief return to her leg swings, she works herself up for the final encounter, doing a dance of pounding, wrenching anticipation.

When the Creature jumps behind her she's ready, and for the first time she meets him face to face. Climbing onto his thighs, she finally gets above him and pushes him down into a backbend, from which he drops to the floor and gives up. She goes to her doorway and takes down the rope. A great calm seems to well up inside her as she leans against one side of the entrance and rubs her hand along its surface. Leaning out, she swings one leg and one arm in wide figure eights, as if swimming through a substance suddenly become light. Finally she steps out altogether and comes forward to the audience, opening her arms.

Once again, perhaps most decisively of all, we see the Graham protagonist coming to terms with her psychological adversary and beating back its advance with her own forceful action. Once again she battles a male who is limiting her freedom to operate, and for Graham I think that threat always implies seduction. It isn't the man's physical strength she fears; she can match him at that or defeat him with her superior wiles. What terrifies her is the man's sexual attraction and the knowledge that yielding to it will put her in a subordinate position. The loss of her own power represents an ultimate humiliation to her. Graham sees the woman who ends up in a subservient sexual relationship as either a pitiful victim, like Jocasta, or as one entitled to become an outlaw, who can violate the morals of society, like Medea and Clytemnestra. This may not constitute a "healthy" or accommodating attitude toward sex. It may indicate that Graham harbored sexual conflicts. But her way of representing her position and the alternatives open to her anticipated some of the most radical feminist ideas of a generation later.

Night Journey (Martha Graham)

Now Graham had found the form. After *Cave of the Heart* and *Night Journey* her achievements lay less in personal revelation than in defining her techniques, in manipulating her theater devices to a variety of ends. The "Greek" works included, among others, *Alcestis* (1960), *Phaedra* and *Samson Agonistes* (1962), *Circe* (1963), *Lucifer* and *The Scarlet Letter* (1975). In the evening-length *Clytemnestra* (1958) the form found its most grandiose realization. Using these devices in various combinations and proportions, she also made lyric works such as *Diversion of Angels* (1948) and *Canticle for Innocent Comedians* (1952), and lighter pieces like *Embattled Garden* (1958) and *Acrobats of God* (1960). Of the tragic works, I will concentrate on *Night Journey* because it is early enough to still be inventive, and yet it has a greater range and complexity of characters than *Cave of the Heart*. Also, an excellent film of the complete dance can be viewed repeatedly for study.

Night Journey is a wonder of craftsmanship. In recent years it has reentered the repertory, with Diane Gray or Pearl Lang in the leading role. Rudolf Nureyev made his celebrated debut as Oedipus in the winter 1975 season and proved at best a curiosity compared to the men in the Graham company, who understand the balanced interrelationship of movement, acting, and staging in which the works are forged. Fortunately the dance was filmed by Graham in 1961, with Bertram Ross, Paul Taylor as Tiresias, and Helen McGehee as the leader of the chorus. Graham's advanced age limited her performance, but she does, after all, play her leading man's mother, so that her condition here is less disturbing than it was in some of the other roles she took at the end of her dancing career.

Night Journey — at least in its casting since 1973 and in the 1961 film — is a tragedy of several characters, not only an exploration of the mind of the female lead. It does begin and end with the queen castigating herself, trying to stave off and finally acceding to inevitable destruction. But the dance in between is a beautifully posed web of four contending forces — all of them except the stolid Tiresias swinging from adulation to agony, from triumph to despair, in relation to the other characters. The work is also superbly condensed, telling the entire story in about six episodes. A person with no knowledge of the Oedipus legend but with a sensitive eye for movement could, I think, understand the basic situation and follow what is happening. With the exception of the opening and closing scenes, all of the action in *Night Journey* involves multiple characters. There are no extended descriptive solos as in *Letter to the World* or *Appalachian Spring*.

After we have seen Jocasta with the prophetic rope suspended between her hands, the blind seer Tiresias enters, making his presence felt by thrusting his staff into the ground at each step. Lifting the staff in a huge arc, he hooks the rope in her hands and pulls it away from her. It is a preview of the gesture with which he later separates the lovers.

Jocasta skitters away, looks helplessly at the sky, then pitches forward to the floor as the chorus of women enters. While she paces back and forth, they dance briefly, their movements sometimes echoing in extreme form the gestures of the main characters. Tiresias stands on a stool downstage right, facing the audience, and the chorus files past him one by one with pleading gestures that he ignores. He goes to stand by an uptilted, skeletal platform that serves as Jocasta's bed. Hunched into his voluminous cloak and leaning forward on his staff, he stands ominously immovable in the shadows while Jocasta dances like a trapped insect. She reels from one side of the stage to another, butting up against the landmarks of her anguish — the bed and the low stool where Oedipus seduced her. She clutches at her breasts, her abdomen, her arms, making almost impatient little up-and-down motions of one foot in recognition and revulsion of her own desire.

She rushes at Tiresias, clutches at his staff, struggles with him briefly, as if she could prevent the destiny he brings. But he shakes her off, lifting the staff high above his head and throwing her into a back fall. She weaves back and forth again, more ineffectually than before, and at last she leans on the bed, exhausted. She climbs onto the bed, her head toward the audience, her lower body closed and twisted. Tiresias leaves.

The Chorus, a group of six women and a leader, ushers in Oedipus. Waving branches of black laurel leaves, they treat him like a hero, a king, and he puffs himself up in broad, arrogant posturings. When he determines to mount a series of graduated low platforms leading to Jocasta's bed, the leader of the Chorus tries to stop him, but again fate refuses to be denied. Drawing his flexed foot high with each step, he marches up — the chorus members slapping their laurel branches on each stair under his foot. (This gesture, which does not appear in the 1961 film, is one of the more noticeable changes among the modifications that constantly appear in Graham's work from season to season. I think it is consistent with the increasingly theatrical tendency of the present Graham company.)

Oedipus lifts Jocasta off the bed and carries her downstage on his shoulder, seating her on the stool. He then proceeds to woo her in the way most Graham heroes do, with a florid display of his physical strength and sexual potency. He doesn't take any pains to flatter her or make more than perfunctory tender advances. He assumes her capitulation, even though — being a queen and widowed — she may require special treatment.

His dance is full of stomping, punching, calling-attention gestures. He jumps with flexed feet in place or to the side, slapping his hip as he lands. Elbows out, he expands his upper body, holding one fist across his chest, then swivels from the waist without changing his pose, asserting and showing all at once. He steps on the bench behind her and, still maintaining his heroic upper body attitude with an upraised fist and expanded chest, lifts one leg as if to march right over her shoulder, but instead lowers it in front of her body, the flexed foot locked over her abdomen. Standing behind her still, he swings his leg up and, leaning on one of her hands for support, he falls above her and kisses her. Then he comes down from the bench and resumes his display, now making even bigger attention-getting flourishes with his cape, a strange, hip-length garment the shape of which is a mystery. Swirling the cape around himself as he turns, almost brandishing it at her, he thrusts his legs, then his arms, through its changing apertures. He wraps it around and around his arm, then, by some ingenious maneuvering, extricates himself from it and winds it around in a new shape.

Every new form of the cape opens a new vessel into which he drives a phallic limb.

Through all this Jocasta sits on the stool holding a laurel branch in each hand. She never takes an active part in the seduction, although sometimes she lifts the branches and holds them imperiously in the form of an X over her head or extends one at arm's length toward Oedipus. In alternation with these commanding gestures, she opens both arms and lowers them to her sides about a foot away from her body. It is when she is thus exposed that Oedipus pounces on her from behind. Once, in a particularly brutal action, he grabs her around the breasts. He approaches her from the front while she's holding the branches assertively, crossed above her head, and falls in a slow, flex-footed arabesque until his head is in her lap, and as he does this she lowers her arms voluntarily.

After this, she capitulates fully, but not before showing off a little for him. With the pitching-forward fall that in this dance in particular seems to signify the utmost homage or submissiveness, she places one of the laurel branches at Oedipus' feet. In an older woman's vain imitation of a young girl's coquetry, she does a series of exotic, angular poses based on Balinese dance. On the stool again, she taunts him, holding the branch beside her hip and sitting in a twisted, closed position. She opens her lower body and brings the branch, like a fan, coyly across her body, then quickly closes pelvis and knee and takes the branch away. Going to him then, she pitches forward at his feet. He swoops over slowly and takes the branch she has offered him.

Finally he embraces her, wrapping both of them in his cape. They dance together inside it for a moment — with his strutting steps and her mincing ones. Then the chorus leader runs in, sees what has happened, and runs out again, covering her eyes. In this interval, Oedipus and Jocasta have gone to the foot of the bed and divested themselves of the cape. Their lovemaking duet is an almost acrobatic series of poses, taken slowly and standing in place, during which they alternate roles: first they embrace as lovers, then Jocasta cradles and supports Oedipus as if he were a baby.

They go up onto the bed, where they find Jocasta's rope, and begin entwining and entangling themselves in a series of erotic poses. The Chorus enters at the beginning of this sequence, covering their eyes with both hands. They dance demonically, tearing the movement out of their viscera, then suddenly holding them-

NIGHT JOURNEY (*Graham, 1947*). *Chorus with Bertram Ross and Ethel Winter. Photo by Martha Swope.*

selves still in distorted shapes. Each time they stop, the audience's attention shifts, cinematically, from their violent motion to the pair on the bed, and we find them each time in a new entanglement suggesting sexual abandon and also recalling the maternal embracings of the earlier part of the duet.

The dance grows more and more intense. Jocasta leads Oedipus down from the bed, curving protectively over his body. They each hold one end of the rope and walk with it in opposite directions until it is stretched as far as it will go. They drop it. Oedipus immediately picks her up and holds her upside down over the rope, which she grasps again in both hands, an inversion of her first pose in the dance. Their passion not yet spent, they return to the foot of the bed and the Chorus continues its dance of agony. When this ends, the Chorus is on the floor. Oedipus and Jocasta are standing enmeshed in the rope but pulling away from each other, each holding one end of it so they don't fall. This is an amazing image, encompassing the inextricable relationship in which they are involved and the paradox into which they have allowed themselves to fall despite the warnings of Tiresias and the Chorus. Now they are so knotted that the thing that is holding them together is the same thing that's about to pull them apart. Their umbilical cord is about to be cut for the second time, this time to cause their destruction instead of their survival.

As they pose there, Tiresias enters, hurling himself onto his staff and jumping like someone in a horrible athletic contest. He understands that his prophecy is being fulfilled — that Oedipus, in marrying the queen, has unknowingly committed incest. Letting his stick fall into the arms of a chorus member sitting on the floor, he wheels and falls around the stage, crawls on his knees, drags himself along the floor by the arms, then rolls with big flinging motions back to the chorus. Taking back the stick, he takes a few small, pogo-stick steps. Then he whirls his cloak over his head with the stick, shrouding his whole upper body with it, goes around to the upstage side of the bed, climbs up on it, and approaches the bound couple while slowly raising his stick in the air. Then, with the accelerating finality of an executioner's ax, he steps off the end of the bed and brings both his stick and his flexed foot down between them. The gesture has immense resonance — it is like Tiresias' earlier snatching of the rope from Jocasta, and it also recalls Oedipus' triumphant subdual of the queen with his foot. It is the same violent idea with which the Ancestress separated Emily and her lover in *Letter to the World*. The maternal/conjugal rope turns to spider silk under Tiresias' blow, and Jocasta and Oedipus topple as it ceases to support them.

Here and in *Letter*, Graham represented what is really a psychological turning point — Emily's decision to abide by tradition, Oedipus and Jocasta's realization of their predicament — with a vivid physical image. In both cases she put the fateful gesture in the hands of a symbolic character, and the action itself takes the form of the severing of an imaginary bond — the breaker-apart doesn't actually attack or touch the victims in any way. In *Night Journey* the power of this image corresponds to the mounting stream of verbal revelations that culminate in Oedipus' discovery of the truth in Sophocles' play. In one metaphorical stroke, Graham created both the moment of revelation and its consequences. I should mention that, in the film, this gesture too is less theatrically grand than it is in live performances now. Tiresias merely touches the rope and it begins to give. By the time he steps off the bed, Oedipus and Jocasta have fallen.

With his staff he finds Oedipus' cape on the floor, and he contemptuously sweeps it away like an unclean thing. Then he leaves with the same step as in his first appearance. Everyone is now crouched on the floor. Jocasta is the first to rise. She wanders back and forth a few times, then climbs slowly onto the bed. Oedipus stands and thrusts the rope away from himself with revulsion. The Chorus, now turned against the king, gathers at the foot of the platform. Oedipus mounts it — his disastrous marriage bed, his pinnacle of power — and falls into their arms. They lower him to the floor and leave, stepping over his body, a final degradation. Oedipus goes to Jocasta, lying on the platform, first pitching down over her body with a kiss. Again Graham invents a wonderfully ambiguous gesture: he stands above her and reaches out toward her throat with both hands. For a second one isn't sure whether he's going to strangle her or kiss her, but he does neither. He grasps a large brooch on her dress and tears it off, then in one ghastly move jams it against his eyes, blinding himself. He backs away, and then, with one hand covering his eyes, staggers out sideways across the back of the stage. His other hand gropes in front of him, passing over the low platforms upon which only a short time before he had ascended to the throne.

Jocasta now has only to complete the tragedy. Symbolically she disrobes, taking off her outer golden garment. She finds the rope and holds it above her head as she did at the opening of the dance. Then quickly she winds it once around her neck, pulls both ends, and falls to her back. Tiresias clumps across the stage once more as the curtain falls.

Some of the symbolic props and movement ideas in *Night Journey* come from Sophocles' play, the idea of seeing and not seeing, for instance. Tiresias, the doom figure, is blind, and so is Oedipus after his error has been made known; but the chorus members keep covering their eyes to avoid seeing the tragedy they know is taking place. In the play, Oedipus keeps trying to find out the truth and equating it with improving his ability to see, and Graham recurrently brings this ironic imagery back to us in movement.

Near the beginning of his seduction dance, Oedipus wraps his head in his cape. This is usually a phallic image with Graham, but here it also refers to his inability to see Jocasta's true identity. At his most dangerous moment, he is most blind. Similarly, at the end of the dance, Tiresias swathes himself in his cloak, reinforcing his own blindness, which is really the power to know the truth, just before irrevocably breaking the bond between the lovers. Jocasta doesn't engage in these visual ambiguities except as she and Oedipus begin their love duet. Once or twice she passes her hand in front of her eyes as if seeing a vision, as if this young hero who has carried her off reminds her of a son lost in infancy — which of course he is.

With the skill of a poet, Graham created movement images that kept accumulating and regenerating themselves in different forms. She not only presents us with the simple meaning of a rope as both umbilical cord and the instrument of suicide. The dancers use the rope and the gestures associated with it to stand for a thread of destiny. We see it first stretched between Jocasta's hands as she contemplates her own death. Tiresias achieves the same position, only magnified, more ominous, when he thrusts away her protest with his staff. When the lovers begin their lovemaking on the bed, Oedipus looms over Jocasta, holding the rope up between his hands, and at the climax of this sequence they take almost the width of the stage to stretch the cord to its fullest.

Each character in *Night Journey* — the Chorus acts as one character, with slight variations by the leader — is given a whole movement vocabulary that distinguishes him or her from the others. Oedipus with his rigid torso, strutting, stamping legs, and crude, peremptory energies. Tiresias, who sees most and least, takes up huge amounts of space when moving or standing still, yet never becomes personally engaged in the tragedy. The Chorus, reflecting, foretelling, reacting to the events, always in extreme body shapes and percussive energies. Jocasta is the only character who is not clear; she's indecisive, passive, doomed from the start. Perhaps in the weakness of this heroine can be seen the first faltering of Graham as a choreographer, even at the moment when her work was most completely achieved.

Balanchine's America

> Four abstract themes, all moving equally and har-
> moniously together like a fugue would convey the
> significance of democracy far better than would
> one woman dressed in red, white and blue, with
> stars in her hair.
>
> — *Doris Humphrey* [1]

*F*OR ALMOST A DECADE, from the end of his association with
the Metropolitan Opera in 1937 to the initiation of Ballet Society
in 1946, George Balanchine was virtually without a company. So
strong was his creative drive that he was able to concentrate his
energies and produce even when his working situation was unstable, and during that interval he made movies in Hollywood,
choreographed operas and Broadway musicals, and made ballets
whenever he had the opportunity. Besides setting *Concerto Barocco*
and *Ballet Imperial* (*Tchaikovsky Concerto No. 2*) for his own dancers, with Alexandra Danilova he did his first version of the Petipa classic *Raymonda* for the Ballet Russe de Monte Carlo in 1946.
He also managed to choreograph *Night Shadow* (*La Sonnambula*) for
the Ballet Russe, *Palais de Cristal* (*Symphony in C*) for the Paris
Opera, and *Theme and Variations* for Ballet Theater.

These ballets, as well as *Apollon Musagète, Serenade,* and *Jeu de
Cartes* and the first *Baiser de la Fée* — the latter two done on an all-
Stravinsky ballet evening during the American Ballet's tenure at the
Met — might all be said to come primarily out of Balanchine's past.
Not that they weren't original or modern. From what I can piece
together of Balanchine's total achievement, his pre–Ballet So-
ciety/New York City Ballet works were already liberated in terms of

form and sensibility; these distinctions he had shown in his work before leaving Europe. But with *Four Temperaments* he also liberated the dancer's body, and this proved decisive in establishing him as a choreographer of and for Americans.

After years of cultivating American ballet dancers, demonstrating that this training could be accomplished far away from the European academies, he was now able to take chances with the dancers' line, succession, attack, phrasing, weight, and balance, yet not have them be mistaken for anything but ballet dancers. Writing about *Jeu de Cartes* in 1940, Edwin Denby spoke about Balanchine's "profounder choreographic gift. His steps no matter where derived are steps that a ballet dancer specifically can do and do best . . . He seems never to violate the real nature of a dancer's body . . . that no matter how odd the movement required, the dancer still remains himself, and does not congeal to an impersonal instrument."[2]

If a major characteristic of American dance is its flexibility of form, then Balanchine began making American dances as soon as he came here or even before. In his first years here he was compelled to work in a variety of media; he served many entertainment masters, and thus gained another American trait, eclecticism. Without ever being untrue to the classical aesthetic, he could graft onto the classical vocabulary the trademark steps or attitudes of show biz, region, period, or social occasion. This practice of incorporating particularized character gesture had been employed throughout the whole history of ballet to lend local color or exoticism to the spectacle. The classical Russian period of Balanchine's background produced the slave dances in the second act of *Raymonda*, the fairy tale divertissements in *Sleeping Beauty*, the mazurka, polonaise, and other national entertainments of *Swan Lake*'s third act. By the twentieth century, whole environments were being re-created, like the Shrovetide fair of *Petrouchka* and the Sultan's harem of *Scheherazade*.

Balanchine's way of using these elements was very different from the prevailing trend, which was operating here very successfully through the 1930s and 1940s via the character ballets of Léonide Massine as well as through the choreographers associated with Lincoln Kirstein in the Ballet Caravan. Except when he was deliberately reconstructing an old ballet like *The Nutcracker*, Balanchine has seldom attempted to re-create character in toto. He has often flavored whole ballets with the gestures of a period — *Who Cares?* and *West-*

ern Symphony are examples — or inserted these gestures into works that otherwise had no direct reference to period — the Charleston steps in *Four Temperaments,* for instance — but he didn't bother with the laborious business of making up a libretto to justify the period or contriving an excuse to introduce exotics into a straight classical work. Some of his early ballets do appear to have done this, but either they haven't survived, like *Jeu de Cartes* (1937), or they've come down to us, like *Apollo* and *Four Temperaments,* without the elaborate costumes and settings in which they were first presented. The very lucidity of these works now, in practice clothes, confirms my impression that Balanchine's mind is almost always on dancing, not on spectacle, even when for box office reasons he does a Production.

But there's another, more unusual and profound way that Balanchine uses "character." He can infuse the classical vocabulary with the energies, the psychokinetic quirks, and the motivations that make movement look individual before it crystallizes into a style. Modern dancers were all trying to catch the feeling qualities of the dance or the character who is dancing, but few ballet choreographers have been able to do it — I think primarily of Tudor and Eliot Feld among the classicists. In ballet it's much more common to invent signature themes that identify a character, like Coppélia's stiff-legged doll walk or Petrouchka's floppy jumps. These do have a feeling-tone, but they are special, set apart again from the business of classical dancing. Balanchine can project this feeling into ballet steps. He doesn't point out the way in which the audience is supposed to identify the strangeness it sees. There's no label of costume or story, not even as indistinct a clue as the footnotes "It was spring" or "She wore perfume" that acompany the dancers' names in Tudor's *Dim Lustre.*

Nor does Balanchine use the body expressively quite as the modern dancers did. The torso may bend but it isn't truly articulate. The dancer may go off center but she always returns to center; vertical alignment is a constant that can be violated but always exists as a sort of touchstone; to depart from it at all becomes an expressive statement. Balanchine's dancers may on occasion drive their body weight into the ground; they may kneel, fall, go barefoot. But they don't move heavily, they don't use their groundedness in the ways modern dancers do. The arms and hands may be distorted, but they are always in play; the limbs count, a lot, whereas they don't always matter in modern dance. For these and many other reasons, we can't confuse Balanchine's modernism with modern dance. He doesn't even borrow verbatim from the modern dance language as some contemporary ballet choreographers do — Gerald Arpino, Glen Tetley, and John Butler, for instance. Yet he was obviously influenced by the existence of a dance form that tried to interpret its time. With the establishment of Ballet Society, Balanchine perhaps felt that his trial and wanderings in America were ending, that with his own company he could settle down and be American. Or perhaps he was doing as he had always done — picking up the currents in which he lived, breathing the life of the moment into a form endowed by centuries.

Four Temperaments (George Balanchine)

When I first saw *Four Temperaments* (1946) (it has at times been called *The Four Temperaments*) it was early in my balletgoing career, and I couldn't really see what relationship the four variations of the dance had to the four medieval humors with which they were subtitled. I still think the ballet has more to do with its fine Hindemith score than with any psychological interpretation of melancholy, sanguine, phlegm or choler, although I see more associations now. Reviewing the ballet when it was new, Edwin Denby said, "It appears to have the dispassionate ferocity of a vital process."[3]

Perhaps because of the expressionism of modern dance, where emotions were supposed to make some sort of appearance in the dance fabric, we are conditioned now to see an actual sad dance when the dance is called "Melancholic." And if the movement doesn't "read" sad, the dancer is supposed at least to *look* sad when he's doing it. All of Balanchine's work presents a problem for the audience to some degree; he just doesn't dramatize things. The burgeoning dance audience of today is still largely looking for theater values or finds its way into the dance through cues used by the verbal or musical theater. It's harder for them to identify with Balanchine because he is about form, not about the romantic expressiveness with which most other theater is still involved.

Hindemith's Four Temperaments (Theme and Four Variations for String Orchestra and Piano, 1940) is a set of variations on three themes, or the three may all be variants of one. Each theme is stated briefly at the beginning of the piece. For each temperament they are presented in a new setting but in the same order, and each theme keeps something of its original character. By the third humor, phlegmatic, the three ideas are beginning to influence each other, and in the last, choleric, they interact quite a bit. The piece ends with one of those majestic codas that Hindemith did so superbly, piling all his themes on top of one another to make a single grand statement.

Without following the score note for note, Balanchine gives a visual translation of the musical idea. Each of the three opening statements is danced by a different couple. The first, square and stately in the music, is a modest demonstration of the dancer's basic equipment: the woman offers her hand, the man holds his out for her to lean on; she points her lower leg, he extends his across it; while he supports her on pointe, she goes into arabesque, she turns into attitude, she pivots with the working foot flexed, then pointed, close to the other ankle. He carries her off in a lift that is as functional as the superstructure of a building, holding her low in front of him with his hands under her armpits. The woman just hangs, arms stretched straight to the sides, with her legs open out in a wide inverted V, her feet just skimming the floor.

The next music is agitated, full of motion created both by its actual speed and by its use of syncopated rushes and suspensions of sound. The second couple does a lot of fast, flashy footwork. The man promenades the woman in arabesque quite fast in different directions; actually, he grabs her around the waist and pulls her so fast he has to hold her back leg like a wheelbarrow, to keep it straight. There is a musical interruption, as there is in each statement and variation of the theme, here expressed as a staccato chord followed by a sort of galloping figure that comes down on the staccato chord again. At this point the woman spreads her arms and and legs and comes into the same lift with which the first woman went out. Except that the man holds her higher, and her legs clang down on his thighs. In this statement, there's the first mention of an idea that will recur — a regular rhythmic base is created by different parts of the orchestra speaking reciprocally. The dancers don't illustrate this idea when it's first heard, but as they leave they wigwag their arms up and down in a similarly responsive fashion.

The third theme is warm and melodic, and the dance seems to be all about adagio — about where the woman places her legs and where the man holds her. The black and white practice clothes in which the ballet is now being done expose the mechanics of the pas de deux to make it quite sensual. There seems to be an extra weight, a lingering care, in the way the man clasps her waist, her thigh. The woman often has to lean back with her whole body against him. And he carries her off folded against his chest, where she's so secure that she can extend her legs forward as she's carried out.

The first actual variation, Melancholic, begins with a male soloist. Each succeeding variation will begin the same way — a soloist, or in the case of Sanguinic a couple, dancing alone, then the entrance of other people as the music gets more active. But each variation develops differently after the appearance of the corps.

The Melancholic man seems to be on a tightrope. A piano and violin are having a dialogue, not an entirely amicable one. The man takes a few teetering steps, then lunges his torso backward with his arms stretched out behind his head as if to gain his balance. He seems to be grasping for huge amounts of space but unable to control it. In a gesture both self-directed and steadying, he rises to half-toe and wraps his arms around his body. He takes another diagonal path, tilts over, falls sideways with his body straight, and just gets his hands under himself in time to keep from slamming into the ground. He whirls as if to rise, but instead falls again, face to the ground this time. Finally he gets up and begins again. At last he goes limp, his whole upper body folding forward, as the music descends from its peak of discord.

The fast theme begins; two women stride on, and with spiky steps they dance around the man. They too travel a lot in the space, but they seem fearless about risking themselves in it. They balance themselves by flinging their arms out into wide diagonals, by pulling a ribcage away to counter a jutting opposite hip. They reach out in front with one leg, then the other, in high battements, or kicks.

What is the relationship of these women to this man? One would like to see them as sympathizers, perhaps trying to pull him out of his pain by getting him involved in their supercharged motion. But they're menacing figures somehow — perhaps it's their assurance and power, their lack of any softness that would make it easier for him to change. He supports them at arm's length, and they lead him almost like a victim toward a new group of women who come in.

I find the music for this dance ominous too. The four women enter to a statement of a third theme in the strings with the piano doing a sort of drum roll underneath. The women appear two at a time, marching by kicking high with an aggressive thrust of the pelvis on each downbeat, knifing their pointe into the ground as the leg comes down. In his dealings with the first two women and the succeeding four, the man keeps giving me the image of someone going through a doorway reluctantly. He holds his arms out to his sides, as if to steady himself or to grip reality for one last time before stepping into the unknown. Sometimes the two women lean on his arms, sometimes he parts the clasped hands of two of the women and climbs between them. He seems to be taking an active role but his partners are always there, weighing down on him, getting in his way. It's hard to say which he needs more: to cling to them or to leave them behind.

After the man makes his way through this formidable group, he seems less stable than before. He takes bigger and bigger steps forward, echoing the women's battements, finally throwing his pelvis so far forward on the kick and arching so far back in response that, like a wound-up spring, he snaps in the middle and folds forward completely, into a ball, at the same time sinking to the floor. The women leave and the music reaches its climax with a series of repeated notes, then slips away still in disagreement — the piano in a descending sequence, the strings ascending, both of them slowing down and getting softer. The argument, if there was one, is exhausted. The man, his torso arched back, his arms reaching behind him, staggers backwards into the wings.

If this variation is not precisely sad, the Sanguinic, which follows, isn't "happy" either. The music, in a moderate waltz tempo, states the first theme in short broken pieces. A man and a woman enter from opposite sides of the stage and gesture to each other one at a time — oh, it's you — yes, I'm here — want to dance? — all right. Arm in arm, they begin a little polite strolling dance.

The whole section that follows seems to be a miniature virtuoso piece, perhaps the kind of dancing Balanchine thinks makes dancers happiest. Quite early the rhythm starts to get syncopated, the accents displacing themselves in the bars. Each rhythmic embellishment seems to suggest some novel footwork to the dancers.

As the theme comes to a close the piano runs up and down the keyboard in a continuous series of trills, and the man picks up the woman and carries her around the perimeter of the space with about three lifts. On each one she opens her legs and pushes her arms slowly out to the sides. If there is one characteristic lift in the whole Balanchine canon, this is it — it appears in the slow movement of *Symphony in C* and in several other works — but here its origin has been clearly demonstrated and it is seen as only one of many possible related shapes that can be used for entirely different reasons.

Four women are ushered in on a series of fast marcato chords. They dig their advancing foot, toe-heel, into the ground on each step and fling their arms in big oppositional arcs. Balanchine uses this small ensemble as background for the woman, then the man, who do brief, showy variations complicated by syncopations they have picked out of the music. The piano accompanies their flights with extraordinary, ornate runs and convolutions from which the original waltz tempo emerges quite soon. This lively pulse continues for the rest of the variation while the other instruments or the dancers tug at its regularity, pushing or stretching the beat to make it move even more.

The music slides right into a version of the third thematic idea, which is sung in a legato but slightly irregular waltz by the strings. After a return to the marcato theme, now also worked out in 3/4 time, the sequence winds up in a contrasting dénouement, the piano in a low register repeating over and over a fast, descending chromatic run, and the strings soaring through the melody. To this placid statement, with its undertone of agitation, the women strut off with their digging, flailing motion, and the man lifts the woman smoothly, arcing her up and around the space.

Unlike the other three temperaments, the Sanguinic variation provides for virtually no contact between the small ensemble and the soloists. The four women serve the same utilitarian purpose as the corps in any classical ballet, backing up the soloists and creating a certain design interest but not an obtrusive one. In this case they also create a supporting movement energy: their strong rhythmic impulse seems to enrich the musical drive that takes the principals into their brief but spectacular solos. But the corps is persistent in its pistonlike dynamism, while the sanguinic pair, who have never succumbed to the ensemble's pushiness, have the capacity to be calm and expansive after their pyrotechnics, and the image of them riding serenely above the corps' organized turmoil at the end is breathtaking.

According to *Webster's* the phlegmatic humor is sluggish, impassive, apathetic, or calm. Balanchine extrapolates the ancient diagnosis from a state of being into action. This phlegmatic person he shows us has a low energy level, so he can be easily led, and a short attention span. You might even think him amiable or playful except that he never gets into things, never sustains an idea. Everything is more or less the same to him, every inspiration has the quality of a whim.

The initial solo is accompanied by a strange, disjointed music. The melody is broken up and taken by different parts of the string ensemble, sometimes playing simultaneously, sometimes alone. The ideas are harmonically more complex, the theme seems to wander desultorily from key to key, but finally the violins find their original home base and keep coming down on it while the other instruments slide up and down a chromatic scale.

The dancer doesn't seem to have any good idea what to do with his body. He takes a few steps, bends over, flexes his elbows in front of his chest, lets one arm go limp, then the other, turns in one knee, then the other, turns them out, stretches his arms to the sides, flexes one wrist, lets the other one droop. He folds his torso toward the ground, in the same position taken by the melancholic man, then does a few changements, his hands imitating the reversals of his feet in fifth position. In fact, he does several other things that are reminiscent of movement we've seen before, but none of them seems to make him comfortable. Finally he comes center stage, bends over, and slowly wraps one hand around one ankle.

As he tries to stand up in this contortionist's pose, the piano begins a lazy sort of *dum de dum de dum* music. Four women enter and engage the man in various games. Like the music, a lot of it seems to be forged in chains — twining in and out of itself but not getting anywhere. The piano drifts irresolutely around until it gets stuck on a seemingly endless two-bar phrase; after about a dozen repetitions of this motif in different keys, the piano seems to get a grip on itself and brings the revolving figure to an end by settling on the first note of it and coming down there again and again. The strings recognize this as a rhythmic ground base and proceed to state the third theme below it and in between the beats.

This creates a jaunty, walking music, and the dance also begins to organize itself more clearly. You see those repeated arabesques in different directions that have occurred more than once before in the ballet. This time the man is in the center of a line-up with the women, and in unison they all step with a rond de jambe into arabesque, then immediately wheel and do the same thing to the other side. The dancers keep returning to that motif every time the music does, after making small excursions to other things. At the end, though, the man is still going his own way, insisting on doing an eccentric battement to the side in his bent-over position, which looks odder than anything else he's done, especially with the women doing it the docile, academic way right behind him.

Choleric is introduced by a series of flamboyant runs on the piano. A woman enters and does a long cadenza in which she seems to be trying alternately to throw all the parts of her body in different directions at once and to gather them all together into the smallest possible package. The piano, in dialogue with the orchestra, quickly alludes to all the main musical ideas of the piece — the marcato marching, the ascending chord progressions, the syncopated conversations, the bitten-off portions of melody and ornamentation, the repeated hammering in of the tonic chord. Toward the end of this display, the sanguinic man enters as if to partner the woman, but each time he grasps her around the waist she flies off again. He leaves but returns with the three men of the opening sections, and each in turn promenades her in arabesque; then they exit. Alone, she flings herself down in the center of the stage.

To a very fast, syncopated pizzicato in the strings, the other four principal women enter and pick their way around her. She seems about to erupt and the piano breaks in with a few chords; then they take over again. Finally the piano launches into another cadenza, and she whirls from their midst and out to the side of the stage. The four women's partners enter, once again encircling the choleric woman. Once again she breaks out, but this last time she exits.

The key changes; the couples execute supported arabesques in the center of the stage. The melancholic man and the choleric man enter, each with his small consort of women behind him, six on one side of the stage, four on the other, and facing the audience they all recapitulate the motifs. Suddenly this begins to look like a big classical ballet. But still it's not quite right, not quite symmetrical, and all the dancers haven't returned. The piano and orchestra speak and answer each other, but one speaks in major and one in minor.

Finally they agree to change to a different key, and there they play a coda, the strings beginning in a low register and repeating the theme cumulatively stronger and higher as the piano marches below them. As the music is resolving itself, the choleric woman and the rest of the ensemble return, and the stage is realigned, with the dancers in two rows facing the audience. The choleric woman, coming forward, makes three smoothing-out gestures with her hands, and we see that the stage has finally calmed down. One by one, the men of the four couples lift their partners high into the open lift, this time the women raising both their arms high overhead. Each couple sweeps through the rows of the ensemble and away as the orchestra tolls triumphantly on the same note with which the piece began.

A musician once asked me what use it was to look at Balanchine, since all he does is depict the music. I had no answer. The musical interdependency in a piece like *Four Temperaments* must be overwhelming to a trained singer or instrumentalist. I'm not prepared to say there is anything in Balanchine's *Four Temperaments* that is not also in Hindemith's. Yet somehow the visualization, the per-

Finale, THE FOUR TEMPERAMENTS (*Balanchine, 1946*). *Daniel Duell and Merrill Ashley and ensemble. Photo by Costas.*

sonification of a score like that, completes its humanity in a way that no amount of verbal analysis, notation, charting, enumeration, comparing, and picking apart of structure can accomplish. The age-old argument for dance — that it is the most human, the most live and immediate of the arts — is strengthened by Balanchine because his mastery of form allows him to deal with the grandest conceptions tackled by any art. The fact that his movement is thematic, academic, makes it richer for me, not imitative or sterile. When he repeats an arabesque or a battement twelve different ways, he's not exposing his own lack of ideas but the arabesque's plenitude of them.

Four Temperaments is cool and unadorned. It doesn't pull your responses out of you, beg for your sympathy. The dancers are merely who they are — agile, daring, responsive, venturesome in space, changeable dynamically. I don't know if these are qualities inherent in American young people or if Balanchine trained them into his dancers, but I know Europeans don't dance this way.

Ivesiana (*George Balanchine*)

On rare occasions, Balanchine concerns himself more with the sound of the music than with its structure. He seldom indulges in the aesthetic sensibility of a score the way he did in *La Valse* (1951), *Gaspard de la Nuit* (1975), and *Ivesiana* (1954). After all, Hindemith's Four Temperaments, besides being elegantly composed, is rather rich and romantic to a post-Webernian or a post-Cagean ear, but Balanchine's *Four T's* is none of that. Perhaps he thinks he needn't point out the obvious, and when the score is of the magnitude of Hindemith, Bach, or Stravinsky he probably has enough to cope with in form alone. But composers who stress color and mood, like Ravel and Ives, have inspired Balanchine to come closer to impressionism.

Two of the original six sections of *Ivesiana* are evidently lost now. In fact, the evolution of this work appears even more wayward than that of other Balanchine ballets. For the most stable and affluent of American dance companies, the New York City Ballet has an extraordinary record of changing, dropping, adding to, and losing choreography, and its productions are preserved even less scrupulously than the steps. *Ivesiana* is one of the worst examples. Only twenty years old (*Swan Lake* is almost one hundred, *Les Sylphides* is sixty-five), *Ivesiana* today is a shadow of its original.*

The real *Ivesiana* was choreographed to six short pre–World War I pieces: Central Park in the Dark, Hallowe'en, The Unanswered Question, Over the Pavements, In the Inn, and In the Night. A year after its première, Balanchine had substituted Arguments for Hallowe'en, then scrapped it and added Barn Dance, which was later omitted. Over the Pavements got junked, too, somewhere over the years. I don't know what alterations have been made in the remaining four sections, although people who saw the original say it was more strange and ominous than it is now. Some say it was the lighting; some say the dancers, or the constricted space on the stage of City Center, where it was made. The costumes may have had something to do with it too. The practice clothes in which it was first given must have made it look exceedingly distorted; the current production, in outfits somewhere between street clothes and classroom apparel, gives the audience an option of contemporaneousness to explain the bizarre things that happen.

Balanchine says he never intended *Ivesiana* to be more than a series of unconnected vignettes, like the music. But what happens between the rise and fall of a curtain automatically creates a sequence even if one wasn't intended. *Ivesiana* now is two dark sections, one light moment, and a return to darkness. What does it mean?

Taking into account what must once have been there and what is left today, I think *Ivesiana* is about a kind of improbable American logic. It is existentialism and theater of the absurd without any European intellectualizing. It is a state of living where unexpected, unwanted things happen and don't matter, where people touch and glance off, where irrational images lurk under the lamp posts, where frivolity dances around the edge of despair and innocence can suddenly become the mute spectator to violence. I suspect the ballet may once have been more balanced between gloom and ironic fun. Now it's all gloom; the levity seems just an aberration.

There's a lot of Anna Sokolow in *Ivesiana*. Sokolow's first work in

---

*In addition to the changes noted, during the 1978 spring season the two middle sections were transposed and Peter Martins' Ives ballet *Calcium Light Night* was inserted before an abbreviated final section.

this genre of agonized noncommunication was *Lyric Suite* (1953). I doubt if Balanchine ever saw that dance or was influenced by it. But he and Sokolow both must have been picking up on the postwar, coldwar disaffection of American youth and on the urban realities that only a few years later were to be glamourized by Jerome Robbins. In this ballet one can also detect the sardonic Balanchine, in that golden age of Graham, Humphrey, and Limón, saying, You think you want modern dance — I'll give you antiballet.

Central Park in the Dark is one of the most eerie scores I've ever heard. The strings slide through what seems an endless sequence of very thin, quiet chords. The progression is arhythmic but unstressed, and creates an odd feeling of tension. The sound is calm but at the same time always unresolved, never letting you anticipate where it will go next. As if from far away, other sounds are heard: a clarinet, a trumpet, an oboe, play their own melodies in completely different keys. Quite near, a piano plays a few bars of dance music. Then a whole jazz band plays a jumbled chorus of a music hall tune, working up to a discordant finale and suddenly breaking off. Oblivious, the strings continue wending their way, and the music ends with them up in the air, still adrift, unaffected by what has been going on around them.

The ballet opens on a dark stage. Dimly in the distance you begin to perceive motion — bodies, faces, coming forward from far away. It's a group of women in dark leotards and tights, walking slowly, very close together. Then the group imperceptibly spreads out, but it's still too dark on the stage to see where they're coming from or how many women there are. All together they do a sequence of motions neither related nor important enough to claim your attention if something else were going on, and in a minute something else is.

Groping her way, a girl enters, then a man, and an enigmatic pas de deux ensues. Ignoring the crowd of women, who kneel, stretch, roll on the floor, and sometimes do more representational gestures that suggest turning a jumprope or other games, the girl pursues the man. They meet briefly in a grappling embrace, then the girl loses herself in the crowd and he tries to find her. Just when the music is getting the most raucous, he catches her and throws her violently down — the other women have gathered in the center and hurled themselves down in a pile, and the girl lands on top of them,

"Central Park in the Dark" from IVESIANA *(Balanchine, 1954). Sara Leland. Photo by Martha Swope.*

like a piece of rubbish. The man leaves. The girl gets up and gropes her way out. The group recedes into the shadows.

Like the music, this pas de deux keeps shifting underfoot. First it seems the couple have a date — perhaps a secret one, otherwise they would have picked a place to meet that was more out in the open. But there doesn't seem to be any tenderness between them when they do get together. Suddenly the man is chasing the girl — did they quarrel or did she think better of her decision to meet him? Or did she perhaps not plan to meet him at all? Maybe she was going to meet someone else and he waylaid her; she became frightened and ran away. Then something violent happens — rape? Yet the girl gets up and goes away without seeming to be hurt or even upset. Meanwhile, the crowd pays no attention, neither sympathizing nor trying to help. Incidents like this happen every day in New York; Central Park in the Dark is the perpetual, unfathomable drama of the city.

The Unanswered Question is a less literal image but such a powerful one that it has since been referred to several times by other choreographers. Musically the piece is a scale — the strings moving very cautiously from one note to the next, sometimes backtracking, sometimes changing out of synchrony, as if some of the instruments were reluctant to move on or some wanted to push ahead faster. They keep being challenged by the woodwinds and a trumpet, which make statements in different keys, sometimes querulously, sometimes stridently. The search goes on regardless.

Balanchine's metaphor for this is a woman held aloft by four men, so that she constantly eludes another man who desires her. The woman is one of those marble American goddesses. She wears a white tank suit, bare legs and feet, her hair is loose, and her perfectly madeup face never changes its perfectly arranged expression. Her four captors or managers are dressed in black and are seldom really seen because the spotlight always aims for the girl on their shoulders. They lift and manipulate her to show her to the man from every angle. She does practically nothing on her own — just poses, sometimes taking a step or sitting on their hands or bending backward — her cavaliers are always there to support her.

According to a 1956 account, the man never touched the girl,[4] but in the current production there is a moment when she's placed in his arms. The embrace is extremely odd, since the man is squatting on his haunches and the girl is all curled up in a ball except for her head, which is thrown back. After a moment her keepers return, she unfolds her body, and, stepping on her admirer's shoulders, she arches backward into safety again.

Most people remembering this dance talk about the fact that the girl's feet never touch the floor. What a powerful image that is, containing both the idea of the ballet dancer's ethereality and the sinister implications of a woman who is a pawn, with no power of her own except the power to attract. As Ives' musical interruptions become more florid, the manipulations do also. The girl is passed horizontally around in a circle as the four men stand in a clump. Another time she stands straight up and suddenly falls backward and disappears behind them for an instant. The lover lies on the floor and the men pass the woman's body directly over him.

The lover yearns for her, reaches, runs around, becomes desperate, falls, and rolls on the floor in frustration. He never actually gets her, but he never gives up either, and as the music ends he's following the cortege out.

In the Inn comes as a welcome relief; for the first time the stage lights come on full, and two dancers bounce in from opposite directions. The duet is jazzy, it seems to be happy, but it's also vaguely disturbing. In the space of four minutes the dancers try out a couple of dozen dance steps and ideas. Then the music just runs out. They shake hands and go off in opposite directions.

The girl is a wiggly, energetic, cheerleader type, her hair in pigtails. The man is collegiate, ready to try anything. Have they come together to try out routines for the fraternity show? Or is their dancing a metaphor for a series of unsuccessful conversational gambits — a would-be pickup that they both think better of after some exploratory small talk. Nothing is concluded between them, yet nothing is especially motivated either. There's no apparent reason why they do the things they do, no reason why they quit when they do, and no resentment left in the air at the end.

A lot depends on the dancers, since there is, presumably, every opportunity for them to make an event out of the encounter. In 1975 Suzanne Farrell was dancing the part, with Jay Jolley. This is an unaccustomed role for Farrell, since it uses her resources of angularity and kicky rhythms but is probably the only jazzy role in which Balanchine doesn't exploit her show-biz sexiness. Working against her own typecasting, she looks clean-cut and uncalculating. She's so relaxed and undemonstrative that you can't think of a reason why she should be doing what she's doing. That is, you can imagine she thinks Jolley is a nice boy, that they might get along well together — but then, why do they part?

Two minutes later the ballet is over and the gloom and mystery have won out. In the Night is a brief, tranquil melody with instants of unrest — like a sleeper stirring without waking — sung by the French horn over a gentle chiming of bells, celeste, and strings. I almost feel as though, if it were possible to end a ballet by playing music, Balanchine would have done that. Since he couldn't, he created something of an outrage.

The stage is very dark, lit by pale shafts of light from the sides near the floor. From all directions dancers enter. Standing on their knees and maintaining an upright position, they walk in straight lines, crisscrossing the space. There are so many of them — thirty-five or so — that, with dim lighting and anonymous costuming and loose hair, you can't recognize any of them or follow one familiar face any distance. Some people reach the other side of the stage and exit, but more keep coming out right to the fall of the curtain.

This final image of *Ivesiana* is the most ambiguous of all. It's so powerful one hardly dares name it. There's more here than the idea of the faceless crowd, the dispassionate, alienated urban millions. The image somehow says that we are also crippled or maimed in our single-focused journeys. And that no one's destination is any more important than anyone else's, no one's path takes him away from the impartial fate that is waiting for all. And that each individual journey, finally, has no effect on the larger journey that everyone travels. Seldom has Balanchine shown his derivation from the Russian fatalists more openly than in *Ivesiana* — and seldom has he spoken more directly to our time and our society.

Agon (George Balanchine)

Not all of Balanchine's Stravinsky ballets are black and white, but *Agon* (1957) is the prototype of a series of dances, extending over at least twenty years, in which the density and particularity of the movement imposed its own décor, its own costume, its own visual imagery. Although he has choreographed the early, coloristic Stravinsky (like *Firebird* and *Le Chant du Rossignol*), Balanchine seems to have more of an affinity for the spare, formal works of the composer's later life. The look of *Agon* — and the later *Monumentum pro Gesualdo, Movements for Piano and Orchestra, Symphony in Three Movements, Violin Concerto* — is possibly severe, but to me it's transparent, alive with motion instead of covered with deadly fabric. The dancers, stripped to their most minimal practice clothes, come before us in a mode for moving. When audiences accepted Balanchine's desire to expose the dancers this way, he was encouraged to reduce the costumes for older ballets as well. Dancing is an absolute proposition, these costumes seem to say; it can't be mitigated or explained or apologized for; these dancers have no need of intermediaries. Not until the 1970s has European ballet been willing to offer the dancer in such uncompromising attire, and often in today's International-style unitards we see a gloss of silky elasticized fabric, a sewn-on decoration or trim, a special tailoring to enhance the body's line. Perhaps it isn't too much to suggest a relationship between these confident, unadorned bodies of Balanchine's and the sense Americans have of being at ease in space. We don't need to be surrounded by artificial vistas, decorative landscaping, or reassuring architecture, because space to us is a limitless challenge, a field for conquest.

Agon is a series of what Lincoln Kirstein has called "unwinnable games."[5] Without Balanchine's translation, Stravinsky's music might be considered neither American nor European but simply a post-Webernian excursion in serialism. Agon is astringent, sometimes even tart; full of cocky fanfares and firm full stops, syncopated riffs, and almost nothing extended enough to be called a melody. The instruments seldom work symphonically but call out, butt in on each other, announce, withdraw, respond, as if for the pure pleasure of declaring themselves present.

Agon seems to me to be as much a jazz ballet as a "modern" ballet or a takeoff on French court dances. It's not that the dancers do anything overtly jazzy, I think, but the way they handle their weight and play around with time. Stravinsky's rhythms are irregular but, as Balanchine has pointed out, his pulse is steady,[6] and the reliable underlying metre supplies all the support that's necessary to open the field for a great rhythmic interplay among the instruments of the orchestra, the solo dancers and the ensemble, and between the dancers and the orchestra. So the ballet really has two lines of imagery to follow: the varieties of rhythmic invention — syncopation, suspension, canonic devices, explorations of the dynamic range from percussive to legato — and the constantly shifting arrangements of dancers in the space and of the dancers' body shapes.

The ballet consists of fourteen little dances for ensembles and soloists, and a pas de deux with its traditional divisions: entrance, adagio, two variations, and coda. Each of these sections is too short to allow for the sort of development we see in *Four Temperaments*. There's nothing memorable about entrances and exits; at appropriate times in the music, dancers leave or arrive on the stage. It's not the thematic events associated with any individual dancer or any part of the ballet that concern Balanchine, but the utterly unsentimental yet witty and assured way the little pieces contribute to the whole.

The work is almost diabolically tight in its structure. Beginning and ending with a line-up of four men across the back of the stage, it first marshals its forces, giving the men's group, then the eight women, their chance to dance as units before combining for the first time. There's a pas de trois for a man and two principal women: they all dance together first, then the man has a solo, the women have a duet, and the whole ensemble dances. A second pas de trois for two men and a principal woman is built the same way, except that the woman's solo follows the men's duet. After the pas de deux, danced by the fourth man and the fourth principal woman, the troops reassemble to make four couples, who are later joined by the four subsidiary women to make four trios. The twelve dancers quickly and ingeniously demonstrate another set of possibilities for two and three collaborators, this time with the small working units multiplying to fill the stage, opening up the audience's field of concentration. When this has been accomplished, the women leave, and the men finish the dance as they began it.

Despite the almost obsessive care with which the ballet is plotted, *Agon* never looks formalistic. Balanchine uses strict forms not to confine himself within limits but as a means of giving himself leeway. *Agon* is anchored to its metric pulse and to its master plan for the arrangement of the ensemble, but within those structures he shuffles things around with great freedom. In fact, one of the things that make *Agon* a major work is the range of its invention within such a reassuring, classical outline. It never pulls us out into exploratory quicksand as *Ivesiana* does. The odd things that happen, especially in the pas de deux, look even odder because of the context they're in. They're like aberrant, harmless jokes, funny hats, or false noses we try on our friends in our daydreams.

The four men we see spaced across the width of the stage as the curtain rises are facing away from the audience. In silence they whip around, and the music begins. To a chorus of tooting brasses, they begin a series of fast, aggressive moves — high kicks, turns in the air, usually in overlapping canons, so that we see one man get set and spring, but our eye flashes to the next man in turn before the first one comes back to the ground. Straining up on their toes, they reach into space to one side, then sweep their arms out and around to the other side, sinking low into the standing leg as they do, cutting a big arc through space, but an arc that is too weighty a gesture to be merely a design. Another time they reach straight out behind with one leg, pulling themselves so far off their center of gravity that they have to dig in the heel of the standing leg to counterbalance. These large gestures recur, sometimes in unison, sometimes in canon, sometimes with the dancers facing in different directions from the way they first performed them. But always the men keep their line-up, their orientation to the audience: a bouncy, athletic chorus line, with a slight swagger of the street about it.

The first of the two big ensembles emphasizes the distinctness of the male and female contingents, the dancers posing, displaying, showing you the angle of a leg, the sweep of a port de bras. For the first time in the ballet we see a pose reminiscent of court dancing: the dancer stands firmly on one leg and raises the other just high enough so that the toe grazes the floor, with the hip turned out to show a shapely calf. One arm hangs easily down along the standing leg and the other curves up around the head. This pose is repeated often thoughout the ballet, sometimes with small changes of placement that give it an entirely different flavor. As we keep seeing it, it becomes familiar despite its variations, and it stabilizes the ballet just as the signature poses do in *Four Temperaments*.

The men and women stay strictly with their own groups, in lines or in formations of four that travel in unison blocks across the space. At one point they do intermingle, forming two lines that face the audience, but no sooner do the lines coalesce than the dancers begin changing places, one by one, until they are separated back into their blocks again. Balanchine manages to take the curse off the rigidity of this idea by arranging the stage asymmetrically a good deal of the time, so that even when they seem to be the most regimented, the dancers work in an off-centered universe.

The tension between symmetricality and asymmetricality, between propriety and unorthodoxy, is a primary source of *Agon*'s energy. In the first pas de trois, the man stands between the two women, steadying one on each arm as they pose, balance, unfold their legs, jump into little lunges. At the end of the coda, he supports them one after the other in a rapid series of pirouettes, out of which they all sweep into a low reverence before disappearing. In the second pas de trois, the woman has two cavaliers; she poses between them, modeling her arabesque in different positions, and they offer their supporting grip from either side, sometimes promenading around her while she balances steadily on pointe. After all their variations, she's thrown in her unwavering arabesque from one man into the arms of the other.

The women's variation is a match to the men's variation in the second pas de trois, while the solos of these two sections also complement each other. The two women first work symmetrically, then move off into a diagonal path, as if playing follow the leader. The two men switch between working in canon and in unison. The canonic phrases are only a beat apart, so what the audience perceives is not so much a reflection as a slight afterimage. The dance seems to be constantly going into and out of focus.

The first man's variation, like all these small ensembles, uses some material associated with other parts of the ballet. Relieved of his partnering responsibilities, he seems for a second as if he doesn't know what to do with center stage. Then he moves out, sweeping into big torso curves and extravagant openings of the legs, using all the space denied him by the task of seeing to the two women. Later, when they come back for their final dance with him, he manages to incorporate some of this expansiveness while enacting his complementary role as their cavalier.

The roles dancers play while dancing together and the roles they dance on their own are very much at issue in *Agon*. Another choreographer would have made a farce of about-faces and topsy-turvy situations — European ballets constantly play this idea for laughs. Balanchine's commentary is contained in the steps. He assumes we already have an idea what dancers do in their conventional transactions and that we will see the wit in his pulling the norms out of shape. So when a man has to grab the waists of two spinning women in turn, in the time he'd usually have to support one, or when the male duo zing through their antiphonal paces, the dancers seem flushed with the trying instead of cocky and on top of the joke.

Many of the tiny interludes in the pas de trois and the pas de deux have false endings (the music does too): the performers will hit a position that looks right for an ending — a supported arabesque, a pretty attitude. An instant later, just after the audience has had time to register the pose and think the dance is over, the dancers change with a click to another pose more bizarre or in a totally different character from the first.

The solo woman in the second pas de trois contrasts high, stabbing pointe work with emphatic sinkings into plié, arms flashing in harmony. The orchestra plays a rhythmic six-count figure over and over on castanets overlaid with a sparse assortment of instruments, and the woman's two escorts stand at the sides of the stage clapping the rhythm while they watch her dance. With the slightest trick of imagination, we could fill in whatever is missing and make it a dance in a Spanish cantina.

The pas de deux, in a way, is the most "modern" section of *Agon;* its distortions of familiar shapes are the most extreme. Again, Balanchine knows the image we have in mind for a man and a woman dancing a classical duet. Linked together in a relationship of great sensitivity and skill, they must know more about each other than most lovers in order to coordinate their moves to the best advantage. Although the classical metaphor is one of romantic love, the event is actually a much more external product. The dancers do this for the benefit of the audience, not really for themselves. A veneer of style, of line, keeps the relationship from becoming literal. It is the remoteness, the restrained intimacy of those decorous holdings and steadyings that Balanchine oversteps in *Agon.*

Without losing track of line and placement, or of the logic that must mold any classical structure, he permits more to happen between the dancers. More parts of their bodies come into contact, their torsos are more articulate, their limbs more twisty. They hold on to or support each other in inversions or exaggerations of the grips we've seen before, and the transitions between grips or positions are prolonged so that not only the end pose but the journey to

Pas de Deux from AGON *(Balanchine, 1957). Jean-Pierre Bonnefous and Allegra Kent. Photo by Martha Swope.*

get there is important. And of course all this aberration is visible, unconcealed by puffs of costume or sleight of hand.

These departures from strict academic form all seem to go in the direction of greater sensuality, both in what the dancers have to feel to achieve the movement and in what the audience perceives. Certain dancers, notably Allegra Kent and Jean-Pierre Bonnefous, have a way of reinforcing the sense of bodily contact, the meeting of surfaces usually held apart, by making their visual spheres smaller, by not having to look where they're moving. As in many conventional pas de deux, the woman's part is very leggy, very stretched. But instead of straight extensions or arabesques directed out in space away from her body, she often opens her legs while the man is holding her in a tight embrace, making the leg gesture more of a peripheral thought to the solidly emphasized center body. She curves her legs around his body, not around the air as in the ordinary attitude, so the leg becomes a frame for his body or an even more personal embracing gesture rather than simply a leg to look at. Once she encircles his head with a curved leg, outrageously doing something arms normally do.

The whole pas de deux seems to be a series of knots and conundrums from which the dancers untangle themselves at intervals to settle serenely, and perhaps a bit ironically, into courtly poses for the benefit of the audience. Each one does two fragmentary solos while the other watches — a few steps, his obliquely stretched and hers tight and finicky, are their nod of deference to tradition. They are constantly changing the way they look — from eccentric acrobats to elegant dancers to preclassic aristocrats with pinkies curled. The woman often turns into a tomboy; hoisting her legs through the small spaces made by their clasped hands, twisting herself into ungainly reaches, she could be climbing a tree. The man could be a species of athlete as he scrambles onto his back on the floor while supporting the woman's arabesque or kneels and bends back as she seems to dive over his shoulder from behind.

At the end, which is a much less emphatic or presentational halt than all the false endings and flourishes that have been sprinkled through the piece, she stands with one foot raised slightly and he kneels on the floor, his body bowed over her bent leg. In one motion she lifts an arm in a gesture of triumphant passion, then folds possessively over him. Scarcely has this had time to sink into our awareness when three other women come running on, then the men, and the ballet speeds to its conclusion.

Four couples quickly swing through some normally adagio positions. As a fugue begins in the orchestra, the four secondary women return. We haven't seen any of them since the opening scene of the ballet; often I've forgotten about them entirely by this time. Each man then briefly partners two women, not as formally as in the first pas de trois nor as adventurously as in the pas de deux. There's a feeling of slight overload here, as if the task is a little more than the dancers can manage. But, as has happened before in the ballet, they go on with it. Then the women are gone and the men remain, to repeat the beginning of their first dance as the music also repeats. The soloing instruments collect into a last downbeat, and the men hit a pose that resembles their first one but seems to lead on to further encounters instead of merely winding us back to the beginning.

Episodes (George Balanchine)

In 1959 the two giants of American dance, George Balanchine and Martha Graham, encountered one another on the same stage for the first and only time. The meeting was more like a mutual acknowledgment than a collaboration. Each conceded the other's rightful territory and agreed there would be no poaching. I think at that time in our dance evolution it could scarcely have been otherwise. I suspect that the two choreographers had more regard for one another, despite their aesthetic incompatibility, than their respective audiences and coworkers had. But production of the work was not easy, and what resulted was a dance about Mary Queen of Scots by Graham, with her own company and New York City Ballet dancer Sallie Wilson; and an abstract ballet by Balanchine for his company with one solo for Graham dancer Paul Taylor. Both parts had music by Anton von Webern.

Graham's contribution to the enterprise disappeared almost immediately after its initial performances, and the Taylor solo was dropped and soon forgotten, since none of the NYCB dancers was able to learn it. Not having seen the whole work, I can only speculate about what it must have been like. From photographs we can tell that Taylor's dance had a shadowy likeness to the Phlegmatic variation in *Four Temperaments* and also to what became Taylor's personal style when he danced and choreographed for his own company during the 1960s and 1970s. It seems to me there must have been an obvious irony in Graham doing a "story ballet" and Balanchine doing a dance about modern movement, even though both of them had previously established their right to deal with the traditional concerns of the other's dance form. I don't know what Graham's dance was like, but there are many things about Balanchine's work in its present form that make me think he was conscious of the polemical nature of the whole project. Even without Paul Taylor's solo, *Episodes* seems often to be referring to modern dance, to be commenting on it, and even to be hinting that Balanchine could go modern dance one better if he felt like it.

The reconciliation between modern dance and ballet — or at least their mutual recognition — was approaching as the 1950s came to an end. *Episodes* was only the most dramatic indication that the two strains of dance realized they didn't have to remain insulated from one another in order to continue to exist. Merce Cunningham for a long time had been using a balletic body attitude as a basis of movement, and his dance *Rune*, choreographed in the same year of 1959, has some striking similarities to the first part of *Episodes*. By 1962 Paul Taylor was choreographing a modern dance ballet, *Aureole*, and Alvin Ailey was working with a ballet company for the first time. Nineteen sixty-two was also the year of one of the first big modern ballets, Brian Macdonald's *Time Out of Mind,* which kept the dancers on pointe and fused their virtuosity with the psychodramatic tensions of Graham. Balanchine undoubtedly took account of this tendency, but having illustrated its possibilities, he returned to what he considered the more versatile form.

Episodes begins a little like *Four Temperaments.* Four couples dressed in black and white practice clothes face the audience didactically and demonstrate the basics: positions, handholds, supports, methods of extending the leg, showing the foot, or using the arms. But something has happened in the intervening thirteen years. The audience is assumed to know something about the academic language, to be able to recognize it and follow it without quite the preparation we needed before. The couples go into a canon after only a few bars of unison, knowing our eyes will be able to comprehend it.

The movement statements are basic, but far from pure. The alignment of the dancers' bodies is distorted; hips jut out, wrists break sharply, upper bodies cantilever away from the center of gravity, feet flex where they should be moving with smooth, pointed efficiency, knees slope together instead of turning out. One supporting position seems to recur most often, the man and woman standing side by side facing the same way, like skaters holding right hand to right hand, left to left. This can create a very open, gracious stance when they extend their arms wide, or a cramped, contorted one when they bend them close to their bodies.

For each of the several short pieces of music (Symphony, Opus 21), the dance elaborates on the idea of a pas de deux being done by four couples on the stage at once. After the first moments of unison, they hardly ever work synchronously again. Sometimes their movements are canonic echoes, made complicated by people facing in different directions or by variations on the established order of entrance. Instead of joining the canonic phrase in order clockwise around the stage, the two couples on the sides may come in together or three couples may work against the principals. Sometime later, when you've lost track of the sequence, a portion ends with all the dancers posing, and you see that two of them have gotten into synchrony but the other two have not.

Some sequences seem to be about contrasts in designs or energies between the principal couple and the three supporting pairs. One section ends with the three women posing in supported, erect attitudes while the principals kneel on the floor with open arms, the man bending back, the woman bowing over forward. Another time the troops promenade back and forth with a kick step while the central woman is lifted vertically and beats her feet together. Two dancers kick with their feet flexed and the other six with them pointed. The principal woman rises into fifth position, her legs tight together; the others sink into a wide second position.

At one point, after they have been working in one place or in very restricted areas of space, people begin running and crisscrossing the space to stand somewhere they haven't been before — a kind of atom-by-atom realignment of their formation, like that in *Agon*. Men come and stand beside a different partner, but just for a minute. Separately, they all run to another new place, and soon each is back to his first partner. There has been so much pulling out of shape of the dance pattern that, near the end, when the women are suddenly upended in the men's arms and beat their feet together in entrechats with arms curved prettily above (below) their heads while upside down, it scarcely looks odd — although it is, of course, very odd indeed.

Maybe because there's a certain amount of standing around in this part of the dance, maybe because it is so plain in its derangement, I have begun to think that the very stance and attitude of the dancers is something quite remarkable. They seem unflustered, unemphatic, settled, not set for doing anything extraordinary. They rest into their own weight, they spend their energy without fuss. They look like people, almost.

The ordinary look of American dancers, the characteristic way they dance as themselves, not as made-up personages, is something we're used to. It's analogous to the unaffected sound of American popular singers like Rudy Vallee, Bing Crosby, Ella Fitzgerald. We notice a distinct contrast when a dancer from another tradition joins an American company: Natalia Makarova always seemed to be overacting when she first danced with Ballet Theater; Peter Martins seemed out of place in the NYCB until he began to relax his princely demeanor. There's a suggestion of bygone aristocracy in the way Europeans dance, a pretext that the dancer's social station is more imposing than that of the audience who's watching him or her. Some of the earliest ballet choreographers in this country tried to bring a more egalitarian look to their work, and most of them did it through character. But I think it was Balanchine who brought this naturalness to classical dancers.

The second part of *Episodes* (Five Pieces, Op. 10) is a kinky pas de deux that not only exploits the movement relationships of the man and woman but makes us look at the roles and attitudes implied by this dancing collaboration. Because some dancers tend to play the dance for laughs, I'm not sure what Balanchine intended — whether his distortions were meant as a mockery of conventional ballet, or a put-down of modern dance, or merely to push the possibilities to their extreme limits.

Each brief section seems like a capsule version of some aspect of the grand pas de deux. First, the yearning approach. The man and woman elaborately tiptoe toward each other from opposite ends of the stage diagonal. Although they could easily go right over to each other, they move as though terrible obstacles were in the way. They reach toward each other, straining forward, but their feet take tentative little tapping steps all around them instead of carrying them forward. When they finally do meet, after this suspenseful build-up, they miscalculate, and instead of holding the arm he has extended for her to balance on, the woman aims too high and practically plunges right over it, doubling up into a half-handstand. As soon as the woman is stabilized, the man walks off nonchalantly, leaving her upside down, posed on her pointes and her fingers. They make another approach, wildly flailing their arms about, grapple, get all twisted up in each other, and in place of a lift, the man lowers the woman by the armpits and runs, pushing her ahead of him with her legs spread apart.

In still another excursion, they begin making witchy, hexing gestures toward each other, and when they meet the man is somehow sitting on the floor with his arms lifted to the sides, and the woman is standing behind him leaning on his hands with hers. This too is reminiscent of *Agon*. But what follows is quite another dance. Very often during *Episodes* we see Balanchine deliberately suggesting the earlier ballet and then doing something completely different, demonstrating that the same key can unlock many doors. As the dancers move from this unconventional gambit, the woman exaggeratedly steps through the circle of their arms with one leg, then the other, until she stands astride his hips. He rolls backward between her legs; since they're still holding hands, this makes her have to bend way back. He returns to sitting and she slithers through to her starting position. They repeat this maneuver once or twice. They extricate themselves and he stands and hoists her to a position on his back. As he stalks across the stage facing the audience, with his arms raised in the shape of a yoke echoed by her inverted legs slung across his shoulders, I can't avoid thinking of the minotaur in *Errand into the Maze*.

The last gambit begins with them standing side by side, cuddling close together and facing the audience. They twine their arms around the head and neck that's nestling right next to their own. They fail to make contact this way too, as they have failed in their previous gropings. Their misjudgments of how far apart they are or how big a movement they have to make in order to touch remind me of the alienation images that Anna Sokolow created so frequently during that period. As if in frustration, the man throws the woman down into a split, steps over her legs as she stepped over him earlier. At last they seem to make one exhausted effort, miss again, and she huddles down, all crouched over, as he drapes himself on top of her.

In the third section (Concerto, Op. 24), a man and woman dance backed by a small ensemble of four women. First there's one of those sensual adages in which Balanchine emphasizes the parts of the dancers' bodies that come into contact as much as the eventual shape into which they're manipulating each other. The woman is very crotch-sprung — Allegra Kent created the role — so she can spread her legs in what seems to be an endless variety of directions while standing or moving in almost any position. Kent, who was still doing the role in 1978, is capable of making her body seem almost boneless one minute and made of thousands of twitchy wires the next.

The four-woman onlooking corps de ballet exits and the pas de deux continues, with the man becoming more overtly manipulative than he's ordinarily required to be. Often he kneels on the floor, where he first holds her standing leg, as the cavalier in *Serenade* does, to create the illusion that the woman is turning in arabesque unsupported. Here, just the opposite process is going on. The man's partnering is not an illusion but a prime element; Balanchine wants us to see the mechanics this time, and he created opportunities so that we can't miss them. Almost every move the woman makes seems to be initiated by the man. Either he literally places each body part into a new position or he starts her into motion. He bundles and elongates her limbs into the most extraordinary lifts, then untangles her again.

The ensemble reenters, and the five women clasp hands, facing out in a circle. The man steps into the circle and continues to partner the woman, his hands around her waist, on her shoulder, twisting and turning her, while she remains connected to the other women. She pokes and jerks her torso in harsh isolations, ignoring the man who's trying to get a grip on her. At the end, the man reaches up into the air, as if he sees at last that he's made a mistake.

The final section (Ricercata in six voices from Bach's Musical Offering) I think of as Balanchine's Doris Humphrey dance, and not only because Humphrey choreographed to Bach so often. The dancers are a principal man and woman and a corps of fourteen women. The dance is orchestral, with the couple and the women, grouped in three unvarying units, making one continuous set of complementary designs. As the music flows, in Webern's orchestration, from one instrument to another, the dance gesture is passed from group to group, sometimes sequentially, sometimes contrapuntally, accumulating at times into larger chordal units.

Balanchine has picked up some of the main elements of Doris Humphrey's group patterning — the monolithic, sculptural use of arm gestures, the idea of people executing the same gestures while positioned on different levels, the prominence given to design when blocks of people work in unison and in place rather than traveling. With the couple, then the woman alone, working stage center in what may be variations on much of the material we have seen earlier in the ballet, the group moves from place to place — nothing at all virtuosic, just a ceremonial walking and rearranging of the floor pattern. What the dance is mainly about is the architecture of

EPISODES (*Balanchine, 1959*). *Bart Cook, Allegra Kent and ensemble. Photo by Martha Swope.*

these arrangements, their musical separateness and family like-nesses, the shifting balances that are possible among them. The man returns for the final part of the music, and from here until the end the principal couple work completely in harmony with the group rather than more prominently.

There is no complete unison work in the whole piece, although the groups begin to coalesce — from the beginning there have been three: four women downstage left and right and six women in a line across the back. Their gestures get to be the same, their timing becomes synchronous. They look as if they might be getting ready to do one thing all together. Still, they face different directions, work on opposite sides of the body. Balanchine refrains from the obvious solution and brings the dance to a nonunison close, every-one doing the same gesture — they slowly bring both arms straight down to their sides in parallel position — with the dancers in the back standing and those in front kneeling.

Adolescents

Echoing through all of rock 'n' roll is the simple
demand for peace of mind and a good time.

—Greil Marcus [1]

O NE SUNDAY EVENING in 1975 when the Joffrey Ballet had
an early curtain, I went to see Jerome Robbins' *Moves* at the
start of their program, then sped downtown to a concert by a young
modern dance choreographer. Her first piece was a dance about
growing up in the fifties. The central character and her companions
in fantasy acted out dreams of teen-age romance to the Keep Cool
dance from "West Side Story." After my first amusement at the idea
of running across Robbins in two different corners of the dance
world on a single night, I began to think about what Robbins had
crystallized that was so important to an adolescent generation, and
by what means he had managed to create such memorable images.

Although he has since gone on to make more "arty" ballets, three
of his early jazz works, *Interplay* (1945), *N.Y. Export: Opus Jazz*
(1958), and *Moves* (1959) have been in the Joffrey repertory for several seasons, and taken together they make clear this phase of our
dance history. It seems appropriate to me that the Joffrey should
have become the repository of these ballets, as it was for Anna
Sokolow's *Opus 65,* which paved the way for them there, and Twyla
Tharp's *Deuce Coupe,* their natural heir.

The Joffrey trades in romanticized images of a society, images
that stress the way we would like ourselves to be rather than in the
piercing observations of an artist about the way we actually are.
People go to the Joffrey not for subtlety or challenge but for clarity,
craft, and for a look into the magic mirror of their illusions. Ameri-

cans, more than most other people, it seems, use their public media and entertainments to project aspects of themselves that can't be openly exploited. Our obsession with sexuality has created an industry devoted to soft-core pornographic publications, movies, spectacles, and advertising. We fulfill other private longings by consuming ballets about homosexuality, drugs, violence, patriotism, or whatever is the current vogue. The Joffrey produces these ballets like any fine American product and updates the models from year to year. In each case they glorify feelings that people might be embarrassed to admit they have, or sentiments too immature, ideals too lofty, drives too destructive. Dance is the main instrument for making these feelings visible, but not the only one; lighting, costumes, music, film, pantomime, and words may all play a part in enhancing the image. I often get the impression that the Joffrey audience feels cheated if it is compelled to watch a ballet that is dance alone or that is "classical." The work seems not to count if it doesn't immediately announce the terms of its identification with the audience.

Perhaps I am making one of several possible definitions for pop art, and since Sokolow, Robbins, and Tharp all fall within this definition, I obviously don't think all pop art is inferior. It is the power of their dance language that makes Sokolow, Robbins, and Tharp supersede the topicality of their material.

Since the beginning of his choreographic career — until some ten years ago — Robbins always had a flexible relationship with the more popular arts, particularly with movies and musical shows. Through the 1940s and 1950s he swung back and forth among the three media, often carrying ideas over from one into another. His last Broadway show, "Fiddler on the Roof," had apparent repercussions in *Les Noces* (1964) and *The Dybbuk Variations* (1974). From the evidence of his ballets and from what he has said about making them, Robbins seems to work always toward the realization of a stage event when he choreographs. Music moves him, certainly, but not in the more mechanistic ways that it does other choreographers. He seems less absorbed with employing and varying the dance language than in seeing how music can make *a person* move. People in a theater frame. Meetings and partings, ebbs and flows of feeling, stillness and motion in space. These are the stuff of Robbins' dance, not steps. And possibly no one in ballet can create more effectively for these elements.

On top of his natural gift for staging, his work in the commercial theater has taught him a great deal. For Robbins, the stage is all that exists; everything that his dancers ever are or do is compressed into that space and time between his meticulously wrought beginnings and endings. George Balanchine has said there are no mothers-in-law in ballet. For Robbins there are no anterooms or closets, no explanations hiding under the furniture or in the room upstairs. His ballets, as a consequence, have a supercharged look. Nothing in them is casual, thrown away. The frame is filled with important incident; if something is not in the frame, it has ceased to be important. I don't have a sense that Robbins dancers go anywhere when they leave the stage or come from anywhere when they enter. They enter because the stage is where they have to be; they leave because they're finished with what they came to do. Robbins heightens this sense of a select, isolated experience by arranging many scenes to bring out the force of a certain gesture or a certain interchange. As if he were making a close-up on a screen, he contrives to magnify that one thing and orient everything else on the stage toward it. Robbins insists that the world is contained within his stage, and he choreographs best when he can examine a world already defined — the sailors' comradeship in *Fancy Free*, the Russian wedding of *Les Noces*, the "inside" life of dancers, the exaggerated, transitory, sealed-off world of the American teen-ager.

Although composed later than all three Robbins works, Anna Sokolow's *Opus 65* preceded them into the Joffrey repertory. In fact, *Opus 65* probably was the forerunner of all the pop-youth ballets with which the Joffrey later became identified. Choreographed originally for students and apprentices at the Joffrey School, with a modern-jazz score by Teo Macero, the ballet was done during the Joffrey's belated "official" New York debut in the fall of 1965 at Central Park's Delacorte Theater. After a decade of homeless touring the Joffrey was then under the patronage of Rebekah Harkness. A year later, when Robert Joffrey was reorganizing after cutting himself loose from his notorious benefactress, he needed an image for the company that would set it apart from other ballet companies, a personality that audiences could grasp. That image turned out to be "contemporary." I suspect it came about less from shrewd premeditation on Joffrey's part than from his taking some chances that succeeded with the public and the popular critics. *Opus 65* was the first contemporary ballet done by the company, but it proved strong stuff.

Sokolow captured the rhythms and moods of the younger generation, a pre-drug generation that had just released its pelvis and its hostilities, that was about to accuse the world of murder and make its case for love. She provided the audience with an image of itself, but the image wasn't always flattering. In *Opus 65*'s best-known sequence, a girl in a bare-midriff costume and a mop of a wig does a dance with several men in which they all rub against one another and turn each other on. But the girl is blasé, the turn-on is only mildly stimulating to her. She yawns and stretches as the quivering men lift her into the air. This dance may be Anna Sokolow's wry comment on the romanticized female image projected in some ballets, notably *Ivesiana*.

But Sokolow could not be funny without being bitter at the same time. In her ballets you have to take your lumps along with your enjoyment. When the Joffrey revived *Rooms* a few years later, it lasted two performances in the repertory. By that time the company had found its formula, a nonthreatening image that stopped short of abrasiveness and offered even its nasties in shiny wrappings. Robert Joffrey's *Astarte* (1967), the first big mixed-media ballet; Gerald Arpino's *The Clowns* (1968), an apocalyptic morality play enacted by lovable funnymen; and *Moves* all entered the repertory within the next couple of seasons and the acrid *Opus 65* was retired.

Robbins articulated the same things that Sokolow did for the Joffrey audience, but his portraits are more finished, invulnerable. His construction of character is impressive, often exciting, but he doesn't strike at the soft, scared parts of the psyche. Robbins also projects an "aesthetic" quality that Sokolow sometimes throws away. Twyla Tharp has this quality too, which is why some critics have been so outraged by her ballets. Sokolow could always be dismissed as a modern dancer, an interloper on the ballet stage who didn't have to be tolerated, but Tharp comes near enough to a ballet aesthetic that she has to be considered even when she is most reckless with ballet values. What all three of them do is represent the humanistic side of the pop coin. Without any fantasy disguises, they show us people dancing about their time and in the idiom of their time.

Interplay (*Jerome Robbins*)

Interplay re-creates the 1940s for me. Unlike so many ballets, it still looks like the period in which it was made. This may be why people call it dated. The idea is simple, even ordinary. The music, Morton Gould's American Concertette, is the kind of symphonic jazz that many serious composers were writing in that period, trying to treat native material as art. Four boys, then four girls, enter one at a time and dance fast, showy combinations. A man does a solo, asking the others to join him for a few bars, recalling the way the different sections of a jazz band in the movies used to come in behind the vocalists for a couple of riffs. There's a slow pas de deux to a blues and finally the dancers choose up sides and have a dance contest in which neither team wins.

As in *Moves* and *Opus Jazz*, the dancers all wear practice clothes, nothing as obvious as bobby sox and saddle shoes. Yet there's a suggestion of period all the same. The men wear black pants and high-neck sweaters, each in a different pastel color. The women wear black leotards with funny bib-vests tied over them — the kind we used to wear in gym so you could tell one team from the other. The colors are pastels to match the men's tops. Their black tights are cut off at the ankles, modern dancer style, and their feet seem to be bare in their pointe shoes. Maybe it's the pony-tail hairdos on the girls, or the look of, the tights, or their sleeves pushed halfway up the forearms, but they don't look quite like today's dancers.

They don't even look quite like ballet dancers, even though their moods — greeting, showing off, romance, competition — are framed in ballet steps. *Interplay* is the first Robbins ballet (*The Concert, Afternoon of a Faun* and *Ma Mère l'Oye* are others) that was essentially about dance, as an idiom with its own slang, poetry, and historical nuance that the dancers know, even if the audience doesn't, and use to communicate with each other.

I've never seen *Interplay* done by technicians. Sometimes I've wished for that, wondered what it would look like if all the feet were pointed, the line perfect, the men's cascade of double tours en l'air at the end were more secure. But finally I see Robbins' reasons for not casting it that way. He choreographed it originally as a number in a Broadway show, Billy Rose's "Concert Varieties," and then gave it to Ballet Theater. In not being didactic about the ballet vocabulary, he allows us to see the work's contemporary shading. Highly classical dancers might not be able to weight the steps ever so slightly, to flash from the end of one step to the beginning of the next without pausing to readjust, to let their arms fail to complete what their legs have started, or to interrupt the long flow of balletic discourse with syncopated gestural remarks. Edward Verso, who danced with Robbins' short-lived Ballets: U.S.A. and did key Robbins roles for the Joffrey, exemplifies the style of these works. He had an easy understated adaptability without being athletic, effeminate, or mannered. Verso is one of the few dancers I could describe as having "grace" and mean something by it.

The actual moments of jazzy dancing in *Interplay* are quite distinct from the balletic continuum of the work, and they usually seem to be there to make a point. Writing in the mid-1950s, Rosalyn Krokover characterized *Interplay* as a subtle put-down of ballet: "It pays lip service to the choreographic amenities, much as high-school kids pay lip service to their teachers, but underneath displays an impatience with, and even a mockery of, the balletic status quo."[2] It's hard to know whether this kind of reaction comes from the way the work was being danced at the time or from the writer's personal interpretation. The piece hardly seems political today.

The 1950s saw the last defense of the various stylistic territories to which the first generation of American dancers had staked their claims, a defense that was doomed and therefore perhaps all the more tenacious. Till then, ballet, modern, and jazz were separate dance entities that came together with trepidation and coexisted self-consciously at best. Thinking about the ways that people had incorporated vernacular dancing into ballets up to 1945, it seems as if jazz could only be used in a character sense, as Christensen had done in *Filling Station* or Robbins in *Fancy Free,* or as a thing set apart from serious ballet. Katherine Dunham was using a ballet vocabulary with a Latin flavor as early as the forties, but she was doing it on Broadway; she was doing entertainment.

So perhaps the early viewers and performers of *Interplay* looked for some polemical justification that would make it all right to do that on a ballet stage. Now, *Interplay* looks like an innocent caper whose language is largely classical, done in a relaxed way, with "period" interjections. The dancers don't seem to be cheating on the ballet steps so much as taking them easy.

But the comment on our cultural xenophobia, soft-pedaled now that it's no longer cute, still marks the ballet. In the middle of the exuberant get-together of the first section, the orchestra breaks into a boogie-woogie beat. The dancers come down to the edge of the pit and peer down, perplexed. One or two of them try a few jazz steps, but none of them really speaks that language, and soon the music becomes more regular. In the second section, a man dances a solo while the other dancers stand casually around the edges of the stage. He wants to show off for them. He does a long series of textbook feats, and every time he undercuts the virtuosity of the steps by breaking off to ingratiate himself with his companions. He

INTERPLAY (*Robbins, 1945*). *Chris Mayer, Bob Thompson, Susan Bourree of Ballets U.S.A. Photo by Martha Swope.*

beckons to the girls to join him in a mock minuet for a couple of bars. He kiddingly bobs up and down in front of a group to get them to do the same thing in response. He reaches for another man's handshake and hugely fails to connect. He throws away the ends of sequences, converting a pose into a sissy's wave of the hand, punctuates a series of pirouettes with fanny wiggles. He comes out of some jumps in arabesque as a big lumbering swan. If you grew up in that America, you learned that artistic tastes or talents were an embarrassing thing to have. Boys especially were thought peculiar, deviant, or even dangerous if they didn't pretend art was a joke and hide their passion for it. Twenty-five years after high school, male classmates admitted to me that they used to sneak off to New York to see the ballet.

But the fear of showing real feelings hangs over all of *Interplay*. After this dance, the boy sinks to the floor, tired out. One of the girls comes over and asks him to dance but he waves away her proposal. Rejected once, she goes to another boy and slowly takes his hand, not quite looking at him in case he should take her too seriously. They dance a pas de deux, romantic out of all proportion to the casualness of the encounter, possibly even a dream. Meanwhile the others pay no attention: the solo boy lies on his back and the others pose in silhouette, catching the beat of the music with intermittent finger-snapping bounces.

At the end of the duet, the couple sit on the floor, leaning against each other. But as if unable to let this elegiac mood go on too long, another boy jumps up and galvanizes the group into action again with his plan for a dance contest. From this point on, the couple never exchange another look. Teams are chosen; the rules are that each side sends out a contender who does a ballet trick — jumps, beats, pirouettes, fouettés, air turns — then the other side has to better the performance. It all happens too fast for the audience to keep score, and both sides act as if they're winning. Finally they all circle the stage in a chorus of piqué turns, and, in some way too intricate to follow, they all end up facing the audience and posing brightly.

N. Y. Export: Opus Jazz (Jerome Robbins)

The bravado that Robbins discovered in youth, the fear of involvement and the desperate need for conformity, the surplus energy that finds its outlet in skittish sexual attractions and athletic displays, became the emotional coinage of many of his later ballets. What is harmless and even a little sweet in *Interplay* here grows brittle and explosive. Playfulness turns into manipulation. Diffidence becomes hostility. A program note that has accompanied *N.Y. Export: Opus Jazz* since its première explains that all young people identify with black and Latin dance music because they feel themselves a minority in a hostile world environment. This is a large and debatable claim, but it probably accounts only minimally for the success of "West Side Story" and its immediate descendant *Opus Jazz* anyway. The ballet as we see it today is so well crafted that we can only think how much more vital and effective it is than the years of show and TV dancing that followed it. Sneaker-clad toughs doing their dance of rape or boisterous conciliation in the shadow of the expressway is now an inescapable cliché. Nothing can lift it out of the realm of the fictional for us.

I think *Opus Jazz* was meant to be a propaganda piece in the first place. Created for Robbins' Ballets: U.S.A., with a hot-jazz score by Robert Prince, it was literally exported to Spoleto and other places overseas, where the company presented this brand of American ballet with great success. It still works best when you accept it as a dance that's *showing* something, not as a dance that *is* something. Its very showiness has some ring of familiarity to us — I think of the energy and competitiveness that were aroused in apathetic ghetto kids during the play-producing days of the first poverty programs.

Opus Jazz magnifies our experience of the urban environment. Commentators have spoken of Robbins as translating "American" energy into theater dance. It seems to me he has absorbed something from the city where he lives, New York. In *Fancy Free* and *Interplay* this comes across as a kind of independence, a readiness for the unexpected, an alertness to the main chance, a mobility to go in any direction, and a resilience to shock or disappointment. By the time he gets to *Opus Jazz*, Robbins has intensified all of this into wariness, suspicion, an instant command of one's body as an instrument of defense or attack, and a rather desperate need to belong to the crowd.

Opus Jazz begins in very much the same way as *Interplay* and *Moves*, with the dancers individually confronting the audience. Here they run on one at a time, stop, and stare out across the

N. Y. Export: Opus Jazz (*Robbins, 1958*). *Joffrey Ballet. Photo by Herbert Migdoll.*

footlights, then step back and slowly squat and touch the floor — their turf — while still staring belligerently at the audience. Robbins used the same gesture ten years later in a quiet, almost meditative way, at the end of *Dances at a Gathering*. I know people who are incensed by it. It is so extreme, so patently phony; no person would ever do such a thing. And yet Robbins insists on its importance; he forces us to accept it as a metaphor.

The first section of the dance takes place against a backdrop of TV antennas by Ben Shahn, drawn, as are the drops for the other sections, with a cartoonlike sarcasm and eccentricity. The dance, however, proceeds without quirks, except for the duet; indeed, it's almost melodramatically predictable. The dancers, all dressed alike in black tights, sneakers, and loose-fitting, brightly colored tops, dance together in the first part, clustered in a tight, front-facing formation, swaying from one leg to the other and snapping their fingers. They break and spread out all over the stage, following some mutually understood pattern of meeting and crossing. Their movement is very isolated and gestural — they walk bent over, on their toes, lifting one hip, then the other; a girl raises an arm, holds it hanging in the air for an instant, then lets a wrist go limp; someone drops into a crouch and simultaneously snaps one challenging finger in front of him. At the end of the dance they all cluster in the center again, reach up high, and suddenly collapse to the floor.

The second interlude takes place on a rooftop. Three boys do a macho display dance. A girl enters, provokes them sexually. Two of them leave and she dances a duet with the third. The two boys return with another boy and suddenly the girl is facing all four of them, fending them off with hands spread out flat on a level with her hips. There's a brief, symbolic rape as each boy lifts and turns the girl in the air. Then all of them pick her up and throw her off-stage, presumably off the roof.

In contrast to this violence, the ballet shifts to the high school gym or some other athletic court, where the kids clown and show off for each other. They crowd around while one after another comes out to the center. Whenever anyone gets carried away by the rhythm and begins a very fast bumping of the pelvis, the others yell "Watch that!" and "Uh, uh!" as if *that* particular gesture of all the suggestive motions they have been doing is forbidden. There is a certain kind of sexual prudery that the teen-age tribe used to exert over its members, a group recognition of drives they weren't supposed to be grown up enough to feel more than a real effort to prevent sexual behavior. In this group the gesture is doubly ironic; their real sexuality is so potent and so threatening that it must be kept secret.

Now, dropped into the midst of this raucous socializing and sexual bravado, like a furtive confession, comes a strange Anna Sokolow–like duet. It was danced in Joffrey productions by Beatriz Rodriguez and Edward Verso, who looked intelligent, smoldering, the kids who would climb out of the ghetto and into law school. The stage is dark, there's nothing on it except a bright collage of ad words in display type: NOW, LOOK, SECR. The dancers walk slowly onstage, he from the audience's right, she from the left, not looking at each other, but aware, savoring the moment their paths will cross. They pause, very close. The music, a muted trumpet, makes its way through fragments of a blues, wandering from key to key, irresolute, noncommittal, stopping and starting again before a melody is complete.

The boy reaches out and touches the girl's shoulder. He pushes it down ever so slightly, as if testing her. He takes his hand away, puts the other hand on her waist; they take a step together. He lowers his face to her chest, as if he were going to kiss her, but instead he pushes her chin up with the top of his head. Without looking her in the face — in fact, their eyes slide away from contact for the whole dance — he pushes at her foot with his foot, her arm with his arm. Each contact is loaded, sensual.

Suddenly they are on their knees facing each other. Chest to chest, they rotate their heads back and around so that their cheeks touch but their eyes don't meet. The man's arms are thrust straight out toward the audience, his hands balled up into fists. Without moving anything else, he uncurls his hands, extending his fingers and palms, reaching in anger or frustration. You don't know what the girl feels. The boy starts to leave, goes back to her, lifts and positions her so that when he stands up, she lies across his back, looking away and holding her foot behind her. Back to back, she sits on his shoulders, then slowly slides down to the floor. They each extend one hand overhead and touch there, behind and above their heads. Then they go out, she to the right and he to the left, without looking back.

This dance, which is hardly a dance but is even less a pantomime, has meant various things to me at various times. Sometimes the performance is harsh and violent, and what assails me about it is the man's manipulativeness and the woman's acquiescence and the dispassionateness of both of them. At other times it seems unbearably sad that they have this intense attraction to each other but are unable to find mutual ease once they are together. I have puzzled over the repressed — almost Victorian — evasion of direct contact or responsibility. Whatever else there is about this pas de deux, it has an overwhelming sense of isolation. The characters can only encounter one another this way when they are away from the protection and rules of the crowd — and their affair may later on cause them shame or regret or just an existential despair.

The tension lifts, the stage brightens. All the dancers return, dressed in the same black tights with white sneakers and white versions of the same tops they wore earlier. They space themselves evenly around the stage and face the audience. They've dropped their city kid personae completely. Robbins seems to have cleared away the character attributes that have gone before, and he starts the ballet again. The group in unison does a slow eight-bar series of movements with no inflexion at all. They do it again, faster, then in double time. As the sequence repeats it becomes looser and an implicit rhythm creeps in. Finally the group rearranges itself and a long set of solo and small ensemble variations begins, climaxed by a fugue that erupts out of a tight formation very much like the one at the beginning of the ballet. Robbins seems to be saying that what we've been looking at as belonging to one particular time and group of people actually comes from the same impulse as all of dance, and can be worked with as seriously by the choreographer as any other movement form.

Moves (Jerome Robbins)

Unlike *Opus Jazz* and *Interplay*, *Moves* has no particular period or place. The movement vocabulary contains no popular dance allusions; it entirely consists of ballet steps and what was called "everyday movement" by modern dancers who were also using it at that time. The dancer didn't always have to move in a stylized way from one prescribed position to another. Sometimes he could just walk, or lift his hand, or turn his head, the way he would in real life. I don't know who first used this device in a serious manner — it's been used for centuries in comedy, and Robbins knew it in that form when he created the role of Hermes in David Lichine's *Helen of Troy* (1942), where he dropped his role as messenger and cupid for some Greek gods and mortals in order to make visual wisecracks to the audience. Certainly Anna Sokolow was most effective in utilizing the plainness of gestures, and Robbins' choreography in *Moves* and the duet from *Opus Jazz* shows a Sokolovian desire to drop the masks of technique that separate the ballet dancer from the audience.

But in place of the good-natured camaraderie of his two earlier works, *Moves* is dark, intense, at times almost fevered. The people in it are no longer adolescents — they are self-assured, self-aware — life is a serious business to them; they have weighed and calculated the probable effect of their actions, and even if things don't go their way, they don't permit disappointment to show. What makes this an heir to the two other works, I think, is that Robbins decided to develop the dance along its own rhythmic lines rather than according to a musical score. The ballet is danced in silence, but the visual music is jazz, maybe the purest, harshest jazz because the dynamics are all there is. You feel the strong downbeat and its momentum surging into the phrase. The staccato interruption, the pauses when a breath stops and is suddenly expelled. The gaudy decoration and the square, matter-of-fact cadence. You feel the drive of it, the sense that nothing can stop it till it's completed. You also feel the dancers straining to stay connected to one another; the shape of the energy is their lifeline. With no aural scenario keeping time for them, they seem automatically to exaggerate the impulses and focuses with which movements arise and succeed one another.

Studying the choreography of *Moves,* I realized how complicated the ballet is compared to the two earlier works. The dance seems almost overloaded with canonic devices and small modifications intended to make the movement look different without having the dancers actually do anything different. It's almost as if Robbins were filling in with visual harmonics for the missing aural dimension.

Moves begins with a little ceremony, Oriental in feeling except for its businesslike tempo. The stage is bare when the curtain goes up, a space enclosed in black drapes dramatically revealed under slowly brightening lights. Ten dancers file onstage across the backdrop, walking at a brisk pace, heels down and firmly set into the floor. They wear practice clothes, pared down and close to the body, but all different, in dark colors and beige, white, and black. Just before she gets to the opposite wing, the girl at the head of the line stops, and the whole line stops with her, spaced evenly apart.

After a pause they all do a slow plié together. A pause, and they all extend the downstage leg, slide it along the floor to the side of them, then abruptly pivot together to face the audience. One by one they begin a slow port de bras. Then they come forward together to the footlights, face the audience for a moment, and all make a little obeisance with their hands and incline their heads. Another pause, then, one at a time they begin to break the formality of the line. Sliding diagonally into a wide plié, each person spreads his or her arms out to the side, twists the upper torso back and forth once from the waist, then pulls back into position. The tension seems unbearable. Slackening it for the first time, one man settles his weight into one hip and folds his arms. Suddenly, twisting their arms behind their backs, as if it were the only way they could tear themselves out of the mold they are creating, one person after another bursts out of the line and runs to a spot somewhere on the stage. One man stops in center stage, wheels, and in a single move throws both his arms out in a commanding gesture toward the woman who led the line. She goes to him, as if magnetized, with fast, traveling turns. The man grabs her and slams her, face down, on the floor. The rest of the group watches this; then they turn, stretch slowly, and leave.

The duet that follows is a lot like the duet from *Opus Jazz*, except that the hostile attraction between the two people, instead of being contained, is allowed to flare and burn itself away to expose the sexual need that lies underneath. Verso, angry this time and taut, danced this with Rebecca Wright and later with Beatriz Rodriguez. First the woman is lying on the floor, on her stomach, and the man stands behind her. With her hands spread beside her as if to support herself, she lifts her head and chest off the ground. While her chest is lifted, she takes her hands cautiously away from the floor. She looks around but not behind her at the man. One toe of a flexed foot digs into the floor, pushing her legs away from the ground, while the other foot makes a flurry of petits battements in the air. Balanced on her foot and hands, she raises her whole body, almost as if she were about to sprint, then continues to bring one leg under her pelvis and out in front of her and lowers herself into a split.

The man lifts her by the armpits from behind into a half-kneeling position. He grabs her wrists and pulls her hands behind her back. Slowly, almost sadistically, he puts one hand on her forehead and bends her head way back. Again he lifts her, into a sitting position that looks contrived and difficult to maintain unsupported: with her back straight, she curves her arms up and to the sides, palms up; one leg extends straight ahead with the foot flexed, the other also points straight ahead, with the knee bent and the foot flat on the floor. These poses are two of many things the women do in *Moves* that make them seem remote, mechanical. Robbins arranges them to exploit their physical beauty — the curve of the calf, the length of the neck, the sinuosity of the upper torso — while limiting their mobility or their capacity for change. The woman's first pose of the duet, on her stomach, is another example.

As she sits, she's inviting the man to manipulate her, and he does. Putting his palm on one of hers, he presses down. Suddenly he seems to become impatient. Stamping hard on the floor close to her body, he now violently picks her up and places her in attitude. Holding her back leg, he lifts her, carries her a few steps, then yanks her into another position. After a few more such tangles, they stand side by side for a minute, touching at arm's length. Briefly they skirmish on the run, taking big swipes at each other that seem filled with venom but are carefully timed or aimed so as not to actually harm the other person. The man comes slashing down to the footlights and makes a fast, complicated cross to the other side, where he lets his body go limp for a minute, then stands watchfully.

The woman comes downstage and pretends to be absorbed in some brisk pliés. All of a sudden she stops, as if she's decided the game isn't interesting anymore. She runs across the footlights and plunges head first into the man's arms — a dive that could also have preceded her first pose on the floor. He puts her down and they stand motionless, close together, exhausted, neither one wanting to signal a truce. Then the woman puts her head quietly down on the man's chest; he drops his head to hers, and one limb at a time she lifts herself and he picks her up. He circles her waist with one arm and leads offstage with the other; she sits there, in an echo of her sitting position on the floor, stretching and bending her legs as if walking in the direction he's taking them.

The duet is followed by a very short dance for five men, another of Robbins' comradely combats, in which they can't achieve complete unanimity because one is always doing something different. Two of them grapple once, then immediately walk away. Two others scuffle briefly. The whole episode has an undertone of dissension and uneasiness. There's work to be done precisely, but someone always spoils it, to the irritation of the others. They reach agreement at the last moment, when they all gather center stage, aim hard blows into the air in the middle of the circle, then wheel and fall forward, away from each other, as the stage blacks out.

Four women then dance basically the same thing, with softer dynamics and twistier, filigreed shapes. I think of the women in this dance as a group you might find in the ladies' room of I. Magnin or having lunch at the Plaza. Sleek and knowing, they avoid direct conflict, preserve alliances when it doesn't matter, but make sure they will be noticed when it comes to open disagreement. They show off their "feminine" wares even though there are no men present, as if to intimidate their future rivals.

Compositionally, the women's dance elaborates on a theme that Robbins has been developing — that of the incompleted pattern or the unfinished shape. Three of the women do a long sequence of moves in which two of them act together and the third makes the same motions alone. Of course, the odd woman's gesture looks different, but in this context what you notice is how alike the women all are. The dance ends as all four women line up in profile to the audience and indicate the woman's final pose from the *Agon* pas de deux. They may have each other, but what's pointedly missing is the man.

In the next section of the ballet, several duos and trios perform simultaneously, doing variations of the same idea. The movement sequence has to do with ballet partnering. Instead of showing you the final poses and skimming over how the dancers achieve them, Robbins emphasizes the mechanical placements and steadyings of balance — a girl puts her hands on the shoulders of a man facing her, goes up on pointe and into arabesque. While she holds the arabesque, another man replaces her partner. Some of the dancers are without partners for some of the time, but they do the same movement as far as is possible. All the dancers perform this together and standing in place, so the audience can really see the choreography in all its different guises.

Another explosive pas de deux comes out of this demonstration, but where the first couple were together even in their disharmony,

Moves (*Robbins, 1959*). *Joffrey Ballet. Photo by Herbert Migdoll.*

this one is jagged, clashing. He is soft and slow, she is quick and nervous. When he wants her, she's not ready. When she's ready, he's out of patience. At the end, she waits, he starts to leave, hesitates, keeps going. She goes out the other way without a sign of regret. While their encounter is taking place, two other couples are dancing in place upstage. They are homosexual, one male, one female. In all three duets, the basic activity is more dramatic than lyrical; it isn't their dance but the development of their relationships, one phase at a time, that we notice.

The last section is reminiscent of the last part of *Opus Jazz* — again the neat, academic ending that ties up all the themes and demonstrates that they are serviceable enough to use in more than one context. But in a way Robbins has been quite didactic all through *Moves*, and rather than seeming excessive, the finale lets the whole ballet open up to space, and to speculation.

The departure of the three couples leaves an empty stage. Then all the dancers run on from all sides, reaching for one spot above the stage. They all meet in the center, reaching up, a visual inversion of the flower-opening fall at the end of the men's dance or the group's sinking-down circle in *Opus Jazz*. Taking their own timing, they reach around a few times and touch the people near them, but it's just a touch, evoking no reaction, a means of rearranging the design of the group. The sequence is fragmented, like a series of stop-action films.

But if the group doesn't seem to act in concert when it is physically in contact, when it breaks apart and each dancer finds his own spot on the floor with space around him, a current seems to pass through them. They stand still for a moment, waiting for the next cue. Then Verso clasps his hands together, stretches them over his head with the palms turned outward, and begins a typical dancer's warm-up, bending to the side, then straightening and bending to the other side. After a few stretches and pliés, he begins a soft jogging in place, limbering up his feet. The other dancers immediately catch his rhythm — those easy, repetitive bounces, those well-loved movements that they treat their bodies to each day; this is as comfortable as breathing to them.

Though they all begin at different times, face different directions, do slightly different motions, their energy is the same. So is their progression from one kind of activity to another, from bending and pliés to faster-paced running in place, to more vigorous twistings and foldings. Their attention is on their bodies, but they listen, as we do, with a kind of third ear, to a tempo created by them all, and gradually everyone comes into congruence with this beat. We become aware of the pace of running feet as they begin traveling through the space. The texture of the sound changes almost before we see that some of them are leaping, then all of them are leaping, and the steady beat is broken as they go into the air. The pauses become longer as women are lifted high above the stage and carried in the air. This sequence is one of the most satisfying things to watch in all of ballet. It is logical, coherent, and simple, and Robbins forces it just enough, condensing the natural time span to make us see how one kind of exercise leads into the next. It's like an elegant lecture-demonstration on ballet technique compressed into about two minutes.

Then, I don't know how they get there, the dancers are spread out all over the stage again, and, reverting to the hothouse dynamics of the earlier part of the ballet, they recapitulate all the themes — the men's stamping theme, the women's narcissistic display of face and torso, the couples' battlings and submissions, the partnerings and posings — in a very short space of time and simultaneously. Almost before you have figured out what's taking place, you see that a line is beginning to take shape across the footlights, and as the last two people step back from their thematic poses, you recognize the same row of dancers that greeted the audience at the beginning; except they are in different places now, and there are twelve dancers in the line instead of ten. Again they make their reverence with their hands and incline their heads, then they turn on their heel and stride away into a darkening stage as the curtain comes down.

That addition of two dancers at the end intrigues me unreasonably. After all, Robbins hardly emphasizes the point; the average audience member, seeing the ballet once, would never notice the change. The careful viewer might feel some dislocation has occurred but not be able to put his finger on just what. But then, when you realize what, the idea is so odd you try to figure out how it happened. Perhaps two dancers were sick when Robbins choreographed the opening, or they were late when the curtain went up for the first performance and Robbins liked the oddness and kept it. Perhaps he wants to make a symbolic point: no pattern is complete even when it looks complete; or most people don't recognize a complete pattern when they see one; or *neither* ten nor twelve people complete this pattern, it is infinitely expandable and compressible.

Deuce Coupe (Twyla Tharp)

Deuce Coupe is a dance of passage. I should say it *was*, because in a world where the survival of any work is doubtful, this one is especially unlikely to be seen again in its original form. *Deuce Coupe* was so big, so unconventional, and so powerful in its impact that one is tempted to see it as a parable of manifold implications, like *Paradise Lost* or the *Odyssey*; and I think even its quick demise was symbolic.

I can't be sure why Robert Joffrey picked Twyla Tharp out of all the modern dance choreographers who might have been ready to venture into ballet in 1973. Tharp took ballet classes, but so do many modern dancers, and the work she had done for her own company up to that time certainly could not be called balletic. It was no longer considered daring, however, for a modern dancer to make a ballet. Anna Sokolow had done *Opus 65* for the Joffrey, though it didn't have any ballet steps in it. Alvin Ailey's *The River* for Ballet Theater in 1970, if not the first, was one of the most clear-cut and successful attempts to treat the ballet idiom from a modern point of view, rather than appending some modern shapes to the classical vocabulary. So fast are we consuming novelty that by now Martha Graham and Murray Louis are choreographing for Nureyev, and in a few years even that may not seem extravagant.

Joffrey no doubt spotted Twyla Tharp's extraordinary ability as a choreographer; he probably also liked the idea that she was working her way through American popular music styles as her accompaniments: Scott Joplin, Jelly Roll Morton, Bix Beiderbecke, Fats Waller, and Chuck Berry have all served Tharp's imagination. As prophetic of public taste as Robert Joffrey is, however, I'm not sure even he realized what a blockbuster he was going to produce.

Deuce Coupe, to rock 'n' roll songs by the Beach Boys, was danced by fifteen Joffrey dancers and the six members of Tharp's modern dance company. Teen-agers recruited from New York's United Graffiti Artists painted new subway-car-art backdrops during each performance. Audiences adored it. During its first season, four per-

DEUCE COUPE (*Twyla Tharp, 1973*). *Joffrey Ballet. Photo by Herbert Migdoll.*

formances were added to the six originally scheduled. The following fall it ran for six performances, and Tharp did a second work for Joffrey, *As Time Goes By*. Then, except for some performances on the road, *Deuce Coupe* vanished. In the spring of 1975 Tharp remade the work for the Joffrey dancers alone; *Deuce Coupe II* bore scant resemblance to its predecessor. But that too is part of the symbolism.

Everything about *Deuce Coupe* proclaimed its disposability. Like the male soloist in *Interplay*, Twyla Tharp has an overwhelming offhandedness about what is most important to her. She has been labeled a smart-aleck, an iconoclast, an intellectual, but underneath the wise guy is someone who cares more than anything else about how dancing is performed and what dancing means. The concept of *Deuce Coupe* is magnificent. It was planned as a fusion of modern dance and ballet, innovation and tradition, fun and morality, free-flowing energy and draftsmanlike construction, ideas and beauty and sentiment, in which all things would be respected, nothing slighted or put down. And it worked. Most important, it worked on the immediate level of entertainment. Those viewers who are turned off by the cerebral aspects of other ballets never had to confront anything heavy in *Deuce Coupe* in order to "get it." I think this is another part of the way we define pop dance; all pop dance aims to offer this kind of gratification to the audience. But *Deuce Coupe* has something below the surface as well.

Two ideas, their polarity and eventual resolution, are the substance of *Deuce Coupe*. They are stated point-blank as the ballet opens, with only three dancers onstage. One of them is doing a lexicon of ballet steps and the other two perform a duet that is much freer in its use of the body but not improvised or formless. The duo don't actually use rock steps but they have a more flexible use of the torso than the ballet dancer; their legs, arms, heads, can move independently of the line of the body; they aren't concerned with placement or delineating a certain space around their bodies — they use space more as a receptacle for changing energies.

For about the first two thirds of the ballet, the classical dancer remains on the scene. She may leave and come back, stay in place a lot, or sometimes travel short distances on the stage. But in her quiet concentration and clarity of line she seems fixed. She creates a kind of fulcrum around which everything else has to revolve or a strong opposing focus against which everything else competes. Her steadiness anchors the restless, transitory energies of the other dancers. At the same time you can see that she isn't immune to their drive and eccentricity; without giving up her own steps, she sometimes catches a vibration or a quirk from the swirling mass around her.

Although the ballet dancer has to perform a didactic task — she demonstrates the steps in a ballet alphabet book — Tharp doesn't quite allow her to capture the audience with either her lesson or the brilliance of her technique. She may hold a star position but there's always a counteraction going on around her, diffusing the impression she makes, breaking up the smooth continuity of her phrase by drawing our eyes away. What is odd about this — for a ballet — is the independence of the two factions. They work apart from one another without trying to change or eradicate what the other is doing. It is this condition of mutual respect that makes the end of the ballet possible.

In the surge and ebb of its collective energies, the larger group of dancers makes its statement about the unruly passions and fads of youth. One of Twyla Tharp's most important contributions to choreography is the way she can show us the appropriate kind of energy for a particular idea and be as convincing as if she had copied the spatial form or pantomimed the action. Most of the sections of *Deuce Coupe* have to do with what the Beach Boys are singing about, the appurtenances, affections, and knee-jerk liberalism of middle-class American teen-agers. More specifically, the Beach Boys refer to Southern California in the 1960s; their songs are elegies to acquisitiveness, to the motorcycle and the surfboard, to the care and gratification of bodies that grew up in a nourishing if polluted year-round sunshine. Theirs is a benevolent world, quite unlike the harsh, potentially violent streets of *Opus 65* and *Opus Jazz*. Their rhythms are regular, their harmonies are agreeable. Nothing abrasive or even suggestive puts an edge on their sentiment; nothing in their Rotarian thought suggests militancy or even a subversively high IQ.

It is this community, who are soon to graduate into ranch house owning, Dodge driving, Saturday night beer-drinking, TV-watching citizens, that Tharp is describing without rancor in *Deuce Coupe*. The ballet celebrates the last fling of undisciplined enthusiasm and mischief before a person enters adulthood. It doesn't take a grim view of this process of socialization, either. The gradual adoption of more formal movement and floor patterns by the dancers could parallel the conversion of the United Graffiti Artists behind them — from outlaws who broke into train yards to paint their names on subway cars into an organization of would-be serious artists or at least entrepreneurs trying to sell their work instead of giving it away. It could even refer to the emergence of Tharp herself from the insecurity of the avant-garde into the more restrained business of being a successful choreographer for ballet.

Tharp shows us this community in so many ways that by the end of the ballet we know quite a lot about it. For one thing, it is extraordinarily self-contained and self-involved. Not only do its members dance their own dance, in utter disregard of the mature aesthetic being demonstrated right before their eyes. They have, as the songs tell us, their own toys and equipment, practically unknown to the rest of society: little Deuce Coupe automobiles, Honda bikes, and surfboards to catch a wave. They have their own codes and their own tribal rites. They read the funny papers, keep their feet in shape with avocado rub, and find their heroes at the movies and rock concerts. They listen to the advice of their mothers and have a curiously unsexual idea of romance. Their entertainments, Tharp shows us, include turning on with pot, roller-skating, and of course dancing. When they become concerned with pollution it's not for humanitarian reasons but because dirty water spoils their swimming.

Despite their insularity and the narrow range of their interests, these adolescents are not conformists. Nor do they pressure their friends to conform. They seem to operate primarily on the level of tuning in to their own vibes. Sometimes this results in competitions, in showing off, or in fragmented, frenetic activity that doesn't coalesce within the stage space. Other times they collect into a single kinetic organism, when they can submerge all their disparate reflexes in the same activity. This can begin with a literal action — like the inhaling of dope ("Papa Ooh Mau Mau") — or it can come to a head out of a boiling mass of motion. In the pot-smoking episode, six people stand at one side of the stage in a tight group. Very slowly they mime taking drags on a marijuana cigarette. When each one feels ready, they begin to grind their pelvises and pump their arms up and down in a sort of slow-motion frug or monkey. They begin to travel across the stage, speeding up as they go, until they reach the other side in an orgy of shudders and shakes and percussive jerks of the body, then flash out of sight. All of the motions in this brief scene are individual, all the participants are completely remote from the others. Yet, in the grip of their collective turn-on, they form one accelerating, intensifying machine that carries them away.

This energy building up to the point where it's irresistible can occur without an initial form to set it in motion, as in "How She Boogalooed It," where a large crowd of dancers are bouncing and skittering around the stage in all directions. They begin to come in contact with one another — clasping hands and swinging, or doing some lifts and slides that look like vestigial traces of the jitterbug. Then the space that has been dense with multifocused activity begins to clear, the directionality of the action crystallizes, and the dancers are snaking in a long chain, weaving back and forth around Erika Goodman, the ballet girl. The chain breaks, but now the audience can follow individual dancers better, as if we were watching people on a skating rink.

In this community the differences between individuals are not great, but differences are tolerated. In Robbins' world or Sokolow's, someone who has something special to say either has to have the conviction to announce it or tells it in private. In Tharp's world, the individual isn't very important; he says his say any old time — to himself, in a crowd, very often while others are talking. His idea may agree with the others' or not, but it doesn't matter because nobody may have heard; he can change his mind the next day and get the same inattention. The varieties of discourse in *Deuce Coupe* are many — people dance overlapping solos, they interrupt each other, they stop in the middle of something and let others continue, they echo each other in canon, they make individual statements against noise from the others. What stands out about the entire ballet is that the dancers never actually dance together; that is, in balletic unison. Nor do they cooperate often as partners.

The fact that the space is almost never unified, that people don't act in concert although they are often doing things at the same time, gives the audience a feeling of restlessness, even vagueness. The scene is not only spatially confused much of the time, it's changing all the time. The dancers' moods shift constantly. They show off, they make jokes, do imitations; they argue, sometimes offhandedly, sometimes angrily; they pretend to be sexy; they are romantic; and most often they are hyperactive. Never calm or introspective, they love speed ("Honda, Honda, faster, faster!"), danger, and disorientation.

Then the ballet has a turning point. Structurally — the audience isn't aware of this, but it's important — Tharp has been introducing certain thematic material at intervals throughout the work. In different forms, all with the incongruous title of "Matrix" and accompanied by versions of the Beach Boys song "Cuddle Up," dancers present this theme material, usually at the same time that other parts of the dance are going on. Then come two overlapping solos, both done to "Got to Know the Woman," in which first Sara Rudner, then Erika Goodman, expresses an idealized image of a woman, each in her own movement vernacular. Goodman then does her version of "Matrix," at the same time finishing the ballet dictionary, and she leaves, not to return until the end of the ballet. The pollution dance ("Don't Go Near the Water") follows: a line of women doing swimming motions with their arms, gradually becoming jerky, spastic, the most fragmented movement in the ballet. This is the one part of *Deuce Coupe* that always seemed too long to me, maybe because the dancers looked so destroyed when they did it. But it's possible that Tharp wanted to emphasize the fragmentation, because out of the middle of this dance the ballet finds a kind of desperation, and out of this desperation a need for order.

Poking and pushing their arms helplessly above their heads, the women lurch offstage. But one of them is left. She staggers across the stage until a boy comes by and, in the standoffish manner they all have with each other, he puts an arm out so that she will bump into it and slow down. Without picking her up or doing anything so definite as putting his hands around her waist to stop her, he succeeds in calming her down so that she can control herself, and they both leave. Another girl takes her place and with a chorus of men behind her she does a joyous, bouncy dance.

This dance begins a long sequence of much more orderly, conventional dancing. Not that the ballet ever gets to look like Petipa. But it does become organized in terms of its own element. Dancers begin taking positions with attention to the space around them; they stop getting in each other's way and distribute themselves more evenly through the space, making room for their gestures to be seen. They begin sticking closer to one spot instead of darting all around so that we lose track of them. And they begin paying attention to the outward appearance of their movement. You sense that they're doing it for each other now, sometimes even for the audience. Compositional forms appear quite clearly, as if they were meant to be shown instead of hidden. You can see that the dancers are adjusting their movements to look more alike, to be more connected to the actions of their companions. These are all signs of a developing maturity.

The boys in this section do a series of balletic phrases, all at different times, while the girl spins and skips around them. Then ten dancers take over the space and state a similar canonic idea, all using the same movement elements, but in this dance they stop and hold still after each piece of the phrase so that the audience can look around and see other people continuing it. It's like the old film technique where the camera skims through the crowd, zeroing in on one face after another.

Tharp herself does the "Matrix" theme then, fragmenting it, flinging it more wildly than anyone, as if she represented its purest, least suppressed form. All the dancers come back, led by Erika Goodman, in a new variation of the procession in which they entered at the beginning of the ballet. This time they pass a movement phrase from one to another, segment by segment, so that the audience's eye can travel along the entering line to see the phrase completed. As the line crosses the stage, it disperses, each person going off to work independently. Once more the space breaks up, gets busy and hard to define. But this time the dancers, or sometimes little groups of two or three dancers, do pieces of thematic material that we have been seeing throughout the ballet.

From the beginning of Tharp's "Matrix," the Beach Boys have been singing "Cuddle Up" — the first time we've heard the words, and extraordinarily banal words they are. The music works up to a big climax, the lover is telling his girl how terrific she is, warm and good . . . and he becomes progressively inarticulate until at the musical high point all he can say is "Honey!" then sort of hum down from it and shyly end with: "I know a man who's so in love, hmmmmm."

Imperceptibly the dancers have been edging over to one side of the stage, and as the music says "Honey!" for the last time they freeze. The stage lights go out except for one spotlight on the group. They're posing as if caught by a news photographer at some event that's crucial for all of them, but we can't quite tell what the event is. People are facing in various directions; some are on the floor, some are standing, one girl is being lifted in the air by several people. Erika Goodman, doing one last ballet entry, is frozen center stage, looking away from them.

Then the moment is over. The music drifts away on a little piano coda, and the dancers too drift away a few at a time. The girl being lifted is placed on the floor. Did she die? Did they all die? Or did the ballet die, as abruptly and unpredictably as it came to us in the first place?

Crystallization II

Afternoon of a Faun (Jerome Robbins)

In some ways *Afternoon of a Faun* is not a ballet at all; but I think Jerome Robbins' contribution to American dance lies somewhere in the dynamic between a reference to dance and a freedom from dance. Robbins has not been an easy choreographer to classify. After his initial success with *Fancy Free*, he relinquished the secure position he undoubtedly could have had as a resident choreographer for Ballet Theater in favor of a much more wide-ranging career. The next thing he did was to turn *Fancy Free* into a highly successful Broadway show, "On the Town," and for the next two decades he divided his time with equally impressive results between ballet and the commercial theater. He has had two long associations with the New York City Ballet, during the first of which he choreographed *Faun* (1953), but he also worked for other companies, including Ballet Theater and his own Ballets: U.S.A. in the late 1950s. Since returning to the New York City Ballet in 1969 to create *Dances at a Gathering*, he has made most of his new works for that company, and he now serves, with George Balanchine and John Taras, as its ballet master.

The New York City Ballet, with its academically trained dancers and its neoclassical identity shaped by Balanchine, seems an odd place for Robbins to have settled, yet his works are extremely popular with NYCB audiences. Even when he seems to be striving for the purity and form that are Balanchine's trademark, Robbins makes drama. He has an instinct for theater that spans all theater forms; no esoteric knowledge is necessary to perceive his idea. Robbins doesn't seem happy confined to a musical form or an academic movement language. His ballets are free-form, as his career has been, even when they have a formal underpinning.

Afternoon of a Faun was choreographed for Tanaquil LeClercq and Francisco Moncion. The nine-and-a-half-minute piece is super-charged before it even begins, for it carries the import of its Debussy score, considered by many to be the composition that inaugurated modern music, and of the scandal that occurred when Nijinsky made his first choreography to the score in 1912. Without ignoring either of these momentous legacies, Robbins produced an independent statement in its own right — entirely different in style from the lush archaism of Mallarmé's poem or the music and the ballet it inspired, yet alluding to all of those precedents through a provocative modern metaphor.

Robbins' *Faun* is a ballet about ballet dancers. The insider ballet is one of Robbins' favorite devices. He not only loves to choreograph about dancers, but about the private world of dancers — the language, behavior, and mythology of the studio and the rehearsal room, as theatrical a world to him as anything created on the stage. The curtain rises on a world within a world: Jean Rosenthal's white gauze room — a ceiling, three walls with the side to the audience cut away — surrounded by the empty, larger space of the actual stage.

On the floor of this luminous but hermetic universe lies a man dressed in tights and ballet slippers. He stretches and flexes a few times, then catches sight of himself in an imaginary mirror that covers the whole "fourth wall." The entire ballet is danced into this mirror, but in putting the mirror wall where it is, Robbins is unavoidably saying that the audience serves a similar purpose for the dancer. *Faun* is about narcissism, the dancer's love for his own image. Robbins makes me ask if the dancer sees himself reflected in the audience too, if his performing is essentially as self-critical and self-gratifying an act as his daily ritual of communing with his body in the studio.

As the dancer surveys himself, trying out different "looks" — front, profile, turned in, turned out, a pose from *Le Spectre de la Rose* — we can see that this vision in the mirror is as palpable to him as the placement of his own bones and the coordination of his muscles. Various dancers in the role have given greater or lesser importance to the man's visual as opposed to his kinetic feedback —

probably depending very much on their own experience of these things — but it is essential to the ballet that the dancer is a sensual being, that he is turned on by his own body *and* by the way he can make his body look.

While he is absorbed in himself, a girl enters from the wings and walks along the outside of the studio tying her tunic. Like the man, she is oblivious to everything except her own reflection in the mirror as she steps inside the studio door. She inspects herself, then goes to the barre to begin some soft pliés. The man sees her and moves behind her along the barre. From the time they become aware of each other's existence, they make eye contact only in the mirror.

They begin a pas de deux. Their bodies are so coordinated and

AFTERNOON OF A FAUN *(Robbins, 1953). Kay Mazzo and John Jones of Ballets U.S.A. Photo by Martha Swope.*

they give each other so few obvious clues that this might be a dance they have rehearsed before. But from the way they twist slightly this way and that, pause an instant after every new manipulation, crane their necks around to see every position from the maximum number of angles, you can tell they are experimenting. Each one constantly checks on his own image, including the other dancer only as an extension of himself.

At some point — and this depends again on the dancers taking the roles — the man begins to perceive the woman apart from himself. Perhaps it's when her long hair brushes against him as he lifts her. Perhaps it's not until they are kneeling face to face, still looking in the mirror. As if they had not been in far more intimate contact for the past five minutes, the man at last takes his eyes from the mirror, looks at the girl, and leans over and kisses her on the cheek. This too the girl observes in the mirror, in the same detached way she watched their enfoldings and embracings. Then she slowly raises her hand to touch her face and, without further acknowledgment, gets up and bourrées out the door and away.

The man thoughtfully returns to his place center floor and, in a languid stretch, lowers himself onto his stomach and lies full length, as if in a dream, and the curtain falls. This last gesture is a direct reference to the final move of Nijinsky's faun, in which he fell erotically on the scarf that one of the nymphs had left behind. This gesture brings us back from what has seemed a very real encounter between two extremely self-preoccupied people to Mallarmé's faun metaphor, and the two ideas begin to merge. Perhaps the girl has been imagined by the dancer, a nymph to complete his fantasy, and her departure is as inevitable as the awakening from a dream or the fall of the curtain. Or perhaps both dancers are real, but their concept of each other is make-believe — what they both understand about their relationship is that it must not transcend the ethereal bonding of the pas de deux.

In any case, Robbins has made a remarkable fusion of ideas in *Faun*. Not the least interesting thing about the ballet is that it's one of the few successful American ballets based on an older work. Considering how frequently the Europeans remake their classics, Americans have undertaken very few raids on the ballet literature for their themes. I find it interesting to compare Robbins' view of a man relating to an idealized female with that of Balanchine. In *Scotch Symphony*, a synthesis of *La Sylphide*, choreographed in 1952, the year before *Faun*, Balanchine made an abstract ballet, with three principals roughly corresponding to James, Effie, and the Sylphide of the Bournonville classic. What happens in *Scotch Symphony*, contrary to Bournonville, is that James not only wins the Sylphide but marries her. In other words, Balanchine's fantasy ends the way of Hollywood — the man gets his dream girl on his own terms; she joins his community, and her rival, his former fiancée, quietly disappears from their life. In Robbins the sylph evaporates at the end of what was always an illusory romance, and both partners are apparently satisfied to have it that way.

Rooms (*Anna Sokolow*)

Anna Sokolow began choreographing in the brief, lost generation of the 1930s. In those days of enterprise and expedience, Sokolow was still a teen-ager in the Graham company. Like so many other artists of her time, she was a dedicated liberal, a joiner and promoter of causes. While continuing to appear with Graham she made dances about social injustice, fascism, and the evils of war. The progeny of the earliest Graham and Humphrey-Weidman groups, or of independents like Lester Horton in California, Sokolow's generation were the first dancers to believe that modern dance was an entity unto itself — a creative point of view, an aesthetic — and that that point of view could continue and even encompass all the individual voices that had enunciated it so far; that, in fact, you could be a modern dancer without being a follower of Martha Graham or of any of the other powers on the scene. These emerging choreographers realized that they didn't have to invent their own systems of dancing; they could use the techniques Graham and Humphrey had devised or make modifications to suit themselves. They could interest themselves primarily in choreography and performance, which at that time meant in messages.

This transitional phase of American dance has never been properly studied; it is ill documented and almost nothing of the actual work was preserved. The reasons for its loss are many. Modern dance had not yet established itself and was still considered a fringe activity; its critics were apologists at best, given to praise and explanation of individual artists but not really concerned with studying larger issues and trends. The dances were conceived on a small scale, and they were topical, frequently pièces d'occasion made for a fund-raising or a rally, for some political or labor union gathering. Perhaps they made more of an impression amid the emotional partisanship of those settings than they would have in calmer times, but without the dances to study now, we can only tell that performers like Sokolow and Tamiris, Jane Dudley, Sophie Maslow, and others showed a dancing image to intellectuals and workers who might not have gone to seek them out in theaters. Margaret Lloyd called Sokolow "a people's dancer,"[1] and this may have been the only period in which dancers really connected with a broad audience until the present time. One possible reason was that, unlike the first modern dancers, many of these artists came from immigrant European stock. They shared left-wing political sympathies with people outside of dance, and they added the elements of poverty, oppression, unrest, and what we would call ethnicity to codes of Anglo-Saxon Americana and aristocratic Europe that formed our dance's beginnings.

Sokolow's early career seems to have been a search for a choreographic identity outside herself, and I have the feeling that's what modern dance was doing, too, in the thirties. After the social protest dances, the bold outcries against Spanish, Italian, and German fascism, against the exploitation of the masses, Sokolow worked in Mexico for long periods of time, teaching, establishing companies and choreographing, meanwhile continuing to show her work in New York once a year or so. Not until 1953, with *Lyric Suite*, did she find the image that was to supply her with her most fruitful source of material: Sokolow began to speak of despair, particularly the twentieth-century angst of loneliness, sexual repression, and all the associated fears and longings of alienation in a conforming, post-Freudian world.

The first expressionistic modern dances had the potential to address the anguish of the age, but for different reasons the idea wasn't carried to any developed lengths until a generation had intervened. Graham's *Lamentation* and probably other small works she did in the thirties suggested a kind of catharsis in which the whole audience could see its inner turmoil made visible and universal by means of abstract movement. But Graham's dance was inescapably personal to her, even after it became more literary. Mary Wigman played the witch-doctor, evoking spirits both psychological and supernatural in her dances. In this country, however, Wigman's style lost its personal quality. During the war, all the German arts and artists lost ground here, and though Wigman's line was carried on by Hanya Holm, who excelled as a teacher, without Wigman's own genius-presence it took on a more abstract character. When Holm's most famous pupil, Alwin Nikolais, began to emerge as a choreographer, he rejected the psychological approach completely in favor of exploring design and pure motion. Doris Humphrey and her successors were true humanists, but they too tended toward specific representations of personal crisis — the bullfighter Ignacio Sanchez Mejias, the matriarch in *With My Red Fires*. When Humphrey got more general, she told of society in optimistic, utopian terms. It was for Anna Sokolow and other Graham breakaways to stand aside from the self-expression and emoting and to develop metaphors, rather than representations, of contemporary life.

Although not the first of Anna Sokolow's mature works, *Rooms* (1955) is probably the best example of her style. When you think of Sokolow you think first of mood. Her dances are overwhelmingly depressed, dark, alienated, sometimes violent, angry, and unresolved. She seems to have had only this to say, and in recent years, though the violence has drained away, somber feelings still pervade her work. I think her choreographic style so appropriately and totally fits the content of her agonized images that she could not convey anything else without reinventing her own dance.

Angst, particularly the angst of the young and disaffected, is a very real component of the American psyche in the twentieth century. I don't think it should be off-limits as a subject for choreography that attempts to reflect the psyche. Modern dance has always perceived itself to be in part a counterforce to the sweetness-and-light aesthetic of ballet. Though Graham dealt with the dark side of experience, she and most other moderns utilized fictional, programmatic structures, and the viewer focused on her heroines, on their situations, so remote from our own. Sokolow doesn't let us shift the blame or the discomfort; she throws anguish squarely into our laps. Like the creatures in a ballet, who are a projection, a personification of joy, exhilaration, power, Sokolow's dancers reflect our fears and frustrations. That's all they're there for.

We see these personae first and always as alone. The way Sokolow structures a dance supports the isolated quality of each dancer's

ROOMS (*Sokolow, 1955*). *Jeff Duncan. Photo by Stephan.*

actions. She usually works in a suite form. With the possible exception of a beginning and ending that relate to each other in some way, the parts of the dance are individual statements that do not depend on what has come before and do not affect what follows. This, again, frequently is the method of abstract ballet. The Sokolow-influenced abstract works of Glen Tetley, Lar Lubovitch, Paul Sanasardo, are an oddly disturbing blend of personal, anguish-expressive movement built on a virtuosic and impersonal balleto-technical base. I find it interesting to note how much dance of the seventies is made in suite form, a sign of contemporary choreographers' preoccupation with style, technique, and mood, rather than content. The performer establishes a rapport with the audience by representing some heightened form of the audience's experience; he doesn't want to transport the audience into another, fictitious existence.

At some point — often right at the opening — we see all the dancers in a Sokolow work, spread out across the space and all facing the same way. They may be standing, crouching, or, as in *Rooms*, sitting on chairs. They begin to do the same thing — all walk toward the footlights, or fling up an arm, or collapse into a fall — but each dancer takes his own timing, which is never on the music if music is playing, and does the move pretty much in his own way. This typical Sokolow scene is much like the opening of *Serenade*, yet so different. In *Serenade* the unison timing and the effort that all the women make to move the same way, face in the same direction, place arms or feet exactly where the others place them, tells us that this is a group, that it has a great degree of consistency and will be able to work together in its tasks. In *Rooms*, the arhythmic timing and individual placement tell you that everyone in the group is independent. The floor pattern that, in Balanchine, suggested cooperation, in Sokolow keeps the dancers apart. The device of assigning each dancer his or her own chair further isolates them by placing a physical object in the space for each dancer to take care of and carry away when a large area is needed for dancing. The chairs are their rooms anyway, metaphorically, and in the opening and closing scenes all their actions are confined to their own tight, immediate vicinity.

Rooms has an atonal hot-jazz score for small combo by Kenyon Hopkins, and before the curtain goes up they play a fast, loud prelude. Then, in silence, we see eight people in simple dresses, pants and shirts, bare feet. A piano and muted trumpet play fragments of an ascending two-note progression, like an exercise, with interruptions of silence, and the dancers slowly rise, look around without seeing anyone else, and sit back down again. They lean precariously over the sides of the chairs, circle their heads around the backs, sit rigidly with their legs stretched straight out in front of them and paddling up and down. Slowly they slide across the chair seats, stretch lengthwise on their sides, and, holding their upper bodies off the floor with one hand, they raise one leg and slam it across the other and down into the floor. Then, drooping across the chair seats, they lower their heads to the floor, lift their arms to the side and let them drop, slapping against the floor with a dead sound. They get to their feet, run in accelerating circles around their chairs, looking sharply around. Suddenly they fall into a split, clinging to the chair seats beside them. They get up and sit in the chairs again resignedly, as if they had made some terrific gesture that they knew would be futile and that they know they will make again. Slowly they lean forward and back in their seats, staring at the audience.

None of this can be called dance movement, but neither is it merely the prosaic activity that it seems to be at first. Sokolow gives these ordinary movements a dancelike character by exaggerating the dynamics and the timing, sometimes beyond "natural" limits. Instead of just raising and lowering a hand, someone might take a very long time to raise it, giving the gesture great importance, then drop it suddenly and heavily, as if, having made all that effort to prepare, there was nothing worth doing with the hand after all. Besides the intensified way everything is carried out, each move or repeated series of moves is a separate gesture that finishes in some way before the next series is undertaken. Movements don't lead sequentially to further developments, only to augmented or diminished versions of themselves. Only one action is going on at a time; frequently only one body part is engaged at a time. The dancer's focus is fixed, usually in the direction of the motion but sometimes pointedly away from that direction. The movement has none of the flexibility or variety or inner conflict of Graham movement, for instance. Sokolow dance ought to be mechanistic, rigid, but it isn't quite. The people sometimes look like zombies; some necessary faculty has been cut off, but they behave as if they haven't found out yet. Their desperation comes from not realizing the extent of their psychic handicap.

Each section of *Rooms* has a terse subtitle. The opening and closing are both called "Alone." After each section ends, the lights dim and the dancers set the stage for the next section by taking away or rearranging chairs, accompanied by bridge music that is usually a variation of the two-finger exercise that started the dance. These bridge sections in themselves are strange and alienated because we see the same driven people depicted in the dance going about mundane tasks very blankly, with no intensity; in a very real way we see how neurotics can function in their daily lives.

Now we see a series of portraits: five individual private torments and two groups of noncommunicants.

"Dream." A man seemingly possessed by the idea of covering space. The bigger the motion or the more he travels, the more he tries to do, until his very motion consumes itself. Dropping his head to the side, he lets its weight pull him off the chair. Once on the floor, the feeling of sliding off the chair continues, and he starts rolling across the stage, gathering speed, until he stops suddenly, kicking off his residual energy by scissoring his legs hard in the air while lying on his side.

Throughout *Rooms* the initiation, accumulation, and spending of energy is very important. You often have the feeling that the dancers don't simply decide to begin moving, but that some irresistible force or impulse sets them in motion, and that they can't stop until they have exhausted themselves or worked themselves into some bind where they can't break out. The man in "Dream" keeps getting himself on different kinds of treadmills — the rolling on the floor is one. He gathers himself up in a ball and rocks back and forth; runs in a big, accelerating circle; and runs in place with big slow-motion steps until he locks one leg and lets it thud into the floor to stop himself. Finally, as we do sometimes with a familiar nightmare, he jerks himself awake and walks over to sit in his chair.

"Escape." A woman in a long flowered chiffon party dress enters. The music is playing something you might hear in a cocktail bar. She too seems to be dreaming — in fact, most of the people in the dance are engaged in either waking or sleeping fantasies, another facet of their isolation from the real world and from one another. The woman in "Escape" imagines a sexual encounter. Her energy is rhythmic, breathy, starting in her head and eventually traveling down to her pelvis. Eyes closed, arms out straight like a sleepwalker, she rocks and sways gently, letting her head circle back. She begins a big reaching-out gesture with her arms that takes her into a running, hip-swaying crescendo of motion. Sitting in the chair, she pumps her legs out to the sides one after the other, flings her arms up and lets them drop, her head thrown back ecstatically.

At this point her self-induced orgy begins to need a focus, and she suddenly comes into awareness, for the only time until the end of the dance. Holding her hands in front of her, she looks at them carefully, scanning them all over, as if inspecting herself in a mirror or reading something. She jumps up and begins dancing around, more excitedly than before. Then she runs to the chairs and sets up two so they face each other, about two feet apart. She sits in one and flirts with the other as if someone were sitting in it. Leaning forward, she passes her arms down the back of the chair opposite as if embracing the occupant. Then, stretched out with her hips on her own chair, she flings one leg up and over the other chair back, then flings it down, across her other leg. After doing this orgasmic motion several times, she becomes quiet for a moment.

Then she comes back to reality with a jolt, sits up, clutches her chair. In a last spending of energy, she pushes the chairs over and whirls fast in a circle, her hands reaching out, touching nothing. Then she drops her arms, rights one chair without looking where she's placing it, and walks off.

Another characteristic of the Sokolow gesture is that it can have several implications. Because her movement is so uncomplicated spatially, each one exerts an unusually palpable effect on the viewer. We are able to experience each one, to find each one's resonances within our own memories and feelings. The woman's climactic flinging her leg over the chair is an example of Sokolow's ability to make movement that is neither literal nor associated with any academic vocabulary but that suggests those possibilities and more. No one actually lies across two chair seats and flings her leg around in this way. The gesture is an obvious symbol of orgasm. It is, equally, another representation — the most emphatic — of what the woman has been doing all through the dance, namely, building an energy pulse that gets released through pushing and flinging motions of various body parts. Compositionally, it is derived from a gesture done by the whole group in the first section, where they hook one leg over the back of the chairs as they stretch across the seats. Other Sokolow moves can suggest one or more representational actions to us, like the woman's scanning of her hands, but always the rationale for the movement comes out of the character's energy patterns, not out of arbitrary dramatic necessities.

"Going." This brief dance is a portrait of a speed freak. It is another feature of Sokolow's psychological accuracy that her messages seem true a generation after they were made, even though they also seem so characteristic of the time in which they were made. In the fifties, this was the kind of kid who played the drums or dribbled a basketball all the way to school in order to release his excess energy. He wears sneakers, pants, a T-shirt and a warm-up jacket. He explodes into the space at a run and slides to his chair like a baseball player stealing home. The music plays a fast, driving bebop that never lets up, and the man bounces and vibrates constantly to its beat. Occasionally stopping tensely, he never really rests. He slaps his foot on the floor, snaps his fingers, lightly beats a fist into the other palm; sits on the chair and squirms from side to side; runs, weaves, and feints like a boxer; takes a few fast rhumba steps, legs tight together, hips swaying; crouches with arms pressed protectively close to the body, turns, looks back over his shoulder, turns, looks back, like an escaping stickup man. Finally he's back down on the floor again, bouncing, clicking his fingers. Then the music stops abruptly, leaving him with his arms reaching up, and after a beat of silence he drops them and the lights go out.

This character has the loose, restless energy of movie tough guys and the kids who imitated them. But the character's basic insecurity, his fear of being left without a beat, is inherent in the crouched, closed wariness of his body, the hunched shoulders, the fixed, inward focus of his jittering, and the brevity of his movement gambits — a few repeated steps or jumps that give way to some new, equally fragmentary idea. I find him the most poignant of all the castaways in *Rooms*.

"Desire." Three men and three women sit on chairs in two rows that face each other — except one man's chair faces a different direction. They are set up to act in couples but they never make contact. Hands stretched straight out like sleepwalkers, they slide their feet rhythmically in and out along the floor in front of their chairs. Their arms reach out and up, and close again across their bodies. They sit, pumping their legs, with their arms crossed over their pelvises, hands clutching their hips — at once hugging themselves and protecting themselves and preventing themselves from getting out of control.

They slide to the floor, and after curling up tight and flopping over from one side to the other, they come to lie full length next to a member of the opposite sex. Never seeing the person next to them, they probe the air with their hands, their legs. Sometimes their limbs become entangled, but they don't seem to recognize that they've touched what they're seeking. Finally they drag themselves back to their chairs and stand on the seats, pivoting from side to side, arms pressed against their bodies, heads drooping, chests sunken in.

"Panic." A man is stretched out full length on a chair, his head thrown over the back. The music plays a single chord that builds to a dissonant crash and stops. The man jerks upright, walks a few steps straight in front of the chair, backs up, and stretches out in it again. A second time, and he reacts more frantically. He runs to the other side of the space, where four people are seated unmoving in chairs. He too gropes for what is right in front of him without seeing it. But he is rigid, his body pulled out into a tense line with one arm reaching and the other pressed to his side, his head immobile as if it were screwed tight onto the end of his spine. This character has only two movement modes: his whole body locks into one position and must move all at once in that position, or he can release himself by shaking violently from side to side. Neither mode, of course, allows any flexibility in seeking or responding.

Perhaps because of the extremity of his behavioral patterns, this man is also the most violent and masochistic in the dance. In order to free his head, he wrenches it back and forth so forcefully that he almost pulls his whole body off balance. He runs in mindless circles, his body bent over and his arms extended to the sides. He falls to his side and bangs his head to the floor. Rolling into a backbend, he grinds the top of his head into the floor. The people in the chairs have gotten up and left one by one, but the man has not noticed. The music, which has been playing random snatches of treadmill motifs and erratic chords, leaves off, but the man is still compulsively shaking his head with eyes covered, jumping, circling. Finally he runs to one of the unoccupied chairs and crouches behind it, clutching the back.

"Daydream." To a sentimental waltz, three women stand by their chairs. They all face front, and in an irregular canon they go through what almost looks like a ballet class routine — lifting and opening their arms, extending one leg as they hold the chair backs for support, then bending the leg back into attitude, which takes them around the chair. I suppose they are being pretty in front of their mirrors. They smile slightly from time to time and always face front. Finally, from behind the chairs they put one leg over the backs and lean their elbows on the raised knee, resting their chins in their cupped hands like some cliché cheesecake models, and make kissy faces at the mirror.

"The End." The woman's hands have some kind of awful compulsion to do her harm. Just when her guard is down, when she is sleeping or exhausted, her hands spread out to her sides and start wiggling uncontrollably, moving toward her throat. She stops them by wearing herself out with shaking or jumping, but the minute she flops over the fingers start their inexorable dance. At last she falls face down across her chair seat. After a pause, she slowly stands on the seat and lifts her arms up and down as if they were wings. I suppose, in her fantasy, suicide is the only way out.

"Alone." The end of *Rooms* is like the beginning, except that now the dancers briefly restate the themes of their solos. Seeing them all together again, seeing how much of their behavior has the same movement origins, I somehow feel compassionate toward them. I see them as forming much more of a community than they have ever imagined, and I find them all the more pitiable for their lack of recognition. Since they have only themes, no development — only rooms, no corridors or common shelter — they will go on doing the same things indefinitely. With five crashing chords, the music ends and the curtain falls.

Revelations (*Alvin Ailey*)

From Ruth St. Denis on, American dancers have been self-conscious about popularity — which may indicate that they are still self-conscious about their art. Until federal and state subsidies to dance made it legitimate — indeed, necessary — to appeal to a large audience, dancers feared for their self-respect whenever they felt themselves edging toward a popular or commercial success. Alvin Ailey has spent much of his career in that forbidden territory.

Like his predecessors Denishawn and Lester Horton, Ailey has never been shy about using glamorous appurtenances to make his work attractive to large audiences. Following his company's first tour of the Far East in 1962, he has aggressively pursued a popular success, and his achievements as a director of dance-as-entertainment have outweighed his contributions as a choreographer.

Ailey's innovations as a modern dance company director are numerous, all in the direction of broadening the appeal of what was, at the time of his entrance into the field, commonly accepted as an esoteric art form. Modern dance was serious in its intent, and the attraction it held for nondance audiences lay almost solely in the personal style of the dancer-choreographers who were its leaders. But Ailey ran his company differently from the beginning.

Only two years after his first New York concert, Ailey broke the traditional one-choreographer or co-choreographer pattern of modern dance companies by reviving a work of Lester Horton's. He took a piece of Glen Tetley's on the first Far Eastern tour, and his expanding company repertory consistently included dances by other choreographers, an idea Ailey formalized some years ago into a program of reconstructing classics by black and white American artists, such as Pearl Primus, Katherine Dunham, and Ted Shawn. Ailey himself retired from dancing in 1965, when he was only thirty-four, making it impossible for the company to draw its identity from his personal dance image.

Ailey was a magnetic dancer, but he didn't feature himself as star. There were no stars in modern dance, in the ballet or opera mode. The original Ailey company was a collection of personalities, dancers of assorted ages, body types, and technical abilities, each of whom contributed in an individual way to the choreography, sometimes even devising their own steps. As the company got into extensive touring, Ailey relied more and more on strong dancers, conventional body types. The Ailey became the first modern dance company to face the opera house audience on a regular basis, and soon it developed a bigger, more externalized performing style that was quite different from the intimate, detailed, even subtle way other modern dance companies performed. Like ballet or Broadway dancers, the Ailey company learned to stress the more obvious physical things, which could be seen in a big auditorium, and, correspondingly, the lighting and costumes played a more vivid part, the sounds, on tape or live-miked, were overamplified. The Ailey even became more overtly balletic, the first modern company to demand ballet training in its dancers. The funky, unpredictable older dancers gave way to guest stars and to resident stars who always played the same types and overshadowed the rest of the company, which began to function as a corps de ballet.

Probably no one until Ailey has moved so freely and unaffectedly between the ballet and modern dance worlds. In 1962 he participated in a workshop sponsored by Rebekah Harkness at Watch Hill, Rhode Island, where he created the ballet *Feast of Ashes,* a dance drama based on Lorca's "House of Bernarda Alba"; and his Duke Ellington ballet *The River* is a favorite in the repertory of American Ballet Theater. In 1971 the Ailey officially became an opera house company itself when it joined the City Center of Music and Drama, taking up residence in the home of the Joffrey Ballet, the former home of the New York City Ballet. The Ailey now gives two seasons a year at City Center and sometimes a summer engagement at the New York State Theater in Lincoln Center. Except that it does not dance on pointe, it operates like a contemporary ballet troupe, with a company school and two "junior" ensembles that train apprentices to go into the main company.

Another important characteristic of the Ailey repertory is its reliance on "pop," from authentic American jazz, blues, and other black music, to the more contemporary mod, rock, and plastic, in décors, costumes, and props. Ailey has said from the beginning that he wanted to reach a mass audience, and as a black artist the theatrical, Broadway-revue type of work done by Katherine Dunham is a respected part of his heritage. A generation of contemporary black dancers took their cue from Ailey, putting equal stress on topical ideas and sources, flamboyant production, and spectacular, high-energy dancing. What is called "black dance" today seems to be derived mostly from Ailey, with additional inspiration from African and Caribbean sources. But Ailey's choreography and his company have nonblack as well as black derivations. The genuine feelings from the black experience that were expressed in *Revelations* have long since been submerged in the company's more general pop-balletic tendency. Ailey grew up in California and learned to dance in the last years of the eclectic, theatrical Lester Horton dance theater. Even in his early choreography, he showed the additional stimulus of Martha Graham. Looking at *Revelations* today, you couldn't trace it exclusively to any one of these antecedents.

In microcosm, the history of *Revelations* recaps the whole process that begins when a dance first makes an impact on us. Some dances change so gradually that, although we realize they aren't doing the same thing to us, we can't quite tell why until they have become almost unrecognizable. By then, what we could almost call a new species of the dance exists, which creates its own fans. These adherents don't understand the disappointment of old-timers. To them, the dance is wonderful as it is now; they can't imagine it ever having been better or anyone wanting it to be better. The old supporters begin to think their memories may have betrayed them; few critics, let alone lay viewers, can remember with precision the facts and the quality of an event they may have seen once or twice years ago. Over the years, since its première early in 1960, *Revelations* has undergone a dramatic evolution to bigger, more set and commercial presentation. Fortunately, Ailey made a television show of it in 1962 that preserves the dance in something close to its original form, and the existence of this filmed record can eliminate arguments of fact, if not of taste.*

What we can see about the old *Revelations* is mainly that it was done with less than half the dancers it now uses and that, although not as strong technically as Ailey's present company, those dancers had a different kind of performing presence, one that seems more sincere and total. But in a larger sense, in evolving toward its present, amplified form, the dance has really come to be a different thing. It has shifted worlds.

Comparing *Revelations* fifteen years apart, one sees that the dance is not changing in the way other dances have changed. Many Graham dances have grown softer, rounder, lighter, more lyrical, and less hard-edged. A Balanchine work tends to bulge out with new ideas in some places and shrink in other places where things get omitted or simplified over the years. Some dances lose their punch; others lose their naturalness and flow. But *Revelations* seems to have entered wholly into that realm of Broadway and television entertainment where the audience's reaction is predictable and can be roused automatically by the dancers.

Somehow, when Denishawn made movies or when Lester Horton did nightclub acts, they must have believed they were bringing an elevated message to their commercial audiences — or if their mes-

*Lamp Unto My Feet, CBS-TV, March 1962.

REVELATIONS (*Ailey, 1960*). *Alvin Ailey and company in early 1960s. Photo by Jack Mitchell.*

sage became hopelessly compromised, they told themselves that this was not what they really did, this was only to get enough money to do what they really did. Alvin Ailey probably still believes in that "higher" kind of communication, but the momentum of hype on which his company has run for years makes a spiritual experience virtually impossible. *Revelations* now is about the intensity of the audience's emotional charge and the skills with which the dancers engineer it. The actual steps in many of the sections of the dance have not changed that much, and I like to remember that audiences were delirious at the end when only seven or eight dancers did "Rocka My Soul in the Bosom of Abraham," without Judith Jamison and a chorus of twenty to whip them into a frenzy.

I feel a great responsibility and a great regret about this dance, which has been so moving a personal experience for me and has given form to such an important part of the American spirit. Under my eyes, I've seen it disappear. As well as I knew the dance at one time, it is nearly irretrievable for me now.

A program note divides the dance into three sections. The first, "Pilgrim of Sorrow," contains dances of meditation and prayer; the second, "Take Me to the Water," is a scene of baptism; and "Move, Members, Move" refers to the more temporal sins and pleasures seen in the light of Christian chastisement and joy. Ailey's movement idiom goes through a roughly parallel evolution, from abstract, Graham-Horton modern to mime to a jazz routine. The dance is built with tremendous skill to modulate from a solemn, almost sorrowful beginning through many emotional changes to its stomping, exultant finale.

When the dance begins ("I Been 'Buked"), we see a mass of people packed close together, standing under a strong, warm light. Although dressed in simplified street clothes — the women in long plain shifts and the men in pants and string tunics — their actions are nonrealistic. With tremendously effective gestures, their arms hovering out to the side like wings, hands reaching out palms to the audience, arms opening straight and sharply from overhead, they suggest supplication, protectiveness, benediction. Much of the dance is done in plié, and in one brilliantly inventive gesture, the dancers pull off center with their upper torsos, one arm reaching to the side and the other hand holding the back above the hip, as if nursing the chronic pain of all cotton-pickers, laundresses, floor scrubbers, mothers, and laborers.

This group stands close together facing the audience and moves in unison except for two brief excursions out into space. They give a strong impression of solidarity and common suffering — in a purely abstract way. Later, in the baptism and jazz sections, the action is much more literal, more pantomimic, until the final "Rocka My Soul in the Bosom of Abraham," which was, even in the beginning, a chorus line.

There are two trios in the dance: "Didn't My Lord Deliver Daniel," a man and two women, and "Sinner Man" for three men, although on occasion Ailey danced it all himself, semi-improvisationally. Both these dances are quite conventional stage pieces, but the duet "Fix Me, Jesus" and the solo "I Want to Be Ready" are unusual. In "Fix Me" the relationship of the man and woman is that of pastor and communicant; their lifts and balances, their goings-away and comings-together, are all presented in this devotional context. This dance has suffered most from the Ailey company's evolution because the dancers who perform it now are technicians. The audience thinks it is seeing a modern ballet pas de deux, since the dancers deliver it with such high technical finish, and it is frequently interrupted by shrieks and applause. The dancers who performed it in the film, Minnie Marshall and James Truitte, were older and they were not technicians. Because of this, the kinetic elements of the pas de deux were much more evident — you didn't see a woman doing a backbend and a développé supported by the man but an image of trust and longing and dependability.

Truitte's solo "I Want to Be Ready," choreographed largely by him, is couched in late-Horton technique, with its pictorial unfoldings of the body, its slow developments and unexpected switches. The dance takes place almost entirely on the ground, and is at the same time showy and very introspective. He alternately cringes in an attitude of abject prayer and reaches hesitantly toward heaven only to fall back in shame. The choreography of this section has changed considerably, but Truitte's successors, Kelvin Rotardier, Dudley Williams, and Clive Thompson, have remained faithful to the spirit of the dance.

The "Honor, Honor" and "Wading in the Water" episodes are interesting compositionally because they are the only part of the dance in which the participants enact a ritual rather than simply suggesting one. This too has been transformed somewhat, and the focus of attention has shifted from the couple being baptized — in the film, Ailey and Thelma Hill — to the lady with the umbrella who assists them. When she took over this part, Judith Jamison borrowed their arm-rippling motion so astonishingly that the audience didn't really notice them anymore. These three principals come onstage in a processional, their attendants carrying mysterious props — a white branch with bells in it, a white chiffon cloth. Ailey has now inserted a repeat of part of the music to give the procession members a dance of their own, and of course there are more of them. The doubling of parts here and the expanding of the action has given the section a more staged, more uniform quality, where in the earlier conception it was individualized and almost spontaneous-looking.

The various changes of scale and style in *Revelations* are reinforced by a wide range of dynamics and mood. In the opening section, "I Want to Be Ready," and to some extent in "Fix Me, Jesus" the action is fixed in one place. The movement energy is concentrated, the mood reflective. The dancers may move out into space briefly but they return to their appointed stations, giving us a visually concrete, stable image that contrasts dramatically with the passing, flowing action of "Wading in the Water" and the action-packed final sections.

The dance progresses in wonderfully theatrical waves of tenderness and excitement, building gradually but logically to its climax. Each section has enough particular interest so that you don't feel the momentum is being held back but that it's being channeled into a different kind of intensity. This varying of mood and gradual building of excitement is also a product of the singers — the Howard Roberts Chorale with rhythm instruments added (the latter sections have even acquired an electric rock base). Gospel singer Brother John Sellers preaches the sermon, "The Day Is Past and Gone," and joins the chorus for the finale.

Aside from the more arbitrary features such as subject matter and costumes, the "black" dance style of *Revelations* is derived from Ailey's use of movement elements that describe or indicate "character," in the Russian classical sense. Ailey's gift was to be able to identify those elements in the black American community, both rural and urban. He was equally accurate in his abstract gestures, like the stooped-over, aching-back motif, and in his mime sequences, like the last sections, where the men and women stroll on as if on their way to church, greet each other, echo the preacher's sermon, and slip easily into a semijitterbug of celebration. Many of the mannerisms, the phrasings, the behavior, must have come from the dancers who created and later refined the dance, and they came so straight and so surely that black audiences greet them with recognition even now, when they have been codified into a depersonalized gesture-language by a generation of younger black dancers.

Summerspace and *Winterbranch* (*Merce Cunningham*)

Although seldom performed and almost never shown concurrently, *Summerspace* (1958) and *Winterbranch* (1964) together exemplify Merce Cunningham's contribution to choreographic style and philosophy. Even the fact that they're given so rarely is typical of his attitude toward his work. Cunningham has made a startling number of dances — nearly one hundred since he began choreographing in 1942 — as well as innumerable films, videodances, and open-space Events; and at least twenty-five of his group works would qualify for major status, though few of them survive in current repertory.

Cunningham's devotion to preserving the immediacy, and thus the transitoriness, of his dance is a key to his longevity as a creator — and also makes it deceptively easy to underrate his serious contribution to the art. We speak of Cunningham so often in terms of what he started — as if he were important only as a precursor of "post-Cunningham dance"; we forget how strong his work is in its own right. To me, *Place, Landrover, RainForest*, and *Field Dances*, for instance, have had as stunning an impact as any Graham drama. It seems almost a violation of Cunningham's intentions to speak of any of his dances as having fixed a style. Indeed, whenever one of his works is revived, people say it looks nothing like its original version. I believe them, but at the same time I believe some authentic sensibility clings to them by which we can recognize their separate identities *and* their common identity as products of Cunningham's hand.

Like his collaborator John Cage, Cunningham called attention to process. The way in which his dances were made — and continued to be made during each performance — was of great interest to him, and he has probably written and said more about this than any other choreographer. It seems he'd rather have us pay attention to how a sequence was arrived at than to the effect it creates or what it "means." His dances are very straightforward; one of the main things about them that impresses us is their lack of artifice or preordained structures in time and space, their intense concentration on making the present real rather than on re-creating some experience that is past. His movement is its own metaphor and, as such, has a very direct, uncompromising expressiveness.

Chance was one of the ways Cunningham anchored himself in process. Many people mistakenly believe a dance created by chance operations is improvised or haphazard. Actually, just the opposite is true. Chance is one of the most concrete and objective procedures by which art can be created. Although the choreographer devises the dancers' movements, everything else is determined by throwing dice, laying out cards, or by some other external device. The choreographer may make conscious decisions about the movement content, but the form in which that content is presented — the duration, speed, density, spatial orientation, sequence, and sometimes the phrasing of the movement — is entirely out of his hands.

He is in a way much more in touch with how his dance comes into existence than the artist working in a quasi-mystical nineteenth-century tradition, who relies on the nebulous and often inexplicable products of instinct and inspiration. The one thing Cunningham almost never talks about is the feeling-tone of his dances. Whether he planned *Winterbranch* to be dark and *Summerspace* light, whether he has overall ideas about narrative development or character before he lays out his charts, he seldom tells us. He is much more likely to have an idea about a movement quality or a task to explore.

Cunningham has written that *Summerspace* was about traveling: "the principal momentum was a concern for steps that carry one through a space, and not only into it." He also mentions that he worked with the dancers individually during most of the creative process, which he thinks may be "what gives the dance its sense of beings in isolation in their motion along with the sense of continuous appearance and vanishing."[2] *Summerspace* is a space atomized, unified, energized, by moving bodies. I think it's Cunningham's most effective statement about neutrality and the way the dancer can create an ordered universe if he starts unencumbered by any spatial preconceptions. Integral to the success of the dance are Robert Rauschenberg's backdrop and costumes, cut from identically patterned and toned pastel-dotted cloth. The dancers are not only in the space, they are *of* it; nothing exists to differentiate them until they move; how they move tells us what the space is.

The dance begins with a woman running into the empty space and circling it. This circular path, repeated in different ways by other dancers, both clears the space and defines it. The dancer is both opening up a field and pulling in the horizons — the dance is to be *in* the space, however the dancers use it, and not restricted to the presentational planes expected in traditional ballet or modern dance. Nor is the circle closed — dancers can enter or leave it from any of six places, and they are usually in the act of dancing when they appear and disappear. When we see them jumping off into the wings, we can assume they are continuing to jump somewhere, not that jumping is only something they start and finish on the stage within our sight. Or, put another way, dancing is not just for stages, and the dancing we see on this stage may only be a part of all the dancing there is, and not even the most important part!

Dancing as we see it in *Summerspace* consists of different, individual activities, another reason — besides the mere fact that it's there — for looking at it closely. The dance doesn't accumulate into lines, cluster, choirs, of any sort, it never gets bigger or makes a point more forcefully than it did at the beginning. Sometimes it echoes itself. A person may sketchily imitate another person's gesture or try out a movement with a different speed. But these are very private impulses; they may be repeated but without transferring themselves back to their origins or pushing toward any new conclusions. In one section, where several people leap across the stage at different speeds, you see that their movements have the same shape, but each leap belongs to each dancer, it doesn't seem to have sprung out of any contagion of rhythm or intensity.

The movement for *Summerspace* underlines this feeling of the dancer's independence. Cunningham's basic movement style is built on a balletically upright body attitude; the emphasis is on the legs and feet, with very little showiness in the upper body. But in *Summerspace* this verticality seems more than usually important for him. The dancers stand on their own two feet; they cover space with purposeful running or striding steps, or with high-energy traveling turns or difficult jumps; they balance on one leg while the rest of the body inscribes careful patterns in the air. They may sink into low lunges or hover in pliés close to the floor, but only once or

SUMMERSPACE (*Cunningham, 1958*). *Robert Kovich and Chris Komar. Photo by Jack Mitchell.*

twice does anyone fall or get lifted or even boosted up by someone else. The basic feeling of the body is open. The body and limbs seem to have a lot of air around them all the time, and the dancers respect each other's constantly shifting territory.

There's a lot of auditory space in the dance too. Morton Feldman's score consists of faint clusters of instrumental sounds that spatter at uneven intervals into the silence. Through this quiet noise we can hear the dancing better, can notice how its rhythms, repetitions, changes of speed, and momentary pauses enliven the space. *Summerspace* is about irregularity, unpredictability. Even when things repeat, we can't foretell how many times they'll repeat, or at what tempo. The dance calls attention to itself by not happening as often as it does by happening. There's a lulling, comfortable feeling about it, as if it could go on and on being there and being not there, being all around us and of only passing interest, for a very long time.

Winterbranch is almost the exact opposite. Dense and oppressive where *Summerspace* takes wing, claustrophobic instead of open, and loud instead of quiet, it does by shock what the other dance does by insinuation. They both arrange their space, time, and dancer-roles in unconventional but totally convincing ways. Perhaps because it makes its point so aggressively, *Winterbranch* is considered a more revolutionary dance than *Summerspace*. Many people are offended and upset by it. Sound and light effects created not by Cunningham but by his collaborators LaMonte Young and Robert Rauschenberg are its most outrageous elements, but the dance itself, if and when it can be perceived at all, is equally disturbing.

Many important contemporary artists and composers have created for Cunningham, perhaps because his basic working method throughout his career has been to compose the dance independently of its musical and decorative components. His desire to give creative artists working with him free rein may have been a reaction to the total control Martha Graham always exercised over her productions. He is convinced that dance doesn't need aural or scenic props to work. With John Cage, he also believes that we can take in several ideas at once, even if they may not be analogous; not even simultaneous contradictory input is forbidden in Cunningham's dances. Scores, costumes, sets, props, and lighting are commissioned and worked on separately from the choreography,

WINTERBRANCH (*Cunningham, 1964*). *Gus Solomons, Jr., and Barbara Lloyd in the 1960s. Photo by Ralph Crane.*

with only the most elementary specifications as to their character. Frequently the dancers don't see or hear the stage environment they will be working in until the dress rehearsal. Particularly during the *Summerspace-Winterbranch* period, Cunningham liked the spontaneity (some of the dancers called it fright) that this added to the performance.

For *Winterbranch* Cunningham asked Rauschenberg "to think of the light as though it were night instead of day," the clashing, deceptive light of mechanized civilization.[3] What Rauschenberg did was to position different types of lighting instruments so that they would create shafts and harsh pools of light, many from the floor or other angles that would cast unflattering shadows on the dancers or glare directly into the eyes of the audience. The lights flashed on and off during the dance according to no perceptible plan. Sometimes the stage would be in almost complete darkness, and it was never completely lit. A dancer would disappear in the middle of a solo, or his lighting would change radically, disorienting the way we perceived him in space. The whole thing seemed designed to tantalize and infuriate the audience, and it did. Since its earliest performances, the lighting has been somewhat moderated and coordinated with the dance activity, but it is still extremely disturbing.

The dance is an auditory shock as well. The first several minutes take place in silence, which makes many people uncomfortable. Suddenly a very loud grinding sound rips into the theater. Later another sound is added. These two sounds, which remind me of train wheels scraping along a curve in the track, are continuous and last until the end of the dance at an amplitude very near the threshold of pain.

These two elements alone, the sound and light, create an atmosphere of violence, unmistakably urban or at least manmade, that mocks the serenity suggested by the dance's title. The dancers, whenever they can be discerned in this harrowing environment, are wearing black sweat suits, tight-fitting helmets, and black smudges of make-up under their eyes. The dance is a succession of images of fixity and condensation — all the feelings induced by crowded elevators, late trains, insomnia, deadlines, and high, narrow streets — images that begin without preparation and end at random, snatched away into the darkness.

The dancers' bodies seem heavy, tightly packed, as if something is always bearing down on them and making it difficult to move, even downward. Cunningham seems to have chosen body shapes that would be anything but upright and open — the dancers are usually either doubled over or straining backward, against the bones of the spine. They're often on the floor, but even there they don't just lie flat; they sit up slowly and laboriously or drag one another half-sitting from place to place. They work together as often as alone, but their groupings don't seem complementary so much as manipulative and impersonal.

The disrupted sequence, so typical of Cunningham's choreography, seems exaggerated in *Winterbranch*. Despite the appalling sound that screeches on without letup, the dance looks so fragmented that any moment might be the end. Each gesture constitutes an isolated fact, without source or issue, without embellishment or mitigation — take it or leave it — that's that. What is slow is inexorably, unbearably slow, so slow that as you're looking at it you keep asking yourself if anything is happening at all. What is fast looks driven and dangerous, the dancers seeming to take needless risks of collisions, injuries. Nothing looks reliable for them. If they're standing or running one minute, they could be collapsing and falling the next. Nothing ever seems finished; no goal once reached cannot be reversed or undone. If they should belong to some larger human group, it will be just as fallible as they are separately — and near the end of the dance they all do cross the space together, clinging together, rushing for a few steps, one stumbling and dragging all the rest down, pulling themselves up and starting again.

This is *Winterbranch* — images of struggle, meaningless accomplishment, loss, beginning again. Images of modern man.

Private Domain (Paul Taylor)

Paul Taylor is one of the most perplexing figures in modern dance. His work can be artful or instinctive, lyrical, funny, grotesque, or demonic — sometimes all in the same dance. Some of his dances appeared quite casually and became trailblazers; others seemed reworkings of his previous material and were thought revolutionary. Musically, he can be inventive or literal. Morally, one can't tell if he's a puritan or a degenerate. He has been considered a major choreographer-director since the early 1960s, yet he has established no school, has few direct descendants, and his perpetually endangered company seldom takes part in the festivals, film projects, and other programs that afford wide visibility and financial reinforcement to other companies. When dancers leave Merce Cunningham to choreograph on their own, many of them choreograph in the Cunningham manner, and most continue to revere Cunningham even if their own work turns out differently. Paul Taylor's alumni almost never choreograph like him, some don't acknowledge any debt to him at all; yet a number have retained an element of wit, zaniness, and ability to yield to the artistic accident that characterizes most of what he does.

Although Taylor has made dances at a surprisingly regular rate, his repertory seems more ephemeral than even Cunningham's. To my knowledge, there is only one publicly accessible film, the early

Three Epitaphs, of a complete Taylor dance.* Because he is suscepti-ble to change and doesn't consider his first idea sacred, he often revises his dances or allows them to lapse altogether. Taylor is par-ticularly good at choreographing for the dancers he has in the com-pany, and he has preserved less of a "company style" over the years than some of the other moderns. Most important, neither Taylor nor significant numbers of his dancers do any extensive teaching, so the Taylor "style" hasn't become systematized and transmitted to non-Taylor dancers. Nor are his works often performed by other compa-nies. Since his retirement from dancing in 1974, his choreography has undergone a rather drastic change, which I believe is still in process, and even fewer of the old works are being performed at present.

Taylor has always seemed to be at odds with the current trend. His most strenuous choreographic efforts to make popular works produced inferior ones. In his new phase, the company is trying to keep up with trendier groups, but what it does is probably too strange and demanding to attract the masses. Just what Taylor's in-fluence is or will be on the course of American dance is not yet clear, but his work is distinctive and significant, poorly remem-bered though it may be.

Although *Aureole* is probably Taylor's best-known work — it has been performed by at least two ballet companies in addition to the Taylor company — it is actually quite atypical of him. Only one or two other Taylor dances are as transparent, as noncommittal about character: *Aureole* and its few relations (*Lento,* a short-lived Corelli suite, *Guests of May*) seem to come straight out of the music, with no prior assumptions having been made about why the dancers are there. He is much more likely to put them there in a context, if even a very slight one. Taylor dancers act as if they have some kind of secret, as if they all belong to some community with a history and a local patois. They do, of course; they all belong to the Taylor dance company. Only Taylor has so openly and consistently drawn on the lore of incident and personality that belong to his company for sub-ject matter. His dances have the look of a closed society, and a large number of them are admittedly about communities or the social be-

---

*A version of *Junction* (1961) by Rudy Burckhardt was put into distribu-tion in 1978.

havior of certain groups, or about the kinds of formalized activity — ritual, myth, art, and theater — that can be produced by generically specialized people. Often he draws on his own repertory, not as formulas for working out plots, as Graham did, but as part of the past that he and the company have experienced and can use as a resource.

The idea of conserving and recycling old dance material through the collective memory of the dance company is shared by Taylor graduate Twyla Tharp, but Tharp's dance is more presentational; it has few psychological overtones, no sense that anything is going on between the dancers that isn't available for the audience to see. Taylor builds roles within roles, leaves references around to his previous dances and collaborators, sometimes in symbolic or even totemic form, without identifying his sources or commenting on them. He sometimes choreographs elements of dancers' real-life personalities into their stage roles. But even when we know its sources, Taylor's dance can look remote to us. There's a faint air of snobbery, a knowingness that shuts us out and at the same time intrigues us.

In spite of his reuse of movement materials and forms, Taylor's dances are always turning up new tones of darkness, new forms of collusion and slightly wayward fun. His comic works, usually in suite form, show a succession of dance and acrobatic tricks in different performing styles, in which the dancers struggle valiantly with intractable material and are defeated, or make memorable impressions by delivering witless material impassively. His dances with plots are full of characters who change identities or undergo drastic role reversals or sex switches, or reveal themselves to be two or three personae more than expected. But is in the plotless "modern dance" dances that Taylor is at his most enigmatic and foreboding.

Scudorama (1963) was probably the best and most shocking of these dances, but it was expanded, revised, and finally consigned to the inactive repertory. I feel that all of Taylor's serious works, and some of the comic ones, are related to *Scudorama*, right up to the 1977 *Dust*. which looks like a pop art version of it. Although he never again made a dance so intensely angry, so desolate, traces of *Scudorama* keep appearing, the goalless flailing and lashing motions; the frequent use of fast crawling and other earth-hugging locomotion that makes the dancers look not like animals but like

tortured humans; the twisting, knotting body shapes and other gro-
tesqueries; the forced speeds at which some risky things are taken;
and the solemn but inexplicably sinister ceremonies that are so
characteristic of his dances. Taylor is one of the last of the old modern dancers. His work shows that it has gone through the agonies
of introspection, and though the personal anguish is gone, its form
remains.

Private Domain (1969) is a dance that could only have been made by
an American. The French would have done it as a joke, the English
as a farce, the Germans as a drama ending in murder or suicide,
and the Dutch would have gone Dada, with plastic props and characters bearing apocalyptic names. Only an American could see a
specific situation, so laden with social implications, as a possibility
for abstract treatment. The five women and three men wear bathing
suits and perform in something like the way people behave on a
beach, at a singles' bar, a gay hangout. The sexual come-ons, the
body displays, the cruising, the not very playful games, are presented in dance episodes as objective as the parts of a ballet.

The entire dance takes place behind a stationary set by Alex Katz:
a drop placed across the footlights and consisting of three archways
with wide panels in between. The stage and everything that happens on it appear only in the partial view afforded from each audience member's seat. As the dance begins, we are inevitably aware
of this restriction of our view, and as it continues, nothing happens
to mitigate this restriction. In one stroke, Taylor and Katz have
made us voyeurs; we're forced to look at something that is partly
hidden, some things are going on that we're not meant to see. At
the same time, the dancers are both concealed and exposed. They
cannot choose which things to hide because a different thing is hidden — and a different thing seen — from each seat in the audience.
The effect this has on the dancers is to make them seem very aware
of their own surfaces and very closed about their interior feelings.
They show only what they will allow to be seen, but a whole lot of
that.

Once you get used to looking at *Private Domain,* you adjust to the
obstructions, as if you'd had the misfortune to buy a badly situated
seat. Metaphorically, this static relationship to the dance's appearances and disappearances is like being in a forest watching something going on beyond the trees. In effect, it's the audience that is

concealed or closed in and the dancers who are out in the open.

You could also regard the permanent blocking off of parts of the view as an op art experience; that is, you could decide that *not* seeing some of the dance is seeing the dance. Merce Cunningham had worked with this idea in *Winterbranch,* and in *Scramble* (1967) and *Canfield* (1969), but he allowed the visual obstructions to shift around the stage; one dance used the absence of direct light and the others used moving props. Other "environmental" choreographers found ways to incorporate architectural obstructions into a theatrical image. But Taylor was completely uncompromising in *Private Domain.* The dance is taking place behind that screen, and the audience is given no relief, no alternative but to comprehend as much as we can.

What happens to the movement when it's cut up this way is a whole visual experience by itself. Someone runs. He begins to disappear behind a pillar. A split second after he disappears — or is it just before he completely disappears — he begins to emerge on the other side. Parts of him do. You're terribly conscious of parts — hands, feet, hips, heads, keep poking into and out of sight, dismembered from torsos. Time does queer things — your eye's idea of time. Someone crossing the space goes out of sight. Much later than you expected she reappears. Did she suddenly decelerate in the interim? Or perhaps she was gradually slowing down and your eyes didn't perceive the change until its continuity was interrupted? When people stay partly hidden for a while, we start imagining what is going on across the space that's blotted out —the mechanics of how a woman can be running one minute and carried in a man's arms the next.

The proscenium barrier in *Private Domain* is in a way simply an actualization of the aura of privacy that veils all Taylor's works. Here he encourages us to speculate about what may be behind the screen. These power and seduction games are not especially attractive — in fact, they're decidedly sleazy — but they're worth looking at nevertheless. When you look at an Edward Hopper painting you're struck by its flatness, by the solidity of the buildings. The way he painted buildings is merciless — and also loving, somehow. Even their flaws are worth looking at — the places where they aren't quite plumb, the clumsiness of the architecture. Hopper's streets are empty, his windows blank, but his foregrounds nearly always project in toward where the painter and the subsequent viewer are standing. He thus invites our speculation about what's going on in the scene even though he seems to be offering it so impassively. Hopper paintings are like stage sets in the instant after the curtain goes up and before the dancers enter — except that what a European would intend as a backdrop, an American sees as the whole show.

I think this is the sense Paul Taylor is conveying in *Private Domain*. Although his landscape has people in it who move, they are just as isolated, just as provocative and mysterious, and just as much the objects of our concentration for their sturdiness, their coarseness, and their impenetrability as any Hopper building. Taylor's original ambition was to become a painter, and nowhere is this inclination more evident than in *Private Domain.* He has allowed the peephole set to flatten out the entire depth of the stage. People seem to be moving always in horizontal planes, their distances from us indicated by the relative sizes when they stop. At the end of the dance, they arrange themselves in the archways of the set and take up poses, not the cute or zany poses you might get up for a snapshot. Settled and serious, they stand in little groups, looking into the darkness, as if they had been composed by Alex Katz.

Men Dancing

My colleague, the American composer Elliott Carter, once said to me that in his opinion only an imaginative mind could conceive itself a composer of serious music in an industrial community like the United States.

— *Aaron Copland* [1]

Since the beginning, the role of the dancing male has been a principal concern of American choreography. We are a country that defined its character largely in terms of how it defined male roles, and the male dancer here has an even greater need to prove himself than his counterpart in Europe, where the ballerina has been dominant for over a hundred years. Dancing is an equivocal activity in any society that places a low value on the arts in general, but it becomes even more dubious where men have been celebrated as kings of the frontier, masters of the gun, the ax, and the plow. The specter of homosexuality — or at least societal inadequacy — haunted generations of American male dancers and still exerts its influence. If society's low esteem were not enough to discourage men from dancing, the great prominence of strong creative women in the field must have presented a formidable challenge as well. In the early part of the twentieth century, neither Isadora Duncan nor Loie Fuller used men in her company, and Ruth St. Denis made her first reputation as a soloist. Men simply did not think to dance — except if they were willing to continue enacting the effete European prototypes.

Ted Shawn and Ruth St. Denis' partnership, formed in 1914, had the appearance of a conventional male-female combination. A marriage, a ballroom duo, a movie couple — these were the kinds of images their dancing together projected. Even their corporate name,

Denishawn, spoke of a mutual submergence of individuality in the interest of the work they could produce together, though of course St. Denis possessed a much greater fame and allure at first. Only a decade later Doris Humphrey and Charles Weidman were able to dance and work together without adopting either the trappings of domesticity or the titular ego-merging that had seemed so necessary to Denishawn.

But, in addition to their glamorous Oriental spectacles and salon portraits, Shawn interested himself in making dances that would celebrate masculinity. He wanted to glorify male qualities just as St. Denis glorified femininity in her *Nautch* dance. Initially Shawn's approach was similar to hers. Working from what visual sources he could find — books, paintings, sculptures, probably — he chose heroic or decorative images of men, from antiquity or foreign cultures, and animated certain signature poses and steps, often adding bits of dramatic byplay to give the dance a focus.

One such portrait, the *Japanese Spear Dance* (later genteelly retitled *Spear Dance — Japonesque*), choreographed in 1919, was performed by Shawn for television in 1960, when he was nearly seventy. The brief salon piece begins with a series of fierce stances and winding-up gestures as the warrior prepares for battle. Suddenly the invisible enemy seems to have struck him, for he throws his long spear down and falls. After binding up an injured hand, he pulls a fan out of his waistband, snaps it open challengingly, and throws it aside. He recovers the spear, winds up again even more vigorously, then stabs his invisible foe definitively, throws the spear away, and poses in triumph. With his Samurai lunges and angular, flat-handed gestures, the handling of the fan, and the way he holds one end of the bandage in his teeth, he conveys a feeling for the character, if only a stereotyped one. But the *Japanese Spear Dance* is more a pantomime than a danced idea.

Quite early Shawn also began making short pieces that had no other illustrative purpose than to depict the music to which they were set. These were called "music visualizations," a term used also by St. Denis and the Denishawn pupil who probably excelled her teachers at it even then, Doris Humphrey. Shawn's efforts in this genre were short, almost like studies, and he probably drew on his classroom work for the up-and-back floor patterns and the sculptural use of the body. Shawn's way of interpreting the music — he used "classical" composers such as Bach and Chopin as well as music composed to order — was a crude anticipation of what Léonide Massine was to do later with huge symphonic works. He created literal, semidramatic gestures and encounters to suit whatever dynamic interplay he found in the music. If the music surged up to a high pitch, the dancers rose on their toes; if it crashed, they fell to the floor; if it was dissonant, they fought; and if there was counterpoint, they traded blow for blow.

Shawn took some of the pantomimic curse off by arranging these gestures in artistic floor patterns. More important, when two or more dancers were involved, he merely indicated that one gesture had caused the other to happen — physical contact did not take place. Or if it became necessary, as in a lift, the dancers flipped as quickly as possible from preparation to lifted pose. So what you saw were men being heroic — suffering, challenging, striking, striving — but not engaged in actual conflict with anyone else. This focused attention on the heroic body image Shawn was so absorbed in; it didn't divert the viewer's attention to a more compelling action, and it minimized any awkward moments when a dance might accidentally pass through an undignified or inappropriate position.

This preoccupation with the look of the body, the insistence that the body should look virile at all times, was Shawn's principal contribution to our choreographic development. He must have decided early on that there was no reason the arms and upper body had to be round, light, and delicate, as dictated by the decorative European ballet. They could be strong and ready for work just as well. As a corrective, his thinking was quite logical. The things men do when dancing *are* strong and do demand great physical endurance, precision, and daring. The whole ballet convention consisted in more or less hiding these attributes, with elaborate costuming, passive role-playing, and that soft, aggression-denying upper body. Frequently, in the nineteenth century, women even took the principal male roles in big ballets. Shawn wanted to restore or complete the energy system that had been emasculated by tradition. The clumsiness of his efforts as choreography doesn't invalidate his vision.

After the breakup of Denishawn around 1930, Shawn formed a men's company, probably the first in our history, and toured the United States for seven years. He added some dances that attempted to document American folk material, particularly of the cowboy-and-Indian genre, but again, his lack of choreographic sophistication was a handicap; Eugene Loring, Martha Graham, and others were already dealing more imaginatively with these themes. Shawn lived, after Denishawn, a kind of seminarian life — he had originally studied for the ministry and obviously had a calling to teach. Jacob's Pillow, his home in the Berkshires of Massachusetts, was built by Shawn and his dancers. It became a major summer dance school and performance center and a refuge for male dance students, who were offered scholarships in return for hard manual labor.

Shawn's closest heir, and the dancer who carried his aesthetic into the most fully realized choreographic style and repertory, was José Limón. A highly intelligent and cultured lapsed Catholic, Limón was a true second-generation modern dancer in that he couldn't identify with any form of dance until he saw the great German modern dancer Harald Kreutzberg. For Limón, Kreutzberg's dance expressed a more direct humanness and masculinity than the balletic and theatrical dancing he had seen. He enrolled at the Humphrey-Weidman school immediately afterward. Limón saw his own dancing not only as a means of personally expressing himself but as a model, a demonstration, of idealized manhood. Referring back to ancient cultures, he found that men had played a much

Ted Shawn's men dancers.

more prominent part in dancing; they had portrayed the gods and heroes of society, not the silly and overdressed ciphers of the eighteenth- and nineteenth-century ballet. In Limón's view, both ballet and popular dancing presented the male in a subordinate and frivolous position that far from reflected his role in society.[2]

Limón quickly became a principal dancer in the Humphrey-Weidman company. With Doris Humphrey he had a perfect artistic symbiosis: at first her star pupil, he later became the executant/creator of her choreography while she acted as artistic director of his company and close adviser to his own choreographic efforts. They had very different temperaments, though. I doubt if Limón could have created the excellent dance dramas that he did — centering around so many powerful literary and historical figures — had he not also enacted the less specific heroic archetypes in Humphrey's works.

Like Shawn, Limón was of robust physical stature, tall and striking, and he seemed perpetually conscious of himself as a noble figure. He too stressed the power of the upper body, but he integrated this attitude much more thoroughly and smoothly into his choreography than Shawn. In addition to specific mime gestures of effort or attack, he developed abstractions, a personal port de bras, that conveyed character in a "masculine" way without being literal. His arms were in constant action, almost always working together in designs abstracted from the virile flamenco dance or in gestures that seemed to suggest work tasks. The arms would lash around or plunge forward with the hands clenched in fury. His hands would be clasped together over one shoulder or lifted laboriously overhead as if contending with some large object, or he'd curve the upper body forward with chest taut and shoulders spread, as if he were bending under a yoke. He made many line and circle dances for a group in which the dancers were joined by locking arms together shoulder high. All these tended to draw attention to the upper body, while, as often as not, the lower body was working in opposition, with swift bourréeing steps or explosive jumps.

In Lucas Hoving, Limón found an ideal partner. As tall as Limón, Hoving contrasted with him in many other ways — pale and Nordic where Limón was dark and Hispanic, coolly austere to Limón's passion. Neither man was really a sensual dancer, but, where Hoving was balletically vertical and rather brittle in his movement, Limón was tight and strong. Employing this duality in their relationship, Limón choreographed several dramatic dances that revolved around a pair of contrasting men. It was probably one of the first such partnerships in Western theater dancing.

As was his habit in his narrative works, Limón painted these characters as bold and static portraits. He chose them to represent situations or emotional struggles of particular interest to him, and they usually had some moral issue at the core. In *The Moor's Pavane*, a weak, shrewd man destroys his rival by finding where he is vulnerable. In *La Malinche*, peasant overthrows tyrant, and in *The Apostate*, the forces of Christianity and paganism vie for a king's allegiance. *The Traitor*, the story of Judas and Jesus, returns to the themes of envy and power, this time with the rivals bound by spiritual love. *Emperor Jones*, probably Limón's most complex character study, shows two outlaws from society competing to gain control of a rogue empire.

In setting up these psychological combats between himself and Hoving, Limón was not only creating great danceable roles. He was elaborating on relationships that were conventionally shown in much cruder terms. Male duets in most ballets were confined to simple battles over women or some other prize, with little account taken of the different types of motivation or inner conflicts the rivals might have. Beginning in the mid-fifties, Limón extended these possibilities even further through a series of all-male group dances, of which *Traitor* and *Emperor Jones* were two. But he never gave up the female contingent in his company, even after Doris Humphrey's death. His greatest sympathy and insight were exercised on the male character, but he was capable of creating fine dramatic roles for women, especially for the gifted Pauline Koner; and he used women well in many of his Humphrey-influenced plotless dances like *There Is a Time* and *Missa Brevis*.

In Limón's choreography, men are not merely the central characters, they are heroes, prime movers. They possess the world's power and talents. They hold responsibility, often for the welfare of many other people — families, communities, kingdoms — and Limón shows them literally bearing the burden on their backs, pulled between opposing loyalties. They are tormented by jealousy, tempted to folly, agonized by impossible choices. He was drawn to man the outsider — the one who can't be part of ordinary society because he's either isolated by his power or ostracized for madness or nonconformity. Interestingly, neither his heroes nor their ene-

THE TRAITOR (*Limón, 1954*). *Photo by Matthew Wysocki.*

mies are artists; they are men of action, soldiers, rulers, crusaders, not the kind of men we associate with dancers. If we think of the vain, idle, nineteenth-century ballet heroes, the fairy-tale kings who sit around in foppish costumes making elegant gestures to their subjects, and the early-twentieth-century exotics, half-slave, half-fantasy sex objects, we can begin to imagine the contempt Limón must have felt for the male dancing image and to understand how sensitively he went about changing it.

It is significant that Limón seldom choreographed in a contemporary mode. For him, the male image was heroic, larger than life, just as the female image was for Martha Graham. Modern man or woman wasn't noble enough. Most ballet and modern dance characterizes people in some sublimated form. The techniques — the bodily idioms in which ballet and modern dancers come before us — are already exaggerations, highly specialized and refined adaptations of everyday behavior. Few choreographers working within the province of conventional stage dancing have been able to reconcile the ordinariness of life with the extraordinariness of dance style. Anna Sokolow has been most consistently successful at this, and more recently Twyla Tharp. It is in the movies and musical comedy that dancing can be an acceptable form of expression for a modern character, and most of the ballets in which we can recognize ourselves and our time have at least a slight tinge of pop about them.

I think the unpretentiousness of musical comedy music and its simpler, more natural rhythms have evoked art dancing that looks more familiar. Show dancing, of course, came largely from jazz and tap, which are more closely rooted in ordinary modern life anyway. The jazz hoofers and tappers were almost all men, so perhaps it isn't surprising that the dancing male found a role easily in movies and musicals. Several roles even. Most of these roles had their origins in either the comedy routines of vaudeville or the pop literature that mass audiences loved — comic books, radio scripts, the sports pages, detective novels. We can see these sources fusing into stage types in the American character ballets of the thirties and forties, like *Filling Station, Billy the Kid,* and *Fancy Free,* and in the frenetic, man-on-the-street solos of Daniel Nagrin, a modern dancer with extensive show experience.

Fred Astaire somehow managed to elude all these stereotypes, probably because by temperament he was neither jock, thug, nor zany. His movie characters projected a male personality who found reasons for dancing in the life he lived, and except that he lived in a fairy-tale world of show business and high society, the things he did were quite ordinary. He could dance about walking a dog, getting caught in the rain — almost anything with any action in it at all. He didn't need the excuse of a sports competition, a fight, or a practical joke to spur him into dancing. Astaire's most important contribution to the role of the male dancer probably is that dancing as an ordinary man didn't make him self-conscious.

Although Astaire found many ways to explore his own tap idiom without adopting any special personae, in ballet men still had a strong tendency to justify themselves through the device of character. As dance in America came to realize that, like the other arts, it could be a vehicle for depicting the contemporary psyche, the male dancer emerged from his previous circumscribed roles to carry a more central and varied share of the dance action. In the dance-dramas of Graham and Tudor the hierarchies were broken; men did not have to be Egyptian slaves or bloodthirsty warriors in order to be discovered dancing.

But until quite recently, pure-dance ballets were the province of women. Males don't just go out and dance, without any other pretext. Even Isadora Duncan, that most idealistic promoter of dancing as social and spiritual enrichment, habitually used the female pronoun when describing her utopian dancing universe.[3] Doris Humphrey did accept men as the dancing equals of women, and her vision of what sexually mixed groups could do choreographi-

Fred Astaire's golf dance from "Carefree" (1938). Lester Glassner Collection.

cally had significant repercussions much later in the all-dancing romantic ballets of Robbins and Feld, as well as in the democratically structured if unsexed modern-ballet works we often see today. Feld and the later Robbins opened the door to the casually discovered, classically virtuosic male.

Dances at a Gathering began a cycle of noncharacter ballets with important classical roles for men, but, long before sex roles became a particular issue in the dance world, Robbins seems to have had a special interest in featuring male dancers. His first choreography, *Fancy Free,* had not one hero but three. The women in that ballet were essentially ciphers who played complementary roles to the showy males, a true reversal of the balletic order of things. Men and women have had almost equal prominence in his work ever since, with men perhaps slightly ahead. One possible reason for this is that Robbins was still active as a dancer when he began to choreograph, and he naturally created roles for himself, roles that his body could understand. The same is true of Feld. Those early Robbins roles were often jazzy or "modern" in the manner of *Four Temperaments.* His ease with contemporary idioms led him into his second, fabulous show career, but when he returned to work exclusively in ballet, he seems to have concentrated on a more traditional language of steps and uncharacterized ideas. However, he still features men in his ballets, and his work has done a great deal for the morale of male dancers at the New York City Ballet, perhaps even inspiring George Balanchine to explore more of his company's male potential.

In a culture where men do not dance, a male bias seems to have some element of special provocativeness; male-dominated ballets can very easily begin to look homosexual, or at least antifeminist. In recent years many dance works have explored the homosexual situation, either overtly or covertly, or depicted a world where women are dealt with unsympathetically while men are seen as desirable. This viewpoint has grown almost endemic in "modern ballet," both American and European. More than any breakthroughs in choreography or dance skill that it accomplished, this pro-male dance has altered everyone's image of how a male dancer should look and what he can do. Baryshnikov's beauty is one of his important attributes, whether he dances a stud in a Glen Tetley allegory or a prince in *Giselle.*

Perhaps the first dance to deal outright with male psychosexual problems was Antony Tudor's *Undertow* (1945). This tortured view of a boy's passage from a traumatic childhood through the temptations of youth became the model for many similar ballets in later years. Tudor's hero, wounded by primal memories of his birth and the early loss of his mother to the affections of his father, is shown observing the flow of life in a town. Every sexual encounter he sees — and most of what he sees carries sexual content to his obsessed mind — is both attractive and repellent. When he finally succumbs to the seduction of a girl, his guilt is so strong that he strangles her. As Edwin Denby interpreted the ballet after its première, "The theme of *Undertow* is that of an adolescent's neurosis, the terrifying dilemma which presents to him the act of manhood as equivalent to murder. The hero of the piece cannot find the normal solution of this, according to psychology, normal dilemma; the image of murder is so powerful in him it dominates and petrifies him, and in his impotence he kills."[4]

In this ballet can be found most of the symbols of the homosexual point of view in dance — the boy's rejection by his first love, his mother, and consequent resentment of his father-rival; his later fear or hatred of his own sexual impulses, especially those connected with women; and his finding an outlet for these impulses in an aggressive act. Perhaps the aggression is only happening in the boy's mind, and murder is his private metaphor for intercourse; either of them could lead to his final guilt and anguish. Although Tudor often returned to questions of sexual repression and inadequacy in his ballets, *Undertow* is his most direct treatment of the subject, and it's significant that he produced it during the same period in which Martha Graham was leading the modern dancers into their deepest psychological explorations.

Shawn's subliminal narcissism and the psychosexual adventures of the postwar period were liberating influences for choreographers. "Serious" dancing and show business began to mix during this time, as Broadway shows felt the influence of choreographers such as Balanchine ("On Your Toes," 1936), de Mille ("Oklahoma," 1943), and Robbins ("West Side Story," 1957); and popular ethnic companies like that of José Greco, Katherine Dunham, and the Moiseyev presented a glamorized male dancer without embarrassment. In the past fifteen to twenty years, many other factors have enhanced our receptivity to the dancing male: the rise of interest in nonverbal communication in general and the loosening up of attitudes toward the body, with greater sexual freedom and a tolerance for nonstandard sexual behavior; the public fascination with performers and performance, especially with stars, and the boost that Rudolf Nureyev gave to the image of the male ballet star; the fact that most of our current movie stars, and other stars in sports, music, journalism, and politics, are male. The American public today admires the man of action, the man *in* action, and, most recently, male dancers have become almost as potent sex symbols as women.

In Europe, Maurice Béjart was choreographing for a large corps of male dancers in the 1950s, but his work and that of his followers always seems to have some political or symbolic pretext, some alternative for the audience member who would prefer not to confront male sexuality outright. Interestingly, in this country it was a woman, Martha Graham, who really faced up to male eroticism first and who has had a major influence on those who are best known for exploiting it today — John Butler, Glen Tetley, Alvin Ailey, and others. Graham had been making display dances for men since she first had men in the company — *American Document* and *Every Soul Is a Circus* (1938) probably contain the earliest examples — and what distinguishes these from a ballet pas de deux or the male solos of modern dance is that Graham didn't gloss over the idea that the woman was physically turned on by what he was doing. All through the 1940s and 1950s, men were Graham's villains, and though to us they may look pompous and grotesque, to her heroines they were fatally erotic.

In her nondramatic dances, where she often didn't dance herself, she was able to develop this sensual awareness, and we can begin to see it in the couple work in *Dark Meadow* and in *Diversion of Angels* (1948) and *Acrobats of God* (1960). *Secular Games* (1962) most fully and frankly exploited these possibilities. In three sections, each about play (the subtitles are "Play with Thought — on a Socratic Island," "Play with Dream — on a Utopian Island," and "Play — on Any Island"), the dance had a group of men, then women, dancing separately. In the last part they paired up. The men's section, which began the piece, was a display of rippling muscles and gorgeous tricks, presented not for female onlookers but for each other. A ball was tossed suggestively among them. The women did nothing very extraordinary, and when the men joined them they were merely compliant. Graham's sinuous movement, emphasizing the body's curves and oppositions, had a much more erotic (and homoerotic) effect when done by a male group than by women — men simply didn't move their bodies that way in 1962. *Secular Games* was considered a sly bit of propaganda by insiders at a time when a homosexual message had to be disguised or at least mitigated by a conventionally paired finale.

By 1977 men could show off on a stage without behaving like football players, and audiences don't particularly categorize or pass judgment on their sexual preferences; sexy men are okay. Young choreographers like Louis Falco and Jennifer Muller have made a very popular genre out of a sort of pan-sexual, swinger mystique, built on a free-flow, casually articulated, and maximally displayed body language slung onto the meagerest of thematic pretexts.

If gender in dance defines itself in terms of sexuality, as it so frequently seems to, some men have chosen the role of androgyne. I suppose this is a throwback to the Spectres and Golden Slaves of Nijinsky — the male adopts a nonaggressive sex role in order to push dancing beyond the limits set by conventional masculinity. The best example of this approach today is seen in Erick Hawkins. Hawkins began as a ballet dancer and choreographed for Ballet Caravan before joining Graham in 1938. Their partnership — and marriage — ended in the late forties, and after a period of withdrawal, Hawkins began choreographing again. Up to this point, his career seems uncannily similar to Ted Shawn's — the effort to find validity as a dancing male, the frustration of trying to work with a dominant woman. But where Shawn's subsequent style stressed the heavy, masterful qualities, Hawkins decided to avoid all aggressiveness and conflict.

Much has been written by his disciples and collaborators about Hawkins' philosophy of movement. After his years with Graham, Hawkins felt that there should be a way to dance that involved less strain and injury. Taking up Isadora Duncan's search for what is naturally beautiful in human motion, he based his system of training on the principles of Mabel Ellsworth Todd, the American proponent of body mechanics and kinesiology. He rejected the necessity for conflict and developed a technique in which "a dancer can learn not to violate the nature of his body, and, therefore, to do 'natural' dancing."[5] In Zen philosophy he found reinforcement for his idea of just letting the movement happen, not investing it with "psychological willfulness and physical tension."[6]

Hawkins' training puts great emphasis on placement, or "centering," on the dancer's developing an acute sensitivity to the intelligent workings of his or her own body, and on a cyclical use of energy, much like that wavelike continuum by which Duncan felt herself in tune with the cosmos. The Hawkins dancer moves with a pulsing of energy, an ebb and flow with subtle gradations, that is never supposed to reach the extremes of total tension or total release and that should never cease and have to be restarted. One writer, the possibly pseudonymous Harvey Rochlein, in a critical essay on modern dance that turned out to be an apologia for Hawkins, said he had "a capacity of stripping movement of everything except its poetry, a kind of pure, naked, bedrock of poetry."[7]

There is much in Hawkins' approach that runs counter to the way we think of the relationship between men and movement. He insists that the body should not be used in pushy, violent, or dissonant ways, which are the ways most men assert themselves on an athletic field or a ballet stage, or in any other place where male physical display is tolerated. Hawkins acknowledges the contemplative, passive Zen way of thinking, a distinctly nonstandard practice in Western countries. And in his preoccupation with the body, with considering the body at all let alone rationalizing about it and trying to find a place for dancing within traditional Western aesthetic-intellectual thought, Hawkins has been rare — a male entering where few men in this country had ventured before.

Philosophically, Hawkins' explorations have led to a paradox. In trying to see the dancing body as a thing in itself, possessing an intrinsic beauty provided it is being faithful to its own natural rules, he comes closer than perhaps anyone to the "objective" goals of modern art, music, and literature. But he is assuming that we can *see* the naturalness and the pure beauty as easily as someone performing in his technique can *feel* it. He asks the audience to separate the literal fact — that real persons, male and female, are doing real actions with inevitable resonances in our experience — from the aesthetic fact — that these persons can be perceived for their form and harmony alone. Instead of suspending our natural affinity for these dancers and placing ourselves at some less personal distance, as Hawkins would like us to do, some of his viewers, myself

ANGELS OF THE INMOST HEAVEN (*Hawkins, 1972*). *Robert Yohn and Erick Hawkins. Photo by Kenn Duncan.*

included, find in these nearly naked, hairless bodies engaging in soft, gentle play not a more human humanity but one that is somehow deficient.

Another reaction against the modern dance of the forties and fifties came from Alwin Nikolais, who expressed a strong aversion to the implicitly feminine psychological probings of Graham and many of the Graham-Humphrey-Horst alumni. Nikolais wanted to relieve choreography of its narcissistic hang-ups. He saw dancing at that time as glorified sexuality — what he called the prince-as-star "Nureyev complex" of ballet and the "foetal, fertile and phallic" neuroticism of modern dance. He thought this attitude was related to a regrettable and false view that man is superior to the rest of the universe. He saw the self-expression of most dancing as a kind of arrogance, "as if one's presence was a self-induced miracle, and each gesture was a radiant gift bestowed upon the environment and whatever existed within it."[8] Nikolais set out to make his dance more "total." He said, "It is not that I don't believe in hero identification, even Nureyev — but I wanted man to be able to identify with things other than himself. This is the day of ecological and environmental visions. We must give up our navel contemplations long enough to take our place in space."[9]

In a sense, Nikolais was after the same thing as Hawkins — to lift from the dancer's shoulders all the accumulated symbolism, lore, and provocative behavior that had distracted audiences from seeing his true, essential qualities. Nikolais was not so interested in the sensually beautiful and the natural, as defined by Hawkins, but in the magic, myth, and imagery that the dancer could invoke as part of an ensemble of evolving stage elements that included light, color, sound, and landscape. Within this artificial but more balanced universe, Nikolais' dancers can manipulate the design, can merge with it and sometimes disappear, and can also be surrounded, enhanced, or even transfigured by it. Sexuality is not an issue, however.

If he has not actually dehumanized his dancers, as he's often been accused of doing, Nikolais has desexed them. Men and women invariably wear the same kinds of costumes, costumes that have been engineered to minimize sexual differences or to eliminate them entirely. In recent years he's used less of the kind of costume construction that totally disguised the dancers, making them look like portable pieces of scenery. But even when he presents them in body suits, seemingly the most revealing option short of nudity, they look flat and hard, their hair often hidden by wigs or helmets, their faces whitened by make-up. Their contacts are physical but impersonal. Even lifting and carrying are not the exclusive tasks of the men. All Nikolais dancers move with great facility and acute sensitivity to their effect on the space around them, but they are somehow unreal. Their dance always has a feeling of being finely engineered and calibrated, their metred rhythms and precut shapes are always reminding us that another person is in control. The only god in Nikolais' universe is Nikolais, and he has created everything in it, including the inhabitants.

Nikolais' detached view of the dancing person seems very much in keeping with our times. In his hands, a dance can be a visual "trip," but it is usually one without emotional content, except on the primal levels of laughter, surprise, awe, excitement. His aim is not to develop these raw responses but simply to make them available to us. In the hands of his less gifted descendants, the facility turns into glibness, the detachment into evasion. I sometimes have the feeling that Nikolais' antic, acrobatic creatures are one more guise, one more persona, through which men can appear on the stage, can be lovable, beautiful, and physically brilliant, without compromising themselves as men.

Another way of defining oneself as a dancer without making a commitment to any sexual image was taken by Charles Weidman, who exemplified the man as dancing clown. In the 1930s, when Weidman emerged from Denishawn to form the Humphrey-Weidman school and company, dance was the last refuge for physical comedy. Talking pictures almost instantaneously wiped out the mime tradition that had reached such a high degree of skill and articulation in silent movies. Weidman was the first dancer to carry on this line; the succession has continued with Merce Cunningham, Murray Louis, Paul Taylor, and the contemporary dancer Douglas Dunn. There were women in the chain, too, notably Katherine Litz, who started as a Humphrey-Weidman dancer, and Nikolais-trained Phyllis Lamhut. But somehow the comic gift has been seen only rarely in women dancers. Viola Farber is capable of it; so is Twyla Tharp; though neither one usually ventures into character, where humor becomes more evident. Men have developed the eye for it much more often and found ways to use it more consistently.

It may be that women don't have as great a need to create a special persona for themselves onstage. The clown wins the audience's sympathy by kidding himself — making himself a "little" man subject to the disappointments and pratfalls of anyone in the audience, he presents himself as much more vulnerable than the superhuman creatures that other dancers seem to be. Modern dance's humanistic tendencies made it a good breeding ground for this kind of clown, but ballet has always had a place for him too in the vulgarian demi-caractère roles such as Alain, the halfwit in *La Fille Mal Gardée* and Massine's Peruvian dandy in *Gaîté Parisienne*.

Weidman began doing comic vignettes early. The Humphrey-Weidman company maintained an unusually open working atmosphere, in which both directors contributed to the repertory —

often choreographing cooperatively or doing sections in each other's dances. Humphrey never fell into stereotyped dance formulas, and Weidman's autobiographical studies, his comic escapades like the silent-movie spoof *Flickers* (1941), were as welcome as the choral and dramatic dances he made in a less personal style. In 1934 he choreographed *Kinetic Pantomime*, initiating a style that was all his. He would begin a gesture that had literal connotations — a dance version of some everyday action or feeling. Just as the viewer began to recognize what he was doing, he would turn his body into something else. This constantly evolving chain of movements — Margaret Lloyd described it as "iridescent bubbles of mirth"[10] — could be funny, and also poignant, surprising, and beautiful, as I suppose all deep comedy is; and even when I saw him do it at sixty-plus, Weidman's timing, his sense of phrasing, and his extraordinarily mobile face and hands could only have belonged to a dancer. Today Weidman is best known for his *Thurber Fables*, a series of dances-with-narration that he began in 1948, when the Humphrey-Weidman association had ended. Like the great American humorist James Thurber, Weidman had a whimsical side, and he was the ideal translator of the little moral tales about the henpecked husbands with secret talents, the empty-headed secretaries, and the wise, mythical creatures that could only be seen by the downtrodden.

In finding new dancing-places for men, Hawkins concentrated on body movement, Nikolais on the total theater effect. Merce Cunningham has viewed the problem from the position of an exceptional choreographer. His solution is probably the least self-conscious since Astaire's. He simply lets the dancers dance. His company is not separated into male and female ensembles; what men and women can do alike, they do, but their partnering proceeds along conventional lines. One seldom sees chic boy-boy or girl-girl couples in Cunningham. Partly you sense his efficiency in doing this — men are stronger than women, so they do the lifting. But also, because there is no other role-playing in his dance, the sensual attraction between men and women comes into our awareness. Post-Cunningham choreographers like Gus Solomons, Dan Wagoner, and Douglas Dunn have allowed their work to become charged with it at times. Cunningham simply lets it be there. His dancers never seem very far from seeming like real people even when they are executing highly technical feats. I cannot remember a time when his company didn't contain a wildly random assortment of sizes, temperaments, and body types. They dance themselves.

Cunningham choreographs for his dancers, not aiming for any standard company veneer or attitude, which is one reason his older works are so hard to revive. Neither he nor anyone else can seem to picture other people in Carolyn Brown's roles, or Viola Farber's or his own. Because they don't play roles other than themselves, the drama of their movement experience is constantly in play on the Cunningham dancers' faces. As if to impress their reality on us even further, Cunningham incorporates "everyday" movement in his choreography. There are times when the dancers abandon strict technique to walk around casually or perform ordinary tasks, like sitting in a chair, taking off or putting on clothing, resting, and watching each other.

Cunningham's dances are about what he and his dancers are doing here for us. Often Cunningham plays the leader, the teacher, the setter-in-motion, and — especially in later years when his speed and agility could no longer match those of the younger dancers — the god, mystery-man, and outsider. Yet these are not special personae that he attaches to himself — nor, I suspect, does Cunningham think of himself as having any special sex role to play. Onstage or off, he is as he appears to us, a man dancing, a dancing-man.

Neoclassicism II

Septet (Merce Cunningham)

Nineteen fifty-three was an important year for Merce Cunningham, who is probably the most influential exile from the expressionism and conflict of Martha Graham's modern dance. The enigmatic Cunningham has done more to obscure the origins and meaning of his work than to reveal them; it seems to me that despite his obvious role as a leader of the avant-garde, he is as closely allied to classicism as he is opposed to tradition. Perhaps only a committed formalist could set up a complicated and laborious structure to prevent himself from becoming too personally involved in the process of his own choreography, or could publish a book of notes and comments about his dances that, although unpaged and typographically eccentric, keeps the material pertaining to a particular dance conveniently together on the same pages.[1]

Cunningham, like Graham, grew up on the West Coast. Whereas Graham's dance education had led in a direct line from Denishawn to her own evolving style, Cunningham began with tap and musical comedy, studied modern, joined the Graham company and simultaneously studied ballet, and began developing his own technique and choreography, all before 1950. Both choreographers appear to have been influenced by the Orient, Graham retaining a predilection for exotic color, costume, design, and movement shapes, Cunningham adopting the contemplative, antiegotistical outlook of many Eastern religions.

Although he danced with Graham until the late 1940s, Cunningham began doing his own choreography as early as the summer of 1942 at Bennington. He made *The Seasons*, to John Cage's music, for Balanchine's Ballet Society in 1947, and he gave concerts in Europe with ballet dancers Tanaquil LcClercq and Betty Nichols two years later. His first "chance" piece, *Sixteen Dances for Soloist and Company of Three,* was made in 1951. The nucleus of the Cunningham Company formed at Black Mountain College in the early fifties, and the company had its first New York season at the Theater de Lys late in 1953. This season saw the first performances of *Septet.*

It is typical of Cunningham's ability to keep many working options open for himself that *Septet* is not a chance dance. He says it was one of the last times he used a "wholly intuitive procedure," [2] and he attached a program note: "The poetic ambiguity of the music and dance titles expresses the character of this ballet, the subject of which is Eros, and the occurrence of which is at the intersection of joy and sorrow." This note seems to me to be as deliberately perplexing as the music and its titles, Erik Satie's Three Pieces in the Shape of a Pear, with sections headed In the Garden, In the Music Hall, In the Tea House, In the Playground, In the Morgue, In the Distance, and In the End. Certainly nothing in the dance refers literally to such settings or to Eros or to any other emotional state, although Cunningham has explained he got the title for the dance from the fact that Satie's music — despite its name — has seven sections. Indeed, *Septet* has almost no relationship to the modern dance of its time; the dance it most resembles is Frederick Ashton's *Monotones,* which was not choreographed until 1965. I've said all this to give some idea of Cunningham's unpredictability, of his refusal to submit to the categories, even his own. This is his most revolutionary characteristic. Other people have made much more unconventional-looking dances, but Cunningham's openness to new forms and methods has shown those more iconoclastic than he what new possibilities there are to be explored.

By 1953 Cunningham had already choreographed several Satie dances. If ever a composer and a choreographer were well matched, these two are — perhaps even more suited than Cunningham is to Cage, who has been his musical director and collaborator since 1942. Aesthetically, Cunningham belongs in the succession of the French avant-garde that began with Satie and Apollinaire and led, through Gertrude Stein, Picasso, and Duchamp, to Cage and Robert Rauschenberg in this country. Cunningham shares with these artists first of all a determination to avoid the emotional and intellectual props on which nineteenth-century art had rested. Cunningham's dance is "abstract" in the sense that it has neither narrative nor descriptive overtones, neither compositional sequence as it's commonly understood nor any intention of being expressive or impressive. Its matter is dance, its environment time and space, its posture cool. Like Satie, Cunningham is a boulevardier rather than a cloistered genius. He appreciates the vernacular as much as the pure — and both are free of emotive implications to him. His dance is sometimes thematic, but it isn't structured for logical development, elaboration, or the evocation of particular audience reactions — even sympathy. Cunningham's lifework is an exposition of dance, and in that he has been as important to American classicism as Balanchine.

Septet has been out of the Cunningham repertory for about a decade, but fortunately it was filmed in 1964 during a performance in Finland, with Cunningham, Carolyn Brown, Viola Farber, Barbara Lloyd, Steve Paxton, and William Davis. Cunningham has cautioned that the dance "didn't necessarily fit the music,"[3] but they are in fact very closely related. Satie's phrasing is modular: the music comes in small units of three or four measures, each unit quite self-contained so that it could work just as easily in another place. It's almost impossible to sing because it has no continuous melodic line. Similarly, Cunningham choreographs segments of motion — usually corresponding to Satie's phrases — that never seem to carry over the bar lines for more than a few measures and that have no climaxes or formal progression. After studying the film and writing about the dance for two weeks, I cannot accurately recite the order of events. The movement, made in modern dance's heyday of tortured, twisted bodies, massive lyricism, and romantic shapes, is upright, light, and placed, more aerial than grounded, serene rather than agitated.

Yet these bodies that look at first so much more balletic than modern don't behave in proper balletic ways. I frequently think of Cunningham's dances as antiballets, but not because I think he is trying to provoke controversy or attack the other form. He seems, in fact, to have a great respect for the classical form, to take the classical conventions as a set of accepted rules against which he plays his contrary games. In *Septet* he often suggests ballet setups and attitudes only to depart from them pointedly, as if to say, "I know this is the way you're used to seeing things, but it can be done another way too."

Septet is a very sparse dance. You get this idea from all aspects of it. Each section is very brief — the whole dance only lasts fifteen minutes — and treats only one main movement idea. The sections are all done by small ensembles, the whole company of six gathering to dance together in only two of the seven sections. There's a relatively large amount of individual movement within the compact group sections, and Cunningham arranges the group in the space so as to emphasize the separateness of each dancer or idea.

Unlike ballet — or the choral modern dances of the time — where the space is kept full and active by the dancers continually massing and shifting, regrouping themselves, and setting up new patterns of organizing the audience's visual field, the dancers in *Septet* gravitate to only a few spots, or they scatter almost without planned pathways through the space. Stressed floor patterns are limited to a small diagonal across the down-left corner of the stage, a line across the footlights, and a spot in the center. Little formations begin to develop, then quickly dissolve. The groupings and pairings of people are not stable either; even the "ballerina," Carolyn Brown, relinquishes her role as the most prominent woman at the very end of the dance, joining the group and leaving while Cunningham is still partnering Viola Farber out.

Most important, the dance is multidirectional. Instead of establishing a "front" toward which they always orient themselves, namely the side of the stage nearest the audience, the dancers take facing positions almost as if at random, or possibly according to how they happened to find themselves in the room when Cunningham started choreographing that particular section. This is not the same idea as pulling the space off center by making a diagonal line. In *Septet*, the dancers often face some oblique quarter of the space or move in crisscross directions against one another without apparently aiming for any specific consolidation point. You are made all the more aware of this erratic orientation because so much of the dance is done in place. Planted in one spot, the dancers attract our attention to their changes of shape or position, like ballerinas being promenaded in arabesque, but often these fixed posings are addressed to unlikely areas of the space.

The dance opens with the three women standing on a diagonal, spaced far apart. Cunningham appears and dances downstage through their line, bowing to them from downstage, where the audience can't get the most favorable view of his gesture. *Septet* is full of bows, gracious nods, and other courtly gestures, which are the only realistic signs in the dance.

This first section is a dialogue between Cunningham and the women. He dances for a few bars while they remain quiet, then they dance while he watches. During the course of the dance they exchange energies. The women begin with slow unfoldings of arms and legs, bendings and turnings of the torso, while Cunningham does springy jumps and runs; later he stretches and lunges slowly while they do a few lively, off-center jumps. The initial diagonal line of women breaks and they reassemble several times, once in a triangular formation facing outward to three corners of the space, once in a horizontal line about midstage, facing the audience. At the end — all the endings come without preparation — he stands up-center and the women gather in a line shoulder to shoulder facing him, with their backs to the audience. After a pause, they tiptoe off together, moving sideward, and Cunningham gazes at them until they're out of sight.

This last little encounter reminds me of *Apollo* — perhaps any twentieth-century dance for a man and three female partners unavoidably recalls the Balanchine classic — and also anticipates Paul Taylor's *Aureole*. Later in *Septet* Cunningham will partner the women in an even stronger, more Apollo-like way and lead them off for a few steps, suggesting Apollo and the three muses on their final journey to Balanchine's Olympus.

When the women are gone, Cunningham begins a lively solo to fast marcato music. The steps he does are quite balletic — consisting mostly of grands jetés and chaîné turns, with a few traveling pas de chat — but his line is casual. He seems more interested in elevation and speed, and in ranging through the space, than in keeping his knees straight and his feet pointed. The movement continues nonstop and is punctuated by very odd gestures — shoulder shakes, contractions of the upper back, a sudden fall back toward his heels and an equally quick recovery. Three or four times, in the middle of a jump or a fast drop into a deep plié, he spreads his hands in front of his face and whips them apart to reveal his mouth wide open, and he dances away with it open, as if he had performed a magic trick.

On the music, he whirls to an abrupt halt down-right after a big circle of jumps. He does not bother to land with his feet in a precise position, and he gives the idea that the dance has merely been interrupted. Four dancers have walked onto the stage and Cunningham stares at them for a moment. Now, in silence, he circles upstage to them and gravely shakes the hand of one, then turns and leaves. Chattily, the woman turns to shake the hand of a companion, and the other couple do likewise. Then all four dancers go off arm in arm in the opposite direction from Cunningham.

After each section of *Septet* there is a little interlude like this, a moment of silence in which the dancers come on and go off with odd, nondancerly behavior. This breaks the formality of the dance, and with it, to some extent, the special persona that the dancer adopts when performing a highly cultivated action. The interlude-skits are also antiballetic in that they call to our attention the changing of characters from one part of the dance to the next, which is either underplayed in ballet — one group of dancers leaves and the other arrives — or achieved with great fanfare. In *Septet* the dancers sometimes nod farewell to their partners before joining up with their next companions, sometimes they meet onstage and do a preliminary swing or step before starting the real dance, and in one case people walk on, wait until they are joined by someone, then walk off, leaving the newcomer behind. Another function of these changing-of-the-guard ceremonies is to neutralize the space, to reshuffle the positions and groupings of dancers, and to allow for the dance to proceed with a completely new arrangement.

Cunningham returns with Carolyn Brown and they begin a slow duet upstage center. They remain in one spot, except at one point they move closer to the audience. The duet is like a ballet adagio, again with a difference. Brown faces the audience, with a calm, unself-conscious look, and slowly assumes several off-center positions, always with her chest open and her arms dropped and slightly spread. Cunningham, standing behind her, supports her with a minute, almost erotic sensitivity to her every adjustment and displacement of line, and she leans back onto him with complete confidence. Once he picks her up, holding her by one bent leg and under one arm, and pivots with her slowly, as much in soft, rocking enjoyment of holding her as to show the audience her elegant form from another angle. He pivots front and carefully sets her down so that she can stand on the extended leg, just the way a ballet dancer puts the woman down so that she's exactly centered on one pointe.

While she balances, now on the balls of both feet, he slowly sinks into a squat, sliding his lightly supporting hand down to her waist. Then he rises. Reaching back without looking at him, she leans back once more and he lifts her onto his shoulder. She closes her arms for the first time, in an embracing circle around his head, and he carries her off.

One of the themes of *Septet* seems to be the utility of dance, the idea that the same thing can keep coming back and be used again by different people. The fourth section, in three parts because the music is, begins with two couples facing into the down-left corner and getting themselves going with vigorous running in place that propels them into jack-in-the-box jumps and running, push-off arabesques. Before you can be certain what their dance is leading to, the men slide into the wings, the third woman has entered, and the women are back in the diagonal formation we saw at the beginning of the dance. Their trio seems to be about replacement, as they change poses while standing in place, always taking the same amount of time to change but sometimes moving together, sometimes in canon.

Farber separates herself from the other two, runs between them, and clasps their hands as if urging them to dance away with her. For a minute they comply, then return to their own preoccupations as she sits on the floor. Lifting her arms and leaning on them, the women take different balance positions on either side of her, leave her, circle around, exchange places, and do the same thing again.

Then the two women leave and two men run on and lift Farber's arms, raising her off the ground and running with her lifted between them. The music returns to its A theme and the dancers begin the same jogging step facing into the corner done initially by the two couples. Their succeeding dance is folky, heels digging into the ground, long striding steps in plié, as opposed to the quartet's aerial excursion. Suddenly Farber dives into the men's arms and they carry her out lengthwise.

The next interlude has people entering and leaving, with long silences in between moves, the audience left in suspense about which dancers will remain and continue. Farber is alone, then three people collect upstage. She turns to join them as another one arrives, and at the last minute Cunningham comes in to make up the full company. The fifth section is the most all-out dancing, a minia-

SEPTET (*Cunningham, 1953*). *Merce Cunningham and Carolyn Brown in foreground. Photo by Stephan.*

ture three-couple ballabile that starts as a sort of Virginia reel, gets all twisted up in space as the couples twirl do-si-do, and turns for a minute into a women-in-the-center-gents-'round-the-outside pattern. Inexplicably, then, they find their partners again and unwind to a stop across the footlights, each man supporting a woman in a different, slowly evolved fall as the music ends.

Two of the women bid their partners goodbye and join Cunningham and Brown in the center. As in the duet, he partners them from that one spot. They take several beautiful poses leaning on or hanging away from his arms, all slowly changing position together and holding the groupings like sculptures for a couple of beats. Most of the women's final poses are balances on one leg, the other leg extended in arabesque or half unfolded, their upper bodies tilted far off center. Cunningham supports them sometimes from difficult positions on the ground, sometimes from a standard balletic fourth.

Gradually they assemble into similar lunge positions, still holding on to one another, and Cunningham starts to lead them away as the music for the last section begins. Just before they leave the stage, Brown detaches herself from them and returns to center stage, where another man is waiting for her. The last dance is really not a dance at all but a line, in profile, across the edge of the stage. The dancers join it, reinforce it with lunges and other flat positions, leave it, change places. Brown circles around through the line, stopping to plunge into a supported arabesque with one of the men, then enters the line again. The dancers begin to leave, continuing the direction of the line into the wings. Brown goes with them. Cunningham holds Farber's hands as she steps backward toward the wings, arching her upper body back, as bizarre and unstable as he is solid and ordinary, piloting her away.

Aureole (Paul Taylor)

In the 1950s, when Paul Taylor's generation began choreographing, modern dance faced a dilemma. It wasn't spoken about much at first, because to speak about it was to admit that modern dance had reached an ideological impasse. It had been from the beginning a dance of resistance, of protest, of individual voice. The Graham-Humphrey generation set out to demonstrate that nonballetic dance could be a viable theater form. Some of their descendants, like José Limón and Pearl Lang, believed that with the force of a strong dancing personality you could extend the work of the original creators. Others, like Anna Sokolow, May O'Donnell, Ann Halprin, Alwin Nikolais, Erick Hawkins, Merce Cunningham, found there was much to discover that the founders hadn't gotten around to. But up to the point where they had to admit the mortality of their leaders, modern dancers had always justified themselves in terms of their individuality. Making something new was the aesthetic of modern dance.

By the 1950s this concept had become academic. For the moment, there wasn't that much new to be discovered, but the audience for modern dance, like the dancers who practiced it, was either exclusively attached to one heroic Graham or Limón-like figure or expected that each promising dancer would emerge as a new choreographic species. Dance composition was taught everywhere, but only Doris Humphrey seems to have thought out a set of real choreographic principles pertaining to movement and space. Everyone else borrowed from music or the plastic arts for models of form, and after Merce Cunningham, composition almost universally became process. The student learned techniques and game plans for working, out of which new movement or dance structures would — almost fortuitously — evolve. No one really wanted to acknowledge that they could use someone else's movement style or choreographic building blocks as a resource for new choreography.

Paul Taylor and the artists of his age group were the first to mature in the period when Doris Humphrey was gone, Hanya Holm had stopped doing concert work, and Graham was slipping into the role of a venerable but no longer innovative matriarch. In their separate ways, Taylor and Alvin Ailey, Donald McKayle, James Waring, Paul Sanasardo, and others became the first moderns to relinquish the totally personal and individual creative roles that had always been thought necessary. This generation made a personal impact in their actual presence as dancers, but their choreography was more eclectic, less distinctive, than the major modern dancers before them. They were engaged in refinement, even elaboration, of the movement asceticism defined by the pioneers. This generation produced the first modern dance *dancers* — Carmen de Lavallade, Mary Hinkson, Ethel Winter, Robert Cohan, Lola Huth, Jaime Rogers, James Truitte, Betty Jones, Ruth Currier — people who were known as performers primarily and later as teachers or company directors, but who did not see success written ultimately in their ability to make individual choreographic statements. For the first time, choreography could be made to service a company, with little pretext beyond providing novelty for a repertory. And for the first time a repertory could include more than one style of choreography. Our present-day modern dance, with its emphasis on performer and performance, not choreography, really began with the Taylor-Ailey generation.

Paul Taylor was not a total independent. Although his style was greatly influenced by his own body and movement preferences, his choreography shows the influence of Graham, with whom he danced for several seasons in the 1950s, and of Cunningham, with whom he appeared briefly. His formality and his feel for music are related to ballet, and he draws extensively on American vernacular dance and other "character" dance styles for his material. But it seems to me that his way of working also resembles Doris Humphrey's, though his dances don't *look* anything like Humphrey's. No contemporary choreographer has had a greater gift than Taylor for combining composition, movement invention, lyricism, and expressive content — and it is interesting to note how many of the currently interesting dance-makers came out of his company.

Aureole was called a white ballet when it was made, in 1962, which seemed either an ultimate tribute or a supreme insult to various sectors of the dance community. It makes few overt references to balletic form, yet it was shocking to some people because of its very acceptance of things the modern dance had — almost religiously — rejected. It is a dance that embodied the uncertainties of its time and survived in spite of them.

It was a pretty dance — not just lyrical or lovely. The dancers wore pristine white practice clothes, with tank tops and short chiffon skirts for the women over bare legs. In not using the standard long skirts or leotards and tights, I think Taylor told the audience to see the dancers as not just functionally beautiful but capable of being slightly idealized, Apollonian. Later he added a ruffle around the neckline of the girls' tops, underlining the point.

Besides the obvious fact of its being a pure-dance work to the music of Handel (selections from *Jeptha* and *Alexander's Feast*), *Aureole* is balletic-looking in its constant orientation to the audience. However, there was a certain reserve about this, an ambivalence. Unlike Cunningham, who had established a frank, extroverted way of addressing the audience, Taylor seemed, and remained throughout his dancing career, somewhat uncertain whether to give out everything. Other dancers were less reticent and the dance later became much more of a performance piece, to the detriment of its particular charm, I thought.

Aureole was one of the first dances I ever saw being born — I watched its first technical rehearsal at Connecticut College during the American Dance Festival — and I have enjoyed it innumerable times since then. Not until I was able to study a work film made of it that first summer did I realize its compositional depth and ingenuity. The discussion that follows is based on that film; although minor changes have been made in the choreography in the interim, the dance as performed by Taylor's company still displays that excellence.

Aureole has five main sections, but the dance is so constructed as to blur the divisions between them. In fact, many of the traditional ways of ordering a dance to help the audience find its way are disrupted. Although there are three clear solo parts, all of the five dancers have implicit solo potential; the brief duets in which the two subsidiary women appear might have been excerpted from some other dance where they played the major roles. Both men have important partnering responsibilities in totally different kinds of ways, and the principal woman spends half her time in a chorus with the other two women. Despite the very small size of the ensemble, Taylor never finds it necessary to make the dance build up to the point where they are all dancing at once. The only time we see the whole company is during a transition between two dance sections: the four make a static formation while Taylor is finishing his solo, and as soon as they have all gathered, he lifts one woman from the floor to activate their group into motion, then dances off himself.

Aureole is one of the most balanced yet off-balance dances imaginable. The stage patterns might have been made by a draftsman so as to avoid attracting your eye to any one dancer or any part of the stage for an undue period of time. In the group sections, people space themselves in neat squares and triangles or tight traveling

AUREOLE *(Taylor, 1962). Paul Taylor (r) and company — original cast. Photo by Jack Mitchell.*

formations or endless diagonals; if one person is singled out, he or she will dance against a unison couple or trio, or will be found alone only briefly, before leading the rest of the dancers onstage.

The movement, for all the dancers except the second male, is based on a flexible torso, with flowing, curving shapes often initiated by one thrusting hip. What makes it look different from the Graham-derived asymmetry that preceded and followed it in other choreographers is its connection to the steady, regular rhythms of Handel's music. The dancers seem to be constantly in motion, usually traveling with a pronounced accent — either weighted skips, runs, or hops or lilting jumps. Even when they are in place, a rhythmic pulse animates their phrasing.

The dance as a whole is extremely active with comings and goings. Except for the solos and the duet section, almost no combination of people remains on the stage for more than a few moments at a time. Dances begin unexpectedly and end before they seem over: some dances seem almost to sneak into action; others begin importantly, only to go into suspension while something else takes place. All these devices work toward deemphasizing the individual dancer or part of the dance, throwing the audience's attention on the dance as a whole.

Aureole begins with an extremely formal, almost intimidating static pose: Taylor and the principal woman (originally Elizabeth Walton) are upstage center, and the two other women stand quietly in the downstage corners. He carries the woman athwart his midsection, and although he makes no pretense at concealing his effort, the woman lies in his arms with perfect repose, as though she were resting on a chaise. He holds her, standing motionless — except for a preliminary turned-in plié — while the other two women crisscross the stage several times in sidestepping skips and twirls. Then he puts her down and they go out in opposite directions. He doesn't return for the rest of the section.

Once it gets going, this dance turns out to be a kind of dialogue between the three women — usually acting as one — and the second man (the roles were created by Walton, Dan Wagoner, Sharon Kinney, and Renee Kimball). The women fly in and out; Wagoner hardly ever dances *with* them but always responds to them, answering each one of their appearances with a little phrase of his own. He seems, at first, happily interested in them, then he grows more excited until he is jumping with an almost deranged exuberance. This dance was infused with the gentle good humor and attentiveness of Dan Wagoner, and is a fine example of Taylor's ability to use the qualities of his dancers to give texture to not only the movement but the dance itself.

Although you could say the first section is a chase, the dancers don't chase each other around. Taylor, cinematically, keeps taking the women off and bringing them on again. Between their visits, Wagoner runs in the direction in which they leave, quickens into a kind of lunging catch-step, and does all his increasingly agitated jumping sequences alone on stage. This way, as if he had a camera switching its focus back and forth, the choreographer can build the excitement without having to fasten on Wagoner all the time and make him seem like a virtuoso trickster.

From time to time Wagoner runs in a circle and the women follow him. At no particular point, he leads them into a diagonal line and they all step into a standing position. After a second, they all turn and walk off along the diagonal.

Taylor now enters a bare stage. He dances an extraordinary solo that is all about positions, scarcely a traveling step in it. Slowly and with great inner concentration he curls and twists his body in a continuously unfolding skein of sensuous and decorative poses. It is the male equivalent of a ballerina dance, and not for another ten years were men commonly to be seen doing such a thing on ballet stages — in the work of another Graham alumnus, Glen Tetley, and others. In the 1970s Taylor gave this role to Rudolf Nureyev, and although the celebrated Russian had the proper sense of plastique, he was not able to achieve Taylor's repose or get the feeling of a great weight in slow but ceaseless flux that was so strange and compelling about Taylor.

Most of the time during this solo he remains in a small central area of the stage, but toward the end he ventures out of it in accelerating spiral-runs that take him up to the group that has entered and is posing quietly. He interrupts his circular travels to stand above the group; for a moment he absorbs their stillness, then he swoops away. The remaining four dancers wind up as if to continue the game they were playing before, but instead they only do a brief reprise, like a chord cadence in between the numbers in a piece of classical music, and disappear, leaving one woman behind.

Her solo begins with an odd, childish but provocative motif of pushing her body from side to side from the hips. It looks as if

Taylor had set her down from the lift in which he held her at the beginning of the dance, told her to keep the same position — body slightly pitched forward and S-curved, arms resting close along the body, and hands flat on the tops of her thighs — and asked her to begin moving from there.

The dance that follows is a sort of analog to Taylor's solo, a dance of big, elaborate curving shapes, but instead of being solidly grounded, the woman keeps her weight buoyantly in motion, rocking from foot to foot, and later progressing into fussy traveling steps — syncopated foot brushes, sideward jumps, and balances that crystallize right out of a run. Where Taylor had molded his body into twisting shapes decorated by the arms, Walton scoops and digs at the air with her hands, allowing her torso to follow the Oriental-looking curves they carve out.

Long before the music is over, the other two women enter softly and she goes out with them. The rest of the dance is a continuous blending and interplay of ideas derived from what has gone before, all seeming completely new, all leading in an almost conversational way into the succeeding incident. Instead of Walton returning immediately, the two other women appear upstage, and they dance a tiny duet of salutation or friendship. They go, and now Walton enters. With little bourréeing hops, never turning away from the audience, she travels in a semicircle from one wing down to the next. When she comes out again, another woman is with her. The women play a modest little sight gag, going in and out of the wings, disappearing and materializing in different combinations, always shoulder to shoulder with the same step. When the possibilities seem almost exhausted, Wagoner joins them.

They take the "Apollo" formation seen in *Septet,* and Taylor makes a whole dance out of what Cunningham threw away in about four bars. The relationship between Wagoner and the women has not changed since the first section, but this time they always approach and leave him in their line, and the rhythm of their bourrée-hops becomes more complicated. Wagoner sometimes chases the women at double their speed; later the step pattern becomes syncopated. Wagoner's excitable jumps in the women's absence become almost virtuosic, and to them he adds turns, running steps, and changing arm designs. At last they all run out.

Once again the space is cleared, and Taylor and Walton enter across the back from opposite sides. They run to the center and stand together where they were discovered at the beginning. Their position is different, but the stillness and formality of their mood are the same. Taylor lifts her by holding her spread-open arms and they dance a few preliminary bars. Suddenly he clasps her around the hips and lifts her flat up against his body, front to front. They stand center stage for a while, then he moves upstage and they stand motionless for a long time. Almost as if he wished not to disturb the air around them, he lets her down and they stand in the same tight embrace, except now their arms are around each other's back and shoulders, and he cups the back of her head with his hand. All during this lift and embrace sequence, Wagoner and one of the chorus women circle toward each other from opposite sides. Advancing and backing in smaller and smaller arcs, they finally meet; he touches her shoulder lingeringly and they part, retreating along the same widening circular path.

When they have left, Taylor and Walton begin again — moving away from each other as if to go, then rushing together in their center spot. Their duet has the sculptural look that both of them have previously shown in their solos, but none of the shapes are quite like ones either of them have achieved before. They move either in unison or responsively — one moving into a new position and the other repeating the phrase in the opposite direction. Although they mold themselves into odd shapes, very Oriental with lots of angularity in the wrists, ankles, knees, and lots of extreme curved-over bodies, this duet is in a way the most symmetrical part of the whole dance. Neither partner makes a move that is not echoed by the other, both in terms of body shape and in covering an equal amount of ground to balance and rebalance the stage picture.

Their folding bodies gradually get close enough together so that they are bowing to each other, Oriental style, heads almost touching. Then they rise, and he slowly picks her up with the same cradling lift we first saw. This, of course, is immensely satisfying because, although the pose wasn't shown to us at the beginning of the duet, Taylor has planted it in our minds firmly by suggesting it, then denying it to us. This time they maintain the lift only long enough for us to see it, then he puts her down and escorts her off with one arm around her shoulders.

Wagoner and the two women walk on in a triangle formation. Now begins the last and most extraordinary part of *Aureole*. Up to now the dance has been moving in increments toward a more complex and idiosyncratic version of itself. Taylor accomplishes this not, as does Humphrey, by adding and connecting elements preserved in something very close to their original form, but by various forms of exaggeration and augmentation of the original elements, by showing you the same ideas in topsy-turvy form. Things seldom repeat in *Aureole*, but they have a close family resemblance, so you're not really aware of how drastically they have changed.

The last section is like the rest of the dance turned inside out. All the original shapes are now thoroughly distorted: the straight and angular ones are precariously tilting zigzags and clownish turned-in, flexed designs; the curves are tight pretzels or wet dishrags. The arms, which have been used importantly throughout the dance, seem no longer integral to the body's changing design but as if the dancers have to lock them into position or they'll fly right out of their sockets. The rhythms and tempos, which have undergone some forcing in each of the preceding sections, are now almost out of control, the dancers sometimes ripping into double-time, kited-over, breakneck runs, sometimes skidding to full stops or sliding into weird, wayward syncopations.

Wagoner is still chasing the women, and now Taylor joins in. However, the chase continues to be seen in fragments. Wagoner dances his odd jumps and his Apollo greetings in the background with the women, while Taylor takes over his solo interludes. At the very beginning of the section, Walton streaks across the stage while Wagoner and the other two women are doing something very orderly. There is something quite disturbing about this cross — its speed and directness and the fact that it doesn't stop in our field of vision to elaborate or entertain us; the dancer just appears and is gone. It happens several more times before the dance is over, and the thought crosses my mind that maybe this was the point of the dance all along — to come in and go out — and all the decoration was merely appeasement. In the last part of *Esplanade* (1975), the first work Taylor choreographed after he stopped dancing, he offers virtually the same dance, without the niceties, and it comes across to me as rage. In *Aureole*, these runs, the fastest, most out-of-whack movement you can make and still be dancing, must at least represent the outer limits of where Taylor has been pushing the whole dance.

The crossings also seem to disrupt the dance's spatial organization, which has remained quite consistent throughout its other dislocations. For the first time the dancers start using the up-left–down-right diagonal, which they have avoided despite frequent use of the other diagonal. This new direction is Taylor's, and in one way you can see in the end of *Aureole* that he is gradually, totally taking over. Not only does he start doing the solo exclamations, he introduces this new diagonal, and insists upon it.

After several minutes of solo and group statements, each more strange than the one before, Taylor comes down his diagonal with running leaps that come to a sudden stop just before he reaches the wings. For a minute he hangs in the air, perched over one foot, then he drops to the floor and rolls over once in the opposite direction, gets up, and goes out with even bigger leaps. The women enter along the more familiar path, moving in very fast chaîné turns that erupt into scissors jumps without any preparation. The next instant they are sitting on the floor on the diagonal Taylor established. He comes running on and hastily lifts each woman by the arms in turn, sending her off and rushing on to the next. When they are all gone, he goes back to the corner and begins another line of leaping runs, and when the curtain falls, the rest of the dancers are following after him.

Early Feld

Eliot Feld's position is one of the most difficult to assess in all of American ballet. His career has coincided with the expansion of dance to a popular entertainment as well as a cultural fixture, and his work has always hovered on the thin edge between those two often contradictory modes. Those who have followed him since the beginning continue to search their memories for the sources of his initial success and to track the steps by which he has seemed to turn away from what we thought was his initial promise. As a critic who was very pro-Feld at the beginning, I have watched him with regret and a great deal of soul-searching.

I think Feld is a classic case of an individual choreographer with serious intentions trying to define himself in a time when choreography is neither highly valued nor particularly well understood. Feld began choreographing in 1967. He was, at the time, dancing with Ballet Theater, but after he had made two successful ballets, he demanded and was refused more authority within the company. Then began a period of trying to find a good working situation. He did free-lance choreography for a year, then established his first group, American Ballet Company, at the Brooklyn Academy of Music. The company lasted two years before Feld dissolved it. Briefly he returned to Ballet Theater, then free-lanced again, and finally formed another company, the Eliot Feld Ballet, under the aegis of Joseph Papp and the New York Shakespeare Festival, in 1974.

Between 1967 and 1970 Feld made six exceptional ballets: *Harbinger* and *At Midnight* (1967), *Meadowlark* (1968), *Intermezzo* (1969), and *Early Songs* and *The Consort* (1970). Soon after organizing the first ensemble, he began to show evidence of considerable pressure to create a varied repertory in the manner of other popular companies. Like the highly personal modern dancers whose era even then was coming to an end, Feld seemed to want to create the entire repertory himself. Although initially he included Fokine's *Carnaval*, Donald McKayle's *Games,* and Herbert Ross' *Caprichos* and *The Maids,* these works gradually were dropped from the repertory as Feld accumulated enough ballets of his own. He began devising little works in all kinds of period flavors, many of which must have been meant to last no more than a season or two. This pattern has continued in the new company. The works of outside choreographers that Feld mounted were interesting and sufficiently different from his own ballets to provide good challenges to the dancers. But he has not built a permanent backlog of either ballet or modern dance classics. The Feld Ballet is now very current, with few pieces in its repertory antedating its own recent existence, except for the standards on which Feld built his reputation.

Having seen all but two of Feld's twenty-five ballets, I think his dance has become increasingly academic, in a way that has confined the emotions and curbed everything that had been personal in his first instinctive efforts. His reasons for wanting to do this cannot be our concern, but it is clear to me that in becoming more skillful at making dances he has retreated from what gave his dance distinction.

I think it always bothered Eliot Feld that as a young choreographer he was compared to Jerome Robbins. Though some of his biographical facts may have related him to Robbins, and Ballet Theater didn't try to dispel the impression it was nurturing another Robbins-phenomenon in its ranks, Feld's artistic derivation appears to have been Tudor and Balanchine rather than Robbins. Robbins' first ballet, *Fancy Free*, carried character ballet into contemporary American terms — a translation into dance of a specific mood and period, and a projection of the personalities, rhythms, and behavior that belonged to that period. Feld's first ballet, on the other hand, was a plotless pure-dance work set to Prokofiev's fifth piano concerto. Even in *Harbinger*, he showed you incident that suggested itself through the music rather than evoking a world that existed apart from music.

The Feld dances in which a continuous, developing "story" can be traced number only four or five, and although he frequently depends on national costume, gesture, and even dance style to color a ballet, he seldom shows you as consistently as Robbins did in his character ballets how intimately people's behavior is bound up with their culture, how their emotional relationships come out of their dance. With Feld, the dance relationship is paramount, and the gesture or anecdote may be completely detached from the dance content or may illustrate an entirely different facet of the particular society from what the dance does. He was most consistent in showing the relationship between incident or "character" and musical expression in his earliest ballets, which were also his least specific ballets as to time and place. No one can say exactly what country or era the dancers in *Harbinger*, *At Midnight*, *Meadowlark*, or *Intermezzo* belong to, but we can certainly see that what they do and how they relate to each other belong to how they dance.

Feld thinks of himself as a classicist. He is interested in form, in manipulating a limited movement vocabulary according to a predetermined, usually musical, structure. He appreciates the elegance and adaptability of a classical line and has often been able to democratize the hierarchies suggested by it without sacrificing the technical versatility it makes possible in the dancer. But there is a duality in Feld. He is not himself the ideal classical dancer, nor does he come from an elegant, aristocratic lineage, either culturally or artistically. Feld is, like Robbins, an urban Jew whose dance training was eclectic and who excels in comic and dramatic roles. As a performer he is earthy, intense, strong; he can create character better than almost any dancer his age. Yet he has never made a narrative ballet. He has not even created more than a few character portraits. He makes vignettes, not dramatic roles. He makes jokes but has not made a comic ballet. All the dramatic works by other choreographers that have been staged for his dancers have been dropped, and virtually all the dancers with a strong dramatic presence have left him after a couple of seasons. I think, as Feld developed, he used his classicism to suppress the dramatic or character strain that is so strong in him.

At first he allowed himself quite a free range within which to interpret music. Without losing a sense of organization, his ballets opened up into space. The ensemble's progress through space was more detailed and less stratified than the lines, squares, diagonals, and spotlit center of traditional ballet. The individual dancer was more daring with the space around his body, reaching and shaping his limbs and torso into areas behind, above, and off his vertical axis. In the early ballets Feld avoided the set-up look in just about every way he could — there were few display solos, preparations were minimized, virtuosity didn't call attention to itself. In fact, he produced few spectacular tricks of any kind. Feld had little regard for the academic vocabulary's peak achievements — multiple pirouettes, intricate beats, high jumps, endless balances. His movement was of a gentler, less competitive, more personal sort.

His one indulgence in the spectacular was in partnering, specifically in lifts. His first attempts in this area, particularly in *Intermezzo*, were astonishing because all the fireworks occurred within the larger shape of the duet. Lifts were not treated as the climax of a dance, the result of a courtship, the pose to picture as the curtain fell, but as an acting out of the natural ebb and flow of the dance's dynamics. *Intermezzo*'s many lifts also drew particular attention to the dancer's weight — the woman would often be literally thrown in the air and caught again — and this reinforced their kinetic impact on the audience.

In the beginning, no one applauded during an Eliot Feld ballet; lifts weren't applauded, nor individual solo passages, nor even the ends of sections of longer works. Performance practice can often control an audience, and even today, at some performances of *At Midnight*, there is such an intensity on the stage that no one out front thinks to interrupt. I think the performing attitude of Feld's dancers had a lot to do with the seriousness of those early works. Perhaps inevitably, as dancers and audience grew familiar with the works, they learned the shape of them, learned where the exciting parts would come, which jokes worked and how the laughs could be nursed along. Phrasing that had been natural became slightly underscored, and character suggested in the movement started to get acted out in the face. This is normally an imperceptible process, and even people who know a ballet well only realize it has happened after a period of time; then something will snap your memory back to the same moment as it occurred in an earlier production, and you see exactly what has changed. Many very small adjustments can alter the whole style of a ballet. All of Feld's works that remain in the Ballet Theater repertory show this erosion-in-reverse, and to a lesser extent his own present company is engaged in a gradual sharpening and intensifying of dynamics, tempos, and effects.

What he did originally had much more in common with the understated flow of Antony Tudor, even though Feld did not make a point of drama. Tudor's early, plotless work *Dark Elegies* is very close in feeling to early Feld. Both choreographers had a way of personalizing movement without characterizing it. Where Balanchine concentrated on putting steps together to match the music's style, and thus differentiated between dancers or ballets, Feld distinguished them by their energy and phrasing, the ways they held their bodies, adapted to space, responded to other people around them, as well as how they fit their steps to the music. If we look at different couples in *Harbinger, At Midnight,* and *Intermezzo,* we see several very different ways that people can team up together.

In the slow movement of *Harbinger,* a man and a woman stand apart from a larger group. They face each other and clasp hands, arms spread wide and slightly above eye level. For much of their pas de deux they work with this kind of an arm-linking or a variation of it. Their partnership seems to be about giving themselves a lot of space or taking in a lot of space together. It contrasts with the brief meetings of the people in the group, who walk around clasping hands with another person, their arms held to their sides and only their forearms extended, and move on to another person without breaking step.

When the music goes into a minor key, the principal couple pull apart, stretching and sliding suddenly angular arms up and down along their own bodies, thrusting a leg out to the side tensely. In a series of lifts, the man tosses the woman high in the air and catches her by the knees in a straight up-and-down grip against his chest. Then, with the woman beside him, he spreads into a wide plié.

HARBINGER (*Feld, 1967*). *American Ballet Theater — original cast. Photo by Louis Péres.*

Holding on to his hand overhead, the woman, in one motion, sits on his thigh and slides over it so she's behind him. He turns and they walk a couple of steps side by side, then she slides over his other leg the same way. He lifts her from behind, grips her tightly around the waist, and runs from side to side while her legs trail along, like grass under water. Finally he stands behind her and in alternation they open their arms and wrap their arms around the woman's chest. In all of these sequences you have a strong sense of anchorage: either the dancers stand still as they spread through space or the man provides a secure mooring for the woman's drift.

This duo is not undisturbed — once, the man and woman separate to become part of the walking-around larger group, and after they meet again, they have the moment of discord I described earlier — but when the dancers do become synchronous, you feel they have all the time and all the room in the world. The couple in *Harbinger*'s first duet are extremely different, yet similar. Their tempo is very fast, full of stops and spurting starts, and they flip from working in unison to close canon to combining shapes. They too use a lot of space, but in this case their intentions differ. The woman reaches, leans, pulls far out into space, away from the man, and a second later he reaches or leans out just as far in order to pull her back. Instead of sweeping through a lot of space on the floor as the slower couple do, they work exclusively along the sides of a tight triangle, between the up-left, down-left, and down-right areas of the stage. They stop a lot, and when they do, what you see is parts of them pointing in a direction *away* from where they are. At the end, though, the man apparently wins, because he succeeds in snatching the woman bodily out of the air as she springs away from him, and the impact of his arm around her waist makes her curl up into a fetal ball. From a performance standpoint, this pas de deux depends on accurate, speedy timing and on the dancers being able to channel their movement so that it is very straight and placed or they will look (and possibly be) all tangled up.

As indicated in the slow duet, Feld wasn't uneasy with two or more ideas going on at the same time. The fourth part of *At Midnight* ("Ich bin der Welt abhanden gekommen" from Mahler's Rückert Songs) poses a solitary woman against a couple of an entirely different emotional tone. The woman, who is perhaps a meditation on the solitary, out-of-tune Hagar in *Pillar of Fire*, swoops and oscillates all over the stage, searching with empty hands and hugging her body with fists of frustration. She reacts violently to the slightest stir from the man and woman who quietly occupy the down-right corner of the stage. This couple's mood is totally unconcerned with the space around them, absorbed in each other. They move very little, and then slowly and smoothly, their touch delicate, their limbs buoyant. Where the slow couple in *Harbinger* was grounded, this one seems almost disembodied. At one point the man lifts the woman into the air and she stays there, kneeling motionless in the crook of his arms, while the solitary woman dances an eternity of questions.

There seem to be countless examples of this kind of emotional texture in the early Feld, but one can also find in those ballets a tendency toward trickiness, cliché, and easy reference to response-triggering situations. His first dancers were either unsure of how to play the choreography or directed by Feld to go lightly on punch lines, and things that now appear arch or contrived looked much less calculated. It was the seeming naturalness that we noticed then, but the gimmicks were lurking. *Meadowlark* was particularly frail. Choreographed for the Royal Winnipeg Ballet, it held a place in the American Ballet Company's repertory, then was revived for the Joffrey Ballet but lasted only a couple of seasons there. Feld's new company has not yet performed it. This was the most formal of his early ballets, set to some Haydn divertimenti. In between inventively composed group dances, Feld put little vignettes — a man swooning after an *Ivesiana*-style dream girl, a flirtatious woman dancing with one, then two, then three eager males. For the first time, it seemed to me, there was a discontinuity, between the lively rationality of the ensemble dancing and the adolescent sentiment of the vignettes.

These interludes of incident were not always jokey — in *Early Songs* Christine Sarry suddenly appeared in a solo of stylized anguish and later was quieted by John Sowinski in a rare, nonromantic pas de deux. But even the best of these episodes were disconcerting. In suddenly suggesting character, they seemed out of character for the ballets in which they occurred. Perhaps Feld's idea was to convey a sort of cinematic or novelistic close-up, a kind of face-in-the-crowd idea.

The first ballets were skillfully constructed to make this temporary role-playing possible. In *Harbinger* and *At Midnight* the soloists were introduced as the protagonists of dance episodes, and only late in the ballet did the whole ensemble appear together, so the scale told you individuals could be considered. In *Meadowlark* and *Intermezzo*, the setting was clearly an intimate social occasion. Later there was less and less indication that anyone might step out of a group and begin acting out hidden fantasies or sorrows. Since Feld had never distinguished the solo dancers from the ensemble in the class-conscious manner of the Imperial ballet, the audience had no preparation for their abrupt changes of behavior. This technique of flashing from the all-alike corps de ballet to the idiosyncratic dances of individual members became standard practice for Feld.

Some of the first ballets Feld made for his own dancers concerned themselves exclusively with "character" traits. *Cortège Burlesque* (1969) was a pas de deux burlesquing and at the same time playing down the circusy pas de deux tradition in classical ballet. *Pagan Spring* (1969) was a stripped-down, nonnarrative essay on some of the themes of *Le Sacre du Printemps*. *The Gods Amused* (1971) drew on "Greek" themes of purity, line, and balance, as suggested in *Apollo*. In these works and many later ones Feld doesn't seem to mind if you notice his sources. His purpose seems to be not to elaborate on what his precursors have suggested, but to encapsulate, to formalize, to intensify, perhaps also to make more obvious what he considers to be the essence of the original work. He seems to be saying that he can tame the most radical ballet conceptions, bring any character style, no matter how incongruous, under the civilizing influence of academic rules.

The Consort, a ballet that begins with slow, dignified, but erotically loaded dances derived from the Renaissance, gradually becomes more and more earthy as the participants shed some of their "proper" clothing along with the inhibiting behavior of the courtly dance. The ballet ends in an orgy, but a curiously static and depersonalized one. The movement is big and flingy, with a heavy, besotted quality, as the women mount the men's thighs and, with legs wrapped around the men's waists, are tossed up and fall backward, upside down, and are pulled back up again into a tight embrace. As spatially wild as this movement is, it's nevertheless contained by the fact that all the couples (originally five, now seven) do the same thing, taking their own timing, not moving out of one spot, and that when the partners separate briefly, the men cluster in the same part of the stage, in the same formation each time. The anonymous, functional way the dancers perform in this section is underscored by the fact that they don't take the same partners with whom they've danced earlier in the ballet. Somehow the pairing of lusty, brawling behavior and uniform, depersonalized, patterned action conveys an air of decadence that overshadows every other intended comment.

Feld's ballets became increasingly organized — the movement compressed into short, repetitive phrases, the floor patterns laid out in lines and small, carefully segregated areas, the group interacting on the simplest levels of unison or two-part canon. Except for the stylized solo and small-group anecdotes, there is nothing to distinguish one dancer from another.

From time to time, Feld continues to make ballets that seem to have a more personal intent. They are usually works in which he himself takes a central dramatic role. *At Midnight* may be the first of this genre, with its three solitary people beating their way through their own loneliness. Three and possibly four later ballets seem related to *At Midnight*. All of them have some narrative development, and they all treat at least one character with compassionate attention. There is a corps de ballet in all of them, but the ensemble plays a minor part; it is the characters and the interactions between them that create the thread of meaning in the ballet rather than the characteristic dance behavior of the group. They all have a feel of autobiography to me, or at least of examining personal feelings.

A Poem Forgotten (1970), the only one Feld did not dance in, had his protégé Daniel Levins as the boy growing up. In *Theater* (1971) Feld gave a moving performance in the mime role of Pierrot, the tragic clown (in its first season he shared this role with John Sowinski). In *A Soldier's Tale* (1972) he was the pimp/master/devil to Levins' naive soldier. And in *The Real McCoy* (1974), in a lighter mood, he imagined himself the suave star of a composite Hollywood musical.

But even in these works, where the personal element seems apparent, where the idea of character can be taken more in a theater sense, Feld clamps down on himself by creating his characters after existing types or models. *Poem* seems to me obviously influenced by Tudor's *Undertow*, *Soldier's Tale* by its existing Stravinsky libretto, and the other two by the conventions of their theatrical antecedents. All the subsidiary characters in these works are two-dimensional, and such plot development as Feld allows is worked out by means of dance action as rigidly patterned as any of his plotless works. All the plots are circular; that is, they all lead back to the same situation with which they began, or they imply that what you have just seen will continue to happen. And although the main characters have some depth, they do not change in the course of the ballet.

I think, for Feld, the closed classical form is a refuge of some kind. In spite of his gift for character, he knows characters can get out of control, and he seems very anxious to preserve order and predictability in his works. This is a very safe place for the audience to be in, too, and Feld's frequent use of the suite form is in keeping with current practice in the undemanding popular ballet. He has become, in fact, one of the most successful exponents of that form.

As Time Goes By and *Push Comes to Shove* (*Twyla Tharp*)

In some ways Twyla Tharp is dance's American dream come true. Having devoted her youth to "my tap dancing lessons, my ballet lessons, my baton twirling lessons, my drum lessons, my gypsy dancing lessons, my piano and viola lessons"[4] and a college education at Barnard, she spent a brief interval dancing with Paul Taylor, then retired to the lofts of Soho, where she endured the poverty and official scorn that we reserve for our rarest artists. Ten years after her first choreographic adventures, she had won not only superstardom but critical acclaim for her ballets. Maybe no one will ever completely know what made her the darling of the slick magazines when she might, just as logically, have found a respectable but endlessly difficult place in the dance world, like Humphrey, Limón, Taylor. Her backstage progress is the stuff they used to make movies out of — and I sometimes think it's the substance of most of her ballets. They all have a happy, effortless style that seems to have been born on the wrong side of the tracks.

Tharp's personal charisma has to count for a lot. She belongs to the same species as the screwball movie heroines of the thirties and forties — smart, fast-talking, irreverent, ingenious, funny, outspoken. Her wisecracks make wonderful copy and her company lecture-demonstrations are invigorating. She can be abrasive, she can be lovable. She is never dull. But her mediagenic personality is not her only attraction.

Tharp has an instinct for pop. She is uncannily in touch with the pulse of our time; she seems to hear it miles away, as if she always has her ear on the track. Her sensing mechanism is so acute that she hardly seems to know she's picking up something special, like those girls in high school who are the first to wear gold chain necklaces or change their hemlines. No one is really sure, afterward, whether she borrowed something from the culture or started a fad herself. Tharp was working seriously with video dance in the early 1970s. For costumes, she abandoned the businesslike dancewear that other experimentalists wore in favor of glamorized but danceable street clothes, so that even when they were dancing on a gym floor or other nonproscenium space, her dancers looked theatrical. Her dancers were moving more like people and less like trained, specialized animals — which they also were — long before she pointed out the obvious by accompanying their loose, familiarly phrased movement with jazz.

Tharp's vernacularisms are so ingrained that they never seem to make a special point. Her dances are not "thematic" in the manner of most ballet repertory: she doesn't pick out "jazz" or "country western" as a novel peg on which to hang the old familiar dance apparatus. Whatever particular things she's thinking about seem to get absorbed into the always greater concept that is the dance, sometimes so thoroughly absorbed that they don't show at all. Much later, in an interview or a lecture-demonstration, she might mention them casually — the references to Balanchine's *Stars and Stripes* in *Give and Take,* her memory of kids carving their names on schoolroom desks when she heard about the graffiti artists who later became a part of *Deuce Coupe·* — but she'd just as soon let the audience catch on by itself.

One thing that allies her to the experimental dancers of our time is her eclecticism, her ability to let a work include references to many unrelated things or to have many meanings even if they seem stylistically disparate. For instance, it probably pleases her that her first work for Ballet Theater, *Push Comes to Shove,* is set to Haydn's Symphony No. 82, "The Bear," and starred the Russian bear Mikhail Baryshnikov, and that the audience first saw him dancing to a twentieth-century American musical form, Lamb's Bohemia Rag, and that Tharp herself was the first dancer to exploit ragtime in her own company work four years earlier, *The Raggedy Dances.* She is much more interested in having her work encompass many things that touch on each other, however glancingly, than in obliging the audience by being more consistent. The raffish, ragpicker jumble of ideas that carries us through a Tharp dance eventually comes to be one element of a new style that is Tharp's alone.

I can't think of another choreographer working today who has an imagination the size of Tharp's. Her naturally experimental mind does not concern itself with success or failure but with working out ideas. She has been remarkably prolific over the past decade but has amassed only a small repertory for her company because so many of her projects were not intended as theater dances at all, or were designed for a single unrepeatable performance situation, or were so magnificent in conception that they could never be executed with existing technologies. She thinks of dance on an expansive scale, thinks of the biggest possible things it could be made to do — she's planned dances that could float down rivers, dances for children from racially antagonistic neighborhoods, dances where policemen would dance with citizens; she's made television group choreography for one dancer, performance pieces in parks, a nine-month videodance of herself during pregnancy, pop art dance films. She thinks on a scale worthy of the more luxurious days of Hollywood. But as a scavenger, she also tries to save whatever bits and pieces she can from old triumphs and disasters, to use her work wherever it can serve.

What is most important about Tharp, though it's often forgotten, is that she's fundamentally a serious artist. She does nothing in jest, in spite of her jokes, jibes, kinetic puns, and the general air of inconsequentiality that comes across in her dances. She has never really tried to conceal her compositional rigorousness; in fact, when she can she tries to expose it. But the air of nonchalance is an American defense: a way of covering up what you care about, or diverting attention from your self-consciousness about being a brainy woman, two steps ahead of everyone in the room, who needs a way to win everybody over when it isn't your habit to be ingratiating.

By the time Robert Joffrey asked Tharp to make a second ballet for his company after *Deuce Coupe*, for his dancers alone, she had established her reputation on three fronts — as an avant-gardist, as a modern dancer with her own fine company and choreographic achievement, and as a successful pop phenomenon. *As Time Goes By* (1973) was not only an important work for the Joffrey, as every Tharp work is for the dancers on whom it is created. It was a milestone for Tharp, too, a ballet made the way she made modern dances, without any little tricks or special efforts to capture the audience's sympathy. She herself called the ballet classical, meaning she thought it would survive other works she had made before it.[5]

Having worked with Tharp earlier the same year on *Deuce Coupe*, many of the Joffrey dancers understood her movement style, its fluidity, its easy-looking complexity, its understated dynamics, all so different from the place-it, punch-it, make-it-look-hard credo of so much traditional ballet. *As Time Goes By* is about that different look and about how that kind of dancing goes with Haydn's music (the last two movements of the Symphony No. 45, "The Farewell"), or with no music at all.

The ballet opens in silence, with no one in sight but a solitary woman (originally Beatriz Rodriguez) wearing a simple brown dress and pointe shoes. In a downstage corner she dances a curious, frenetic solo. She looks wound up, almost out of control, as if she were trying to do three times as much movement as is comfortable for her. As she stabs and tweaks at the air, she tips off center. All the large balletic curves and elongations get straightened out and foreshortened; the gestures get smaller and closer to the body and also more run in together. She pauses frequently in her scribbles and takes a very deliberate and clear balletic position, as if calming herself by reestablishing the familiar. Then she speeds on again.

Tharp has more than a slight tendency to didacticism, but she also has a full bag of diversionary tricks to prevent her dances from looking rigid. In fact, some of the delight we feel when watching Tharp comes from knowing that she is simultaneously being serious and poking fun at her seriousness — or, as may also happen, concealing her wit under a gloss of rectitude.

After the first solo in *As Time Goes By*, the woman is joined by five other dancers and the music starts. They line up in proper balletic fashion, facing downstage, women in front, men behind them. But they're clustered close together rather than spread out. Without traveling away from the spot at first, they do a dance that resembles the solo — a fast breeze-through of eccentricities with momentary returns to home in the form of textbook positions, preparations that don't lead anywhere, quick but conventional partnerings that break off abruptly or suddenly detour into an entirely different direction. But the dancers seem able to fall into any sort of motion and recover from it coolly, no matter how unlikely or precarious. What the audience sees is not a series of jokes but a buzz of simultaneous activity during which odd scenes keep popping into focus.

Later on they scatter to obscure parts of the stage and go on in the same vein, and with more space around them it's somewhat easier to see their dislocations. But even when you're looking at only two or three dancers, Tharp doesn't allow you the leisurely, logical kind of event you find in ballet. For a period, Tharp appeared determined not to do anything obvious, and her use of space in *As Time Goes By* seemed a deliberate attempt to deny the hallowed rules of stage deployment. Almost nothing in this ballet respects the established proportions and stresses of group arrangement; center stage is consistently ignored; people are always bunched up somewhere to the side or crossing in unruly herds; and whether the action for the moment is going on in a small or a larger space, your attention is almost always divided between competing ideas or themes. One of the reasons for the even more tremendous success of *Push Comes to Shove* is that for most of it Tharp treated the space conventionally enough for the audience to feel comfortable about knowing where to look. In Tharp, I think, the urge to upset the norms comes not only from her general orneriness, but from a desire, like Balanchine before her, to get the audience to pay attention.

The third section of *As Time Goes By* is called "The Four Finales," and in four very brief episodes, the first six dancers are joined by another eleven, including a new male soloist, who won't be seen solo until the fourth section. This blurring of distinctions between soloists and corps is another way Tharp prevents the audience from using well-known landmarks to skim through the ballet.

Each of the four finales has a featured dancer, but they are not distinguished by the usual means, like clearing away the space around them or setting them off in spatial and rhythmic counterpoint from the corps. In fact, the whole section is harder to see than the rest of the ballet. It seems that, with more people, the dance has become thicker, busier. Even when it organizes itself into some semblance of unison, there are always slight variations in tempo and placement among the dancers, there are always contradictory motifs diluting the effect of total unanimity. Again, the whole section is an expansion of the previous one, bigger but not necessarily any clearer.

What you can discern, within the meshes of movement, is one cliché curtain scene after another, all taken out of their ballet contexts and pulled askew by Tharp. This is a ballet to Haydn's Farewell, after all, and to Tharp, the standard rituals of the ballet repertory are as good a source for movement as any other, a correspondence in this case so appropriate to her that she doesn't see the need to underline it. Other people, without Tharp's copious access to related materials, may not consider her many quotations at all obvious or to be taken for granted; hence, the hints of preciosity sometimes made by even her sympathetic critics.[6]

One of the essentials of Tharp's classicism is her relation to music. It is also the hardest to see because she works with music so analytically. Her basic musicality is evident in her rhythm and phrasing, but the structure of her works often comes from an almost musicological understanding of a score, and without film *and* score to study, one can't grasp the fullness of her musical ideas. There are simply too many other distracting things on the stage. Tharp once said in an interview that her main reason for doing *As Time Goes By* was to capture the way Haydn built the fourth movement of his symphony to a huge climax, then allowed the whole piece to subside and fade away.[7] This is the work in which the musicians leave one by one, until only two violins are left to play the last bars. Tharp's ballet does the same thing. After "The Four Finales" the stage gradually empties, the dancers drifting in clusters through remnants of what came before with fragmentary greetings, shadowy partnerings, casual crossings and departures. One man remains throughout, making glancing contact with various women who all eventually straggle away. At the end, even after the end of the music, he's still dancing in a fading light.

This continuous adagio solo is one of Tharp's most remarkable inventions, an achievement due in large part to Larry Grenier, who created the role. Conceptually a neat opposite number to the ballet's opening dance, it is companion-piece, analog, and inversion, as if

As TIME GOES BY *(Tharp, 1973). Ann Marie de Angelo, Larry Grenier, and Christine Uchida of Joffrey Ballet. Photo by Herbert Migdoll.*

the peculiarities of the first solo had gradually been smoothed out and contained by the bodies who pursued its energies in between. Where Rodriguez was hurried but precise, Grenier was indulgent in space, letting his motion slide easily into its own fluctuating rhythms. Instead of trying to hit a multitude of tiny positions, he let the movement course through his body and limbs, taking him into big spirals and curves. The force of a gesture seemed to recede gradually as he stretched into soft sinuous lunges or sank in elastic pliés, or allowed the last bit of energy to float out through his fingertips or his head, even as a new surge of motion was being generated somewhere else in his body.

Nancy Goldner has pointed out the essential "femininity" of this solo; she says its "lyricism speaks for all men who see in the swan queen a reflection of their own lyrical impulses."[8] What Tharp made possible for Grenier, and for other men in her dances including Baryshnikov, was very different from the narcissistic "feminine" movement of the post-Graham choreographers. Theirs is all about showing and loving to show; hers is about feeling and not caring if it shows.

Push Comes to Shove (1976) was a huge, and hugely successful, ballet. It seems to sum up and extend all Tharp's major assets — her appeal to the audience, her innate consideration for dancers, and the fact that each ballet is a new challenge she sets for herself. Because it is a dance-farce, the most uproarious of all Tharp's screwball ballets, it temporizes with the one important issue I can think of concerning her development as a maturing artist: whether she will ever be able to deal with profound emotions, especially between people.

Tharp can choreograph how dancers feel about themselves, but not how they feel about each other. They always end their negotiations by giving each other the brush-off or flopping vacantly into each other's arms. Their handling of each other can be considerate, exasperated, brisk, or good-natured, but always there's a faint air of defensiveness between them, a subconscious dread of getting too involved, with an accessory stream of kidding-around behavior to soothe any abrasions. The one objective of any encounter seems to be for both parties to walk away unscathed. I think the lack of interpersonal elaboration is what may give us the occasional feeling that her dances aren't getting anywhere — especially since they literally *don't* get anywhere in terms of carrying out most of ballet's traditional game plans. In *Push* she had so many other things on the fire that the courtly pretense isn't important; in fact, its absence may even be an asset. The audience loves to see its stars behaving in such a disarmingly casual manner.

And in a way, this kind of revelation is what *Push* is about. The ballet is an amazingly direct statement of the condition of American Ballet Theater, and much of American ballet, at the time it was made. In the mid-1970s' race for survival by public subsidy, Ballet Theater had evolved into a large institutional mechanism for satisfying a new public's rudimentary but avid taste for prestige ballet. The company's vanilla versions of the old Russian classics have become a staple in a repertory where the remaining few American and contemporary European works occupy a distinctly minor place. Choosing to direct the audience's attention to glamorous, publicized stars rather than maintaining the detail and style that such an audience cannot see, ABT became the most popular dance organization in the country, if not the most satisfying to ballet lovers.

There were rumblings of discontent among the dancers, more serious than the griping and gossip that permeate any backstage milieu. American dancers who had grown up in the company or joined it to be able to perform what are still considered the ultimate classical roles felt they were being neglected in favor of transient foreign guest stars. There were defections to other companies, mutterings of a strike. Shortly before the winter 1975–76 New York season, when *Push* was premièred, ABT's reigning home-grown ballerina, Cynthia Gregory, began a long, off-again-on-again retirement. Young Gelsey Kirkland, only a year after she left the New York City Ballet to dance with Baryshnikov at Ballet Theater, was suffering a strange decline. Both women seemed to be casualties of the star craze that ruled the company. But though morale was low, the company was riding high, with the Russian superstars Baryshnikov and Makarova firmly established as its main attractions.

Into this loaded situation stepped Twyla Tharp, and unabashedly made a ballet about it. *Push Comes to Shove* not only documents the troubles at Ballet Theater, it makes very plain that the trouble is not with the dancers. Tharp not only puts her bets down squarely on the dancers but demonstrates the enormous success that can be won just by giving dancers what they need.

*

Push is, of course, Baryshnikov's ballet. Tharp uses him to make a political statement — and also to make a hit. Yet the ballet doesn't seem at all opportunistic, both because of the care and affection with which she molds *him* into an American-style dancer and because she has required the other dancers to carry at least half the ballet. If Baryshnikov is superstar, he shares billing with the female soloists, male and female featured dancers, bit players and corps. Tharp makes us *see* all these people, see that they all have essential roles to play. She makes us appreciate each one of these components, all over again, as if they had not become worn out and neglected and nearly invisible.

The ballet takes a symphonic form, which Tharp worked out in her own special, unpredictable way. It has two openings, the second a variation of the first. Baryshnikov is the "star" of both these sections; then he appears only as a walk-on during the next two sections, which feature his two female partners. They each lead one of the middle sections — Marianna Tcherkassky with another woman heads the big corps de ballet, and Martine van Hamel with Clark Tippet reigns at a social gathering of some kind. Baryshnikov finally comes to the fore again in the last movement, but by this time the prominence of all the other dancers has been so surely established that he can be scarcely more than an escort.

Tharp has not assigned categorical roles to any of the principals, and, in true Tharp fashion, they don't form any fixed relationships with each other. Yet, almost from the beginning, roles suggest themselves. Baryshnikov, of course, is the hero; Tcherkassky is a born ingénue and van Hamel a queen. They are introduced in turn, meandering across the footlights in what could almost be a vaudeville routine, to ragtime. But, like the music, blown up for full pit orchestra, the dance is a little hyped. Despite the understated movement, small, sensual, and detailed, and the offhand way the dancers fool around with each other, they are stars after all, and their costumes are party clothes of some indefinable period. The audience loves what they are doing, but there is a tension behind the laughter, an exquisite suspense that comes from knowing how much more there must be. Before they've slunk into the opposite wing from where they appeared, the seeds of the ballet have been planted.

It's not always clear why Tharp's recent fans seem so convulsed by the antics on her stage. In this case, though, she establishes immediately that — at least on the top level — she's doing a send-up, a turnabout. Not only does she present the stars in unaccustomed guises, but they pass around Baryshnikov's black derby in a suggestive manner, so that you can take it as a symbol of either his sexual desirability or his top banana status. But the sly tone of this transaction also indicates that more than what meets the eye is going to go on.

After their exit, the Haydn music begins and the curtain opens on a full stage. Baryshnikov is there all alone, ready to do what we expected him to do in the first place, dance a spectacular solo. This he does, but in a way that resembles neither his accustomed classical solos nor the shimmying, Tharpian ragtime he did before the curtain. Tharp has threaded together a dance out of big classical steps — the jumps, fantastic spins, space-eating leaps, and elegant gestural adornments — that Baryshnikov is currently the master of, and small, parenthetical motions assembled from his life-dancing — disco steps, rehearsal behavior, conversational phrases. It's like a speeded-up kinetic process, a dancer bursting into ideas for steps, running out, thinking, erupting, changing his mind, beginning again, letting his mind wander for an instant, beginning again. Aside from the breathtaking suddenness and power with which Baryshnikov can rip into all this, Tharp has choreographed it so that the normal emphasis is reversed. The ballet steps are made to seem effortless and the fist-pounding-into-palm or fingers-pushing-through-the-hair are as commanding as the musical trumpetings that accompany them. It is a feat for a dancer of enormous authority, and Baryshnikov, rather than make all these switches into jokes, sells them with complete seriousness.

The solo is brief. He ejects himself into the wings, only to amble on again a minute later. By this time van Hamel has entered, and he circles her at a distance, not used to having someone else take his spotlight, but not competing outright for it either. Tcherkassky comes in, and again he seems disconcerted rather than angry. If there is anger, none of them shows it, and eventually the women leave and he finishes dancing in big bursts of energy, with an almost sardonic bow.

Then occurs the first of several strange intervals in the ballet. While Baryshnikov is still acknowledging applause, the lights change, making the stage somehow darker and more artificial, and two women from what is to be the corps de ballet walk on. They do a few steps with Baryshnikov, he goes out, and the stage brightens for the entrance of the rest of the corps. Two or three more times the cast of characters changes like this. It's almost the direct opposite of Merce Cunningham's scene changes in *Septet;* instead of softening and blurring the division between sections of the ballet, Tharp dramatizes them, and she does it differently each time so that it can't become another unseen ritual.

Choreographically, the next section is the heart of the ballet. It is a meticulously planned exposition of classical ballet gone haywire; the dancers have to be more precise and musical in their mistiming than a lazy corps that stays sloppily in unison. The ensemble —first a group of eight women with Tcherkassky, then a second group with another soloist (originally Kristine Elliott), then both together — is another one of Tharp's riots, where so much is going on that you don't know where to look to find the jokes, but when you're not expecting them, there they are. Yet this is one of the most spatially organized group dances she's ever made; its disorder is clearly patterned, even though that may not make it any easier to comprehend. It seems to me just as classical, and just as daring for its time, as *Concerto Barocco.*

The two groups of the corps wear different-color costumes, one blue and one beige, and they usually divide the stage between them according to some logical system. One or two women get into the wrong group; their color coding exposes their mistake — and incidentally singles them out as individuals even if they're functioning as part of a mass organism. Within the line-ups and formations there's always something wrong going on — the first, second, third, and fourth members of each line do a four-part counterpoint instead of whole lines being in counterpoint with other lines; the movement is often not pretty, the women throwing themselves too hard into things that are supposed to be "graceful"; for no good reason, people relax their poses and walk to new positions.

Baryshnikov enters and starts dancing with Tcherkassky at one side of the stage. Some of the corps dancers bow and all of them leave. During the next interval, Baryshnikov and Tcherkassky do a dance about making up their minds whether to get together, very close up and fast as a jitterbug. Behind them, other dancers make tentative entrances and leave again.

These new participants are definitely not a corps de ballet. Unlike the filmy cocktail dresses of Tcherkassky, Elliott, and the corps,

PUSH COMES TO SHOVE (*Tharp, 1976*). *Marianna Tcherkassky, Mikhail Baryshnikov and ensemble, American Ballet Theater. Photo by Martha Swope.*

these women's costumes are long and severe, in smooth, opaque fabrics, less modern but more consistent with van Hamel's gray halter-top dress. The men wear costumes like Baryshnikov's soft jersey top and pants rolled to just below the knee with leg warmers underneath. Even though these costumes are basically contemporary clothes, they all have small touches of decoration or an extra elegance of cut and fabric that suggest dressing up, becoming a character. If Baryshnikov is the prince and Tcherkassky the princess, this last group must be courtiers, and van Hamel, now partnered by Clark Tippet, is perhaps the resident Black Swan.

Now van Hamel and Tippet dance a duet backed by a continuous, distracting series of courtly greetings, assemblings, and dispersals among the oblivious nobles. I'm reminded of the Ballet Theater corps milling around on a particularly dull night in the first act of *Swan Lake*. Van Hamel and Tippet seldom move in harmony.

Their dance is a competition, each trying to make a move that will top the other's last one. The pas de deux where the male gets revenge for all those hours spent in undignified positions while showing off the ballerina is a favorite parody subject for choreographers. Tharp's version, as one might expect, is based a lot on timing, the dancers breaking into each other's line, trying to fit more steps than necessary into the musical opportunity. What you also notice about this competition is that it doesn't leave any hard feelings and that the whole ballet has been seething with rivalries up to this point. Even the docile corps de ballet girls at one point gather on opposing sides of the stage and hiss at each other with the two-handed, close-to-the-body clawing gesture of the cats in *Sleeping Beauty* — the gesture also used by the hot-tempered Mexican women in *Billy the Kid*. The two corps leaders later scratch at each other the same way.

It seems at this point that the ballet can only mobilize itself into further and further chaos. But it is Baryshnikov himself who engineers a different conclusion as the final section starts, by leading on two of the corps women for a bow. Then follows an orgy of choreographed bows, overlapping, interrupting, and incorporating dancing by everyone. Somewhere the derby has reappeared, and as Baryshnikov dances briefly with the corps alone, it gets tossed in the air from dancer to dancer. All the others return, and as the music punches at one closing sentence after another, they pose and re-pose as if for snapshots. On the last one, you glimpse *two* hats in the air as the curtain is falling. The company's problems may not be permanently solved, but this ballet at least goes out with a great self-congratulatory bravo.

Chronology
Notes
Bibliography
Index

Chronology

A selected listing of important first performances and other events in the development of American dance.

1926 *Flute of Krishna* (Graham)
First of *Negro Spirituals* (Tamiris)
First Graham concert in New York

1928 *Air for the G String* (Humphrey)
Water Study (Humphrey)
First Humphrey-Weidman concert

1929 *Life of the Bee* (Humphrey)
Death of Diaghilev

1930 *Lamentation* (Graham)

1931 *Primitive Mysteries* (Graham)
The Shakers (Humphrey)
Last Denishawn concert

1933 First Astaire & Rogers movie, "Flying Down to Rio"

1934 Bennington School of Dance, first summer
Catherine Littlefield Ballet formed (Philadelphia)
School of American Ballet established

1935 *Serenade* (Balanchine)
Frontier (Graham)

New Dance (Humphrey)
Kinetic Molpai (Shawn)

1936 *Chronicle* (Graham)
With My Red Fires (Humphrey)
Lynchtown (Weidman)
Ballet Caravan debut at Bennington College
Musical, "On Your Toes" (Balanchine)

1937 *Trend* (Holm)
How Long, Brethren (Tamiris)

1938 *Filling Station* (Christensen)
American Document (Graham)
Passacaglia (Humphrey)
Billy the Kid (Loring)
Frankie and Johnny (Page-Stone)
Page-Stone Ballet formed (Chicago)

1939 *Every Soul Is a Circus* (Graham)
Ballet Theater founded

1940 *El Penitente* (Graham)
Letter to the World (Graham)

Song of the West begun
(Humphrey)
The Great American Goof
(Loring/Saroyan)

1941 *Ballet Imperial* (Balanchine)
Concerto Barocco (Balan-
chine)
Three Virgins and a Devil (de
Mille)
Dust Bowl Ballads (Mas-
low/Woodie Guthrie)
Jacob's Pillow Dance Fes-
tival incorporated

1942 *Rodeo* (de Mille)
Pillar of Fire (Tudor)
Flickers (Weidman)

1943 *Deaths and Entrances* (Gra-
ham)
Suspension (O'Donnell)
Romeo and Juliet (Tudor)
Musical, "Oklahoma" (de
Mille)

1944 *Appalachian Spring* (Gra-
ham)
Hérodiade (Graham)
Tally-Ho (de Mille)
Fancy Free (Robbins)
Musical, "On the Town"
(Robbins)

1945 *Interplay* (Robbins)
Undertow (Tudor)

1946 *Four Temperaments* (Balan-
chine)
Cave of the Heart (Graham)
Dark Meadow (Graham)
*Lament for Ignacio Sanchez
Mejias* (Humphrey)

1947 *Errand into the Maze* (Gra-
ham)
Night Journey (Graham)
Day on Earth (Humphrey)
Theme and Variations (Balan-
chine)

San Francisco (Civic) Ballet
formed

1948 *Orpheus* (Balanchine)
Symphony in C (Balanchine)
Fall River Legend (de Mille)
Diversion of Angels (Gra-
ham)
The Beloved (Horton)
Thurber Fables begun (Weid-
man)
Musical, Kiss Me Kate (Holm)
American Dance Festival
begun, Connecticut Col-
lege
New York City Ballet es-
tablished in City Center

1949 *La Malinche* (Limón)
The Moor's Pavane (Limón)

1950 *The Exiles* (Limón)
Age of Anxiety (Robbins)

1951 *La Valse* (Balanchine)
Cakewalk (Boris)
*Sixteen Dances for Soloist and
Company of Three* (Cun-
ningham)
Night Spell (Humphrey)
Games (McKayle)
The Cage (Robbins)

1952 *Scotch Symphony* (Balanchine)
*Canticle for Innocent Come-
dians* (Graham)

1953 *Septet* (Cunningham)
Ritmo Jondo (Humphrey)
Masks, Props & Mobiles (Ni-
kolais)
Afternoon of a Faun (Rob-
bins)
Lyric Suite (Sokolow)

1954 *Ivesiana* (Balanchine)
The Nutcracker (Balanchine)
Western Symphony (Balan-
chine)
The Traitor (Limón)

1955　*Seraphic Dialogue* (Graham)
　　　Rooms (Sokolow)

1956　*Nocturnes* (Cunningham)
　　　Suite for Five (Cunningham)
　　　Emperor Jones (Limón)
　　　There Is a Time (Limón)
　　　The Concert (Robbins)
　　　Joffrey Ballet established

1957　*Agon* (Balanchine)
　　　Square Dance (Balanchine)
　　　Here and Now with Watchers
　　　　(Hawkins)
　　　Indeterminate Figure (Na-
　　　　grin)
　　　Musical, "West Side Story"
　　　　(Robbins)

1958　*Stars and Stripes* (Balan-
　　　　chine)
　　　Antic Meet (Cunningham)
　　　Summerspace (Cunningham)
　　　Clytemnestra (Graham)
　　　Missa Brevis (Limón)
　　　N. Y. Export: Opus Jazz
　　　　(Robbins)
　　　Death of Doris Humphrey

1959　*Episodes* (Balanchine/Gra-
　　　　ham)
　　　Rune (Cunningham)
　　　Rainbow Round My Shoulder
　　　　(McKayle)
　　　Moves (Robbins)

1960　*Revelations* (Ailey)
　　　Liebeslieder Walzer (Balan-
　　　　chine)
　　　Monumentum pro Gesualdo
　　　　(Balanchine)
　　　Crises (Cunningham)
　　　Acrobats of God (Graham)

1961　*Aeon* (Cunningham)
　　　Dreams (Sokolow)
　　　Insects and Heroes (Taylor)
　　　Establishment of Judson
　　　　Dance Theater and the
　　　　"post-modern" dance

1962　*Feast of Ashes* (Ailey)
　　　Phaedra (Graham)
　　　Secular Games (Graham)
　　　Time out of Mind (Mac-
　　　　donald)
　　　Aureole (Taylor)

1963　*Bugaku* (Balanchine)
　　　Story (Cunningham)
　　　Imago (Nikolais)
　　　Scudorama (Taylor)
　　　First large foundation grant
　　　　to dance: Ford Founda-
　　　　tion gives $4.5 million to
　　　　New York City Ballet &
　　　　School of American Ballet

1964　*Winterbranch* (Cunningham)
　　　New York State Theater
　　　　opens at Lincoln Center

1965　*Viva Vivaldi* (Arpino)
　　　Don Quixote (Balanchine)
　　　Variations V (Cunningham)
　　　Les Noces (Robbins)
　　　Opus 65 (Sokolow)
　　　National Endowment for
　　　　the Arts established
　　　New York State Council on
　　　　the Arts becomes perma-
　　　　nent agency of state gov-
　　　　ernment

1966　*Place* (Cunningham)
　　　The Winged (Limón)
　　　Orbs (Taylor)

1967　*Harbinger* (Feld)
　　　Astarte (Joffrey)
　　　Somniloquy (Nikolais)

1968　*RainForest* (Cunningham)
　　　At Midnight (Feld)
　　　Tent (Nikolais)
　　　Public Domain (Taylor)

1969　*Canfield* (Cunningham)
　　　Intermezzo (Feld)
　　　Dances at a Gathering (Rob-
　　　　bins)

Private Domain (Taylor)
Medley (Tharp)

1970 *The River* (Ailey)
Trinity (Arpino)
Who Cares (Balanchine)
The Fugue (Tharp)

1971 *Dances for Isadora* (Limón)
The Goldberg Variations
    (Robbins)
Big Bertha (Taylor)
The Bix Pieces (Tharp)
Eight Jelly Rolls (Tharp)

1972 *Landrover* (Cunningham)
Watermill (Robbins)
The Raggedy Dances (Tharp)
New York City Ballet Stra-
    vinsky Festival

1973 *Deuce Coupe* (Tharp)
As Time Goes By (Tharp)

1975 *Le Tombeau de Couperin* (Ba-
    lanchine)
Rebus (Cunningham)
Esplanade (Taylor)
Sue's Leg (Tharp)

1976 *Union Jack* (Balanchine)
Push Comes to Shove (Tharp)
First of nationally televised
    Dance in America series,
    funded by the National
    Endowment for the Arts,
    the Corporation for Public
    Broadcasting, and Exxon
    Corporation

Notes

REHEARSAL (*pages 1–10*)

1. In Nesta Macdonald, *Diaghilev Observed* (Brooklyn, Dance Horizons, and London, Dance Books, Ltd., 1975), p. 15.
2. *S. Hurok Presents* (New York, 1955), p. 15.
3. Ruth St. Denis, *An Unfinished Life* (1939; reprint ed., Brooklyn, Dance Horizons), p. 131.

THE DENISHAWN SUCCESSION (*pages 11–22*)

1. Two sayings of Ruth St. Denis in Jane Sherman, *Soaring* (Middletown, Conn., Wesleyan University Press, 1976), p. 23.
2. St. Denis, *An Unfinished Life*, p. 323.
3. Elizabeth Selden, *The Dancer's Quest* (Berkeley, University of California Press, 1935), pp. 47–48.

BEGINNINGS (*pages 23–48*)

1. Quoted in an interview with the Minneapolis *Tribune*, January 16, 1932, in *The Mary Wigman Book*, ed. Walter Sorell (Middletown, Conn., Wesleyan University Press, 1975), p. 149.
2. Selma Jeanne Cohen, *Doris Humphrey: An Artist First* (Middletown, Conn., Wesleyan University Press, 1972), p. 73.
3. Ibid., p. 254.
4. Louis Horst and Carroll Russell, *Modern Dance Forms* (San Francisco, Impulse Publications, 1961), p. 18.
5. Margaret Lloyd, *The Borzoi Book of Modern Dance* (1949; reprint ed., Brooklyn, Dance Horizons), p. 87.
6. Ibid., p. 88.
7. Ibid., p. 165.
8. Biographical sketch by Robert Sabin in *Martha Graham*, ed. Karl Leabo (New York, Theater Arts Books, 1961).
9. Article by Lincoln Kirstein in *Martha Graham* (1937; reprint ed., Brooklyn, Dance Horizons), pp. 25–26.
10. Christena L. Schlundt, *Tamiris, A Chronicle of Her Dance Career* (New York, New York Public Library, 1972), p. 76.

RITUAL (*pages 49–67*)

1. "Typical Dancing," from Edward Deming Andrews, *The Gift to Be Simple* (1940; reprint ed., New York, Dover), p. 16.
2. Cohen, *Humphrey*, p. 94.
3. Ibid., p. 95.
4. Ibid.

NEOCLASSICISM I (*pages 68–107*)

1. Lincoln Kirstein, *Flesh Is Heir* (1932; reprint ed., New York, Popular Library), p. 146.
2. Lloyd, *Modern Dance*, p. 95.
3. Clive Barnes conducted an unfounded and reprehensible attack on Humphrey for years. "Miss Humphrey, not an especially gifted choreographer in her own right, knew exactly what to do with and for Mr. Limón" (from Limón's obituary notice, New York *Times*, December 4, 1972). ". . . she was probably not a major choreographer" (from a review of the Limón Company season, New York *Times*, spring 1975). Repeated slurs of this type have undoubtedly sunk into the public's consciousness and debased her reputation during a period when there were few works of hers available to prove otherwise.
4. Cohen, *Humphrey*, pp. 238–241.
5. Ibid., p. 242.
6. Ibid., pp. 222–232. Cohen discusses the reconstruction of *New Dance* and the difficulties of preserving the Humphrey repertory.
7. John Martin, *Introduction to the Dance* (1939; reprint ed., Brooklyn, Dance Horizons), p. 262.
8. Louis Horst, *Pre-Classic Forms* (1937; reprint ed., Brooklyn, Dance Horizons), p. viii.
9. George Amberg, *Ballet in America* (New York, Mentor, 1949), p. 45.
10. Lincoln Kirstein, *Blast at Ballet* (1937–39; reprint ed., Brooklyn, Dance Horizons), pp. 11–12.
11. Ibid., p. 105.
12. Ibid., p. 83.
13. Ibid., pp. 105–6.
14. Quoted by Grace Robert, in *The Borzoi Book of Ballets* (New York, Knopf, 1946), p. 74.
15. Edwin Denby, *Looking at the Dance* (New York, Horizon Press, 1949), p. 237.

AMERICANA BALLET (*pages 108–137*)

1. Quoted by Robert Kimball and Alfred Sloan, in *The Gershwins* (New York, Atheneum, 1972), p. 35.
2. Fairfield Porter, *Thomas Eakins* (New York, George Braziller, 1959), p. 24.
3. Pittsburgh Ballet Theatre, January 5, 1976, press release.
4. Lloyd, *Modern Dance*, p. 337.

5. Quoted by Gerald Weales, in "Popular Theatre of the Thirties," *The Drama Review* (Summer 1967), p. 52.
6. Kirstein, *Blast at Ballet*, p. 108.
7. Ibid., p. 107.
8. Lincoln Kirstein, *The New York City Ballet* (New York, Knopf, 1973), p. 50.
9. Amberg, *Ballet in America*, pp. 56–57.
10. Denby, *Looking at the Dance*, p. 64.
11. Anatole Chujoy, *The New York City Ballet* (New York, Knopf, 1953), p. 114.
12. Amberg, *Ballet in America*, p. 128.
13. Ibid., p. 129.
14. Ibid., p. 133.

CRYSTALLIZATION I (*pages 138–174*)

1. "Essays before a Sonata," 1920, in *Three Classics in the Aesthetics of Music* (New York, Dover), p. 15.
2. Martha Graham to audience at performance of December 16, 1975, Mark Hellinger Theater, New York.
3. Lloyd, *Modern Dance*, p. 76.
4. Sound track of *The Dance Theater of José Limón*, produced by Jac Venza for WGBH-TV, 1965.
5. Horst, *Pre-Classic Forms*, pp. 7–16.
6. Thoinot Arbeau, *Orchesography* (1589; reprint ed., New York, Dover), pp. 57–66.

THE EPIC GRAHAM (*pages 175–209*)

1. Score of *Letter to the World*.
2. Selden, *Dancer's Quest*, pp. 162–164.
3. Lloyd, *Modern Dance*, p. 67.
4. *Selected Poems and Letters of Emily Dickinson*, ed. Robert W. Linscott (New York, Doubleday Anchor, 1959), p. 30.
5. *Emily Dickinson*, ed. John Malcolm Brinnin (New York, Dell, Laurel Poetry Series, 1960), p. 53.
6. Denby, *Looking at the Dance*, pp. 312–314.
7. Lloyd, *Modern Dance*, p. 43.

BALANCHINE'S AMERICA (*pages 210–242*)

1. Cohen, *Humphrey*, p. 252.
2. Denby, *Looking at the Dance*, p. 221.
3. Ibid., p. 49.
4. Rosalyn Krokover, *The New Borzoi Book of Ballets* (New York, Knopf, 1956), p. 161.
5. Lincoln Kirstein, *Movement and Metaphor* (New York, Praeger, 1970), p. 242.
6. *Stravinsky in the Theater*, ed. Minna Lederman (1949; reprint ed., New York, Da Capo Press), pp. 75ff.

Adolescents (*pages 243–270*)

1. Greil Marcus, *Mystery Train, Images of America in Rock 'n' Roll Music* (New York, Dutton, 1976), p. 158.
2. Krokover, *Ballets*, pp. 156–157.

Crystallization II (*pages 271–304*)

1. Lloyd, *Modern Dance*, p. 214.
2. Merce Cunningham, *Changes* (New York, Something Else Press, 1968).
3. Ibid.

Men Dancing (*pages 305–323*)

1. Aaron Copland, *Music and Imagination* (New York, Mentor, 1952), p. 103.
2. José Limón, "The Virile Dance," in *The Dance Has Many Faces*, ed. Walter Sorell (New York, Columbia University Press, 1966), pp. 82–86.
3. Isadora Duncan, *The Art of the Dance* (1928; reprint ed., New York, Theater Arts Books).
4. Denby, *Looking at the Dance*, p. 122.
5. Beverly Brown, "Training to Dance with Erick Hawkins," *Dance Scope* (Fall/Winter 1971/1972), p. 9.
6. Ibid., pp. 9–10.
7. Harvey Rochlein, *Notes on Contemporary Dance* (Baltimore, University Extension Press, 1964).
8. *Nik — A Documentary*, ed. Marcia B. Siegel (Dance Perspectives #48, 1971), p. 9.
9. Ibid., p. 10.
10. Lloyd, *Modern Dance*, p. 103.

Neoclassicism II (*pages 324–363*)

1. Cunningham, *Changes*.
2. Ibid.
3. Ibid.
4. Twyla Tharp, script for *The Bix Pieces*, 1972.
5. Radio interview with Jim D'Anna, July 11, 1975.
6. "If you wish, you can make an even more specific *danse à clef* out of it. I find the insider's view of ballet distasteful, but in fairness to Tharp it should be said that even a novice balletgoer will get the jokes" (Nancy Goldner, in the *Nation*, December 3, 1973).
7. D'Anna radio interview.
8. Goldner, in the *Nation*.

Bibliography

General

Amberg, George. *Ballet in America*. New York, Mentor Books, 1949.

Balanchine, George, and Francis Mason. *101 Stories of the Great Ballets*. Garden City, N.Y., Doubleday, 1975.

Cohen, Selma Jeanne. *Doris Humphrey: An Artist First*. Middletown, Conn., Wesleyan University Press, 1972.

Cohen, Selma Jeanne, ed. *Dance As a Theatre Art*. New York, Dodd, Mead, 1974.

———. *The Modern Dance — Seven Statements of Belief*. Middletown, Conn., Wesleyan University Press, 1966.

Croce, Arlene. *Afterimages*. New York, Knopf, 1977.

———. *The Fred Astaire and Ginger Rogers Book*. New York, Outerbridge & Lazard Inc., 1972.

Denby, Edwin. *Dancers, Buildings and People in the Streets*. New York, Horizon Press, 1965.

———. *Looking at the Dance*. New York, Horizon Press, 1949.

Johnston, Jill. *Marmalade Me*. New York, Dutton, 1971.

Jowitt, Deborah. *Dance Beat*. New York, Marcel Dekker, 1977.

Kirstein, Lincoln. *Dance — A Short History of Classical Theatrical Dancing*. 1935. Reprint. Brooklyn, Dance Horizons.

Krokover, Rosalyn. *The New Borzoi Book of Ballets*. New York, Knopf, 1956.

Lloyd, Margaret. *The Borzoi Book of Modern Dance*. 1949. Reprint. Brooklyn, Dance Horizons.

Martin, John. *America Dancing*. New York, Dodge, 1936.

———. *The Modern Dance*. 1933. Reprint. Brooklyn, Dance Horizons.

Moore, Lillian. *Artists of the Dance*. 1938. Reprint. Brooklyn, Dance Horizons.

Padgette, Paul, ed. *The Dance Writings of Carl Van Vechten*. Brooklyn, Dance Horizons, 1974.

Robert, Grace. *The Borzoi Book of Ballets*. New York, Knopf, 1946.

Selden, Elizabeth. *The Dancer's Quest*. Berkeley, University of California Press, 1935.

Siegel, Marcia B. *At the Vanishing Point*. New York, Saturday Review Press, 1972.

———. *Watching the Dance Go By.* Boston, Houghton Mifflin, 1977.
Siegel, Marcia B., ed. *Dancers' Notes.* Dance Perspectives #38, 1969.
Stewart, Virginia, and Merle Armitage. *The Modern Dance.* 1935. Reprint. Brooklyn, Dance Horizons.

Rehearsal

Dumesnil, Maurice. *An Amazing Journey.* New York, Ives Washburn, 1932.
Duncan, Irma. *The Technique of Isadora Duncan.* 1970. Reprint. Brooklyn, Dance Horizons.
Duncan, Isadora. *The Art of the Dance.* Ed. Sheldon Cheney. 1928. Reprint. New York, Theater Arts Books, 1977.
———. *My Life.* 1927, Award Books edition, 1966.
Fuller, Loie. *Fifteen Years of a Dancer's Life.* 1913. Reprint. Brooklyn, Dance Horizons.
Grigoriev, S. L. *The Diaghilev Ballet 1909–1929.* 1953. Reprint. Brooklyn, Dance Horizons.
Hurok, S., with Ruth Goode. *Impresario.* New York, Random House, 1946.
Kochno, Boris. *Diaghilev and the Ballets Russes.* New York, Harper & Row, 1970.
Magriel, Paul, ed. *Nijinsky, Pavlova, Duncan.* 1946 and 1947. Reprint. New York, Da Capo Press.
Oliveroff, Andre. *Flight of the Swan.* New York, Dutton, 1932.
Seroff, Victor. *The Real Isadora.* New York, Dial Press, 1971.
Steegmuller, Francis, ed. *Your Isadora.* New York, Random House and the New York Public Library, 1974.
Svetloff, V. *Anna Pavlova.* 1922. Reprint. New York, Dover.

The Denishawn Succession

Cohen, Selma Jeanne, ed. *The Dance Theater of Lester Horton.* Dance Perspectives #31, 1967.
Schlundt, Christena L. *Into the Mystic with Miss Ruth.* Dance Perspectives #46, 1971.
———. *Ruth St. Denis & Ted Shawn.* New York, New York Public Library 1962.
———. *Ted Shawn and His Men Dancers.* New York, New York Public Library, 1967.
Sherman, Jane. *Soaring.* Middletown, Conn., Wesleyan University Press, 1976.

Beginnings

Armitage, Merle, ed. *Martha Graham.* 1937. Reprint. Brooklyn, Dance Horizons.
Davis, Martha, and Claire Schmais. "An Analysis of the Style and Composition of Water Study." In *Research in Dance,* New York, Committee of Research on Dance, 1968.
Kagan, Elizabeth. "Towards the Analysis of a Score: A Study of Three Epitaphs and Water Study." Unpub., 1974.

Leabo, Karl, ed. *Martha Graham*. New York, Theatre Arts Books, 1961.

McDonagh, Don. *Martha Graham*. New York, Praeger, 1973.

Morgan, Barbara. *Martha Graham — Sixteen Dances in Photographs*. New York, Duell Sloan & Pearce, 1941.

Schlundt, Christena L. *Tamaris, A Chronicle of Her Dance Career*. New York, New York Public Library, 1972.

Sorell, Walter. *Hanya Holm*. Middletown, Conn., Wesleyan University Press, 1969.

Weintink, Andrew Mark. "The Doris Humphrey Collection: An Introduction and Guide," *Bulletin of the New York Public Library*, v.77 #1, Autumn 1973.

Ritual

Horst, Louis, and Carroll Russell. *Modern Dance Forms*. San Francisco, Impulse Publications, 1961.

Neoclassicism I

Humphrey, Doris. *The Art of Making Dances*. New York, Grove Press, 1959.

Americana Ballet

de Mille, Agnes. *Dance to the Piper*. Boston, Atlantic–Little, Brown, 1951.

The Epic Graham

Graham, Martha. *The Notebooks of Martha Graham*. New York, Harcourt Brace Jovanovich, 1973.

Mueller, John. "Notes for the Film Night Journey." From *Films on Ballet and Modern Dance*. New York, American Dance Guild, 1974.

Balanchine's America

Chujoy, Anatole. *The New York City Ballet*. New York, Knopf, 1953.

Kirstein, Lincoln. *The New York City Ballet*. New York, Knopf, 1973.

Taper, Bernard. *Balanchine*. New York, Collier Books, 1974.

Crystallization II

Cunningham, Merce. *Changes*. New York, Something Else Press, 1968.

Men Dancing

Siegel, Marcia B., ed. *Nik — A Documentary*. Dance Perspectives #48, 1971.

Neoclassicism II

Cohen, Selma Jeanne, ed. *Time to Walk in Space*. Dance Perspectives #34, 1968.

Index